INTERVENTIONS AND ADAPTIVE REUSE

To the many students of adaptive reuse that we've taught at RISD Interior Architecture about the importance of responsible practice

INTERVENTIONS AND ADAPTIVE REUSE

A Decade of Responsible Practice

edited by Liliane Wong
Markus Berger

Birkhäuser | Basel

Cover Design_Ernesto Aparicio
Layout + Design_Mukul Chakravarthi
Redesign Volumes 1–3_ Abigail Furlow

Acknowledgments
The Int|AR Journal is an annual publication by the editors in chief: Markus Berger + Liliane Wong and the Department of Interior Architecture, Rhode Island School of Design. We thank the Board Members of the Int|AR Journal for their commitment to our decade of architectural journalism: Heinrich Hermann, Uta Hassler, Brian Kernaghan, Niklaus Kohler, Dietrich Neumann, Theodore Prudon, August Sarnitz, Friedrich St. Florian and Wilfried Wang.

We are grateful for the contribution of the Associate Editors over the years: Heinrich Hermann [Volumes 01 and 02], Maya Marx [Volumes 03 and 04], Sunila Galappatti [Volume 04], Damian White [Volume 05], Jeffrey Katz [Volume 06], Patricia Phillips [Volume 07], Nick Heywood [Volume 09].

Our gratitude to the teams of assistants who have contributed to the production of the journal:
Volume 01_Chia-Yu Chang, Lauren Gueli, Seung Hwan Huang
Volume 02_Justin Bazar, Sarah Frank, Clara Halston, Lili Hermann, Eun Lee, Abigail Luley
Volume 03_Nick Dufresne, Dinah Fried, Clara Halston, Patricia Lomando, Caitlin Santone
Volume 04_Sarah Burgett-Leutner, Christina Chanter, Nick DuFresne, Michelle Duesterhoeft, Clara Halston, Eun Song Kim, Jennifer Krauser
Volume 05_Sarah Burgett-Leutner, Cathy Ha, Clara Halston, Pamela Harrington, Yoon Kim, Khanh Luu, Lindsay Windstead
Volume 06_Alaina Bernstein, Mariana Bender, Clara Halston, Pamela Harrington, Lea Hershkowitz, Nick Heywood, Liming Jiang, Jin Hee Kim, Jisoo Kim, Ben Shuai
Volume 07_Jenna Balute, Mariana Bender, Clara Halston, Lea Hershkowitz, Min Hee Kim, Francesca Krisli
Volume 08_Cara Buzzell, Amy Doyle, Clara Halston, Iris Kuo, Toban Shadlyn, Sungkyu Yang, Jeremy Wolin
Volume 09_Anna Albrecht, Amy Doyle, Clara Halston, Xiangyu Liu, Xin Ma
Volume 10_Mukul Chakravarthi, Amy Doyle, Xiangyu Liu, Libby Smith

We especially thank our Graphic Design Editor, Ernesto Aparicio, who brought our ideas to life through text and without whom the Int|AR Journal would not be what it is.

CONTENTS

07 PREFACE

11 INTRODUCTION

22 APPROPRIATION

76 AUTHENTICITY

128 ECOLOGY

174 EQUITY

200 IDENTITY

238 MEMORY AND REDEMPTION

294 COLOPHON

Int AR
Vol. 01
Interventions Adaptive Reuse Autumn 2009
Department of Interior Architecture, Rhode Island School of Design

Int AR
Interventions Adaptive Reuse Vol 02
Department of Interior Architecture, Rhode Island School of Design

Int AR
Interventions Adaptive Reuse Vol 03
Department of Interior Architecture, Rhode Island School of Design

DIFFICULT MEMORIES RECONCILING MEANING
Int AR
Interventions Adaptive Reuse Vol 04
Department of Interior Architecture, Rhode Island School of Design

RESILIENCE AND ADAPTABILITY
Int AR
Interventions Adaptive Reuse Vol 05
Department of Interior Architecture, Rhode Island School of Design

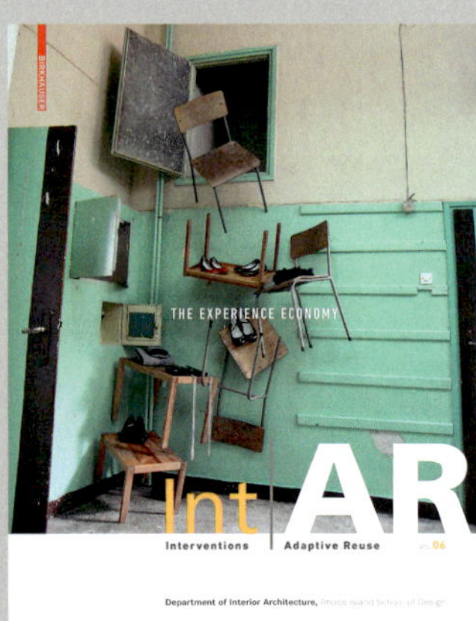
THE EXPERIENCE ECONOMY
Int AR
Interventions Adaptive Reuse Vol 06
Department of Interior Architecture, Rhode Island School of Design

ART IN CONTEXT
Int AR
Interventions Adaptive Reuse 07
Department of Interior Architecture,

WATER AS CATALYST
Int AR
Interventions Adaptive Reuse Vol 08
Department of Interior Architecture,

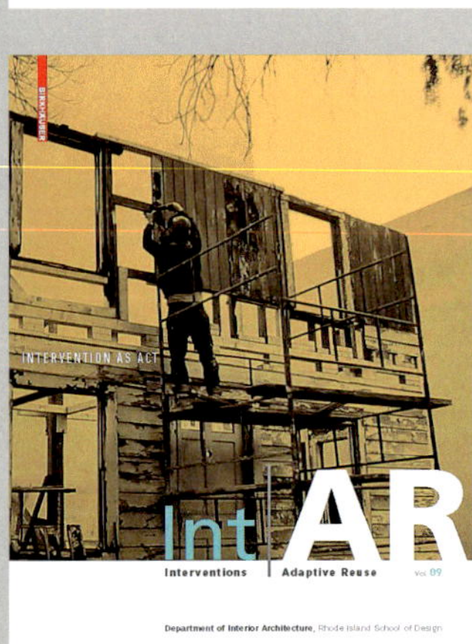
INTERVENTION AS ACT
Int AR
Interventions Adaptive Reuse Vol 09
Department of Interior Architecture, Rhode Island School of Design

IN-BETWEEN
Int AR
Interventions Adaptive Reuse Vol 10
Department of Interior Architecture, Rhode Island School of Design

PREFACE

A DECADE OF ADAPTIVE REUSE JOURNALISM

by LILIANE WONG

A decade is a mark in time that invites backward glances — glances that reevaluate objectives, re-review production, summarize accomplishments and assess relationships in the context of years. The ten volumes of the *Int|AR Journal*, released annually each autumn from 2009 to 2019, invite such speculation not only on the physical volumes but on the development of the publication's fundamental premise: adaptive reuse.

The *Int|AR Journal* has its origins in the Department of Interior Architecture at the Rhode Island School of Design. With humble beginnings as a course in Interior Decoration in 1912, the department was formed through a long and tumultuous history in which the topic of study was often questioned or repositioned within the pedagogy of other departments including Architecture, Furniture and Industrial Design. The Department of Interior Architecture came into its own under the leadership of 1955 Department Head Ernst Lichtblau, who gave it the name it has today. Assuming the position in 1947, Lichtblau was an architect, a designer and a student of Otto Wagner, grounded in the sensibilities of the Vienna Secession. He changed the name of the department and its professional orientation, from that of Interior Design to Interior Architecture. This change was transformative and brought 'an entirely new set of issues and values,' influencing the direction of the department through the 21st century. This repositioning distanced the department from Interior Design, as an application of surface materials, and emphasized the need for a "thorough study of the principles of modern architecture, construction and technology of materials,"[1] so as to prepare the student "to design a building from the interior to the exterior. An intelligent understanding of the design of the structure as a whole [...] can only be accomplished when the same principles are applied conscientiously to all of its parts." [2]

While the department flirted with interior design in the post-Lichtblau years, it returned to Lichtblau's philosophy under the headship of Brian Kernaghan in 1996, albeit in an evolved form. From the late 1990s, the department consolidated those concepts of the relationship of interior and exterior as adaptive reuse, defined as the "reuse of an existing structure for new purposes"[3] and embracing the interior retrofit as well as the addition. This pedagogy of altering architecture would be the hallmark of the Department of Interior Architecture in the millennium.

It was in this context in the autumn of 2008 that Markus Berger, Heinrich Hermann and Liliane Wong, faculty colleagues at the Department of Interior Architecture, lamented the dearth of published material on adaptive reuse. Often relegated as a subset of architecture, adaptive reuse at that time did not merit recognition in the field of architecture or in architectural publications. The founding of the *Int|AR Journal* resulted from the receipt of a miniscule grant to introduce this subject to the field. In the joint editorial of the inaugural Volume 01 of *Int|AR*, adaptive reuse is defined as a "field of practice [that] is rich and varied and its importance includes not only the reuse of existing structures but also the reuse of materials, transformative interventions, continuation of cultural phenomena through built infrastructure, connections across the fabric of time and space, and preservation."[4] Released in 2009, the first volume of the *Int|AR Journal* was followed by nine subsequent issues, each with its own focus: Adapting Industrial Structures, Emerging Economies, Difficult Memories/Reconciling Meaning, Resilience, Experience Economy, Art in Context, Water as Catalyst, Intervention as Act and In-Between. In 2019, a colloquium was held to celebrate both the release of Volume 10 on the "In-Between" and the achievement of a decade of adaptive reuse journalism. This event, hosted at Rhode Island School of Design's Fleet Library, itself an adaptive reuse of an early 20th century landmark bank building from the heyday of Providence as a center of commerce, included participants from academia as well as the architectural community. The discussion focused on the breadth of the subjects of the ten issues and the decade they encompassed, with a closing by Friedrich

St. Florian stating that this endeavor extended the legacy of Ernst Lichtblau.

Why did three architects teaching in the Department of Interior Architecture choose to co-found an academic journal on "adaptive reuse" in 2008? At that time, the term adaptive reuse was established but not commonly used. A Google search of the term then would have yielded no results. While the first recorded use of the term adaptive reuse is recent, the practice has its roots in earlier centuries, where reuse was often necessitated by a scarcity of resources. The first noted use of the term in 1973 curiously coincided with the global oil crisis, which triggered an awareness of natural resources. Until recently the reuse of existing structures was most often associated with renovation and refurbishment, previously considered as a bread-and-butter staple of architectural practice not meriting design recognition. With a global focus in the millennium on the effects of climate change, and the acknowledgment that "buildings are the major source of global demand for energy and materials that produce by-product greenhouse gases,"[5] the practice of adaptive reuse came into its own. In 2007, Carl Elefante, an architect with a practice focusing on preservation and sustainability (and eventually the 94th president of the American Institute of Architects), coined the phrase "the greenest building is one that is already built,"[6] in an article of the same name for the *Forum Journal*, a publication of the National Trust for Historic Preservation. In this article, Elefante connected environmental stewardship to architecture by underscoring that architects, despite their embrace of carbon-neutral buildings, could not build their way to sustainability. Citing statistics from Ed Mazria's Architecture 2030 organization, with its goal of carbon neutrality, Elefante stated that a millennial building boom would result in 28 billion square feet of new construction by 2030 while, simultaneously, 54 billion square feet of the existing building stock would undergo renovations. This was the context for the coining of the greenest building phrase. Four years later, in 2011, the National Trust would substantiate Elefante's statement by quantifying the environmental value of building reuse through the Preservation Green Lab of the National Trust. It found that "it takes 10 to 80 years for a new building that is 30 percent more efficient than an average-performing existing building to overcome, through efficient operations, the negative climate change impacts related to the construction process."[7] Although this quantification would be in the future, in 2008 simply the existence of Elefante's turn of phrase on the greenest building caused great excitement in RISD's Department of Interior Architecture. This convergence of sustainability and reuse captured the essence of the department pedagogy. Through Elefante's phrase, the department's educational mission would gain recognition in the field. This visibility triggered an awareness of the woefully scarce quantity of material on the subject, written or otherwise, despite this recognition. It was the impetus for crafting a grant proposal that would seed the inaugural volume of *Int|AR*.

The inaugural issue of the *Int|AR Journal* was a sampling of adaptive reuse ideas that served as both a 'testing of the waters' and an enticement for further exploration. In 2008, as the first issue was assembled, there was no indication of how the future of adaptive reuse would evolve, or how it would fit into the contemporary construct of the design world. One could not have predicted the convergence of history, politics and economics in paradigm shifts and its effect on adaptive reuse. The confluence of deindustrialization and climate change science and its effect on adaptive reuse practice are also strongly apparent with hindsight. Without this knowledge, the subjects touched upon in the inaugural volume are prescient. The breadth of subjects represented in the table of contents set an agenda for the future of the practice. Beyond case studies, the articles expanded into urban renewal, historic preservation and art, all viewed through the lens of reuse. The inaugural cover depicts a transformation by Franco Albini of the former convent of the Eremitani to the Musei Civici degli Eremitani in Padua, Italy. Albini's modern steel stair intervention, viewed from a steel-reinforced, classical stone rondel, conveyed the optimism of this new subject as dialogues between new and old, past and present.

The plans for the production of Volume 02 began in earnest months before the publication of the inaugural volume in 2009. Again, looking backward, its subject, Adapting Industrial Structures, paralleled history. It reflected the phenomenon that began at the end of the 20th century, emerging in 2009. A remnant of textile manufacturing in a town of southern France, an outmoded slaughterhouse on the outskirts of Shanghai, a defunct electrical factory complex in western Massachusetts, a decommissioned ammunition factory in Beijing and the last grain elevator in Philadelphia, these articles on abandoned and decommissioned industrial buildings reflected the repercussions of deindustrialization. While Volume 02 focused on the perspectives of the developed countries left with empty structures for reuse, Volume 03 instead looked to the less developed countries that were the recipients of this shift. As the place of relocated industries, emerging economies became the focus of Volume 03. The viewpoint of the BRIC countries (Brazil, Russia, India and China) was represented with projects of reuse from India to Brazil and other nations such as Poland, Saudi Arabia, Slovenia and Pakistan. The issue was bracketed by "Submerging," on one end, a glance backward at lessons learned in developed countries such as Italy, and, on the other, "Luanda's New Frontier," speculations on the economic divide in the peri-urban communities of Angola.

A reflection of the name of the journal, Volumes 01 – 03 focused on design interventions in existing structures. The release of Volume 04 in 2012, however, ushered in a new direction. In a departure from topics of reuse in decommissioned or abandoned structures, Volume 04 focused on Difficult Memories: Reconciling Meaning. As an investigation of the uncomfortable and difficult inheritance from places of genocide, imprisonment, mental illness, natural disasters and racism, this issue expanded the focus of adaptive reuse studies beyond that of bricks and mortar. Termed 'negative heritage' today, in 2012 such a term did not exist to describe projects of trauma. Articles such as the one on *S.21*, a Cambodian school and an unwitting site of torture transformed to a genocide memorial, extended the discussion of adaptive reuse, liberating it from its formal dictionary definition. Volumes thereafter embraced critical contemporary topics such as climate action, service economics and race politics: Resilience (05), Water as Catalyst (08), Experience Economy (06), Intervention as Act (09). In Between (10) was interpreted broadly from urban contexts to interior space. Through the lens of adaptive reuse, these topics were explored as media that comprised, in each case, an existing structure and its context. The latter proved to be the critical connection that would launch adaptive reuse practice into prominence.

Context, in the case of adaptive reuse, has its physical manifestation as built form. The paradigm shifts that marked the end of the 20th century and the beginning of the millennium left behind such built manifestation of the past as factories, jails, slaughterhouses and mental asylums. In addition to issues of pure construction, the reuse of such structures is laden with the values of a past existence. Sam Mockbee, founder of Rural Studio, stated that "[a]rchitecture, more than any other art form, is a social art and must rest on the social and cultural base of its time and place."[8] A thoughtful application of the Venice Charter principles in adaptive reuse that conservation (and in this case, reuse) would best be served "by making use of them for some socially useful purpose,"[9] implies a choice of new use that would relate to the social and cultural context of the present society. In this sense, where an existing structure represents the values of a past social context in which it was built, its reuse in a new social context yields an intersection of past and present values. It is an opportunity that invites critique of the old through the new.

The various subjects of Volumes 04 through 10 are reflective of the social context of the first two decades of the millennium. Concerns related to the environment and climate change fueled Volumes 05 and 08 and resulted in explorations of resilience and sea level rise. Volume 07 focused on the evolving role of installation art and exhibition in context as a means to connect to the past through aesthetic interpretations. Volume 09 was inspired by the political context in the US of 2018 that prompted a call to "act."

The selection of the cover is a complicated process at all times. For Volume 09, it was a clarion call for action with a cover depicting the *Rosa Parks House Project* and referencing the 'first lady' of American civil rights activism. Volume 10 on the In-Between speaks to the fluidity of our society at the end of the second decade. While each volume addressed its particular focus, threads of similar themes were discernible across the ten issues that connected them in time. These themes reflect the preoccupations of a millennial society absorbed in its particular causes. The decade of adaptive reuse journalism was, in retrospect, more than simply an architectural inquiry.

NOTES

1 "A New World: Good taste and good design Ernst Lichtblau in Providence" in *Ernst Lichtblau Architect 1883–1963*, organized by Otto Wagner Archive, Academy of Fine Arts, Vienna, and curated by August Sarnitz and Samuel B. Frank, Providence, RI, 1994, p. 33.

2 Ibid.

3 https://www.merriam-webster.com (accessed January 13, 2021).

4 Editorial, *Int|AR Journal* Volume 01, 2009.

5 http://www.architecture2030.org (accessed December 7, 2015).

6 Carl Elefante. "The Greenest Building Is One That Is Already Built," *Forum Journal*, Summer 2007, Volume 21, No. 4, p. 26.

7 "The Greenest Building: Quantifying the Environmental Value of Building Reuse," a Report of the Preservation Green Lab, National Trust for Historic Preservation, 2011, p. VIII.

8 http://samuelmockbee.net/about/quotes/architecture-more-than-any-other-art-form/ (accessed December 15, 2020).

9 Article 5, International Charter for the Conservation and Restoration of Monuments and Sites (The Venice Charter, 1964) from IInd International Congress of Architects and Technicians of Historic Monuments, Venice, 1964.

INTRODUCTION

THE SOCIAL AGENDA OF ADAPTIVE REUSE

by LILIANE WONG

Environmental stewardship was the defining characteristic of adaptive reuse in the first decade of the millennium that brought this practice to the forefront. Through this lens, adaptive reuse was a call to adaptation, recycling and transformation — as opposed to a destruction of the past to make way for the new. Through this lens, adaptive reuse was poised as a responsible alternative to building anew, one truly contributing to a net zero carbon future. Such a position was unique to the urgent concerns of the day.

As adaptive reuse practice is millennia-old, other concerns of the day have prompted reuse of different kinds over the centuries. From iconoclasm to displays of power and equitable land use, adaptive reuse has the unique characteristic of serving as a vehicle that reflects the agenda of its times. In this sense, adaptive reuse practice is distinctive for its mutable nature, a mutability derived from its reliance on existing structures. Design decisions in adaptive reuse are predicated on pre-existing conditions stemming from the host structure; each host structure is defined by a particular historic, economic and cultural context that, in turn, influences its reuse. From early civilizations to the present, adaptive reuse practice is a product of these shifts of context.

Towards the Forefront of Sustainability and Design

Early examples of adaptive reuse are derived from the evolution of civilization from one cultural society to another. Factors that include trade, colonization, religious conversion, social dominance, natural disaster and invasion resulted in the elimination of one civilized group by another. Each of these conquests was accompanied by victory and its resultant spoils of war. These spoils of looted goods, prisoners and existing infrastructure form the basis of early material reuse. Plunder of a different nature is found within the vanquished cities. Occupied by victors, the remnants of the cities became sites for adaptive reuse. New styles of habitation, the hallmark of a foreign culture, were introduced into the remaining structures and infrastructure — structures whose purpose and importance in one society are made obsolete by the customs of another. Domestic structures are overwritten by a slow occupation that embeds itself over time. Accommodating mundane, quotidian needs, domestic structures are knit into and inbetween grand structures of old, creating a patchwork in the fabric of the city. Driven by the needs of the new culture, these small interventions are made without consideration of the purpose

(FIG. 1)

(FIG.1)
Geometry is used as commentary in Studio Libeskind's reuse of an armory as Dresden's Military History Museum

or organization of the existing architecture itself. Rather, these domestic host buildings become simply an economy of means. By contrast, civic and religious structures, representative of the values of the vanquished, are often the site of an adaptive reuse of iconoclasm. Adaptive reuse as a byproduct of power shifts can be seen in ancient sites of worship, from Luxor to Córdoba. New occupation manifests itself through religion as iconoclastic interventions overwritten upon the existing worship sites. These interventions of new use rely on and reference the history and cultural context of the existing structure. Such interventions are visible in ancient sites, but power shifts are not limited to the distant past or to religious sites. While religious structures are no longer centers of power, other structures representative of contemporary seats of power become the host structure for iconoclasm of a different sort. In the geometric skewering of the Dresden armory in its new life as the Military History Museum, or the cathartic stake driven into the Nazi Party Rally Grounds in Nuremberg, now transformed in part to the Nuremberg Documentation Center, adaptive reuse interventions are utilized as commentary on past modes of power.

Adaptive reuse is in service of power through patronage in the 16th century, as evidenced in the projects of Michelangelo for various popes from Clement X to Pius IV. His Florentine projects are a panoply of adaptive reuse types from interior renovation to façade and rooftop additions, each commissioned by a member of the Medici family for their glorification. The new Sacristy of San Lorenzo is part of the San Lorenzo complex, where work to memorialize the Medici family spanned two centuries. The new Sacristy, completed in 1555, is an interior retrofit that is predicated on the design of the existing old Sacristy of Brunelleschi, completed in 1440. The geometric and volumetric interplay of Brunelleschi's sacristy serves as the starting point of Michelangelo's Medici chapel, where the themes of Brunelleschi become the springboard for Michelangelo's inventions in the classical language of architecture. The two sacristies demonstrate the relationship between adaptive reuse interventions and existing context. The Laurentian Library, a rooftop extension in the same complex of structures, was intended to display the intellectual leadership of the Medici family. Michelangelo's intervention here is limited by the structural requirements for supporting an addition over the existing monastic quarters. The design for the vestibule with its iconic orders (and staircase) is a stratagem of load transfer from new to existing supports, demonstrating a critical aspect of the relationship between adaptive reuse and the host structure.

Michelangelo's move from Florence to Rome in the 1530s brought him commissions of a different scale that further advanced the practice of adaptive reuse. His project for Pope Paul III to reimagine Capitoline Hill as a symbol of Rome for a visit of Charles V exhibits adaptive reuse practice at a grand urban scale. The Piazza del Campidoglio is a planning project involving not a single host structure but a group of host structures. The design for the grand piazza that we know today was predicated on the existence of two structures, the medieval Senators' palace and the Quattrocento Conservators' palace, each with its particular character, style, placement, geometry, volume, etc. These existing conditions were the basis of Michelangelo's façade renovations, additions and landscape interventions that together constitute one of Rome's most important landmarks. Michelangelo's 1561 project for Pope Pius IV to transform the Thermae of Diocletian to the church of Santa Maria degli Angeli e Martiri is exemplary as a first intentional conversion of one programmatic use to another. In a Christian Rome of the late Renaissance, it was a conversion of a semi-intact pagan ruin to a Christian basilica. The Thermae were the largest baths of ancient Rome and accommodated over 3,000 visitors at one time. Their remains, as depicted in artists' renderings from Étienne du Pérac to Piranesi, attest to a colossal scale with monumental architectural features. As an abandoned structure, its potential lay in these characteristics, which Pope Pius IV viewed as architectural features common to both the pagan baths and the Christian church. Michelangelo's church was built with minimal new exterior construction inside the frigidarium and within the existing cross vaults, some still standing today. Adapting the remains of three vaulted rooms, Michelangelo created a Greek cross with a monumental transept of more than 90 meters, derived from the colossal forms of the existing baths. This project was

(FIG. 2)

groundbreaking as an architectural intervention into an existing structure. Surprisingly, there is no formal entrance to this impressive basilica. It is accessed instead through the remains of a coved apse of the Thermae, left in its original, ruined form. The relationship of intervention to existing structure and the decision to retain the ruins as a temporal reference are far-thinking. A conversion of this scale would not be attempted again for centuries. Through the patronage of the powerful in this period of history, the architectural achievements of Michelangelo, each a unique adaptive reuse project, advanced adaptive reuse practice in an unprecedented manner.

From conquerors of ancient civilizations to the ruling families and clergy of the Renaissance and Baroque periods, adaptive reuse as an instrument of power brought a monumental form of the practice into view. Buildings and structures and the manner in which they were reused were advanced through the machinations of power. In subsequent centuries, the concept of power would change dramatically with the wane of monarchs and clerics. Projects of reuse, at the scale and significance of Papal Rome, would not re-emerge for more than 400 years. Until the last decades of the 20th century, adaptive reuse was limited to minor projects of reuse, primarily driven by economy. There was in this hiatus, however, indirect development in the concept of adaptive reuse through the formation of ideas of preservation. These ideas date to late 18th century

(FIG.2)
In an act of exorcism, the new Documentation Center Nazi Party Rally Grounds is a glass shaft driven through the Nuremberg Nazi Party rally grounds

(FIG. 3)

France, where revolutionary ideas of power led to the fall of the monarchy and the rise of the people. One direct result of the French Revolution was the damage inflicted upon thousands of structures from jails to church property and palaces. In the aftermath of this destruction and the restoration of the Bourbons in 1830, the position of Inspector General for the Historic Monuments of France was established to oversee the inventory of damaged historic monuments and to begin the process of restoring them. By 1849, the 934 monuments enumerated in the first 1840 inventory of buildings in dire need of repairs had grown to 3,000 monuments. The attempts to understand the plight of such historically significant structures led to polarized views of what should or should not be undertaken with historic structures. These were conversations on the restoration of heritage from which emerged concepts of conservation and preservation as regulatory practices.

From cathedrals to excavated archaeological sites, the debates that began in the late 19th century became all the more urgent in the 20th century with the destruction wrought by the power struggles of the two World Wars. The formation of international agencies such as UNESCO and ICOMOS led to the creation of charters and policies on preservation and restoration. The introduction and adoption by many countries of the Athens Charter of 1931 and the Venice Charter of 1964, together with the establishment of the organizations dedicated to global cooperation in the field, mark a major moment in the international development and consolidation of conservation policies. At the heart of these policies was the issue of the reuse of heritage structures. The General Principles of the Athens Charter that "recommends that the occupation of buildings, which ensures the continuity of their life, should be maintained but that they should be used for a purpose which respects their historic or artistic character,"[1] and those of the Venice Charter stating that "[t]he conservation of monuments is always facilitated by making use of them for some socially useful purpose"[2] provide the foundation for the adaptive reuse of significant structures. Without direct reference to adaptive reuse, a term yet undefined at that time, these policies provide an implicit set of definitions and regulations pertaining to a type of reuse practice. Other important developments followed that impart nuanced interpretations of heritage and reuse, including the 1972 UNESCO Convention for the Protection of World Cultural and Natural Heritage, the 1981 Burra Charter of ICOMOS Australia that provided guidelines for cultural heritage management, the 1983 Appleton Charter of ICOMOS Canada for the Protection and Enhancement of the Built Environment, and the 1994 Nara Document on Authenticity. More recently, the role of the international organizations has been instrumental in further expanding the scope of heritage, with the 1997 Proclamation of Masterpieces of the government to

(FIG.3)
The first Earth Day, April 22, 1970

"investigate and define a form of preservation," the 1998 establishment of DOCOMOMO International (International Committee for Documentation and Conservation of Buildings, Sites and Neighborhoods of the Modern Movement) and the 2003 UNESCO adoption of policy for Safeguarding Intangible Heritage. Each development in preservation and conservation also contributed to expanding the breadth of the adaptive reuse of heritage.

In 1973, nine years after the Venice Charter, the term 'adaptive reuse' was formally defined.[3] This acknowledgment of the reuse of existing structures coincides with a burgeoning awareness and activism for the environment. Earth Day was celebrated just three years prior, in 1970. Power struggles in a different part of the world brought these issues to crisis point in the US with the oil embargoes of the early 1970s. The issue of energy and the global entanglement surrounding oil production provided the impetus for exploring alternative and renewable sources. The decade of the 70s witnessed the birth of environmentalist issues with the 1972 United Nations Conference on the Human Environment as a turning point for international participation. In the next decades, environmental issues proliferated with the acknowledgment of global warming and, eventually, climate change science as we know it today. A direct mandate for adaptive reuse based on environmentalism would not be linearly established until Carl Elefante's 2007 article "The Greenest Building Is One That Is Already Built."

As a term of the 1970s, adaptive reuse references a time in which the scarcity of resources emerged as a global issue, but also a turbulent time of change which witnessed the manifestation of many idealistic protests of the previous decade. In the realm of urban planning, it was a time of opposition to urban renewal programs introduced in the 1940s and 1950s that authorized "loans and grants to localities to assist locally initiated, locally planned and locally managed slum clearance and urban redevelopment undertakings"[4] "to aid in the ... elimination and prevention of slums."[5] While Jane Jacobs' seminal 1961 *Death and Life of Great American Cities* voiced early opposition to this type of urban renewal, which often affected the most disadvantaged, it was not until the early 1970s that this disaffection became action. In particular, the US Department of Housing and Urban Development (HUD) enacted the Community Development Block Grant in 1974, which allocated funds for the rehabilitation of housing and commercial buildings. In this context, one of HUD's longest-running programs, large cities such as New York pursued various initiatives, including one to "Reuse Vacant Space in Existing Buildings."[6] Art entrepreneur Alanna Heiss pioneered adaptive reuse practice as we know it today in her efforts to rehabilitate "derelict warehouses and unused city-owned property in an

(FIG. 4)

(FIG.4)
IUAV University entrance, Venice, Italy

(FIG. 5)

environment reeling from blight and decay, creating nonprofit art spaces that blurred the lines between studio, gallery, theater and community center."[7] These initial instances of adaptive reuse included the 1972 founding of an artists' gallery in the clock tower of the 19th-century McKim, Mead & White New York Life Insurance Company Building in Lower Manhattan (designated a historic landmark in the 1980s) and the reuse of the abandoned First Ward School or Queens Public School No. 1 (PS1) in Long Island City as the Institute for Art and Urban Resources, Inc., an organization devoted to organizing exhibitions in underutilized and abandoned spaces across New York City, which would eventually become MoMA PS1, an offshoot of the Museum of Modern Art.

Elsewhere in the latter half of the 20th century, adaptive reuse projects were sporadic. The oeuvre of Carlo Scarpa in the Veneto stands out with exemplary adaptive reuse projects that encompass interior retrofit, addition and conversion. The transformation of the medieval castle to the Museo di Castelvecchio in Verona, the renovation of the Querini Stampalia, the addition at the Gipsoteca Canoviana Museum, the retrofit for the Olivetti Showroom are timeless and classic works of architectural poetry in existing structures. But they are not the norm. Other notable projects at this time are scant. La Fábrica in Barcelona, Spain, a 1973 conversion of a concrete factory to an office and residence by Ricardo Bofill, is one notable example. In the following decade, Lina Bo Bardi's SESC Pompeia, the transformation of a barrel factory in São Paolo, Brazil, to a cultural art center and social programming complex, is another.

In the next decades, free trade agreements of the 1980s led to the relocation of labor-intensive manufacturing to less developed nations with lower wages and work standards. Predicted by Daniel Bell in his 1973 book *The Coming of Post-Industrial Society*, these changes in industrialized societies brought about by the shifting of labor would contribute significantly to the development of adaptive reuse practice. In addition, technology introduced a new element into the workforce of industrial robotics. Together, these developments led to a deindustrialization crisis in developed countries of unemployment and defunct industrial complexes. The disappearance of industrial processes from industrial nations left a vast number of vacant factories and plant-type structures behind, such as textile mills, printing companies, meatpacking plants and armaments factories. New forms of energy production and agricultural practices added to the collection of decommissioned structures with defunct gasometers, coal mine extraction

(FIG. 6)

(FIG.5)

La Fábrica, Barcelona, Spain

(FIG.6)

SESC Pompeia, São Paulo, Brazil, a conversion of a barrel factory to a cultural center by Lina Bo Bardi

(FIG. 7)

facilities, grain silos and slaughterhouses found in many countries including Europe, the USA and China. These existing structures would either be demolished or reused. Bofill's and Bo Bardi's projects were the first examples of the adaptive reuse of industrial structures. These would be followed by groundbreaking projects such as the 2000 reuse of a decommissioned power station in London as the Tate Modern Museum, the 2001 conversion of gasometers in Vienna as housing, the 2007 transformation of the Zollverein coal mine industrial complex in Essen, into a cultural center, the 2006 renovation of a Polish textile manufacturing complex into Manufaktura, a multiuse project of hospitality, culture and commerce, the conversion of a munitions production factory to the 798 Art District in Beijing, the transformation of a Danish grain silo to waterfront apartments, the conversion of a slaughterhouse in Shanghai to a shopping and cultural center. Completed in the last years of the 20th century and the beginning of the millennium, these adaptive reuse projects have now become the standard bearers of industrial conversions. In the first decade of the millennium, marked by its preoccupation with urgent climate change action, this wealth of decommissioned buildings, together with Carl Elefante's coining of the phrase "the greenest building is one that is already built," catapulted adaptive reuse practice into the forefront of sustainability and design.

(FIG. 8)

(FIG. 9)

Hosts, Guests and Current Social Discourse

In Book III of *The Ten Books on Architecture*, Vitruvius introduced a parallel between the human body and buildings. In the spirit of such a parallel where a host is someone who receives guests, a host building is a structure that receives a new use for a defined or undefined period of time. Just as a host contends with the various social circumstances of their guests, a host structure also contends with the social conditions relevant to new use. Host buildings are wrappers of different kinds, manifested as physical construction into which new life is introduced. Their ability to sustain a new use depends on many specific and individual factors: their condition, their potential to support additional load, their spatial fit with the demands of a new use, their memory, their placement in context. Often, the factors determine constructability. The last two factors, however, posit the host structure as a vehicle for social commentary. Many concerns of the day that are the hallmark of current social discourse — just and equitable societies, climate change, identity, systemic racism, post-truth, migration, redemption and resilience — can be communicated through the language of bricks and mortar. As the reuse of an existing

(FIG.7)
The transformation of gasometers to housing in Vienna, Austria

(FIG.8)
798 Art Center, transformed from a munitions factory in Beijing, China

(FIG.9)
Andel's Hotel, hospitality in a decommissioned manufacturing complex in Łódź, Poland

(FIG. 10)

structure for a new purpose requires adaptation to an imperfect host structure, the design intervention is a tool for bridging architectural imperfections but also for critiquing the hosts' past context(s).

Six Themes

Six common themes mirroring those of society in the millennium were discernable across a decade of adaptive reuse practice: appropriation, ecology, equity, memory and redemption, identity, authenticity. Expressed through the vocabulary of design and reuse, they speak to the social issues of a decade.

Pertaining to the action of inserting a new program of use within the old, **Appropriation** is an apt theme for the reuse of existing structures. Michelangelo's Santa Maria degli Angeli e Martiri in a pagan bath, Ricardo Bofill's private residence in a site of material production, Lina Bo Bardi's cultural complex in a factory, Gae Aulenti's Musée d'Orsay in a train station, Toyo Ito's reuse of a ventilation shaft as installation art are new occupations of existing constructs that reveal changing societal values. Privatization of the industrial as home interior or the employment of production as facilities for culture offer new views of domesticity and entertainment. These appropriations are reflections of our shifting beliefs and social mores. In time, these conversions, too, will be replaced in another reuse serving the needs and values of a future society, in a continuum of adaptive reuse practice. If this trend can be seen in Michelangelo's appropriation of a civic pagan structure for Christian worship in the heyday of the Renaissance, today we see the trend reversed in the reappropriation of many Christian churches for concert venues, breweries and gyms.

The United Nations states that "climate change is the defining issue of our time and we are at a defining moment."[8] Relating to our physical surroundings, the topic of

(FIG.10)
Musée d'Orsay, a museum in the former Gare d'Orsay, Paris, France

Ecology is critical in the built environment. The effects of climate change as they impact structures will be a crucial aspect of adaptive reuse practice. The future of coastal structures and cities and those affected by increased climate-induced disasters will require rethinking and retrofitting. The embrace of renewable energy and the resultant rejection of energy sources harmful to the environment will provide in itself an entire typology of decommissioned structures for adaptive reuse practice. The reuse of heritage gasometers in Vienna or the coalmine complex in Essen constitutes the beginnings of a shift in society as it necessarily moves forward, prioritizing environmental concerns.

In appropriating structures of the past or rethinking those affected by climate change, what constitutes an equitable practice? Who are the beneficiaries of reuse? Who participates in the decisions regarding change? What of inclusive processes? From physical shelter to intangible knowledge, the potential exists for the consideration of **Equity** in both the concept and the implementation of reuse.

With the changes wrought by so many shifting past norms from deindustrialization to climate change, what is the role of the past as we look to the future? This is a question that was at the heart of the debates of conservation and preservation from the third decade of the 19th century and it remains with us today. Debated furiously in the late 1870s between the advocates of theorists such as Viollet-le-Duc, John Ruskin and William Morris, this question eventually led to the beginnings of the conservation/preservation movement. Today, beyond the need to recognize and preserve the past, we acknowledge and reckon with heritage of a different nature; negative heritage — trauma, genocide, systemic racism — demands a different accounting of **Memory and Redemption**. The structures that were the sites of such atrocities hold memories that cannot be erased. They are silent witnesses of horrific events in the past but also of continuous and systemic inequalities. The reuse of structures imbued with these memories places a responsibility on adaptive reuse practice. Can a structure be an instrument of healing and justice? Can bricks and mortar play a role in redemption?

Shifting norms in the built environment, appropriation of decommissioned and abandoned structures, redefining memory, redemption through reuse — these actions prompt a reflection of **Identity** in the midst of metamorphosis. An existing structure, with its past histories, is a palimpsest on which new histories are grafted. These recombinations parallel the complexities of contemporary identity discussions from collective to political and from gender to racial. In the built environment, reuse becomes a means to query the status quo and to contribute to an evolving conversation. A structure with an agricultural

(FIG. 11)

(FIG. 12)

(FIG.11)
Nikolaj Art Museum in the former church of Saint Nicholas, Copenhagen, Denmark

(FIG.12)
The Zollverein Coal Mine Industrial Complex in a former industrial mining site in Essen, Germany

past in Switzerland, named Yellow House for its iconic color, is whitewashed as part of its transformation to a cultural center; its identifying color removed, the Yellow House retains its name, referencing the change and its new identity.

In the 19th century discourse on preservation and restoration, John Ruskin argued against any action on our monuments, claiming: "We have no right whatever to touch them. They are not ours. They belong partly to those who built them, and partly to all the generations of mankind who are to follow us. The dead have still their right in them: that which they laboured for, the praise of achievement or the expression of religious feeling, or whatsoever else it might be which in those buildings they intended to be permanent, we have no right to obliterate. What we have ourselves built, we are at liberty to throw down; but what other men gave their strength and wealth and life to accomplish, their right over does not pass away with their death: still less is the right to the use of what they have left vested in us only. It belongs to all their successors."[9] Ruskin represents one extreme viewpoint of **Authenticity** — that it belongs only to the untouched original. Ruskin's view precludes new lives for existing structures. Between Ruskin and Viollet-le-Duc, who spoke of restoration as "a completeness which could never have existed at any given moment,"[10] there is a spectrum of viewpoints. What is authentic in adaptive reuse? What of the aura defined by Walter Benjamin? How does adaptive reuse practice maintain authenticity of the original? How do the new identities claimed through adaptive reuse forge their own authenticity?

(FIG. 13)

The Evolving Context of History

The rich variations of adaptive reuse practice are derived from the evolving context of history. Responding to changing norms over time, adaptive reuse is a response to shifting ideas and momentous events. In 2020, we witness a shift caused by the sudden and compressed events of the pandemic crisis. Paradigm shifts today are a response to the havoc the pandemic has wrought on all aspects of life. In the built environment, existing structures are reused in unconventional ways as temporary emergency responses. Ice rinks as morgues, gymnasiums as temporary hospital, car washes as drive-through testing sites, hotels as housing for health workers unable to return home; this novel reuse of existing structures establishes a new category of adaptive reuse practice — pandemic reuse. While these uses are hopefully temporary, there will not be a return to life pre-March 2020. The shifting norms of working from home or remote learning will have post-pandemic repercussions. Office towers, the classroom, nursing homes will all be revised in post-pandemic life through adaptive reuse.

(FIG. 14)

(FIG.13)
The *Rosa Parks House Project*, displayed in WaterFire Art Center in Providence, RI, USA

(FIG.14)
Yellow House, Flims, Switzerland

(FIG. 15)

While the effects of the pandemic on the built environment are easily discernible due to the swift and drastic way it transformed everyday life, the impact of other, less rapidly moving trends are only visible in hindsight. Adaptive reuse practice has had moments of glory in fits and starts since the beginning of time. In the 21st century, it gained recognition and importance as a responsible practice at an urgent time of climate change. The story of ten seminal years of adaptive reuse practice in the 21st century is found in a decade of journalism at *Int|AR*. It is in reviewing the work of these years that a whole picture emerges of this practice, where it has come from, why it was important in the past, why it is important now and how it will be part of our future. In *War and Peace*, Tolstoy wrote of Russia during the Napoleonic wars some 50 years after the subject of his novel. In looking back at this time from such distance, he said that it was "a period whose scent and sound are still perceptible to us, but remote enough for us to contemplate it unemotionally."[11] It is in looking back over the articles with their various themes of 10 years that we gain a perspective of adaptive reuse and its ascent as a responsible practice, one of enormous relevance both to the past and the future.

(FIG. 16)

NOTES

1 General Principles, The Athens Charter for the Restoration of Historic Monuments-1931, from First International Congress of Architects and Technicians of Historic Monuments, Athens, 1931. https://www.icomos.org/en/167-the-athens-charter-for-the-restoration-of-historic-monuments (accessed January 13, 2021)

2 Article 5, International Charter for the Conservation and Restoration of Monuments and Sites (The Venice Charter 1964), from IInd International Congress of Architects and Technicians of Historic Monuments, Venice, 1964.

3 https://www.merriam-webster.com (accessed January 13, 2021).

4 Summary of Provisions of the National Housing Act of 1949, Committee on Banking and Currency U.S. Senate, U.S. Government Printing Office, Washington, DC, 1949, p. 1.

5 Public Law 560 - August 2, 1954, U.S. Government Printing Office, Washington, DC, 1954, p. 1.

6 Economic Recovery, New York City's program for 1977 – 81, U.S. Department of Commerce NOAA, p. 48.

7 "Introduction," *The Artist in Place: The First 10 Years of MoMA PS 1*, https://www.moma.org/interactives/exhibitions/2012/artistinplace/ (accessed January 30, 2021).

8 https://www.un.org/en/sections/issues-depth/climate-change/ (accessed December 23, 2020).

9 John Ruskin, *The Seven Lamps of Architecture*, George Allen, Kent, 1889, p. 197.

10 Viollet-le-Duc, *On Restoration*, Samson Low, Marston, Low and Searle, London, 1875, p. 9.

11 Henri Troyat. *Tolstoy*, transl. Nancy Amphoux, Grove Press edition, New York, 2001, p. 275.

(FIG.15)
The Tuol Sleng Genocide Museum in S.21, the former Khmer Rouge security prison, Phnom Penh, Cambodia

(FIG.16)
FRAC Dunkerque, France

APPROPRIATION

Appropriation is a defining action of adaptive reuse practice. In reusing an existing structure for a new purpose, adaptive reuse is distinguished from architecture and the act of building form where there was none. Appropriation implies possession but, in the continuum of adaptive reuse, a temporary one. Dependent on the presence of a host structure, adaptive reuse can continue indefinitely in a cycle in which a host structure evolves from actively re-usable space to semi-ruin and ruin. In this act of appropriation, the re-inhabitation of physical space is accompanied by an inheritance of memory.

24 **Preservation through Transformation: The Granary [Volume 02]**
Deborah Grossberg Katz and Brian Phillips

30 **Appropriating Architecture: Digital Graffiti as Temporary Spatial Intervention [Volume 09]**
Dorothée King

38 **Coming Home: A Conversation with Do Ho Suh [Volume 07]**
Lea Hershkowitz

52 **Postindustrial Spectacle: Reconnecting Image and Function [Volume 06]**
Patrick Ruggiero, Jr.

58 **Informal Annexations [Volume 10]**
Rafael Luna

66 **City as Hotel: Pixel Hotel [Volume 01]**
Markus Berger

PRESERVATION THROUGH TRANSFORMATION

THE GRANARY

by DEBORAH GROSSBERG KATZ AND BRIAN PHILLIPS

Industrial conversions have become a crucial component of urban revitalization strategies in cities across the United States. Typically, the developer-driven approach to industrial adaptive reuse reprograms the high-ceilinged, open-plan spaces of defunct urban warehouses and factories as artist studios, high-end condos, or live-work lofts. But some industrial buildings, those with unusual structural features tailored to specific roles in industrial processes, have proved more difficult to convert. Because residential and commercial uses commonly represent the most economical conversion potentials, industrial structures that cannot be reused for either purpose face long-term neglect, demolition, or at best a specialized cultural program reliant on economic subsidies. Structures such as power plants, wharves, and grain silos have been systematically underutilized, abandoned, or torn down to make way for new development. Even buildings protected as historic structures can meet with demolition if developed with private funds.

A fresh look is required at how a wider variety of existing industrial structures can be adapted to become generators of urban development. This type of strategy would value the preservation of existing built spaces both as a method for reducing energy expenditure on new construction and as a tactic for saving historically valuable buildings that might otherwise be demolished. The re-commissioning of specialized industrial buildings should be more widely considered by developers, architects, and the historic preservation community,

Perspective view of the Granary from 20th Street

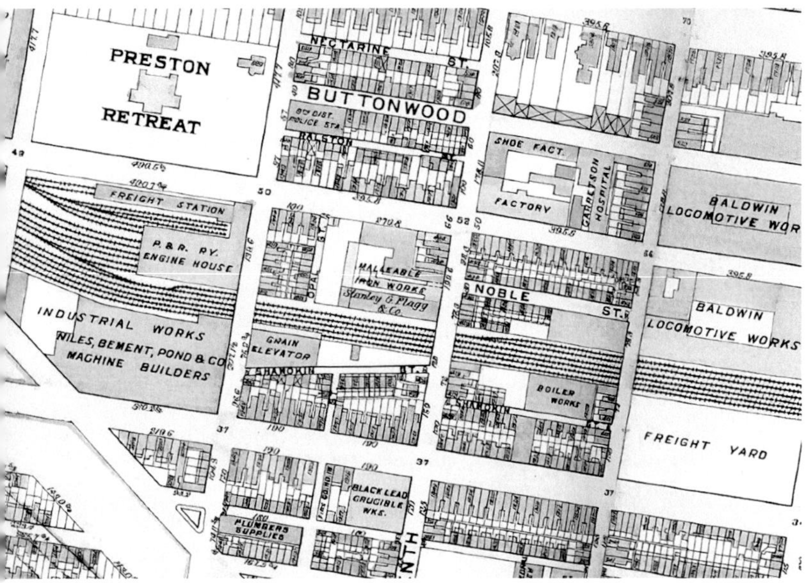

even if radical physical changes must be made. Architects should become advocates for the potential value these seemingly outmoded structures can bring to the development equation. A comprehensive plan for adaptive reuse of the Granary, one of Philadelphia's last remaining grain silos, points to the possibilities and complexities of such advocacy.

In the 19th and early 20th centuries, Philadelphia was one of the nation's foremost manufacturing cities and possessed a rich and diverse stock of industrial buildings and infrastructure. In particular, the city's highly developed railroad and seaport infrastructure rendered it an important hub for grain harvested in Pennsylvania and the Midwest. Philadelphia's granaries supplied other East Coast cities while serving the needs of thriving local businesses. From the mid-1860s through the mid-1950s, the Granary at 20th and Shamokin Streets served an important role supplying the city's bakeries and breweries. Taking advantage of its siting adjacent to the Brewerytown neighborhood and the railroad connecting the western countryside with eastern seaports, the building became a major distribution point in the local and national grain trade.

The first granary on the building's site was constructed of slate-sheathed wood in 1862. Grain was stored in its silos and gravity fed to railcars that pulled directly into the building's basement on tracks below grade. In 1924, the building was destroyed in a massive explosion caused by highly flammable grain dust, and the following year it was rebuilt on the old foundation out of reinforced concrete. The new structure, designed by architects at the Reading Company, was planned to withstand future grain dust explosions, with 17-inch-thick concrete walls organizing 70 eight-by-eight-foot silos. In addition to the hefty walls, six-foot-diameter supporting columns were placed about 16 feet on center at the building's base, tapering to two- and three-foot widths on upper floors. Six high-ceilinged floors sandwiched the silos, providing space for wagons and trucks to pull in at street level, and for machinery above.

The 1925 Granary structure served as a functioning grain elevator through the middle of the 20th century, when manufacturers and residents began to flee the city for the suburbs. The building was decommissioned in the late 1960s and was sold to a warehouse company in 1970. In 1977, after brief periods as a restaurant and later a disco, the structure was sold at sheriff sale to an interior designer, who converted the bottom two floors into a design studio and the top two floors and rooftop machine towers into a private penthouse residence. From 1986 to 2007, the building was owned and occupied by an architecture firm. Throughout its postindustrial history, the Granary's six-story grain silos have gone unused.

Today, the Granary site faces development pressure for the first time in half a century. It lies one block north

TOP
Historic photo of the Granary
MIDDLE
Sanborn Fire Insurance Map, 1910
BOTTOM
The Granary, present day

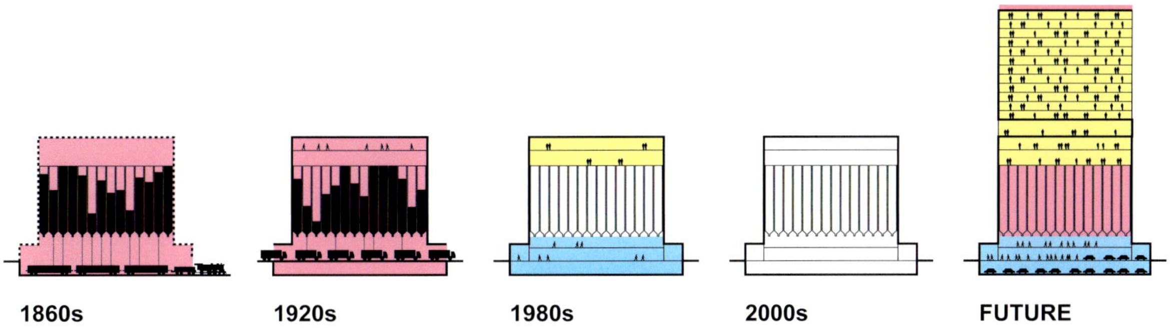

of the Benjamin Franklin Parkway, the diagonal traffic axis and civic armature developed in the early part of the 1900s to link Philadelphia's central City Hall with the Philadelphia Art Museum to the northwest. Over the past decade, a new development initiative along the

Parkway has led to the current and planned construction of a variety of cultural institutions immediately adjacent to the Granary site. A new home for the world renowned Barnes Foundation art collection designed by Tod Williams Billie Tsien is currently under construction across 20th Street from the Granary, and a significant expansion of the Free Library across Callowhill Street is proposed for construction in the next decade.

In 2007, Philadelphia-based developer Pearl Properties acquired the Granary. For two years, Pearl tried to find a tenant for the building's limited usable space on the top and bottom floors, without success. Today, in the face of increasing development pressures, the building is poised for change. Conversion to a cultural destination or other use that would keep it completely intact is unlikely. Demolition, to make way for more flexible, modern development, is a realistic possibility. In 2010, Interface Studio Architects (ISA) was retained to study the potential for integrating the Granary into an economically feasible reuse scheme.

ISA's approach for the adaptive reuse of the Granary was to repurpose the unusual, robust structure of its silos. Although the building is the equivalent of 12 stories tall, only six of those stories represent easily usable space. The remainder of the building—the tightly packed grid of windowless silos rising 60 feet up from the 3rd floor—cannot be reused for residential or commercial functions. A major interior demolition and reconstruction to create living spaces would be prohibitively expensive, and would destroy the oddly compelling silo spaces. It would also require the creation of façade apertures to allow light in—an unacceptable alteration by any standard.

Conversion in a traditional fashion is difficult due to the silos' robust structure and shape. But these potential drawbacks could be leveraged as strengths for a variety of non-standard environmental and cultural functions in which their over-designed structure could again be put to productive use. The ISA proposal employs the Granary's bulky structure as a literal platform for development and repurposes the silos as rainwater cisterns, heat exchange labyrinths, art galleries, historical installations, and climbing walls, among other temporary and permanent uses. These architectural and programmatic additions would bring sufficient density to the site to support development, enhance the energy-efficiency and cultural life of the building, and for the first time open the extraordinary interior to the public.

The proposal avoids costly demolition or alteration of the building by treating the Granary's structural grid as a massive foundation for a 12-story, 100-unit residential 'overbuild.' Proportion, materials, and massing are key design challenges in overbuilding the Granary. The design balances the existing building with a new addition of a similar size and shape. Old and new components are wrapped by a continuous architectural element, which serves as an armature for green walls on the north and west façades and a solar array on the roof. At grade, the program wrapper erodes into canopies and street furniture, reactivating the streetscape and creating a covered dining terrace, valet booth, bike parking, and public seating.

The 'overbuild' is also an opportunity to experiment with emerging construction technologies. To simplify logistics and control costs, ISA proposes the use of a prefabricated, modular construction technique, in which components are fabricated in an off site factory, trucked to the site, and craned into place. Factory installation of mechanical systems and finishes minimizes on-site labor, and the existing 16-foot column grid of the Granary aligns well with the dimensional limits of modular construction. Since the Granary represents an important early example of slip-form concrete construction, a retrofit with an equally innovative 21st century construction method would be fitting.

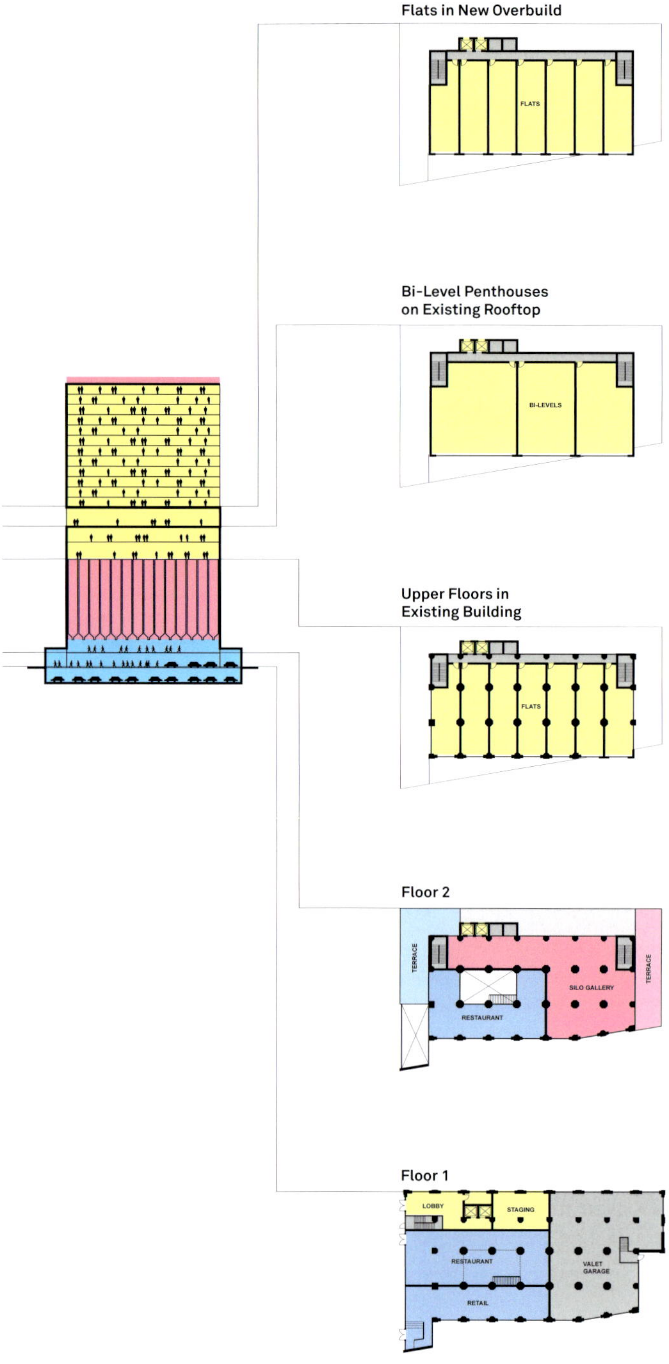

In addition to the 'overbuild,' the design converts the six existing floors of usable space into new restaurants, retail, and community facilities at grade and new apartments above the silos, with bi-level penthouses replacing the machine tower level on the existing building's rooftop. A second-floor silo gallery displays the new environmental and cultural uses of the silos to visitors, and public access points allow silo programs to connect with nearby businesses and cultural institutions. By forging extended programming partnerships with neighborhood fitness centers, groceries, museums, and libraries, the project aims to engage directly with the community and cultural network surrounding the Parkway.

The project proposes a number of bold, atypical moves, which are crucial to its feasibility. The proposal aims to preserve the Granary— not as a building shell devoid of internal function, but rather as a productive actor in the contemporary life of the city.

In an economically fragile city like Philadelphia, the challenge of preservation is to protect the rich inventory of historic structures while leveraging it for the future growth of the city. Unfortunately, the Philadelphia preservation community has opposed this development plan, clearly stating that the building should not be modified. Such an all-or-nothing point of view may actually endanger the building, since it constrains the potential for a more nuanced approach to the future of the Granary. For historically designated buildings, the lengthy preservation approval process can create a situation in which it is more economically efficient to demolish a historic building and build anew than it is to save and convert it for appropriate contemporary uses. As exemplified by the Granary, where financial hardship can be demonstrated by private developers, a historic designation may make a building's demolition more likely by disallowing economically necessary alterations.

The argument for a more flexible view of preservation revolves around the definition of value in historic buildings. A more traditional viewpoint argues that the Granary's architectural value is in its façade — its blank massiveness, elegant proportions, and crenellated roofline. Although these attributes must be recognized, the building's highest value lies in its unique industrial history, best expressed by its extraordinary interior. The spatial, material, and sensory qualities of the grain silo grid provide the most salient architectural experience of the building, while simultaneously containing the potential to tell the story of its past. ISA's proposed design emphasizes preserving and exposing the role buildings play in the story of the city — how they came to be, how they were used in the past, and how they will be used in new ways in the future. A flexible, nuanced definition of architectural value would encourage and promote adaptive reuse of historic buildings as a means to tell the evolving story of our built environment.

Typical plans and section

REFERENCES

"Reading Company Grain Elevator / The Granary." National Register of Historic Places Inventory Nomination Form, U.S. Dept. of the Interior National Park Service, Feb. 28, 1980. Item 8, p.1

"The Granary / Tidewater Grain Company Elevator / Reading Company Elevator." Submission to the Philadelphia Historical Commission, 1980. p.4–5

Ibid. p.4

The structural capacity of the building is more than adequate to support the proposed addition, according to the Harman Group, consulting engineers on the project.

"The Granary / Tidewater Grain Company Elevator / Reading Company Elevator." p.1

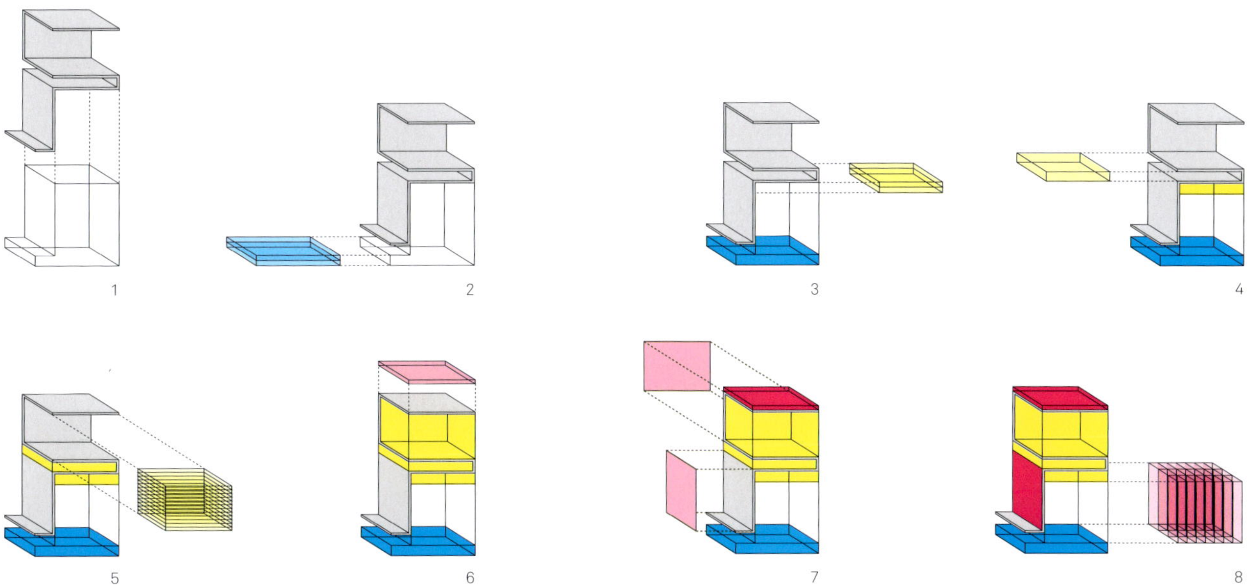

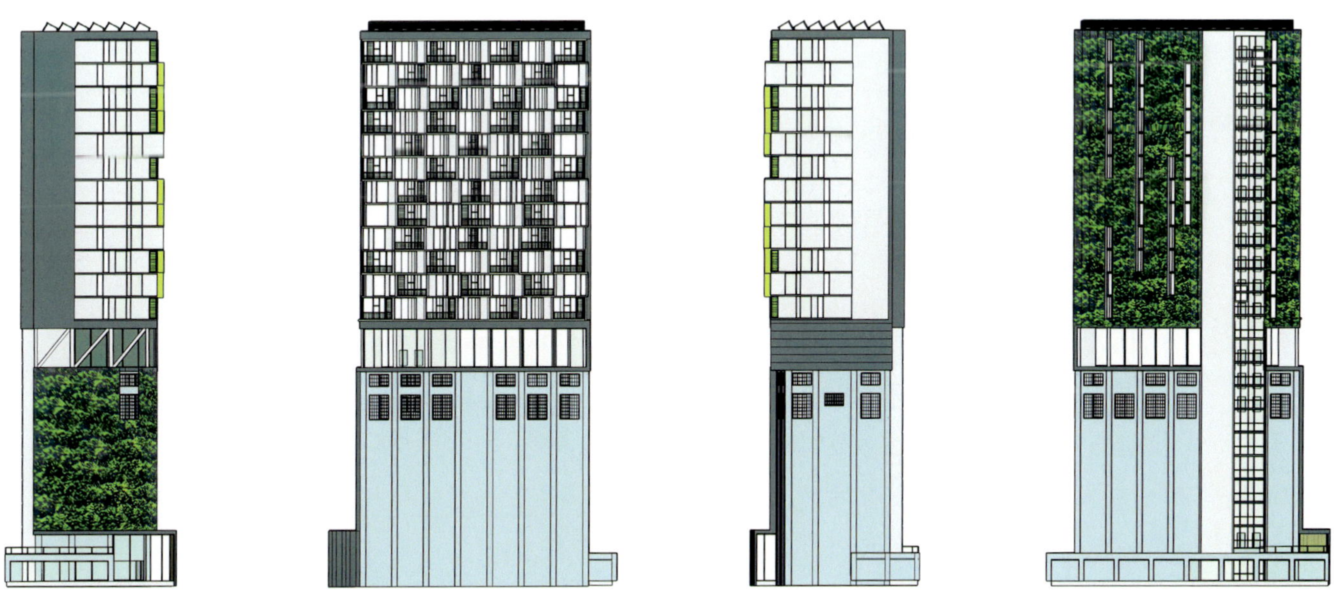

TOP

Granary Wrapper Sequence Diagram

BOTTOM

Granary elevations

Shamsia Hassani, *Dream Graffiti*, 2015

APPROPRIATING ARCHITECTURE

DIGITAL GRAFFITI AS TEMPORARY SPATIAL INTERVENTION

by DOROTHÉE KING

In the classic first essay on the importance of graffiti in the 1970s in New York City, Norman Mailer tells us the joke about the importance of a mediated visual reality. Two Jewish grandmothers are meeting on a street. The first one is pushing a stroller: "Oh," says the other, "what a beautiful grandchild you have." "That's nothing," says the first, reaching for her pocketbook, "Wait'll I show you her picture." [1]

We might not fully notice what we directly and sensually perceive in reality – yet we react very strongly to a mediated visual reality. Graffiti artists use this knowledge to display messages they do not want to be unconsciously, but consciously acknowledged. Playing with size, colors, and remarkable calligraphy, graffiti artists publicly apply layers of mediated visual realities with the hope to provoke real change in society. Graffiti developed as a cultural technique, cheap and available to the suppressed, to react to political and social constraints. Until now most graffiti artists use their publicly visible imagery to protest against authority, inequality, racism, supremacy, or ignorance. Graffiti is a tool of intervention. It comments on and criticizes existing cultural parameters.

The change-provoking, reality-mediating aspects are also true of digital graffiti. [2] Yet there are differences, which digital graffiti manifests in its temporality and its material. Digital graffiti is ephemeral in a way which physical graffiti is not. Messages are displayed temporarily. In traditional graffiti, information is scratched, scribbled, painted or sprayed on all kinds of mostly publicly visible surfaces, with the intention that the graffiti would be there for a long duration of time (if not forever). In digital graffiti the protest is no longer permanently applied to architecture. Graffiti in the form of digital images of writing, calligraphy, drawing, or painting is temporarily projected onto facades of buildings or other visible parts of constructions. While traditional graffiti might be associated with long-term vandalism and its messages might go out of fashion quickly, digital graffiti has the advantage of being removable and can be updated. Its other notable characteristic is its digital materiality in relation to the digitalization of our environment. Digital media makes us relate differently to space. Pictures, video, and sound are portable information, available at all times, embedded in carry-on every day gadgets and mobile phones. As the architect Anastasia Karandinou notes in her research on ephemeral qualities of architecture, "the traditional binary opposition between the sensuous and the digital is being currently reversed."[3] We have come to a point where technology does not only change the way we interact virtually, but also alters the physical architecture surrounding us. This seems to be the next logical step: to picture digital imagery from carry-on gadgets, projecting them in greater size and thus making them publicly visible interventions. With digital graffiti, we may mediate our visual environment digitally.

Some examples may serve to demonstrate the potential of digital graffiti as a form of intervention, and also show cultural differences in community engagement, mediation, and aesthetics within the realm of digital graffiti. First, I shall look at political initiatives that use digital graffiti professionally to formulate broader political statements. These initiatives choose distinct architecture to appropriate, linking the 'projection screen' with their messages, and appealing to the viewers to imagine change. Secondly, as an example of a digital graffiti community project, I will discuss 'Calligraffiti', which includes Berlin-based refugees from the Arabic world. This community project links to the politics and aesthetics of graffiti that showed up during the Arab Spring, and at the same time relates to the Arabic cultural tool to concatenate written words or calligraphy with the facades of public buildings. Thirdly, I will show the work of the Afghani graffiti artist Shamsia Hassani, who uses digital graffiti in the form of photoshop projects, applying colorful and peaceful elements to heal the broken architecture and communities in her war-ridden home country.

Digital Graffiti

In 2014 the environmentalist group Greenpeace projected the message 'Listen to the People, Not the Polluters' on the United Nations building in New York City, shortly

Team Vulvarella, US Embassy Berlin, March 8, 2017
***Planet Earth First Projection*, 2017**

after hundreds of thousands of people demonstrated on the streets to demand climate action. The projection was later translated into different languages and was shared instantly in digital media with communities around the world, who also held marches and protests drawing attention to climate change on the same weekend.[4] Through using the UN building as projection screen, Greenpeace literally appealed to the nations to unite, addressing global responsibility for climate control. Another example is Greenpeace's 'Planet Earth First' digital graffiti campaign seen 2017 in Hamburg and the Vatican, following the US president's travel to the G20 summit and a meeting with the Pope.

On Women's Day, March 8, 2017, the feminist activist group Team Vulvarella projected two huge images of a naked woman with a face mask on the façade of the US Embassy in Berlin. Deliberately choosing time and place, the activists protested against sexual harassment and the US travel ban against citizens of several countries in the Middle East.

In both cases the projection screens are chosen upon the basis of a calculation. The message to be spread is linked to the place which represents its cause. Digital graffiti is addressing the pedestrians walking by, and additionally the larger institutions, whose facades are used for the projections. Also, the graffiti acts digitally in two ways: firstly, through the technique of digital projection and, secondly, through the massive viral impact on digital media that follows the actual projection event.

Digital Calligraffiti

During the Arab Spring graffiti was an often-used tool to formulate visible protest against political oppression. Graffiti was seen in such diverse forms as fast scribbling, slogans, and scenic murals.[5] Voices that were silenced or whitewashed become louder through recurring graffiti.[6] One special form of this graffiti is Calligraffiti. Looking back to a 1400-year-old Muslim aniconic culture of emphasizing the depiction of words over the representation of animated beings, it appears to be a logical step to combine traditional calligraphy with graffiti. Another twist is applied by projecting calligraphy as digital graffiti.

In the summer of 2017, the Berlin based Public Art Lab, a platform for urban art projects, organized a project with migrants from Syria, Afghanistan, Iraq, Senegal, and other countries.[7] The main idea was to transform the urban environment into projection screens and communication platforms. Subway stations and public building interiors and exteriors served as boards for calligraphic messages. The projection tool was a simple live projector named 'Infl3ctor', developed by the artists Michael Ang and Hamza Abu Ayyash.[8] The messages spread were written primarily in Arabic and German. Calls were made for love, art, and peace. Yet also more concrete political messages were spread,

TOP
Vatican, *Greenpeace Planet Earth First Projection*, 2017

BOTTOM
Hamburg, *Greenpeace Planet Earth First Projection*, 2017

Shamsia Hassani, *Dream Graffiti*, 2015

such as "It's amazing to take pictures in the street without being stopped by police." [9]

In this case of digital graffiti, the messages and the aesthetics of the digital graffiti are an important factor in the acknowledgment of the cultural heritage of the new Berliners. Calligraffiti serves as a community builder. Through appropriating public space, one belongs to a community. This is true for digital graffiti in 2017, as it was true for graffiti in 1972, when Hugo Martinez, who organized the first graffiti association, stated that "graffiti writing is a way of gaining status in a society where to own property is a way to have an identity." [10]

Digital Dreaming Graffiti

Shamsia Hassani is a famous graffiti artist in Kabul. Being a professor of sculpture at Kabul University, she has brought street art to the center of her home town. She uses colorful graffiti to cover up the negative reminders of the war on real architecture and also in the minds of the people. She claims that "image has more effect than words, and it's a friendly way to fight."[11] Shamsia Hassani also presents her ideas digitally. Her project 'Dreaming Graffiti' is a series of photoshopped images. She paints and decorates war ruins from Kabul and shares these images online. She imagines a different environment through interacting virtually with the physical architecture surrounding her. Though this subcategory of digital graffiti may not be tangible in the physical space, it has the power to change the way in which the community sees the potential of its environment.

Conclusion

Is digital graffiti the new tool for the generation of digital natives to resist, protest, and engage? With the examples above we see that going digital allows a "displacement and assemblage of space," [12] and leads to a reorganizing of the aesthetics of architecture with all its symbols and power structures. Digital graffiti is a powerful tool for protest and intervention. And the practical advantages of digital graffiti over traditional graffiti are obvious. One does not have to get close to the architecture onto which one intends to project. Even fenced-in buildings can be turned into a projection screen. One may even choose the building in relation to the message of the graffiti. Also, digital graffiti does not cause damage to property and is therefore not a criminal act.

We return to the joke about the picture in the pocketbook. Now is the time to get our pocketbooks—aka phones and tablets—to show our environment the real truth. This time we are not only showing our mediated reality to our friends. This time our messages are projected, are publicly visible, and go viral. All one needs is some courage, maybe a good projector—but usually a flash light does the job.

NOTES

1 Norman Mailer, *The Faith of Graffiti* (Westport: Praeger Publishers,1974), ch.1.

2 There are non-protest versions of digital graffiti, such as street festivals and commercial advertisement. For this article, I want to focus on digital graffiti as interventions and political acts.

3 Anastasia Karandinou, *Theories and Practices of the Ephemeral in Architecture* (Surrey: Ashgate, 2013), preface.

4 Molly Dorozenski, "Greenpeace Delivers People's Message on Eve of Climate Summit," September 23, 2014. http://www.greenpeace.org/usa/greenpeace-delivers-peoples-message-eve-climate-summit/.

5 Pascal Zoghbi and Don Karl aka Stone, *Arabic Graffiti*, (Berlin: From Here to Fame, 2011), 57.

6 Rana Jarbou, "The Seeds of a Graffiti Revolution," in *Walls of Freedom – Street Art of the Egyptian Revolution*" ed. by Basma Handy, Don Karl (Berlin: From Here to Fame, 2014), 9–12, 9.

7 "Digital Calligraffiti," *Public Art Lab*, accessed November 11, 2017, http://www.publicartlab-berlin.de/blog/2017/09/05/digital-calligraffiti-2/.

8 "Michael Ang, Infl3ctor, Michael Ang," accessed November 11, 2017, http://www.michaelang.com/project/infl3ctor.

9 DJ Pangburg, "*Activists Are Projecting Digital 'Calligraffiti' Onto Walls in Berlin*," accessed November 11, 2017, https://creators.vice.com/en_us/article/nz57wz/activists-are-projecting-digital-calligraffiti-onto-walls-in-berlin.

10 Norman Mailer, *The Faith of Graffiti* (Westport: Praeger Publishers,1974), ch.1.

11 Shamsia Hassani, interview with auopsiart, accessed November 12, 2017, http://autopsiart.com/shamsia-hassani/.

12 Karandinou, 201.

***Drury live in the subway, Berlin*, 2017**

SOS

COMING HOME

A CONVERSATION WITH DO HO SUH

by LEA HERSHKOWITZ

Named Wall Street Journal Magazine*'s 2013 Innovator of the Year in Art, Do Ho Suh received a BFA in painting from the Rhode Island School of Design and an MFA in sculpture from Yale University. As a Korean man living abroad, Suh describes his feelings of "cultural displacement"* [1] *when first arriving in the United States as a student at the Rhode Island School of Design; these feelings became the springboard for his* Home *series, which comprises some of his most coveted works today. The "so called transitional spaces,"* [2] *such as staircases and doorways, represent the physical space separating the United States and Korea, as well as the space that we all create within different cultures.*

Interested in the malleability of space in both its physical and metaphorical manifestations, Do Ho Suh constructs site-specific installations that question the boundaries of identity. [3] *Through full-scale fabric installations, Suh recreates specific domestic spaces informed by his experiences. These spaces include his childhood home, a traditional hanok-style Korean house; a house in Rhode Island, where he lived as a student; and his apartment in New York City. Dreamlike and captivating, Suh's work is one that meticulously encapsulates memory by replicating such interiors that address some of our most vulnerable feelings.*

Do Ho Suh's works are housed in several globally prestigious collections such as: the Guggenheim Museum, New York's Museum of Modern Art, The Whitney Museum, LACMA, and Tate, London. [4] *Suh shares with Int|AR author and RISD graduate student of Interior Architecture, Lea Hershkowitz his experiences of the city of Providence and of RISD while discussing the impact of place on artists and designers as they strive to*

348 West 22nd Street, New York, NY 10011, USA – Apartment A, Corridors and Staircases (Kanazawa version)
2011–2012
Polyester fabric, stainless steel
Apartment A: 690 x 430 x 245 cm / Corridors and Staircases: 1328 x 179 x 1175 cm
This and all subsequent illustrations are the work of Do Ho Suh

allow their personal questions and longings to manifest while maintaining the logic and ethos of a universally relatable work.

Do Ho Suh: The first place that I ever lived outside of Korea was Providence, to go to RISD. The experience of leaving home and going somewhere to study without knowing what was going to happen in my life was something to chew on for many years. I'm still fascinated by it. It was a physical and spiritual experience, rather than an inspirational one.

Lea Hershkowitz: You've mentioned the idea of transitional space[5] as the focal point for much of your work. I imagine this stems from the feelings of cultural displacement that you just alluded to. These ideas are literally represented in your *Home* series and mirrored by your placing of your homes in Korea and Providence within the walls of a gallery. In this sense, does the gallery become your new home, rather than the work itself?

DHS: Each time I show my work in a different space I know the piece will somehow contain the memory or the experience of that particular space. That trace of movement from one space to the other has always been in my mind from the very beginning of the project. It's hard to see it in an obvious way, since the physical change might be subtle.

My fabric pieces are very ephemeral. The museum people probably hate to hear this, but the color of the fabric fades once it has shown for several months in the museum context. Simple wear and tear as well as

Each replicated space is precisely measured, wrapped in paper, and then rubbed to generate an imprint of every scratch, notch, or smooth surface within the space.

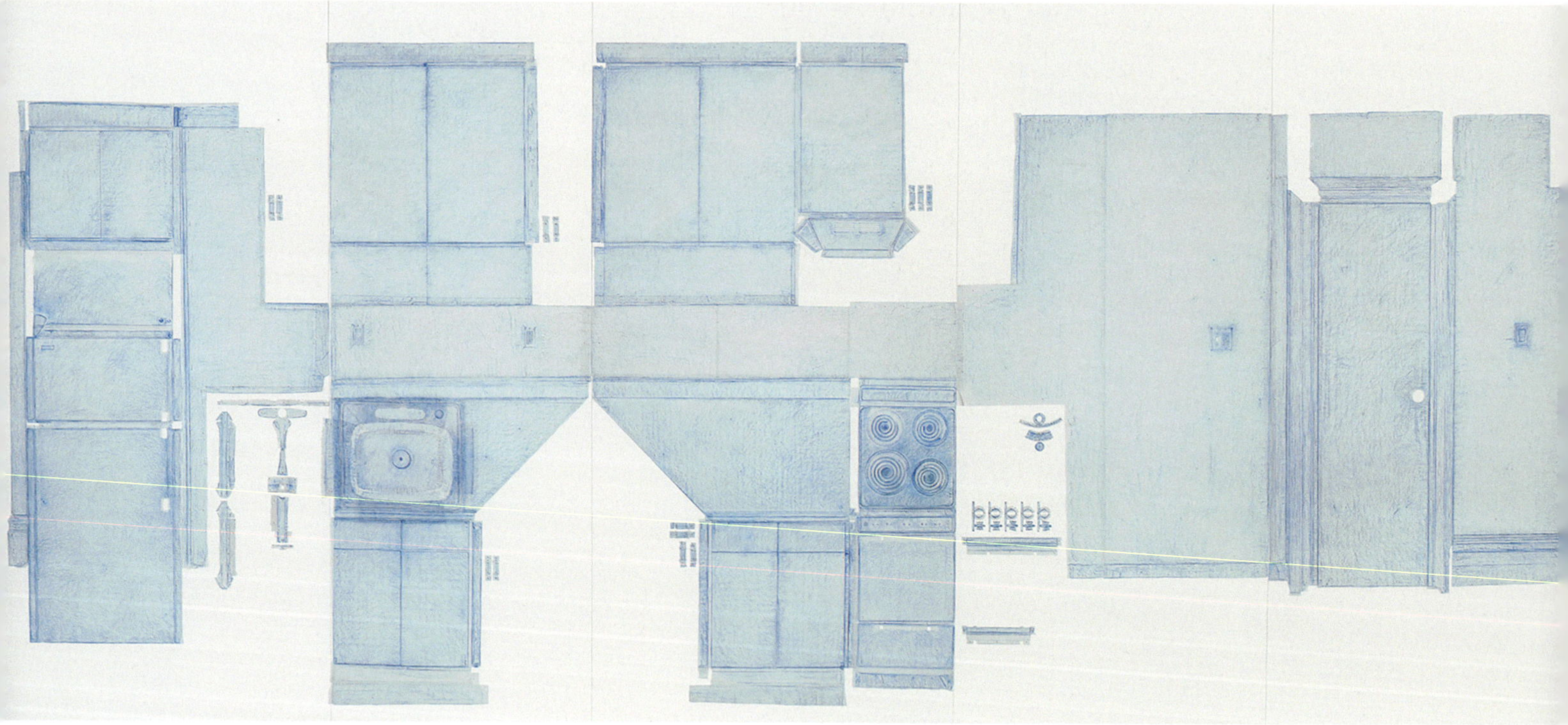

Rubbing/Loving Project: Kitchen, Apartment A, 348 West 22nd Street, New York, NY 10011, USA
2014
Colored pencil on vellum pinned on board
363.9 x 843.6cm (143.25 x 332.125 inches)

aging accumulate the more you show the work and the more the work travels to different places. That is what happens to the physical piece.

For me, it is how I remember the space; it is the memory associated with that particular space and that particular piece. These intangible elements become visible layers that my pieces start to possess. It is a very complex experience. In a way, the piece itself is a catalyst. You bring your work to show somewhere, but ironically, the final product is less about the piece being shown somewhere than it is about the process of organizing, traveling, and communicating to get the piece there. Each particular process of showing the work gets added onto the piece.

LH: That is what is most fascinating. You scrupulously replicate the space through your papering process, creating volumes rather than objects in the space. You've mentioned that the intention behind building your childhood home out of fabric was to be able to carry it everywhere with you. You once said, "I want to carry my house, my home, with me all the time, like a snail."[6]

Typically, when people travel and want to be reminded of home, they bring memorabilia with them, maybe

Specimen Series: Stove, Apartment A, 348 West 22nd Street, New York, NY 10011, USA
2013
Polyester fabric, stainless steel wire, and display case with LED lighting
741/8 x 361/8 x 35 inches

a book or a photograph, maybe a stool. You've done the opposite and found a way to take the space with you, rather than the objects. Was your reasoning that the space holds memory in a way that objects cannot?

DHS: I think so. Don't get me wrong – I have obsessions with or attachments to certain objects as well. What struck me since first moving to the United States was how different cultures construct space and environments, which is directly related to how different cultures see the universe and understand the world. There were many stimuli all at once; it was not just a single object, it was the space that I responded to.

I think I moved nine times over the course of my three years at RISD, and your first impression is always the space without anything in it. I didn't like the process at the time, but it gave me a lot to think about. Then, when I moved to New York, I lived in one place for 18 years, which was a little different. I started traveling a lot, and my New York home became my home base. I have been traveling like crazy for the last decade, and I have started to develop certain attachments to objects within the building. It has been an interesting development.

From the beginning, it was always about the space. I was a painting major at RISD, so I didn't have the means to realize my ideas in a three dimensional way, but I really wanted to make something spatial. I wanted to make something at a 1:1 scale. I didn't want to make anything smaller scale because, for me, everything that I experienced was really physical.

LH: You wanted something you could be in.

DHS: Right. So the very first series of works and experiments that I did at RISD, which still resonate with me, dealt with measuring my studio. Measuring the corridors in the Met Café and measuring my apartment without really knowing what I was going to do. I really spent time with those particular measurements and came up with something. While I was developing an understanding of my environment, I was learning the techniques that I needed to realize my ideas in a three dimensional way.

Fallen Star 1/5
2008–2009
ABS, basswood, beech, ceramic, enamel paint, glass, honeycomb board, lacquer paint, latex paint, LED lights, pinewood, plywood, resin, spruce, styrene, polycarbonate sheets, and PVC sheets
Approximately 332.7 x 368.3 x 762cm (131 x 145 x 300 inches)

The rubbings are transposed onto silk or polyester, rung on metal wire, and hung to represent, in a 1:1 scale, the documented space that a viewer can occupy.

Home within Home within Home within Home within Home
2013
Polyester fabric, metal frame 1530 x 1283 x 1297 cm

Apartment A, 348 West 22nd Street, New York, NY 10011, USA
2011–2014
Polyester fabric, stainless steel tubes 271.65 x 169.29 x 96.49 inches / 690 x 430 x 245cm

Maybe because I did not come from architecture or sculpture I had the flexibility to approach the problems I saw in a more naïve way. Making something in fabric is almost impossible in construction: A whole house, a three story building at a 1:1 scale, in fabric?

LH: From the outside, your work is a precious object, which is typically not occupied by people. You've mentioned that your inspiration came from the way you interacted with people in different cultures and the way that people interact with the spaces within which they exist. I'm wondering if you have an opinion regarding what happens in the spaces that you create once people interact, touch, or engage them, because those interstitial spaces are then dissolved.

DHS: It is interesting that you mention the absence of people. With any work of art, there is no one there when you are creating something; you are alone. Once you put your work out, and it starts to interact with people, my presence as an author and theirs as the user is always there.

LH: As if in the absence of a person, you know that there is the presence—

DHS: — presence of the person, yes. It is related to the things that I mentioned at the very beginning: that you only see the sheer fabric, and it seems like there is nothing attached to it. But, for me, there is this invisible memory with many layers attached to it. It's an interesting question, because I hardly ever see my favorite architecture without any people in it.

LH: It's impossible, yet that is typical of how the completed space is displayed within a firm's portfolio.

DHS: When it's being documented, there's no human presence. I think that's a really interesting thing. It's kind of a modernist tradition.

LH: Once you add a user, the nature of the space changes: it potentially implies a new author and, with her or him, the possibility of a change of function to the form, maybe different from what the architect intended.

DHS: Exactly. I've been trying to fight against that tradition in many ways. First of all, the use of ephemeral fabric is against this modernist attempt to preserve and monumentalize. My works, my pieces, are about the anti-monument. The monument is immobile.

LH: It's a dead thing.

DHS: It's on a pedestal. It doesn't really matter where you show that piece – as long as it is on the pedestal, it is the same piece. That's how the modernists see their work. For me, each and every time I show work in a different place, it becomes a different work, because it's in a different context.

LH: When I first began to think about you and your work, meticulously measuring, documenting, and papering each aspect of the building or room, it seemed almost a preservationist technique. But it sounds like you would not consider yourself a preservationist.

DHS: I don't think so! My work is not about being an immobile static sculpture. The work is about the beholder's movement throughout the different spaces. Lately, when I've shown my work, I have used video. The interaction of my work within different contexts, and with different viewers, is important, and that makes the experience of the work differ from one place to the other. It is about the subtle changes of light and movement of the people. In different cultures, people behave differently at the museum, and that also makes the work a different piece—a completely different piece. I think the ironic thing is that the original space is an extremely private place. As art, it becomes a highly public space with a transformation of both the space and its functionality.

LH: What *is* the function of the space? It was meant to be your home, but what is it now?

DHS: Once I occupied the space, my old apartment became my own intimate space. The audience has never lived in or even seen my old apartment. If the audience includes people from New York or the West Coast, the apartment might be a different spatial configuration and have different hardware.

LH: The objects you've chosen to feature—the stove, for example—are very utilitarian, but they also create an emotional connection, because everyone experiences those objects. This is why at the beginning of the interview, I asked about objects in space rather than just space. Your idea that the space you've transposed is unique while also being universal comes through in these typical appliances; they hold your memories but can also hold mine.

DHS: At the moment, I'm in London, renovating my old apartment. It's quite interesting; this is the first time I've had the opportunity to make a lot of decisions based on my own taste.

The structure of the building is already given; it's really limited for the architect. There are many unforeseen discoveries that force us to change the design as we take the walls down, for example. It's almost a karmic experience. How many people can afford to create their own space from scratch? Most of us cannot. But the original appliances in the apartment were not my choices; they were already given and are probably the most generic things.

LH: They look like mine in Providence, which probably look like yours did when you were in Providence.

DHS: And somehow we created this collective memory based on these sorts of mass produced products, which is fascinating.

LH: Going back to this idea of being able to create or design your own space being something of a luxury: On one end of the spectrum, I think of your work in relation to primitive man or nomadic architecture. On the other end, and more relevant in today's context, I think of refugees. Though you've elevated this idea, your work references what is currently happening throughout the world, as people are being forced to carry their homes with them.

DHS: Let's put it this way: I think that going to the United States was probably the most important experience in my life, and a lot of my work comes out of that experience. Interestingly enough, no one really asks me about my work prior to what I did in the United States. It's very strange.

LH: Well, what was your work like prior to coming to the United States?

Heavy in process, the work reflects how the pieces are experienced by the artist and how the pieces are constructed.

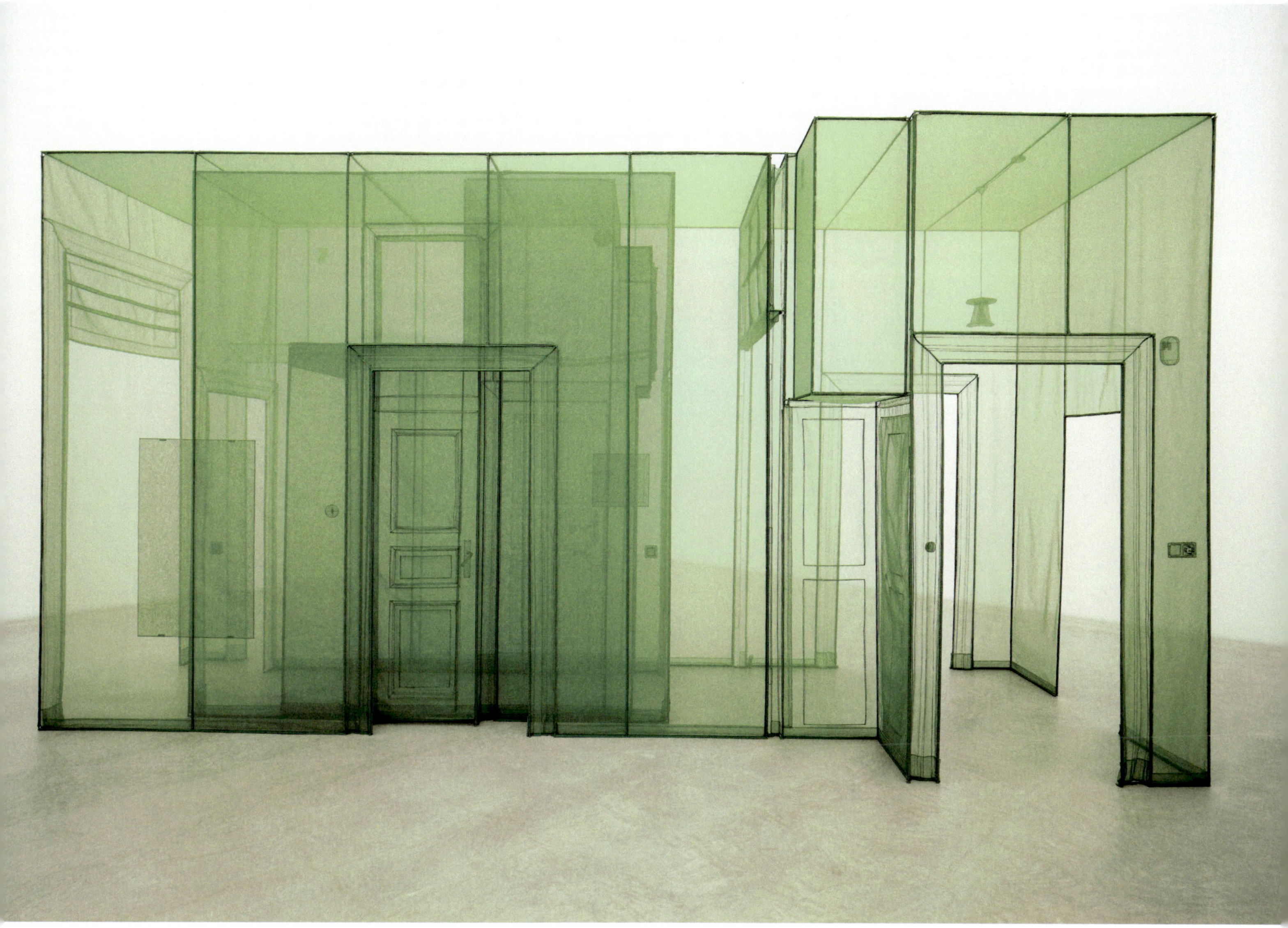

DHS: I was a painting student.

LH: Because your father was a painter?

DHS: Yes. I studied the more traditional medium of ink and brush on paper. However, the pieces that I was making were installations that dealt with the idea of transporting space from one place to another. My point is that, before I left, the seed was planted in Korea but it was nurtured by my education at RISD. That's how all of this work started.

In Korea, I was making a piece using a balloon, blowing it up in my studio. The idea was that the air inside the balloon was representative of the space in my studio. I put the balloon in a very large plastic bag and then transported it to the gallery space, but it was not just sitting in the gallery. The balloon traveled from one gallery space to the other. It wrapped around the partitions from one gallery space to the next, so that at first glance within the gallery spaces, the piece was difficult to see in its entirety. In this sense, I was transporting the air from one particular space to the other. This was one example of how the ideas I'm working with now first developed in Korea.

When I went to the US, I started again as a painting student. It didn't occur to me to continue to work three dimensionally, and maybe the reason was that I just wanted to learn something completely new. The strange thing was that when I look back at my old sketchbooks in Korea, there are some old sketches that are very relevant to what I'm doing now. I didn't even realize that connection until recently.

Wielandstr. 18, 12159 Berlin, Germany – 3 Corridors
2011
Polyester fabric, stainless steel tubes
655 x 209 x 351cm

LH: The connections our brains make before we are consciously aware of them are fascinating. It sounds like that's what you're describing.

DHS: It was great to discover these old sketches. Did I really think about this back then? At the same time, it's scary; you're kind of trapped with this one idea for a long time, and you have to wonder, how did it happen?

LH: As if we choose these paths or topics based on our experiences, something innate.

DHS: Yes. However, I'm pretty sure someone would have done this work if I hadn't done it. But I happen to be the person, and I've only just barely scratched the surface. In this way, I know that it didn't happen without any reason, because these ideas are a consistent thread throughout my life. I completely forgot about my old sketches, and I came up with some great ideas. I'm happy about them, only to look back at my sketchbook, and the drawing is already there. I know that I didn't intentionally look back in my studio just to create this piece ten years later. Maybe that idea or that sketch has been in me on a subconscious level for ten years, and then reemerged. I'm not sure how those things work.

I also think there are particular spaces that I'm more drawn into, and I'm trying to understand why and what triggers that. You probably have experienced this sense of déjà vu? Whenever I remember my dreams, the spatial background or the places and spaces are always the same. For example, my childhood home in Korea is different than the real house or home. Some part of the house is similar to the real home, but it is otherwise different.

LH: But it has the same feeling, is that what you mean?

DHS: The sensation in my dream tells me that the space is my home, but there is a very strange, different feeling. It feels completely new. I'm almost lost within my own home, but that particular space, as a home, comes often in my dreams. Somehow my brain or my consciousness puts this information together, and it creates this...

LH: Whole new space?

DHS: Yes. So when I have a dream, I think, 'oh not again, that's the same space that's not home.' I know that 100%, but in my dream setting, that is my home. In real life, sometimes I go somewhere and feel the same way. I strongly believe that I've lived there in my previous life because there is no way I would know it otherwise. But in the dream, my studio is always in the same place looking down to the sea; the experience is just so vivid and real. The more I think about it, the more I think it is probably unerased memory from many different past lives.

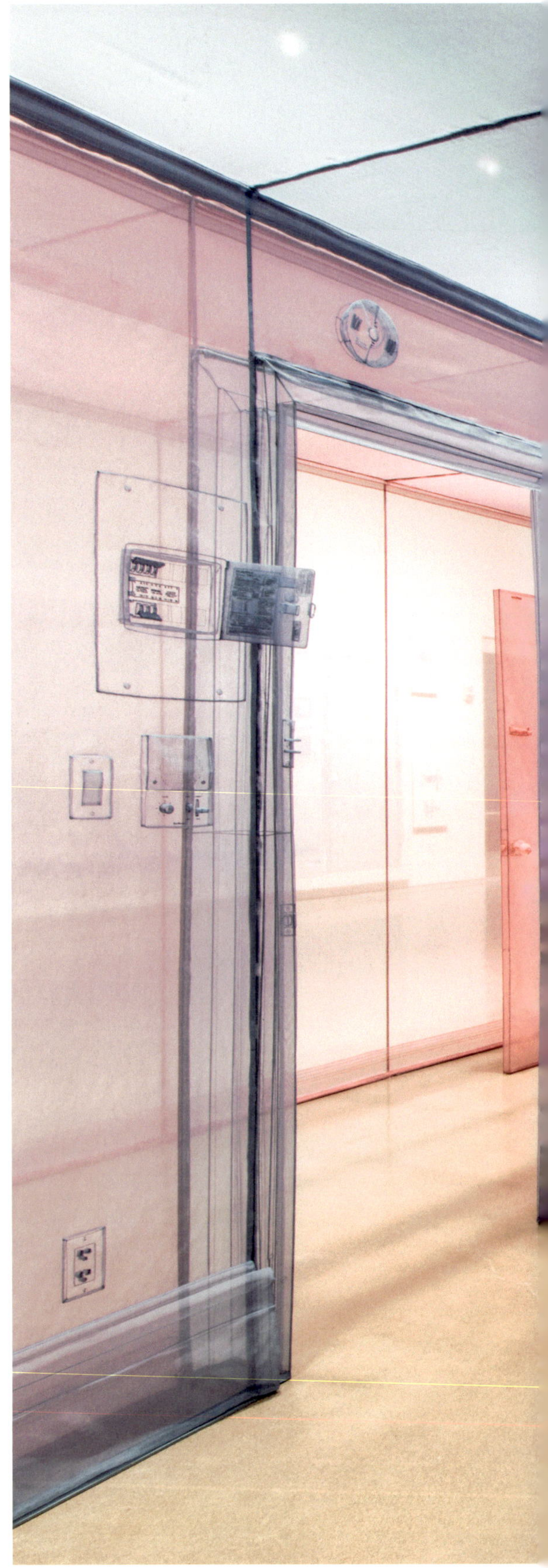

Apartment A, 348 West 22nd Street, New York, NY 10011, USA
2011–2014
Polyester fabric, stainless steel tubes
271.65 x 169.29 x 96.49 inches / 690 x 430 x 245 cm

LH: I once read that individuals with impaired facial perception do not dream of faces.[7] Maybe it's possible that individuals with heightened spatial perception dream only of space, or create new spaces within their dreams. Yet what you're saying is that maybe the spaces we create come from our past lives and our past experiences.

DHS: I think the mechanism of dreaming is very interesting. I'm not in a position to completely understand how it works, but what I find fascinating is that I remember this space within the dream over and over again. This space exists in me, and in a way, that makes it more real.

LH: Have you ever built it?

DHS: I've made some sketches about it, but I think in a way the work I'm doing now might be a quest to find that space that I've been dreaming of. I don't know whether I will find it. I think the conceptual gesture of working with the spaces I live in is itself an accumulation of the fragments that make up the space that appears in my dream.

LH: What I hear you saying is that you cannot create that space because you have not found it yet, and your whole conceptual method is: existing within these spaces first, developing memories, and then transposing those spaces. Rather than saying, 'I dreamt of this space and I want to construct it,' which is very much more of an architectural practice!

DHS: There is probably a long history and tradition if you're an architect that becomes a limitation.

LH: To draw a conceptual link here, you are adaptively reusing your memories rather than developing a new construction of your dreams. And that is *The Architect's Dream*[8]: this perfect, complete world built of tradition that was dreamt and then created.

DHS: Right, and I don't have that, so I can do whatever I want to do! Art and architecture have their own limitations. I was traveling in Tokyo, and I saw the Frank Gehry and Norman Foster exhibition. From Tokyo, I went to Los Angeles, and I saw the other Frank Gehry exhibition at LACMA. The Tokyo show of Frank Gehry had a lot of models, but it was more focused on the technology that he created to design his buildings. The LACMA show was more traditional. I was thinking that I would like to have an exhibition like that. I really like architecture exhibitions. It was perfect for me to see how the models were made, and I would love to have an exhibition of just models and drawings.

LH: Your recent show at MOCA Cleveland included a lot of your sketches, the paper you used for imprinting, as well as video. The idea of documenting and displaying your process seems particularly interesting for your work because the final form, as well as the process, makes up the total memory that is on display.

DHS: The process is becoming more and more important to me. The process has always been there, but I just didn't want to share it, or I just didn't think that it was something that people might be interested in.

LH: But now that you've found that sketch, you know that it's probably really important.

DHS: I think you're absolutely right, because the chain of thoughts, the threads in my old sketchbook, have always been there. I'm still making manageable pieces, even though the scale is large. There are pieces that are completely impossible to make in real life due to the scale, so I've been thinking of making models and drawings and bringing all of those things together to have an exhibition like those of architects.

LH: Something that is important in making models is how to get the viewer to really experience the space when it's very small, or when it's just a model, and the materials are not exactly what you imagine them to be. The model becomes a completely new and unique challenge, rather than being able to make the space the way that it really should be at a 1:1 scale.

DHS: I think that's a unique kind of challenge. For me, people have been experiencing my installation versions of the spaces, so I think people could make a connection from my model to the other full-scale versions. It's kind of a retrofit too. I just recently opened an exhibition at the Contemporary Arts Center in Cincinnati, and for that show, I made a few models, very intricate models, of the piece that was being made but then destroyed. Not many people were able to see it and experience it as a permanent piece. So I made a model. It's not a study model to realize that project; it was more a replica of the actual piece that no longer existed.

LH: Talking about Modernism, Le Corbusier used to say that the model is the ideal form of the architecture. You can't touch it, and nothing happens to it. You are flipping that statement on its head and saying, 'Well, I created the actual thing, but I destroyed it, and now I only have the model to show you.'

DHS: Right! So, I've been documenting the pieces through film. In Cincinnati, I showed a documentary of the making of the piece with a model and that's probably the closest experience one could have of the work without actually being there. It's a challenge for me when my work is really site specific. I think that my work, as well as that of many architects, deal with three-dimensional space, yet everything is becoming virtual.

LH: Do you know Oculus Rift? You put these goggles on and in a couple of seconds you can be anywhere, including home. I was wondering too what you thought about that because you spend enormous time doing these amazing, almost historic processes, and there are people on the other end of the spectrum that are using technology to try to replicate a similar experience. I wonder if you see the potential for that kind of thing in your work, or if integrating these kinds of technology is something that you'd like to stay away from?

DHS: I'm actually looking into it. Those technologies have been evolving so rapidly. I remember when I was at RISD we got a tour at some kind of media lab at Brown University. They were experimenting with virtual reality and it was so primitive. Now, we have 3D filming as well as virtual reality. Before 3D filming had the chance to pick up, virtual reality has really taken off. In my work, I would pass by the 3D filming and just go directly into virtual reality. It is really affordable now and I think it is perfect for documenting space. However, I still think that it cannot replace the physical experience. I have a collaborator who has been helping me to document my work and almost make video art so we've been talking about it.

LH: Which is really interesting as an architectural practice to create space without actually having to make space.

Being in Providence, I'm wondering if there are certain spaces at RISD that you found to be particularly inspirational?

DHS: Providence is a really beautiful place. I went back maybe 5 or 6 years ago, and I scanned the whole building I used to live in on Benefit Street. The landlord is actually an architect from RISD Architecture, practicing in Providence. He knew my brother, who also went to RISD, and he helped me access the building to do the documentation. There's a hidden staircase that goes up to the top of the building. I don't know how they did it. They just probably chopped the space into 6 or 7 units but originally it was meant for one very rich family. There are two different staircases; probably one was for the family, and the other was for the servants, but they closed it off and that staircase was behind the refrigerator in my flat.

LH: Did you know it was there?

DHS: I had no idea. I knew there was a space, but I had no access to it.

LH: The architecture in Providence has such amazing history, for reasons you've mentioned; it was a colonial town, lots of really wealthy families. Some of the most amazing structures have been converted into the craziest units.

DHS: There are a lot of details, half buried in the plaster. It's fascinating when you're measuring those spaces. It was a total coincidence, but the building I used to live in was also where my brother used to live when he was at RISD before me. When I first moved to the US, I lived in one of the school dormitories, but it was too small. So I was looking for an apartment, and someone called me to show it, and it happened to be my brother's building.

LH: Talk about building Karma?

DHS: I think there is something that is not just superstition. I really like Providence because it is associated with good memories. I really worked hard, learned so much, made good friends. You know, you see RISD graduates everywhere, and we still keep in touch.

LH: It's really nice to hear about your experience, as I am about to leave RISD and Providence.

DHS: Did you drink the water from that fountain on Benefit Street, the one outside of the court building?

LH: I have not, but maybe I should?

DHS: If you drink the water from that fountain, you will never leave Providence.

And maybe Do Ho Suh never has, as he continues to take 388 Benefit Street with him wherever he goes.

NOTES

1 http://www.pbs.org/art21/artists/do-ho-suh, accessed February 03, 2016.

2 https://www.youtube.com/watch?v=xYEF_GXilu8, accessed February 01, 2016.

3 Do Ho Suh Biography from the Lehmann Maupin Gallery website, http://www.lehmannmaupin.com/artists/do-ho-suh, accessed April 05, 2016.

4 http://www.lehmannmaupin.com/artists/do-ho-suh#13, accessed February 03, 2016.

5 https://www.youtube.com/watch?v=xYEF_GXilu8, accessed February 01, 2016.

6 http://www.sothebys.com/de/auctions/ecatalogue/2010/fusion-contemporary-art-and-design-n08748/lot.63.html, accessed February 03, 2016.

7 http://www.ncbi.nlm.nih.gov/pmc/articles/PMC2814941/, accessed March 08, 2016.

8 http://www.explorethomascole.org/tour/items/91/about, April 04, 2016.

POSTINDUSTRIAL SPECTACLE

RECONNECTING IMAGE AND FUNCTION

by PATRICK RUGGIERO, JR.

Replacing an Industry

The decline of manufacturing industry in Rust Belt cities has led municipal governments and real-estate investors to look to tourism and entertainment as new engines of economic growth and recovery. With major producers of tax revenue and jobs now defunct, stakeholders are taking active ownership in both the rebranding and reprogramming of deteriorated properties at the heart of their towns. The emerging design work in many of these redevelopment sites straddles the interests of both developers and the public—*"Retain our heritage, but attract people to create jobs and spend money."* The resultant urban environments capitalize on the *image* of industry in a fetishized, spectacular way, using it as a billboard to attract business.

With entertainment and commerce as core programs, redevelopment offers a destination where tourists and residents alike can escape their everyday life in an environment that is exciting and in contrast to the realities of the everyday. These sites contain a unique opportunity to leverage the machines of industry within contemporary culture's obsession with the spectacle. By creating a simulated environment based on authenticity, these sites engage visitors through a false notion that what they see is real. Like the experience of a reality TV show or overzealous advertisement, one knows that the steel company, mill, or factory is no longer in business. However, through the signs and images presented the visitor is caught up in the latent memories of the industrial.

A successful simulation of this type of environment requires an array of signs, representations, and simulacra that points to the activity of an activated social

scene. For architecture to accomplish this, the uneasy relationship between how things appear and how they function must be considered. On one hand, the architectural language and ornamentation recall the past, addressing the dormant memories of the local culture. On the other hand, the buildings must function in a contemporary commercial role. In this context, form and function are no longer related—*the image* rules all as an applicable face to commerce. What these industrial sites miss, however, is the opportunity to connect image and content in a more sophisticated and recursive relationship.

Connecting Image and Content

While spectacle cannot be avoided, my project, *The Simulator of Mechanized Authenticity (SoMA)* reconsiders the missed opportunity to relate the image (architectural imagery) and content (function) in reuse urbanisms. *SoMA* distinguishes itself by putting forth a spectacular image that contains many potential readings. Through the use of irony—contradictions between content and image—as well as the sampling and integration of historical and contextual precedents, the production of these connections serves as a generative means of developing a discourse and solving the architectural problems of site.

The Tower, *SoMA: The Simulator of Mechanized Authenticity*

The Redevelopment of the Bethlehem Steel Site

The Bethlehem Steel Corporation, headquartered in Bethlehem, Pennsylvania, was once the world's largest producer of steel, producing the first railroads and, later, structures like the Golden Gate Bridge and the Empire State Building. After failing to upgrade technologically and suffering from complex issues with labor unions, the company officially closed its doors in 1995, leaving behind one of the largest brownfield sites in the world. The city is in the process of redeveloping the ten-acre campus that includes over 20 structures.

City planning officials have publicized a three-staged planning strategy for the redevelopment of the site that includes 1) increasing commerce with entertainment venues, 2) anchoring the commerce with business tenants, and 3) re-zoning in order to create residential housing that will support the other programs.

Situated at the center of town, most of the site is within walking distance of large neighborhoods of former working class housing in the South Side of Bethlehem. In 2006, the Las Vegas Sands Corporation purchased the site and began the construction of The Sands Casino Resort, which would necessitate cleaning up large swaths of land that were otherwise unusable due to toxic waste. Enticed by tax incentives, the casino has gifted parcels to arts organizations, designated areas as public plazas, and constructed a convention and events center. High-profile commercial tenants are anticipated to occupy renovated building shells.

While the built (and planned) work tries to honor the heritage aspect of the site, perhaps it is obsessed with these acts of recall: theatrical lights illuminate the buildings as backdrops for concert venues; shells of industrially purposed structures are renovated for non-related uses; undeveloped buildings are fenced off and strictly guarded; and new construction features exposed materials and structure. It is as if these elements conspire to imply the continued existence of the steel company. While simulating social activity, these elements create a mask of distraction unrelated to the function of each building. Functioning at the campus scale, these simulacra become integrated into the site's context and local vernacular.

What's the problem with this? Why shouldn't Bethlehem celebrate the company that its parents, grandparents, and relatives grew up in? Naturally, the accommodation of heritage is positive; there are two critical reasons to address this phenomenon. The first

Fenced-off buildings litter the redevelopment campus

is to ensure the campus' integration with the existing city fabric, and the second to introduce a framing of the industrial imagery that avoids a mask of inauthenticity.

Integrated Context

One of the parcels that was gifted to the city by the Sands Casino has recently been deemed "The 21st Century Town Square." This new civic center is characterized by a plaza and concert shell, and is backed by four iconic blast furnaces. The plaza is host to all major civic activities including mayoral addresses and city festivals, and the site adopts the trends of similar redevelopment sites that are engineered to attract consumers. But Bethlehem's 21st Century Town Square lacks framing devices—a way to alert the occupant that the site is not meant to be read as reality.

Such framing mechanisms are used in places such as Las Vegas, a mirage in the middle of the desert that perverts the basic reality of themed localities; Disneyworld, a complete contrast to reality, which is reached on its own highway after progressing through lines, gates, and fees; and Venice, an island with as many tourists daily as there are permanent residents, which reflects a basic reality of a Renaissance town. Jean Baudrillard, in his essay "Simulacra and Simulation" elaborates these three types of experiences, focusing on the way they use simulacra to convey various understandings of "the real." He goes on to describe a fourth type of experience, dissimulated inauthenticity (read: a state of denial), whereby the signs and images of a site mask the fact that something is no longer there. The industrial simulation in Bethlehem is that of Baudrillard's fourth type of simulation, one that contributes to a denial of the fact that its major industry has left.

Reconnecting

In order to shift the site's understanding of authenticity toward the experiences of Disney, Las Vegas, and Venice, and to avoid Baudrillard's dissimulated inauthenticity, newly implemented design must frame the imagery. While on a macro level this framing would interrupt the integration with the site and town, a building-specific critical framing would alert visitors that what is going on in Bethlehem is extraordinary.

This is where *SoMA* interjects to create value in commercial mixed-use real estate. The project proposes a series of renovations that reconsider the relationship between the architectural image of reused buildings and their programmatic function. A commentary on both the spectacularization of architectural imagery and an exploration into the potential of architectural representation, the project demonstrates how a richer, framed reading of spectacle can contribute to reclaimed urban environments. Each of the project's five buildings seeks to simulate, in its entirety, a previously existing condition. The form, material and architectural language all serve as simulacra, or signs/evidence to support this. The project differentiates itself from the site's existing context by producing a framed understanding that the spectacular experience is manufactured, establishing the connection between image and content.

The Stage | Transformation

The Stage takes a critical stance towards Bethlehem's fascination with lighting—projecting onto, making backdrops of, and illuminating the ruined buildings of the steel company. The building is programmatically divided into three distinct parts: the Seating Area, the Point of Purchase (POP) Facade, and The Back-of-House. Materially, *The Stage* contrasts the projected image and formed concrete that is smooth and unfinished—a canvas for the temporal expression of false ruin. A crane structure spans the Queue Pad and POP Facade, supporting lighting and projection equipment that sporadically projects a ruin texture onto the concrete, giving the area a ghostly sense of being of another time. The ephemeral quality of *The Stage's* image is contrasted with the hardness of its detailing. Its action is sporadic and natural. Like Yellowstone's Old Faithful, it runs on its own schedule and cycles in an unpredictable fashion.

The formal organization of *The Stage* is a machine for commerce: waiting line, service counter, and back of house. Its attraction is the spectacle of a ruin projected onto a new construction. *The Stage* honors the history of the site through a reverberation of readings. While discernibly produced of modern construction techniques, the form recalls what could have been a staging yard for forged components awaiting shipment.

The Tower | Hyperbole

The Tower is a critique of Bethlehem's rush to enclose, partition off, and preserve any building remains for as long as possible—even in the face of their eventual destruction. Fenced-off and condemned buildings litter the redevelopment campus, establishing a landscape of inaccessibility and surveillance. *The Tower* is a nine-story office building, built of steel, glass, fencing, walls, and barriers. Each floor contains a full luxury office suite with 270° views of the Bethlehem Steel Campus. At the ground floor, the tower is enclosed with existing walls and security fencing systems. *The Tower* will be the premier office space in the second phase of the city's redevelopment.

The Tower borrows the architectural language of the iconic blast furnaces. Conveyed as Bethlehem Ironworks' first building of the 19th century, *The Tower* honors the history of the site by blurring new and old. While constructed with modern techniques and means, the building's language vacillates between contemporary building systems and iconic artifact. *The Tower* frames itself through the unrelenting use of barriers, enclosures, partitions and fencing. This amplification of an existing phenomenon conveys its inauthenticity.

Prototype

Both *The Tower* and *The Stage* seek to combine commerce and heritage in the critical framing of spectacle as intervention in the Bethlehem Steel Redevelopment Campus. Each does this in different ways: while *The Stage* produces an ephemeral reading that is temporal and transformative, *The Tower* establishes its permanence through layers of security and hyperbole. Both aim to engage consumers with a nuanced reversal of their understanding of authenticity. The interventions use spectacle to both honor heritage and fuel commerce.

SoMA is a prototypical project: a test for addressing the redevelopment of sites involving heritage and the reuse of multiple culturally significant buildings. *SoMA* exemplifies an opportunity to develop ordinances and guidelines for designers, connecting the imagery with the programmatic use and content of each proposed building.

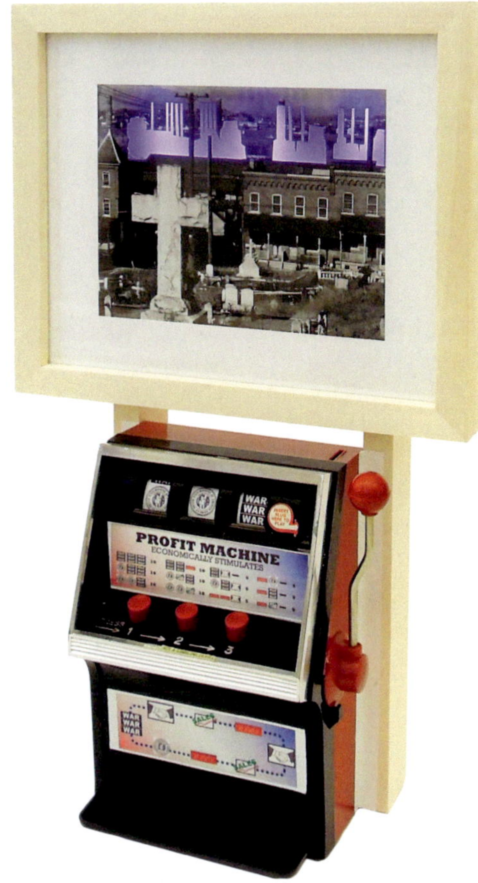

Establishing a connection between image and function

INFORMAL ANNEXATIONS

by RAFAEL LUNA

A critical development occurred during the 19th century in the spatial relationships of our cities when the paradigm shifted from city form to city management. The parcelization of the city by the implementation of grid standards allowed multiple cities to produce a management tool for taxation and property control. It was popularized by the iconic projects of the Commissioners' Plan of 1811, Haussmann's plan for Paris in the 1850s, and, most importantly, theorized and published as the "General Theory of Urbanization" by Ildefons Cerda for the expansion of Barcelona. These models were repeated all over the globe as urbanization expanded. Yet parcelization could not have foreseen the informalities of the city in the space that happens between parcels and between buildings. Such is the case in Seoul, in the district of Hongdae where the leftover space between the parcel and the building is appropriated as an interior extension, giving rise to a whole neighborhood economy of illegal marketable space. These spaces are used as shops, restaurants, galleries, through an extension of the ground level. This essay will review how the in-between space has not only produced an interesting neighborhood condition but a variety of interior spaces that have adapted to maximize the residual spaces of parcels.

In the continuing process of urbanization, much emphasis has been placed on the development of city form through the implementation of grid design. The grid has been equated to a method for establishing city form, as well as a political tool for managing the growth of cities. The grid in itself could be studied independently as an urban artifact with its roots as a control tool developed by the Roman Empire during its expansive colonization. The parameters that founded each of these imperial colonies followed two axes; the *cardo* and *decumanus* embedded a directional logic onto the system with parallel streets, a system of subdivisions for development and public squares. Aside from providing a geometrical strategy for organizing citizens, the formation of these cities through the grid developed the important distinction between *res publica* and *res privata*. These Latin terms defined that which is public and that which is private. They politicized the land and the managerial aspect of maintaining such land; that which was maintained by the state would be considered *res publica*, or public with access to all. This is one of the embedded fundamental aspects that needs to be addressed when discussing the nature of our cities – both as a separation of privacies through the grid and the resulting implications on the efficiency of urban space. The grid, therefore, should be defined not as a direct geometric operation of design that is imposed on a field, but as the primary infrastructural network that shapes the public realm of a city and its parcelized privacies. The space in-between the parcels is arguably the most important factor in defining the city, as it represents the area of discrepancy between the public infrastructure and private buildings. In between the parcels and buildings exists the political, contested space between private land and public access—the space for appropriation. It represents a hidden value of urban efficiency, one that unearths the inadequacies of understanding a city as fixed spaces through grids and parcelization.

Understanding urban efficiency through the in-between space created by the parcelization process

Storefront extensions hide the legal border of buildings and give the appearance of a larger store

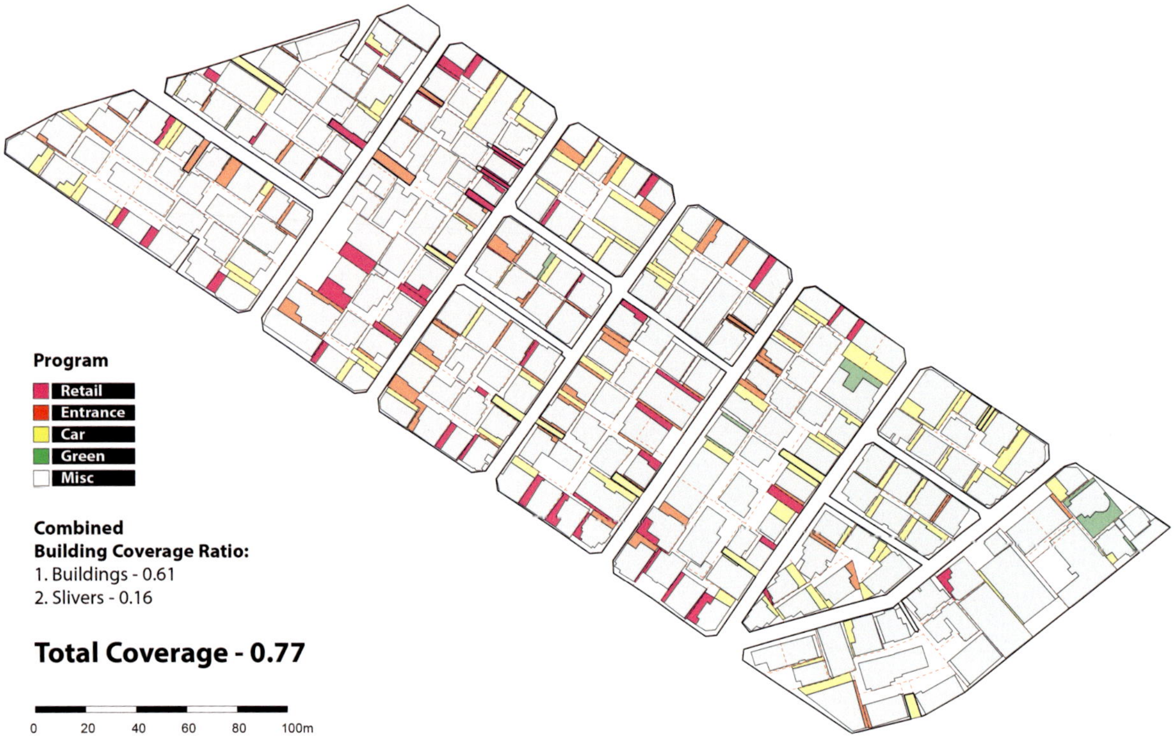

requires a review of contemporary methodologies for reading a city. Systems like GIS (geographic information system), for example, have been in development since the 1960s. They record what has been legally documented as public infrastructure, the subdivisions of parcels, and the perimeter of buildings inside parcels. Although GIS is the most popular method for visualizing and working with open-source data for mapping, for architects it is mainly used to demonstrate building coverage area and two-dimensional urban forms, such as a Nolli map. Urban efficiency in this scenario could be described through the density of the urban fabric of a city as an indicator of walkability and, therefore, density of amenities for occupancy. In his book *Walkable City: How Downtown Can Save America, One Step at a Time*, Jeff Speck argues for the need of a healthy building density that allows for higher usability of the space by its residents.[1] The further the separation of the in-between space of buildings, the less efficient the city, as walking distances between buildings are longer and the city more car-oriented. This argument is exemplified by projects such as the "taxonomy of urban fabrics," generated by the urbanization.org group at the Institute for Advanced Architecture of Catalonia.[2] The intent of this project is to create a classification of urban fabrics from around the world as an open source to allow for collaborative comparative studies. Although a comparative study of this kind would provide valid information regarding densities, it would not demonstrate the in-between condition that occurs by informal occupations.

The ad-hoc appropriations of public space for private use are common in a dense city like Seoul. In their book *Borrowed City*, Bruno, Carena, and Kim analyze the condition of appropriation of the public space in Seoul as a social contract among the residents and local government. "Borrowed City can be simply defined as the way private citizens use public space for their own personal benefit.... Most of these "negotiated" activities are illegal, but at the same time they are the result of a mutual agreement among citizens, which is a fundamental process in any democracy. For this reason, in a public space debate, informal occupations should be considered more as a resource to exploit than a problem to eradicate."[3] "Borrowed City" describes the condition in Seoul that exists out of the demarcated limits of a grid. Pop-up shops or tents may happen on the sidewalk, alleys, or between buildings as common occurrences regardless of their legality. Although they are not accounted for as legal building spaces or registered commercial activity, they provide amenities that may not be present inside legal buildings but are ingrained in the daily use of the city.

Another methodology to note is the mapping generated through the visualization of big data. In computation, big data refers to large data sets that could be analyzed to reveal patterns. These data sets have been incrementally increasing through the internet and the process of digitalizing our environments. The Civic Data Design Lab at MIT has been producing such mappings to evaluate the real estate speculative development

Diagram of in-between programming of Hongdae Block

occurring in China.[4] The visualization of data sets from social network apps reveals urban voids. These areas lack amenities and therefore become unsustainable communities, contributing to a phenomenon labeled as Ghost Cities. Urban efficiency is presented as a model of proximity to amenities for local residents.

These methodologies present an understanding of urban efficiency as an expression of density and proximities within legal parameters, be it recorded survey of buildings or licensed business operations. These methodologies operate within the public and private limits demarcated by the grid system. Yet in a dense urban environment, the public boundaries are sometimes blurred through appropriations of the in-between spaces as shown in studies like *Borrowed City*. These appropriations or occupations uncover the need for an additional understanding of the in-between, not just as a function of space but also of time. In 2002, Groupe e2 formed an international ideas competition to explore the notion of the in-between urban condition. Although the connotation of the "in-between" in the brief may have been preconceived to connote the space between two things, Bernard Tschumi offered a separate observation of the importance of understanding the in-between also as a time reference.[5] The in-between can be conceptualized as the progressive layering effect that builds the city over time, implying a new dimension; the lack of this dimension in the Nolli plan methodology explains its failure to capture the city in its totality, one including ad-hoc occupancies and temporal events.

The inadequacies of understanding a city through its grid and parcelization as fixed spaces rather than its in-between spaces are further studied by Solomon, Wong, and Frampton in their book *Cities Without Ground: A Guide to Hong Kong's Elevated Walkways*,[6] a demonstration of the endless three-dimensional connections that occur in Hong Kong's pedestrian networks. The in-between space is completely blurred through the appropriation of public infrastructure for private commercial use. The space between buildings becomes irrelevant as a two-dimensional ground condition because public infrastructure is extended into the private interior spaces, offering a continuous urban experience instead of a compartmentalized parcelization of two-dimensional space.

In both scenarios of appropriations, Seoul and Hong Kong, the need for space has led to an understanding of urban efficiencies beyond the political implication of the grid. The grid still represents the bundled, sunken investment of a city with an intrinsic path-dependency and limited possibilities of change to its formal structure. This implies that once a grid is laid out, variation can only come from its subdivisions and the evolution of the architecture, currently seen occurring in dense Asian cities through informal occupations.

The city of Seoul, for example, experienced a period of rapid urbanization in its postwar of the 1960s, 1970s, and 1980s, which generated a milieu of urban fabrics within the city. The development of the different housing types was a direct response to the rapid incoming and growing population. This led to the production of a quantity of buildings regardless of the quality of urban space. As the city stabilized its growth in becoming a 21st century post-industrial cultural city, there has been a growing emphasis on the quality of urban space. In Seoul, this can only be produced through the appropriation of void spaces in the given variety of existing grids.

One specific case study is the dense commercial neighborhood of Hongdae, where the in-between has evolved beyond the parcelization of the grid system to appropriate the setback spaces of buildings as extensions of the interior commercial spaces. Although setback areas are legally owned by the property owner, their purpose is to serve as easements for safe passage in case of emergencies, to separate buildings in case of fire or earthquakes, and to provide natural ventilation and lighting. Setbacks are technically private property but serve a public safety function, making them an ambiguous semi-private space. Bypassing the legality of building within the setbacks, many of the buildings on the main streets of Hongdae extend their volume as commercial sheds using temporal and light materials that afford them a dubious legality.

The setback as an entrance

The presence of these occupations relates to the grid implementation of the neighborhood, which appears on city survey maps during the 1970s. The area is flanked by Hongik University, which was established in 1946, and hints at informal dense settlements that occurred before the development of the parcels. This parcelization process of defining informal settlements within legal parcels resulted in buildings that are separated through setbacks ranging in average from two to four meters. This leaves spaces of one to two meters for each neighbor's side. The area is typologically characterized by low-rise buildings three to four stories high. As the neighborhood continued to densify due to its appeal as an arts and music scene anchored by Hongik University, there was a need for buildings to expand into the only remaining void spaces: the in-between setbacks. Bounded also by the subway Line 2, commuter train Gyeongui–Jungang Line, and the Airport Line to Seoul station, the area thrives with a constant inflow of tourists and a younger population of students, making the area one of the most active commercial areas in Seoul. In order to benefit the most from this retail context, stores use every available space to capitalize on the display and vending of their merchandise. The mapping of the in-between spaces reveals five typologies of appropriation: retail extension, entrance extension, green space, car-oriented spaces, and miscellaneous storage.

The first appropriation type, retail extension, derives from the adaptation of garage spaces and the extension of the ground-level storefront. These are the most interesting examples among the five typologies, as the interior volume makes use of the additional setback space for an interior effect. Garages of buildings that are raised on pilotis for ground level parking are transformed into boutique retail spaces. The one-meter setback in this example becomes a highlighted rack space, naturally lit through a polycarbonate roof that encloses the setback. This is a typical scenario that technically maintains a

A ground-level parking garage transformed into boutique retail space

legal use. Some of the storefront extensions hide the legal border of the building by constructing a decorated façade, using the additional area to give the appearance of a larger store. Inside, these tend to be covered with polycarbonate roofing to maintain the feel of a naturally lit sliver. Some shed-like setbacks that have more than two meters build an enclosure with aluminum panels or light construction as if it were a temporary construction without insulation.

The second appropriation type is the use of the setback as an entrance to the building. Exterior stairs do not count in the calculation of legal FAR (floor area ratio), and by moving the entrance to the second or third floor on the side setback, the ground floor can gain extra square meters of interior retail space.

The third appropriation type includes a social agenda, as the setbacks are used as green space. Because the width of the setbacks would not allow for a proper private garden, the notion of using these spaces as a green space has a larger social role that benefits the neighborhood more than the individual. In the previously mentioned competition from 2002 by Groupe e2, a Japanese entry proposed using these one-meter setbacks as a way of creating a perimeter ring of green around Tokyo. As a semi-private space, these slivers, vertical gardens between buildings, could play a larger infrastructural role as green lungs for the city, especially in large cities like Seoul that suffer from pollution and bad air quality.

The fourth adaptation is that of driveways transformed as advertisement entrances instead of for car parking. Due to parcelization, some buildings occupy the middle of the block without any street front other than a narrow driveway. These driveways are highlighted as part of an entrance sequence to commercial spaces in the back. They extend the interior experience to the street.

Lastly, the miscellaneous spaces are used for extra storage or just left empty. The use of light materials like polycarbonate roofing allows inventory to be kept outside of the building. Laundromats, for example, will extend their operations into these spaces, using them for drying racks.

Although this phenomenon seems unique to Hongdae with its retail density, this condition is repeated in other neighborhoods like Itaewon or Sinsa-dong, which have similar urban fabric makeup of low-rise buildings separated by two to five meters of shared setbacks. Analysis of the actual usage of setback space among the selected case study blocks in Hongdae indicates about a 10 percent increase in usability. This is a higher efficiency of use than that recorded by traditional methods, and it relies on the ingenuity of interior design to work within the legal parameters. This case study also suggests a potential need for understanding the spacing that generates an unplanned urbanity.

In order to compare the condition of the unplanned appropriation of the in-between in relation to grid types, 15 grid types within a 0.25 km^2 boundary are compared based on building coverage ratios. These 15 types of grids represent a cross-section of time in the development of Seoul. The grids closer to the inner core have been in transformation since the inception of Seoul in 1392. The original streams in the inner core formed informal urban fabrics that remain today. The grids further from the inner core represent areas that experienced rapid development during the decades of the 1960s, 1970s, and 1980s. These grids were laid out on empty land as a tabula rasa condition in a "western development" style of regular grids. The variation in distance between buildings among the various grids showcases an interpretation of urban efficiency through appropriation. Areas that already have 50 percent area coverage leave little room for intervention. Yet areas that have very low coverage ratios, below 20 percent, as in Apgujeong, Yeouido, or Jamsil, have separations between buildings that exceed 40 meters. These are areas made up of high-rise apartment complexes inside megablock infrastructure with no clear demarcation of parcelization. These developments resemble socialist blocks such as the Superquadra in Brasilia, where the privatized in-between is completely lost. In his essay on Brasilia in the Typological Urbanism issue of *AD*,[7] Tarttara explains Lucio Costa's intention of generating a socialist space through the displacement of linear housing blocks, raised on pilotis, in order to democratize the ground as public space. The amenities found on these superquadras follow social infrastructural agendas like public schools, daycare centers, community centers, or athletic facilities, rather than privately developed commercial retail spaces like cafes or restaurants. The relationship of *res publica* and *res privata* is flipped vertically as the entire ground is intended for public use, and private development is lifted to allow unobstructed views and free pedestrian flow throughout the entire block.

The 15 different grids allow for a conceptualization of the in-between space as a political space based on the distance of separation between buildings. Conceptually, the further away the buildings are from each other, as in Jamsil, Yeouido or Apgujeong, the more the parcelization process is lost. These developments are scaled to the size of the megablock and built as individual projects. This type democratizes the land and makes appropriations more difficult, while tighter urban fabrics privatize the ground and the subdivisions take on a more important role allowing for free market appropriations.

As discussed by Pier Vittorio Aureli in his description of the grid in the *[re]Form: New Investigations in Urban Form* symposium at Harvard, it is the subdivisions of the grid[8] that become the most important part of shaping the urban form, an idea consistent with gridded development in history. Aureli offers the possibility of escaping the dependency of subdivisions through "island" urban occupations such as the *acampada* in Madrid. These informal settlements, like the Occupy Wall Street (OWS) movements, created urbanities of the in-between informal settlements in urban voids. In cities like Seoul, where informal occupations are not rare, as previously discussed in *Borrowed City*, the island development effect can take place in the large in-between grounds as a second layer of informal amenities.

As a speculative scenario, new smart infrastructures may allow the customization of the urban space. Large open grounds between buildings could potentially allow for informal occupations controlled through digital technologies. Antoine Picon discusses the discrepancy that is occurring between the notion of "smart city" or

The driveway transformed to commercial entrance

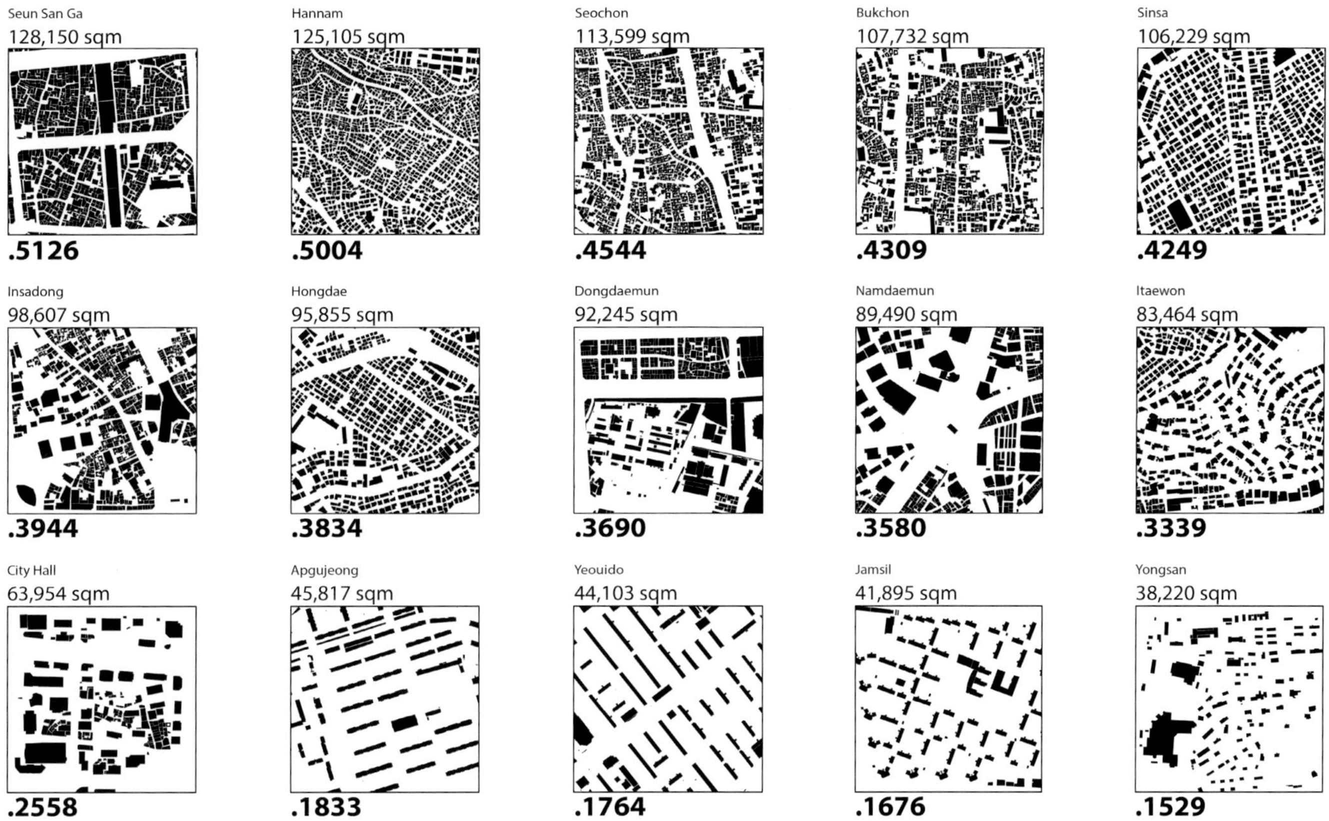

"smart infrastructure" and the actual urban makeup.[9] Our cities still maintain a known form based on a grid logic that no longer reflects the advances in technology shaping our daily lives. As previously mentioned, the path dependency of the grid will not allow much of a spatial transformation, but the in-between space of appropriation can quickly become the adaptable space for these new tendencies enabled by the technology of mass customization. The larger in-between spaces could be regulated for other activities, operating as temporal islands, as smart devices allow for multiplicity of use for the same setting. Smaller spaces, such as the ones in Hongdae or Sinsa, can also become integrated as virtual commercial spaces. Spaces of one meter to two meters in width can offer the virtual platforms for shopping while the interior displays physical goods. The hidden values of the unaccounted-for setback space of the in-between offers a whole new field of operations as an independent layer of the future city.

NOTES

1 Speck, Jeff. *Walkable City: How Downtown Can save America, One Step at a Time*. New York: North Point Press, 2013. P10.

2 http://urbanization.org/project.html?project=5.

3 Bruno, Marco, Simone Carena, and Minji Kim. *Borrowed City: Private Use of Public Space in Seoul*. Seoul: Damdi Publishing, 2015. P15.

4 http://civicdatadesignlab.mit.edu/#projects/GHOST%20CIT-IES%20-%20BEYOND%20THE%20IMAGE.

5 Perrault, Dominique, Bernard Tschumi, Michel Desvigne, and Nasrine Seraji-Bozorgzad. *E2: Exploring the Urban Condition*. Paris: Groupe E2, 2002.

6 Frampton, Adam, Jonathan D. Solomon, and Clara Wong. *Cities without Ground: A Hong Kong Guidebook*. Berkley: Oro Editions, 2015.

7 Martino Tarttara, Brasilia's Prototypical Design in *Architectural Design*, January/ February 2011, Volume 209. P.46–55 8 https://youtu.be/0L7Anlsu2A4.

8 https://youtu.be/0L7Anlsu2A4

9 Picon, Antoine. *Smart Cities: A Spatialised Intelligence*. Chichester: Wiley, 2015. P11–14.

CITY AS HOTEL

PIXEL HOTEL

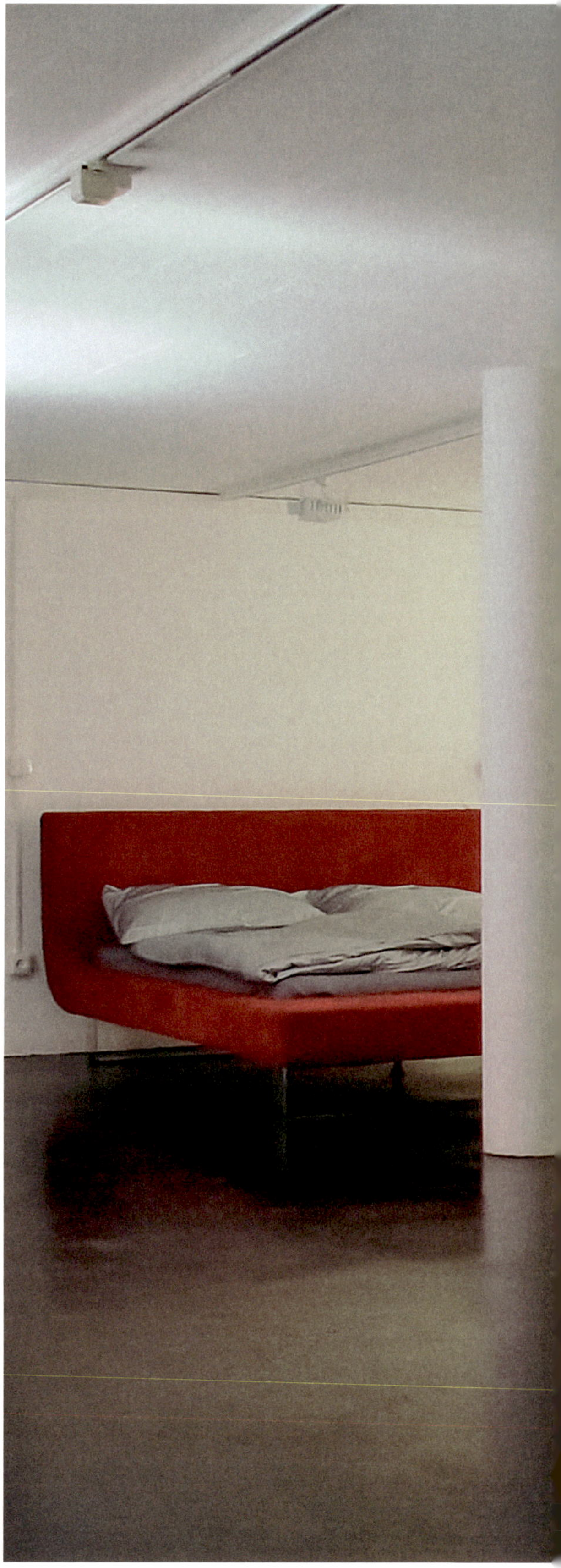

by MARKUS BERGER

Since its designation as the cultural capital of Europe in 2009, visitors to the Austrian city of Linz are being offered a new form of accommodation. The Pixel Hotel consists of rooms that are no longer in a single building. Instead, the individual rooms are spread out, or 'pixelated,' throughout the city. This is a project of adaptive reuse that reinvents the concept of hotel in its relation to the city, a concept that revitalizes old and empty spaces in the urban landscape, and gives unique expression to the historical and cultural transformations of the different parts of this city on the Danube.

By breaking down the conventional idea of a hotel and placing the rooms or pixels into the larger 'picture' of the city, a new relationship is forged between hotel and city. In stark contrast to the reception desks in conventional hotel lobbies where one retrieves room keys and hotel information prior to proceeding to one's room, the pixel lobby is essentially the city itself. Upon arrival in the city, one meets a receptionist in a public place, such as one of Linz's grand cafés, or a museum where one receives keys, a necessary city map to find

Bed and caravan

one's pixel, breakfast vouchers for the neighborhood cafes, a public transit ticket, and information on the city's activities. As guests make their way to their pixel units, they form first impressions of Linz and immediately negotiate the city's character. While the pixel itself offers the usual features of conventional hotel rooms—like TV, internet access and daily cleaning service—guests have to make their way to the neighborhood bakery or cafe around the corner for breakfast, to a neighborhood pub for a drink, and to the city's restaurants for lunch and dinner. Thus the pixel takes the hotel room out of the mediating generic spaces of the conventional hotel—lobby, corridors, breakfast buffet, hotel bar, etc.—and instead places the hotel room directly inside the life of the city.

The Pixel Hotel is the concept of a group of young architects and designers in Linz who form A.ORT.A (Architecture. Place. Analysis). As an initiative that attempts to generate new ideas in the study of the urban landscape, the Pixel Hotel emerged from a branch of A.ORT.A which focused, in particular, on urban renewal (the Verein zur Reurbanisierung und Stadtreparatur). Its goal was to re-activate void spaces within the urban fabric and to create connections between them. Cultural tourism became the vehicle for realizing this idea. The group investigated numerous empty and unused spaces across the city for suitable pixel locations—from vacant retail spaces, lofts and workshops, industrial hangars, business premises, council housing, to galleries and public spaces. The task to select between these options was difficult, as every unused space in the city had potential and a story to tell. According to Michael Grugl, one of the architects of the project, it was ultimately through word of mouth and fortuitous accidents that the present six locations of the Pixel Hotel came to be realized.

For the designers of the Pixel Hotel, this was "an art project for the temporary use of existing empty spaces." Their artistic interventions were targeted towards the repair, renewal and reconnection of these empty spaces to their individual and specific urban environments, while simultaneously fulfilling the functional needs of paid lodging. Each architectural detail of the interior was redesigned to connect with the historical and cultural context of the host building, its neighborhood, and the city-at-large. Each pixel is thus both a new expression and an integral part of this larger changing picture of the city of Linz.

According to Michael Grugl, "design decisions were usually taken as a means to transform and visualize certain historical and recent characteristics of the [city] zone, the building and the spaces we occupy." While the "old" existing history of the pixel's space and its surroundings was important, the intent was to allow the different hotel rooms to become narrative spaces telling stories of historical transformations and cultural meanings. The design interventions were thus acts that interpreted the past and, in doing so, enabled a renewed experience of the city in the present. The following descriptions of each of the six pixels will examine the distinct expressions achieved with each interpretative act and reuse of spaces in different parts of the city.

Pixel im Hof (Pixel in the courtyard)

Marienstraße 10a

The Pixel im Hof is located in the heart of downtown Linz, a short walk away from Linz's main square (Hauptplatz) and art museums, on a narrow little lane called Marienstraße. The room is part of an early industrial building, constructed in 1786. Due to numerous renovations and expansions, the character of the building has been in a constant state of transition. The room itself was originally a cabinetmaker's workshop. Over the years it was occupied in succession by a workshop for mending pots & pans, a photo studio and most recently an auto repair garage. It has now been transformed into a 90m² (900sf) hotel room. The pixel maintains the historical industrial character of the place in the rooms which are 2.2m (7'–2") in height, with original mastic-asphalt floor, minimal furniture, and a walk-in closet built into the former industrial-freight elevator. The transformation also adds a specific expression to the pixel – that of the mobility that marked the postwar years in Europe. To give historical and artistic expression to this theme, a 1960s vintage camping trailer (bought on eBay) is placed in the pixel, to serve as an adjunct living room that provides additional beds when needed. The trailer and the open space around it thus transform the room into an experience of industrialization and the mobility it engendered.

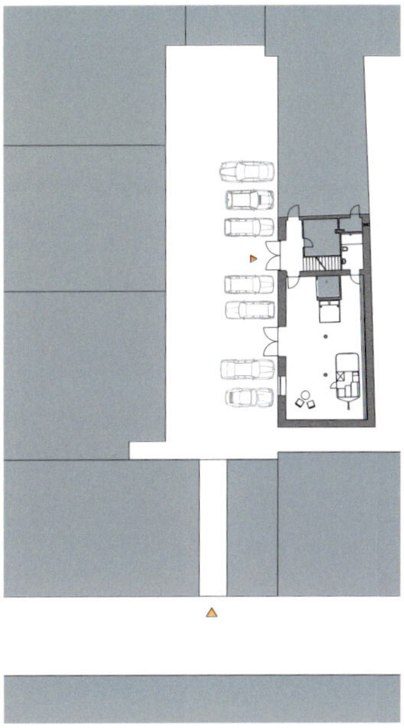

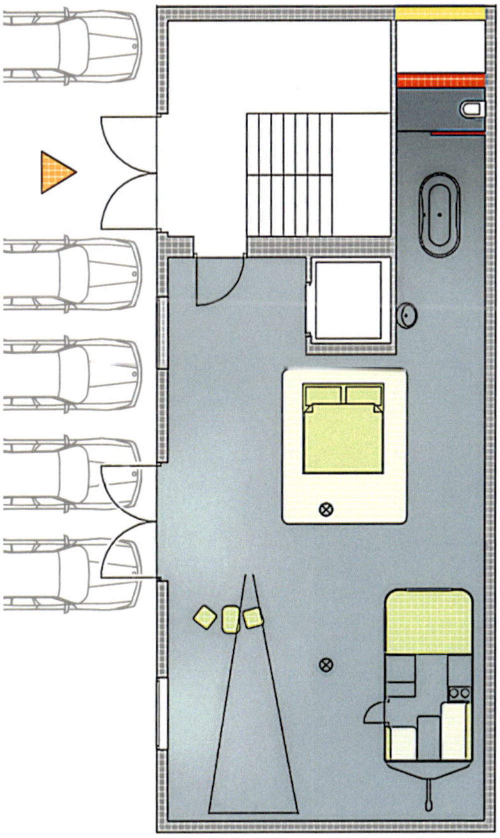

BOTTOM LEFT
View from Outside
TOP RIGHT
Site Plan
BOTTOM RIGHT
First Floor Plan

Pixel in der Textilpassage (Pixel in the textile passage)

Graben

The Pixel in der Textilpassage is located in the centre of the oldest part of Linz, near the Hauptplatz and the art gallery which supplies the Pixel Hotel with artwork for its rooms. Situated inside a small courtyard, this building was a horse stable which in the 19th century was changed into a textile workshop. That remained its function until its pixel transformation. The theme of 'textiles' is central to its design, with heavy textiles, suspended from wood, MDF and steel cables, that define the multiple levels for sleeping, living and playing. The original 1.5m (4'–11") high office room on the top of the old workshop floor has also been reused and refurbished with pillows and a games console to form a kid-size play room called "Neverland." The history of the space has contributed to a dramatic new expression and use for the present.

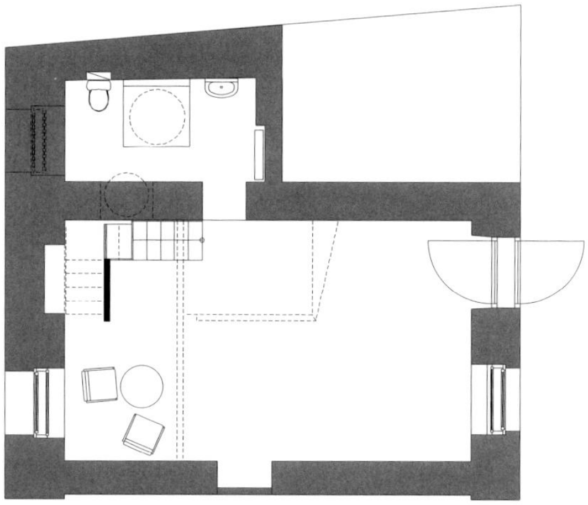

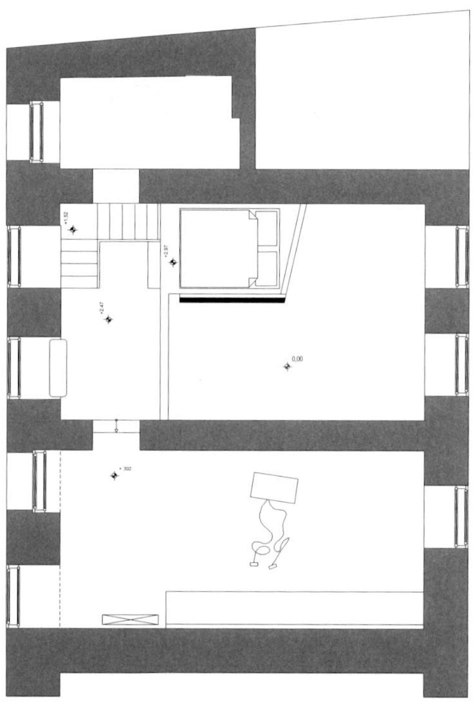

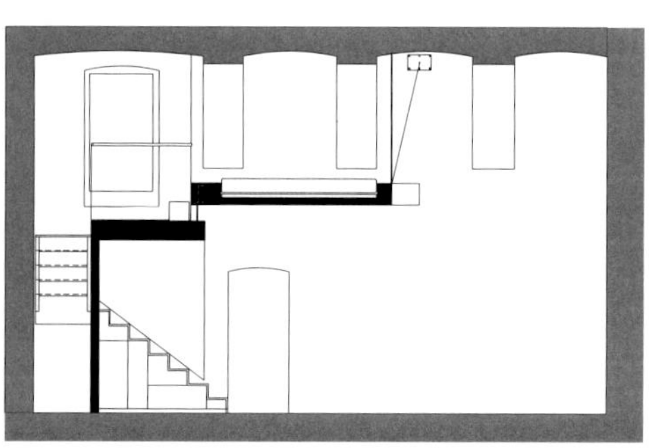

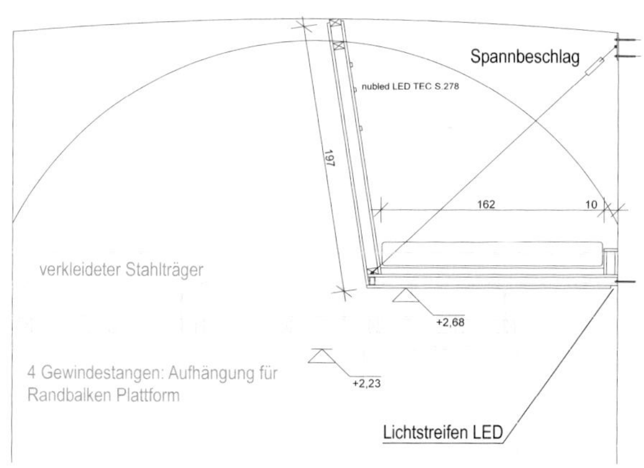

TOP
Plan at Entrance
MIDDLE
Plan Upper Level
BOTTOM
Cross Section

Bed Detail

TOP LEFT, BOTTOM LEFT

Interior Views of Levels

TOP RIGHT

Lounge

BOTTOM RIGHT

Detail, Upper Level

Pixel in der Galerie (Pixel in the gallery)

Hirschgasse 17

Pixel in der Galerie is perhaps the most published of all the pixel rooms. It is a temporary transformation of a pre-existing art gallery which has been converted into a hotel room for the year 2009, and will revert back to its original function in 2010. But even as a hotel room, the pixel is designed to give the experience of living in an art gallery. The walls display paintings and photographs by Thomas Feichtner, the gallery owner and artist, as they would when functioning as a gallery. In addition, the furniture is designed to be used not simply as functional fixtures but to be appreciated as artwork. The Schlafmöbel (sleep furniture) in particular is such a sculptural statement that combines both art and habitat. In one sense this pixel is adaptation at its minimum: it makes a conceptual statement about living with, rather than simply looking at, art (in this case, literally sleeping in it).

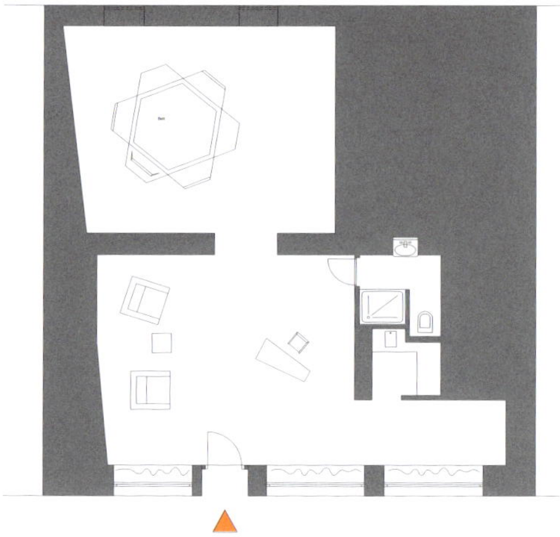

TOP

First Floor Plan

BOTTOM LEFT

Specially Designed Bed

BOTTOM RIGHT

Gallery Furnishings

Pixel am Wasser (Pixel on the water)

Linzer Hafen

The river Danube defines the city of Linz as no other natural feature. The busy traffic of excursion boats, barges and private water vehicles makes the river very lively in the summer. Pixel am Wasser, located on MZS Traisen, an old tug and pusher boat, captures this very specific aspect of Linz. MZS Traisen was launched in 1958 and remained in service until 1996. In 1997 it was purchased by the Österreichische Gesellschaft für Eisenbahn Geschichte, the Austrian Society for the History of Trains, and now three former cabins have been restored to form a suite for two people. In adapting it for purposes of a hotel, the original details have been kept intact and, as such, it is perhaps the least interpretive of the pixels in terms of contemporary design. However, the innovation lies largely in expanding the experience of the city, by bringing the pixel onto the Danube and giving new life to an old boat.

TOP RIGHT
Bow MZS Traisen
BOTTOM
Detail Bedroom

Pixel mit Garten (Pixel with garden)

Wimhölzelstraße 25

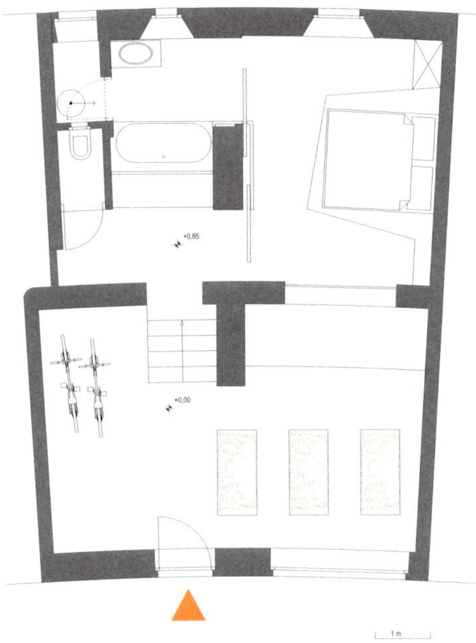

The Pixel mit Garten is located right in the heart of Linz's working class neighborhood, the Franckviertel, where an apartment and storefront of a housing complex have been combined to form this pixel. The building was part of an ambitious public housing project that was started in 1919 to build 1,200 small flats. Because of the severe financial crisis of the interwar years, only 160 of these apartments were completed. Despite the high-density low-cost housing program, they included communal gardens for residents to grow their own produce. Thus in the pixel, the retail space has been transformed into an indoor garden with green peppers, gooseberries, lettuce and herbs for the guests to savor. In addition, the bedroom and bathroom in the former apartment have a sound & image installation reminding guests of a time when most apartments in Europe had no bathrooms and the use of public bathhouses was a common practice. And finally, authentic wall patterns, a feature of working-class aesthetics, are a theme within the pixel, accentuating the textures and colors of working-class living spaces in the city.

TOP

First Floor Plan

BOTTOM

View from Bedroom

Pixel in der Volksküche
(Pixel in the community kitchen)

Herbert-Bayer-Platz 1

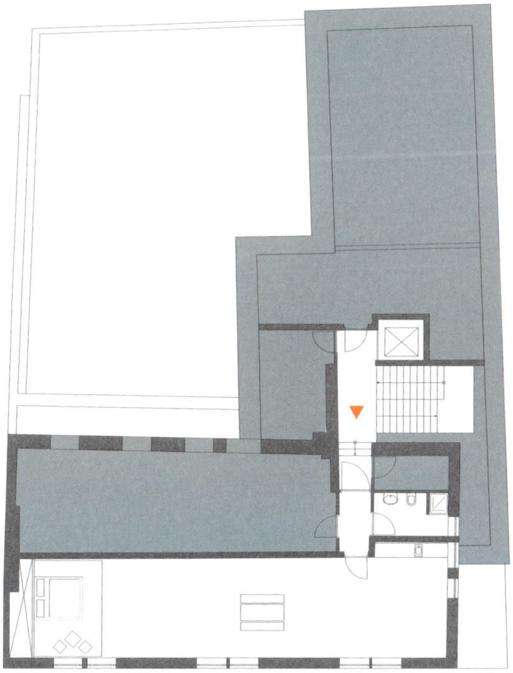

The Pixel in der Volksküche is located in the Altstadt Ost (the old eastern part of the city), in the building of a former communal kitchen. In 1887 a coal warehouse was turned into a soup kitchen for the poor. It was continuously enlarged until the First World War, when it became financially impossible to keep it open. The kitchen was taken over by the city, reopened in 1927, and remained operational until 1968, when it finally closed and was converted into an office building for the city's power company. In recent years the building housed a center for architecture and an art gallery, before its present use as a pixel. The mechanically controlled bed that can move and be concealed behind panels is a more elusive social and historical statement than similar design gestures in other pixels. The pixel attempts to refer to the past and its simplicity through the extensive use of fiber-cement boards, but the resulting white abstract spaces and its contemporary look connect it more to its present neighbors than its interesting past.

TOP
Interior View of Bed
BOTTOM
First Floor Plan

AUTHENTICITY

At the heart of adaptive reuse practice lies the balance of past heritage and present time. New narratives extend the lives of structures belonging to one age through design interventions of another. Determined in part by the vagaries of time as they act upon a host structure and in part the actions of the designer, the extent of such change impacts the original whose presence Walter Benjamin maintains "is the prerequisite to the concept of authenticity." Geopolitical and societal shifts as much as the architectural forms themselves place the author of adaptive reuse practice in a role as mediator of authenticity.

78 **Faraway, So Close | FRAC Nord-Pas de Calais: On Cloning and Duplication**
[Volume 09]
Stefano Corbo

84 **The Past Embodied in Action**
[Volume 09]
Laura Gioeni

94 **Absent Matter: An Interview with Edoardo Tresoldi**
[Volume 10]
Liliane Wong

106 **Skin Deep Conservation Versus the Imagination of Preservation**
[Volume 01]
Federica Goffi

112 **Counterpreservation: Between Grimy Buildings and Renovation Rage**
[Volume 01]
Daniela Sandler

118 **Cultural Ambassadors: Allopatric Adaptive Reuse and Secondary Narratives of Huizhou Ancient Dwellings**
[Volume 10]
Hongjiang Wang

FRAC Grand Large, Dunkirk, France

FARAWAY, SO CLOSE

FRAC GRAND LARGE: ON CLONING AND DUPLICATION

by STEFANO CORBO

> *One egg, one embryo, one adult – normality. But a bokanovskified egg will bud, will proliferate, will divide. From eight to ninety-six buds, and every bud will grow into a perfectly formed embryo, and every embryo into a full-sized adult. Making ninety-six human beings grow where only one grew before. Progress.*[1]

In his novel *Brave New World*, written in 1931, writer Aldous Huxley envisions a new model of society characterized by a peculiar process of cloning: the so-called Bokanovsky Process. Thanks to this fictional example of ectogenesis – imagined by Huxley as a method of human reproduction in which a fertilized egg can be split into as many as 96 embryos – any government or political power can program the number of humans, their behaviours and their actions. As in a futuristic Panopticon, social control is achieved through biological techniques and proto-genetic engineering. Ninety-six embryos, as pointed out in the novel, mean 96 identical machines: by creating and manipulating an artificial working class, the Power will assure itself an infinite prolongation of the status quo.

Whereas for Huxley cloning is a medium to preserve and instrumentalize social vigilance, in many recent design strategies cloning has served as a main tool to liberate architecture from programmatic predeterminations and, at the same time, to establish renovated relationships between one or more buildings, their history and their functioning. Contrary to the scenario imagined by the English author – a world based on fear and control – architectural cloning can be an instrument of freedom: freedom as a deliberate and active appropriation of space.

Cloning, in fact, is the interpretative key to describe one of Lacaton & Vassal's latest projects: the FRAC Nord-Pas de Calais in Dunkirk, France. A winning proposal of a competition held in 2009, the FRAC is a hybrid program, being an archive and an exhibition space at the same time. The starting point of this project is an old boat warehouse (Halle AP2), located in the port area and built in 1949. Rather than altering or modifying its formal characteristics, Lacaton & Vassal decided to duplicate the existing building, and to juxtapose to the Halle AP2 a new structure with the same dimensions and the same volumetry. If the warehouse is a massive concrete structure, its clone is a prefabricated and transparent envelope. Moreover, the whole program of the FRAC collections is condensed within the new construction: it provides 9,357 sqm in addition to the 1,953 sqm available in the old structure. By doing so, the Halle becomes a built void with no specific function: a flexible space, open to change and evolution. It can work as an extension of the FRAC activities, but can also have its own programmatic autonomy (concert, fairs, shows, etc.). Its life is separated but, at the same time, combined with that of the new structure.

The reuse of the Halle, inscribed within a wider process of redevelopment of the Dunkirk Port, makes the FRAC not simply a museum or an archive, but a collective catalyst: its abstract and symbolic character will function as a visual magnet in the postindustrial landscape of the port area. Second, its flexible program aims to attract the local community and at the same time to host international events. In the Halle AP2 no radical interventions or modifications have taken place: not only its structural integrity but also its raw, non-finite and industrial atmosphere has been preserved. Whereas the Halle is an enclosed vacuum to be colonized, its cloned structure follows the same compositive strategy that Lacaton & Vassal have been testing in one of their most successful projects: the Nantes School of Architecture building. In a similar way as in Nantes, the FRAC is conceived of as a vertical promenade that from the exterior takes the visitor up to a panoramic "belvedere": in other words, an example of vertical urbanism.

Elevators and a public staircase connect the different levels of the building. The new structure is a combination of different irregular spaces: café and exhibition rooms on the ground level, then administration areas, a double-height forum, and the belvedere on the last floor. The archive area, on the contrary, works as a repetitive stacking of levels: it is partially isolated and disconnected from the public circulation of the

Interior view from Halle AP2

building. A lift, located in the middle of the complex, will allow the transportation of the artworks from the ground floor to the three-storey archive.

As seen before, the main difference between the old and new structure does not reside exclusively in their divergent spatial articulation, but mainly depends on their opposite materiality: in the new building, in fact, we can find some of those elements that made Lacaton & Vassal's projects so distinguished: exposed concrete, polycarbonate panels, greenhouse-like structures, etc. The choice of these materials responds only partially to aesthetic reasons: movable polycarbonate panels, for example, work as efficient thermodynamic devices as well. Thanks to their use, it is possible to control some climatic parameters within the building – temperature, humidity, pressure – and to optimize its energy behaviour. In many cases heating and air conditioning systems become unnecessary.

There is no indulgence for complex constructive models or expensive materials: Lacaton & Vassal are not interested in the phenomenological aspects of the design process. They don't work on the creation of atmospheres, and don't believe in the cathartic function of architecture. Their projects deal with time and performance.

In Dunkirk, apart from the idea of cloning as generative strategy, old and new structures are conventional constructions: their symbolic impact is not reached through a spectacularization of the design gestures, but through a method of intervention based on a strong conceptual component, which allows a connection of past and future, history and technology, memory and information.

For the materials employed and for some of the spatial and compositive techniques adopted in this project, one may say that the FRAC represents a coherent fragment in Lacaton & Vassal's long trajectory. Starting from the beginning of the 1990s, in fact, the French firm has been experimenting with the evolutionary and adaptive character of their architectures. When working on existing structures, their projects turn into neutral palimpsests, capable of being customized according to the users' needs. In absorbing the lesson of Cedric Price, whose Fun Palace has always constituted one of their main sources of inspiration, Lacaton & Vassal question not only architecture and its traditional status, but also the role played by the architect in the design process. While Price explored in his projects the possibility of defining architecture through a constant practice of manipulation, based on cycles of assembly and destruction, Lacaton & Vassal address their efforts towards the progressive dismantlement of the architectural discipline in favour of its dilution within social and performative parameters.

Interior view from the Belvedere

As claimed by Price, architecture can only exist as a sequence of events, and not as a fixed point immerged into space: it should trigger appetites, desires, and inject them within the urban structure under the appearance of a collective Situationist game. The Fun Palace (1961), but also the InterAction Centre (1972–77), responded to this logic: if the idea of function can be subject to infinite potential modifications, and if form is free from tectonic and stereotomic constraints, architecture can be finally interpreted as a participatory or interactive machine, whose configuration depends on the dialogue between users and its components. At the same time, by assuming its ever-changing character, architecture will always contain a certain degree of indeterminacy, which will guarantee unexpected appropriations.

Consequently, in Cedric Price's opinion, even the role of the designer – a deus ex machina imposing his own worldview through the project – will disappear for good. Creativity, intended as a romantic vehicle of inspiration, is replaced by the precision and efficiency of new technological devices: well-known was Price's interest in cybernetics, game theory and information science. Porous, temporary and constantly evolving: that's how he envisioned his proposals, and projected architecture into a new dimension, where time and change shape an open notion of form. Similarly, in their projects Lacaton & Vassal express their perplexity for any sort of static, definitive and assertive approach to design.

In Bois le Prêtre Tower (Paris, 2011), or in Saint-Nazaire Housing project (2014–16), for example, the French duo confront Cedric Price's quest for adaptation and active participation. These two proposals shared a similar starting condition: an existing high-rise block built in the 1960s–1970s. Instead of demolishing these buildings, Lacaton & Vassal decided to transform them by proposing a radical extension of each apartment. New self-supporting structures are added on the old facade of the towers, in order to create terraces and loggias. These secondary parasitic structures, made of polycarbonate panels, do not offer only extra space, but at the same time work as thermal filter between the interior and the exterior, by allowing them to reach personal conditions of comfort.

Price's concern for temporality and spatial flexibility also influenced the project for the Palais de Tokyo, a modern Art Centre opened in 1937 and progressively abandoned after the completion of the Centre Pompidou in the 1970's. Here Lacaton & Vassal applied some of their consolidated strategies: the use of exposed and raw materials – the original structure of the building was liberated by superfluous decorative strata and brought to light, the interest in time as a material of the project – patina is preserved and dramatized, the free colonization of the space. Contrary to many other galleries, in Palais de Tokyo the circulation pattern is not based on dictated routes. Visitors are free to invade the whole building: from the basement, converted into a sort of habitable cave, until the upper-level exhibition spaces. The necessary technological apparatus displayed in the building is counterbalanced by its roughness, in the best of the neo-Brutalist tradition. In an analogous fashion to other projects from Lacaton & Vassal, Palais de Tokyo

TOP
Exterior view of FRAC Grand Large
BOTTOM
Nocturnal view of FRAC Grand Large

is an infrastructural support that doesn't impose any functional or spatial decision, but rather suggests a way to interact and engage with the artworks. Subtle or even invisible marks become thresholds or boundaries: ramps, variation in slope, doors and staircases.

Opposed to any modernist tradition, contemporary design is not anymore a process of tabula rasa. By recycling, modifying forms, re-interpreting existing messages, architecture engages with the strategic appropriation and manipulation of elements even proceeding from alien territories. At the same time, the traditional separation between different disciplines tends to evaporate, and architecture blurs into a constellation of innocent and ephemeral installations, extemporary episodes whose ultimate goal is simply to describe a certain temporary condition.

Against such a reassuring and innocuous vision stands the work of Lacaton & Vassal. As we have seen, when reusing existing structures, their projects are the paradigmatic expression of an alternative worldview: post-production can turn into an operative instrument of change and civic activism.

In Dunkirk, by preserving the spatial integrity of the old warehouse, Lacaton & Vassal emphasize again the unstable character of their architectures: in the same way as in Saint Nazaire's social housing tower, or in the Bois le Prêtre, the French office works on the idea of design as an open process. But if in the past any of their projects of reuse implied a physical and material contact with the old structure, in Dunkirk their strategy becomes more abstract and conceptual.

At the same time, reuse is not articulated anymore as an operation of reaction to the physical, perceptive and spatial characteristics of an old building; nor is it dictated by functional requirements or constraints. Through a project of reuse, Lacaton & Vassal apply for action: for a more participative and effective role that users can play in the making of their own environment and, by consequence, in the making of the city.

In other words, one may say that users become ecological tools: through their actions they can shape a new and sustainable modus vivendi.

NOTES

1 Aldous Huxley, *Brave New World* and *Brave New World Revisited* (New York: Harper Perennial, 2005), 17.

Palais de Tokyo, Paris, France: Interior view from the basement

THE PAST EMBODIED IN ACTION

by LAURA GIOENI

Space is not merely a geometrical issue and a pure dimensional entity given before the body and its movement. This important lesson came not from my architectural studies, but from the theatrical school, based on the methods of Jacques Lecoq, where I trained as actor and mime. That idea remained long submerged in my unconscious until it soared free, clear and distinct, during my philosophical studies. It is summarized by Ludwig Wittgenstein's observation that "architecture is a gesture" and that "not every purposive movement of the human body is a gesture. Just as little as every functional building is architecture." [1]

Unlike other arts, architecture addresses itself not only to our sight but to our whole body, configuring itself, so to speak, as the double rebound of our gestures. As almost an extension of our body, architecture becomes its further limit, the reflecting surface where body and the world simultaneously mirror themselves; in pragmatic terms we can say that the authentic meaning of architecture resides exactly in our practical replay, in what architecture invites us to do. In this way, architecture reveals its deeper sense and makes us connect to a building's past. The architectural environment activates our physical response, linking us to the chain of gestures of its designers, builders and tenants through material

The remains of the first two lateral chapels from the 17th century and the angular columns of the pronaos of the temple, embedded in the new glass facade, delimit a kind of open vestibule to the cathedral

traces left behind. Every modification provides the existing building with new interpretations that constitute its evolving authenticity, historical value and meaning.

Referring to architecture as "mimesis of the body" in his seminal book *The Eyes of the Skin*, Juhani Pallasmaa argues that "architecture is communication from the body of the architect directly to the body of the person who encounters the work, perhaps centuries later."[2] Referencing Henri Bergson's research, Pallasmaa reminds us that "there is an inherent suggestion of action in images of architecture, the moment of active encounter, or a 'promise of function' and purpose," a possibility of action which implies a "bodily reaction as inseparable aspect." As designers and users, this bodily experience of architecture is linked to our memory. In the "Lamp of Memory," John Ruskin remarked that our faculty of remembering relies on architecture. In a similar way, Pallasmaa observes that "the body knows and remembers. Architectural meaning derives from archaic responses and reactions remembered by the body and the senses."[3] Thus, "a meaningful architectural experience is not simply a series of retinal images" and architectural elements are not only visual components, but "confrontation that interacts with memory."[4]

Reflecting on the interplay between memory, body and act, Edward Casey underlines the role of "body memory" as the "natural center of any sensitive account of remembering,"[5] as privileged point of view able to illuminate the nature of our relationship with the past. He defines "habitual body memory," as a pre-reflective, tacit and pre-articulate dimension of human experience, where the remembering resides just in the performance of actions. Casey reflects that "in such memory the past is embodied in action. Rather than being contained separately somewhere in the mind or brain, it is actively an ingredient in the very bodily movements that accomplish

View from the naos of the Temple of Augustus towards the remains of the choir and apse of the Baroque church of Saint Proculus

The new marble altar and ambo dialogue with the remains of the classical monument

a particular action."[6] Likewise, architectural design, far before its drawn expression, arises from this interplay of body and memory. Speaking from experience, this is one of the most interesting offspring of Lecoq's theatrical pedagogy when applied to architectural teaching.

Jacques Lecoq is one of the most influential pedagogues of modern theatre. Nevertheless, his contribution to architectural education is little known and quite underestimated. Lecoq began to apply his research on mime, gesture and movement to architectural pedagogy in 1968, when he was invited to teach at the École Nationale Supérieure des Beaux-Arts in Paris: since then and for over 20 years, he developed a mimodynamic approach to the training of architects. Lecoq's pedagogy focused on the fundamental relationship between architectural space and body movement and gestures, investigated through the miming practice. His method is based on the study of movement, embodiment and improvisation. Lecoq conceived of miming as a universal background for our relationship with the world, as knowledge process that leads to the rediscovery of the dynamic meaning of life. Mimodynamic method represents a universal pedagogical tool, useful not only for actor training but, in general, in every field of knowledge, including architecture: "Every true artist is a mime," Lecoq writes." Picasso's ability to draw a bull depended on his having found the *essential* Bull in himself, which released the shaping gesture of his hand. He was miming. Painters and sculptors are outstanding mime artists because they share in the same act of embodiment (...). This is why I could move from teaching theatre to teaching architecture, and how I invented 'architect-mimes'."[7]

In the architectural field, Lecoq aimed to improve the design skills of architects: to build in a better way means to consider the dynamics of the body and its movements. According to Lecoq, architectural education, like every other form of artistic training, should always be founded on bodily awareness. Only through the involvement of the point of view of the body in the observation of reality and by means of the embodiment of creative process can one reach what he called "the universal poetic sense."[8] The moving body is intended by Lecoq as the center of a space-time interrelation projecting a field of forces and creating the space. Every gesture played by human beings happens in a relationship with the space around them. The external space is reflected in the inner space, provoking an emotional feeling and a motor response. The natural and the built environment mime themselves in us and make us move. Lecoq's pedagogy shows in practice the body as the mirroring margin of the world and architecture as the living threshold between our gestures and the environment.

The creative process springs from a narrative bodily action, starting from the interplay of the present of the situation and the past of the memory, so that "the

The gap between the reconstructed rear pediment of the temple and the lunette vault of the Baroque chancel

dynamics of the memory are more important than the memory itself." Lecoq writes that when one is confronted with a new place for the first time, "suddenly memory is triggered (...); you are in an image of the present and suddenly an image of the past appears. Out of the interplay between these two images comes the improvisation." [9]

These bodily roots of memory as action emerge in our natural mimodynamic embodiment of the world and constitute the fundamentals of the architectural design process and the architects' drawing gesture. In consonance with Lecoq's teaching, Pallasmaa underlines that "the making of architecture (...) is a specific embodied mode of thought that takes place through the senses and the body" and configures architecture as "projection of the human body and its movement through space." [10] According to Pallasmaa, we need to understand the space in terms of dynamic interactions: "basic architectural experiences have a verb form rather than being nouns." [11]

The mimodynamic origin of architecture, involving body and memory in action, shows its haptic dimension in opposition to its characterization as immaterial and "retinal." Likewise, bodily and gestural dimension plays the main role in the architectural design process, when the drawing action of the "thinking hand" designs, cuts, incises, decides, and starts to trace limits between the domain of possible and the kingdom of necessity.

Corinthian capitals emerged from the walls of the Baroque church after the fire which ravaged the building in 1964

Focusing on this gesture, Pallasma explains how the natural hand-eye-mind connection works in drawing, when the tip of the pencil becomes almost an extension of fingerprints and a bridge between mental and physical space.

This phenomenological approach to the architecture and design process, which accords the greatest importance to the dynamics of the body, gestures and actions, shares with pragmatism the same concept of meaning as "purpose of action." This leads to a reconsideration, together with the traditional idea of meaning and space, of the classical concept of time, in a renewed attitude towards history and historical heritage, taking into account the dynamic nature of our relationship with the past. Following Friedrich Nietzsche and Michel Foucault, this new perspective can be called Genealogy. Genealogy embraces a hermeneutical view towards the issue of temporality: past, present and future do not constitute a simple succession of atomic, unrelated instants; rather, they are in a circle where the past, according to Heidegger, is waiting at the gateway of the future. So a genealogical approach recognizes the hermeneutical and projecting character of the memory, which, in architecture, as memory in act, is activated through a chain of bodily actions and reactions between designer and user.

The authentic and living meaning of history resides in how we respond and correspond to the past in a practical act, a behavior, a habit. In this way, even historical monuments lose the eternal present of their origin, acquiring a new sense as a (re)collection of the chain of their interpretations. Certainly, intervention on existing architecture must grow from respect for authentic material components, from which the architecture also takes, in a broad sense, its historic value, and its identity; but, at the same time, we have to acknowledge that usefulness is part of architectural meaning and identity. Use forms part of the identity of architecture: an identity which is not invariable and changes according to the transformations of its past by a memory which, as interpretation and project, looks and aims to the future.

The case of the conservation and reuse of the temple-cathedral in Pozzuoli, Naples, is an expression of the ideas above: one of many acts over time, mediating identity through continuous use over millennia.

When, in 2004, the professional team led by Marco Dezzi Bardeschi won the international contest for the restoration of the ruined temple cathedral, the palimpsest communicated, in the polyphonic and fragmented state of anatomic dissection, an incomparable documental and emotional richness. I was a member of the team entrusted with the ruin. The building told us of its three main archaeological layers: the first composed of relics of the Republican Roman Capitolium and Temple of Augustus; the second, the ruin of the Christian cathedral with the Baroque Holy Sacrament Chapel and Chapter Hall; finally, the third layer exhibited the scars from a destructive and unfinished intervention undertaken in 1968, aimed at reconstructing the Roman temple after a devastating fire in 1964. Further, the site and surrounding urban context were emptied of inhabitants after an earthquake and continued seismic activity during the 1980s.

The project team faced two main tasks. On one hand, we rejected any aspiration to re-establish the lost formal unity of the original building and instead focused on guaranteeing the legibility of the historical document in its complex material stratification; on the other hand, we aimed at bringing life to the site through two seemingly opposite goals, cultic and cultural: providing

Corinthian half column of the pseudo-peristyle emerges in the gap between the wall of the temple and the Holy Sacrament Chapel

the monument with reuse as a place of religious worship aimed at a social and urban level, and creating a living cultural center as museum and archaeological site.

In places the conservation project leaves fragments and discontinuities, which, as stones on a path, make the memory stumble, while elsewhere contemporary elements complete broken forms, which, as polished terrazzo, make the memory slide into the now.

Thus, structural glass walls, with the silhouettes of the destroyed columns of the pronaos, the new bell tower, which hosts three historic bronze bells, the new inclined floor of the cella, almost a theater parterre with site-specific wooden furniture, interact with the ancient remains and act as invitation to use, as suggestion of action, as gesture, pushing to enter, sit down, walk around, look at the sky, and discover, in these bodily attitudes, the past embodied in action.

NOTES

1 Ludwig Wittgenstein, *Culture and Value: A Selection from the Posthumous Remains*, 2nd Ed. (Oxford & Malden: Blackwell Publishers,1998), 149.

2 Juhani Pallasmaa, *The Eyes of the Skin: Architecture and the Senses* (Hoboken: Wiley, 2005), 67.

3 Pallasmaa, 60.

4 Pallasmaa, 63.

5 E.S. Casey, *Remembering: A Phenomenological Study*. (Bloomington: Indiana University Press, 2000), 148.

6 Casey, 149.

7 J.G. Carasso, J. Lecoq, and J.C. Lallias, *The Moving Body: Teaching Creative Theatre,* 2nd Ed. (London & New York: Bloomsbury, 2002), 23.

8 Carasso, Lecoq and Lallias, 5.

9 Carasso, Lecoq and Lallias, 31.

10 Pallasmaa, 44–45.

11 Pallasmaa, 63.

A floor raised to its original height connects the lower level of the chancel which hosts the seats for the faithful

ABSENT MATTER

AN INTERVIEW WITH EDOARDO TRESOLDI

by LILIANE WONG

In 2016, Italian artist Edoardo Tresoldi constructed a monumental wire mesh installation at the archaeological park of Siponto, in the southern Italian region of Puglia. Abandoned in the 13th century, the site includes fragments of Apulian-Romanesque architecture and the remains of a Paleo-Christian basilica. *Basilica di Siponto* offered a contemporary interpretation/re-interpretation of the basilica that earned him worldwide acclaim. The installation also served as a new provocation for innovative approaches to preservation and heritage. In 2018, Tresoldi was awarded the Gold Medal for Italian Architecture—Special Prize to Commission by the Triennale di Milano for this bold and visionary intervention that crosses and connects disciplines from sculpture and preservation to public art. Tresoldi has since engaged in new projects that further probe complex issues of intervention and site, not only in Italy but in cities around the world, from France to Spain and from the USA to the United Arab Emirates. He shares his thoughts with Int|AR on his path to Siponto, new work in Paris and Rome, explorations of material and investigations beyond time and space, all of which offer us thoughtful and insightful new views of adaptive reuse. In "Absent Matter," Edoardo Tresoldi takes us on a journey in which "places, instants and beings are narrated."

***Basilica di Siponto*, a permanent installation commissioned by the Ministry of Cultural Heritage and Activities and Tourism, Manfredonia, Italy, 2016**

This and all subsequent illustrations are the work of Edoardo Tresoldi

Int|AR: You operate in between numerous and varied dimensions: time & space, art & archaeology, classical & modern, place & absence, limits & the unbound. With a background in fields including cinema, music, and sculpture, can you speak to the influence of these many creative areas on your heterogeneous vision of art?

ET: I come from the world of cinema, where I worked as a scenographer for seven years. So yes, it certainly had an influence on my next career, especially in composition and in a spirit of cinematographic "framing" that pushes me to immediately consider how a work will be reproduced.

I have many musician friends with whom I have several projects in the pipeline. We spend hours in my Milan studio experimenting and discussing how music's creative process can be adapted to that of sculpture—after all, they are structured in the same area of the brain—and how music and sculpture can strike similar chords. What we find most stimulating is not so much an understanding of how to combine them, but rather how a musician designs architecture, how an architect composes a song, or how a musician sculpts.

Int|AR: The Int|AR Journal focuses on the subject of adaptive reuse, defined as the practice of giving new purpose to existing structures. Our exploration of this subject has, at times, been analogized to the idea of palimpsest such that different architectural interventions in existing context are viewed as adding layers in time. In your projects involving heritage structures such as the Archaeological Park of Siponto, what type of layer would you term your interventions of wire mesh forms?

ET: They certainly belong to the contemporary, to the present. The ephemeral is an essential aspect in my poetry and my work. The *Basilica di Siponto* project, for example, was designed to "exist" for several years, but with no claim to impose itself on subsequent

***Aura*, a temporary installation at Le Bon Marché Rive Gauche, Paris, France, 2017**

Aura, a temporary installation at the Le Bon Marché Rive Gauche, Paris, France, 2017

Aura, a temporary installation at Le Bon Marché Rive Gauche, Paris, France, 2017

generations. I believe it is necessary to respect unequivocally the place and the passage of time.

In general, my interventions are based on the temporal existence of a place; their duration depends on the type of project, the place, the purpose, and the type of narration.

Int|AR: Your work is achieved primarily through the use of a single material: wire mesh. And you speak of it as 'absent matter.' How and why did you choose this material? Were you working with other materials before focusing on wire mesh?

ET: I have been drawing since I was five and for my entire career I have been in contact with materials of differing nature and characteristic.

I discovered wire mesh when I was a scenographer and was immediately struck by its potential to convey a light and subtle tale that could merge with the surrounding environment. I started with figurative sculptures and then delved into the architectural realm.

Int|AR: The project at the Archaeological Park of Siponto is premised upon the remains of the Paleo Christian basilica. It is a novel direction in working with history, heritage, and legacy. How does your intervention relate to the ruins? To the remaining Romanesque church?

ET: First, I studied the historical documentation with a team of archaeologists and researchers. Gradually I realized that I had to suggest the reappearance of the basilica, not by faithfully reconstructing it, but redesigning it in the air according to its own language. It is important for me to generate an intervention that does not require any specific knowledge to be fully accessed and assimilated.

I then tried to make the emotional and physical aspects of that place my own; I considered it as a character and outlined the narrative elements. Starting from the identification of the lines that recall the original identity, I worked on the morphology to give life to architectural echoes and tensions that relate to the landscape

***Basilica di Siponto*, a permanent installation commissioned by the Ministry of Cultural Heritage and Activities and Tourism, Manfredonia, Italy, 2016**

through transparency: the tree, as well as the conformation of the landscape and the Romanesque church have become fundamental elements in the design phase.

Int|AR: Would you categorize your work in what is today sometimes termed 'experimental preservation'?

ET: I would define it more as dynamic conservation: intervening in an archaeological site allowed me to build a contemporary landmark, able to dialogue with the pre-existing in a new way. Siponto has turned out to be a cultural operation in which art, landscape, history and the environment merge through a strongly empathetic interpretation with regard to visitors.

Int|AR: The term 'ghostly' is often used to describe your work. Is this an accurate description? How does such an adjective apply to heritage and ruins?

ET: It is. The 'Absent Matter,' narrated through the wire mesh, and what I have defined 'Metaphysical Ruin,' its application on the historical substrate, are the object of my research aimed at projecting onto the real something that is not there, or that existed and has since disappeared.

The *Basilica di Siponto* is an expression of the Metaphysical Ruin: a sculpture–architecture that suggests the original forms of the monument but is contaminated with the context both visually and spatially, thus delineating itself as a profoundly contemporary artifact.

Int|AR: Your work is read entirely differently when seen in daylight or at night. Does this duality inform the conceptualization of your projects?

ET: Lighting is an integral part of my work in the design phase and, obviously, in its perception. Solid and void are born from light and shadow that impact the wire mesh, sculpting it or merging with it.

Basilica di Siponto, a permanent installation commissioned by the Ministry of Cultural Heritage and Activities and Tourism, Manfredonia, Italy, 2016

During the day, atmospheric agents make them dynamic spaces where the boundaries between inside and outside fade away, while at night, artificial lighting enriches surfaces and volumes, characterizing them in suspense and majesty.

Int|AR: In the installation at Le Bon Marché store in Paris, identical forms are displayed but in two different materials: wire mesh and steel. This is the first time that you introduce a second material. What is the significance of this action? Given the properties of each of the materials, the resulting form, though conceptually identical, offers contrasting aspects of the volume. The wire mesh speaks of an ethereal space, while the steel reveals the confines of surface. How do you wish your audience to view the two structures?

ET: I am fascinated by most industrial materials. For some time, I wanted to experiment with corrugated sheet metal and found the perfect opportunity with *Aura*, structured on a continuous conceptual dichotomy that I also applied to the material.

Aura is in fact a reflection on the concept of art and architecture, ruin and disintegration, on the passage of time and the transformation of matter through the contrast between classical form and contemporary materials.

The project in wire mesh expresses the spirit of the architectural form, through which absence is evoked, while that in corrugated sheet metal is an organic relic, the empty shell of the architecture. While expressing a dichotomy, the two works are in continuous dialogue with each other: both are pure structural essence and narrate a space-time dimension that does not belong to the present.

Int|AR: In *The Work of Art in the Age of Mechanical Reproduction*, Walter Benjamin states, "That which withers in the age of mechanical reproduction is the aura of the work of art." You deliberately give the name Aura to your project at Le Bon Marché. Can you speak to your intentions in doing this? How do the two domes of different materials reference (or not) Benjamin's idea of 'aura'?

ET: With the two installations of *Aura* I returned to the subject of architectural ruins: one narrates the spiritual dimension, the other the physical.

As fragments of the past and an integral part of the Western imagination, in constant balance between form and anti-form, I believe that the ruins are steeped in the 'aura' defined by Walter Benjamin, "the unique

Aura, a temporary installation at the Le Bon Marché Rive Gauche, Paris, France, 2017

appearance of a distance," the magical and supernatural force which emanates from their uniqueness.

Int|AR: Your project *Sacral*, a classical volume of arches, columns and domes, is installed within the industrial setting of the Leonardo da Vinci National Museum of Science and Technology, whose mission is "to narrate the past, interpret the present through new languages, and outline new dimensions through a constant interaction with the surrounding world." It is the only one of your sited installations that contrast the classical language of architecture with the vocabulary of its host context. What was the impetus for this contrast? And, do you see this strategy as a development from your previous projects working within existing ruins?

ET: *Sacral* was presented in 2016 for the exhibition, *Il Paradiso Inclinato*, at the Ex Dogana of Rome, an industrial space, and was thus born in full contrast with the location. While in Rome, I was fascinated by the potential co-existence of classical forms, materials, and industrial locations; in the Science Museum of Milan this co-existence was an opportunity to remind visitors of the historical nature of the building, which over the years was a Benedictine monastery, an Olivetan monastery, then a hospital and a military barracks, until its inauguration as a museum in 1953. It is a tribute to the space's capacity to adapt to transformations.

Int|AR: You identify as a sculptor. What do you see as the relationship of sculpture to adaptive reuse?

ET: Intervening in the "life" of architecture is simultaneously stimulating and delicate, and requires multidisciplinary approaches for dealing with complex issues in an organic way. Contemporary interventions are enormously interesting as high-profiled proposals related to technology, materials and the concept of respect for the existing, all with the capacity to enhance and validate artistic applications.

***Sacral*, a temporary installation, *Il Paradiso Inclinato* at Ex Dogana Curated by Luca Tomio, Rome, Italy, 2016**

Sacral, a temporary installation, *Il Paradiso Inclinato* at Ex Dogana
Curated by Luca Tomio, Rome, Italy, 2016

Nils Ole Lund, The City as Scenography, 37x49, 1983
(From *Collage Architecture,* 1990)

SKIN DEEP CONSERVATION

VERSUS THE IMAGINATION OF PRESERVATION

by FEDERICA GOFFI

A critical look into current approaches to the conservation of iconic buildings in the Western world, with a focus on façadism, helps one understand some of preservation's inner contradictions. Looking into the practice of re-clothing a body contained, as an imaginative form of conservation, might contribute to critically rethinking the notion of preservation — beyond mere conservation as is — toward unveiling a meaningful form of invention, embodying a duality of preservation and design.

The idea of adding to, subtracting from and altering an existing building is well received within the context of contemporary adaptive reuse practice. Altering industrial sites for the purpose of retaining history, while sustaining our built environment in adapting it to new necessities, is now a well-established practice.

When the building in question is of recognized heritage value though, alterations are, if considered at all, viewed with suspicion, even when change is absolutely necessary. If required, structural improvements are, as far as possible, performed in a mimetic way, to maintain exterior likeness as is, equating this to a preservation of essence.

Norwegian architect Sverre Fehn (1924–2009) poignantly observed that 'the religion of the present day is the denial of death.'[1] Historic buildings are not allowed to die or even change, but rather are treated as museum objects.

Reconstruction of a one-time likeness seems the only possible way to resurrect identity. This focus on exterior likeness significantly contributed to making façadism a widely accepted practice, reducing the perception of what constitutes heritage to a skin deep facade.

Façadism is possibly the clearest example of the divorce that took place between architecture and conservation. The divorce is quite literally materialized at the dividing of a skin-deep façade preserved as is, and an entirely new building erected behind it, where the building-fragment rarely engages in a meaningful dialogue with the new.

Façadism should be critically interpreted as a cosmetic form of conservation, where only exterior likeness is preserved, reducing architecture to a simulacrum, i.e, a void shell. This is the case with countless interventions of urban conservation, claiming the preservation of historic streetscapes, without regard for the interior of the building erased from memory.

Danish architect Nils Ole Lund (b.1930), author of 'The City as Scenography' (Fig. 1), presents a poignant visual metaphor for the reduction of streetscapes to artificially propped up scenographic displays.[2]

Recent scholarship has pointed out the positive influence of sustainability on adaptive reuse, toward the need for sustaining the fabric as a whole, beyond the mere appreciation of the exterior façades. This is largely due to the acknowledged value of embodied energy.[3]

Even though we are moved to think critically about how to sustain our environment, and making the best use of present resources for future use, architects often do not view historic buildings as likely canvases for their creations, predisposed as they are to a culture of instant making; nor are they allowed to do so when the building considered is an iconic one, and protected by heritage designation. The sustainability approach offers reflections primarily focused on measurable efficiencies and does not contribute to a broader understanding of architecture as a vessel for meaning.[4]

Santa Prassede, a spolia Corinthian column emerges from its Baroque vestment

Meanwhile, modern icons, such as the Ville Savoye at Poissy-sur-Seine, by Le Corbusier (1929 – 30), conceived as instant architecture, are to be preserved as is, requiring significant resources to sustain a past time-frame. Nickolaus Pevsner, arguing in his article "Time and Le Corbusier"[5] for the preservation of the villa, inadvertently pointed out its inadequacy in sustaining itself through Time.

In disrepair after the war, the villa was restored. Mark Wigley[6] explained that "white as newness" is the key to understanding the time dimension of this building, because of its associations with purity, simplicity, and health.[7] The unpleasing, premature decay prompted Pevsner to state: "They do not make beautiful ruins, and there is no reason why they should have to, within a quarter century of their erection." He criticizes government authorities, who should guarantee the conservation of this modern icon. He argued that Corbusier's buildings make "bad ruins." Ironically, they do need frequent makeovers and adequate upkeep to preserve a still image of eternal whiteness.

Wigley comments that "replacing the degenerate layer of decoration that lines buildings with a coat of whitewash" is the compelling moral duty envisioned by the modern master. The modern instant building places itself outside the influence of time, perpetuating the original image. Is the building born in a state of perfection or is it the result of a Dorian Gray syndrome? Dorian's essence was inscribed in his exterior appearance, not his actual body.

Architecture should sustain itself through time. The owner of the 1922 Villa at Vaucresson, by Le Corbusier, added a pitched roof to make it more sustainable, as a criticism by action of its unsustainably frequent need of maintenance.

The recent focus of architectural representation on the production of photorealistic renderings also contributes to the false belief that, with design and construction, a building reaches a state of completeness, corresponding to a still image, prefigured by a final likeness, unalterable by time. The realistic enhancement of digital drawings, aiming to emulate photographic techniques, becomes the physical embodiment of the stillness of architecture.

This generated the illusion that the past can be fully preserved, through instantaneous still shots, eluding the question of whether likeness is sufficient to preserve essence.

Digitally rendered architectural still shots reduce architecture to a skin-deep design, i.e, a dressing of 2D images onto a Cartesian empty space, where inner workings are seemingly unquestioned, and outer image is imposed onto them.

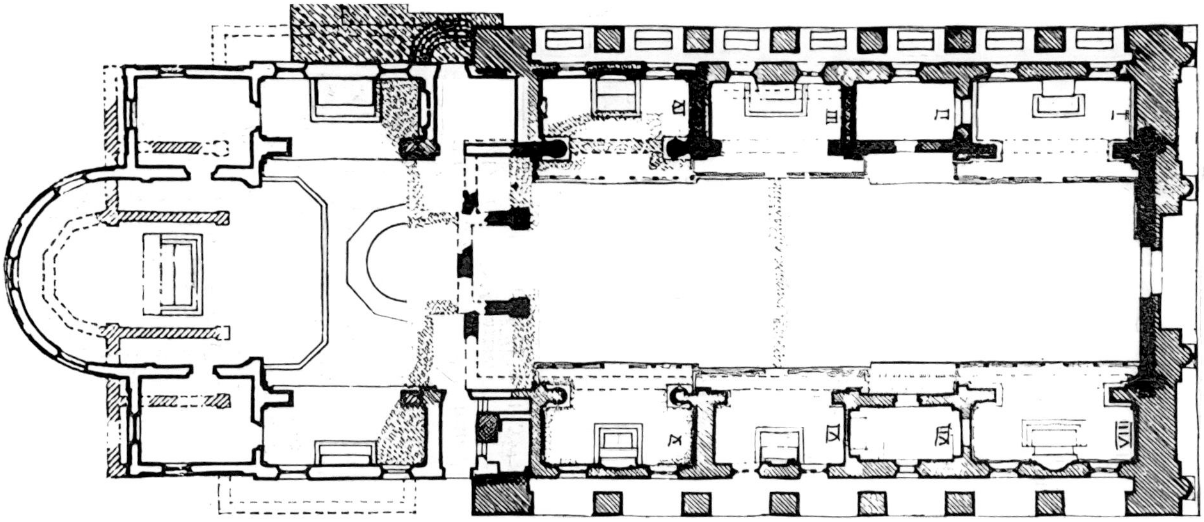

Digital technology is progressively replacing hand drawing within design schools. Students can instantly produce 'images of' architecture — without any knowledge of architecture as an art of making.

This reduces the architect's work to the application of a rendered skin. The implication is that the traditional anatomical reading of architecture, embedded in Renaissance practice and theory, suggesting a meaningful relationship between the layers constituting body/building — i.e, skin, muscular system, skeleton structure, etc. — that allows for a reading of the anatomy and poetry through the skin, is perceived as negligible.[7]

The outer 'skin' of Renaissance architecture was a metaphoric representation of the imperishable body of Architecture. In the Tempio Malatestiano, Renaissance architect and theoretician Leon Battista Alberti (1404 – 1472) projected his architectonic imagination onto an existing building facing the problem of conservation.[8] His objective was to preserve the existing church, treated as a relic, while celebrating the Malatesta family, which wraps itself around it, like a reliquary (Fig. 3).[9]

Leon Battista Alberti's treatise "On the Art of Building in Ten Books" (1988 [1450]) is fundamental to understanding the anthropomorphic architectural theories of the period and their application in the phenomenology of conservation. Architecture is described as a second body that we wear as a coat in winter weather, or a linen dress during the summer, appropriate to circumstance.

Alberti's theory is based on suggesting metaphoric relations between the body and a building's fabric. The building as a microcosm relates to the world as the macrocosm, through the medium of the body. He affirms, based on the writings of Aristotle, that change is the natural life of things.[10]

Medieval and Renaissance discussion on material continuity is relevant. Questions regarding the resurrection of the body allow for dealing with the imagination of change. The reliquary preserves holy body fragments until the end of time, extending their life into sempiternity. Sempiternity, i.e. an eternity with a beginning, is the cosmological time dimension of the human soul.[11] For a building to be sempiternal meant that its life had a beginning but not an end. Its survival within time entailed constant changes.

Wrapping was a metaphor for resurrection: "For this perishable nature must put on the imperishable, and this mortal nature must put on immortality."[12]

The habit — clothing of the body — from the Latin *habere*, to have, is a representation of what one is constituted of, meaning of what one is.[13]

Icons were often clothed with permanence. This was the case with the Sancta Sanctorum (ca. 600) in the Basilica of St. John in the Lateran, dressed with a silver casing (ca. 1200).[14] Sempiternal existence was made visible using durable materials. Immortality was put on as a garment. Wrapping conveyed permanence.[15]

A similar treatment was applied to architectural spoils, clothed with imperishable vestments. The incorporation of spoil columns in Santa Prassede (817 – 824) in Rome within Baroque vestments is an example (Fig. 2). The column capital emerges from its vestment, just like the face of the Sancta Sanctorum from the silver casing.

René Magritte's 1961 *La Folie des grandeurs* presents the fragmentary torso of a classical statue contained within another body fragment. Magritte makes visible an invisible process of creation as recreation, providing a visual metaphor for the imagination of the 'body contained.'

Floor Plan of the Tempio Malatestiano. It is possible to see the separation between the inner walls of the Church of San Francesco and the outer walls of the Tempio

The Tempio Malatestiano wraps itself around the preexisting church literally and metaphorically. The burial places of the members of the Malatesta family are located under arches around the exterior perimeter.[16] Alberti's project entails the making of a reliquary. Triumph over death is denoted by the motif of the Roman triumphal arch in the façade (Wittkower, 1988).[17]

This is very different from the modus operandi of instant architecture. The battle of materials against time is the result of a very different time-cosmology, aiming at a building's sustenance into sempiternity.[18]

In my opinion, the column was originally developed to support the roof. Yet it is remarkable that mortals, once they had developed a passion for nobler things, grew concerned to construct buildings that would be permanent and, as far as possible, immortal. They therefore built columns, beams, even entire floors and roofs of marble. Materials were chosen for their durability, guaranteeing sempiternity. Beauty contributed to permanence by inspiring admiration and preventing destruction.[19]

When American artist Christo wrapped and unwrapped one of the most symbolic 'relics' of German history, the Reichstag in Berlin (1991), he created the equivalent of a symbolic rebirth. By wrapping the object, Christo shows the object, drawing attention to it. Wrapping marks the passing over a particular threshold in German history, revealing the relic-like nature of the building fragment at the time when Sir Norman Foster's renovation was about to begin. The Reichstag was later reopened as the the new house of Parliament. The construction, in 1999, of the new dome as a transparent metal-glass structure, is to be interpreted as the finding of the right dress for a particular time, becoming a metaphoric projection, symbolizing the transparency of democracy.[20]

CONCLUSION

Conservation is a creative process which allows for a building to change over time and is concerned with the problems and modes of combining the old with the new. Currently the practice of conservation has turned into a form of 'still-preservation'. The belief is that a building can and should maintain its likeness in perpetuity in order to preserve its heritage. The past is frozen into still shots.[21]

In Renaissance understanding, conservation does not preclude the possibility of letting a building evolve physically into a new form, which is an essential part of the imagination of conservation. Several Renaissance examples assure conservation through re-creation, through wrapping, such is the case with Alberti's Tempio Malatestiano, but also with the Rucellai Sepulchre in San Pancrazio, Florence and even New St. Peter's in the Vatican.[22] All projects used re-clothing to achieve conservation of a body contained.

Modern and contemporary conservation carry the Renaissance stamp of sempiternity by wrapping existing structures with a second skin. Carlo Scarpa's new façade for the Banca Popolare in Verona (1973), Bernard Tschumi's 'in between architecture' at Le Fresnoy (1992), or even Peter Zumthor's recent project for the renovation of St. Kolumba (1997–2007) do not differ in their intention from a Renaissance desire for sempiternity. Immortality is put on as a garment. The wrapping of the object conveys permanence.

Wrapping existing buildings with renewed 'skin' is a form of conservation that extends a building's life imaginatively, and can be used as a model to critically reassess contemporary practices of conservation, which focus on likeness as is to preserve essence.

NOTES

1 Gennaro Postiglione & Christian Norberg Schulz. *Sverre Fehn*. The Monacelli Press: 1997.

2 Nils Ole Lund. *Collage Architecture*. Ernst & Sons, 1990.

3 Kessler Mark. "Sowing Seeds of Diversity: The Influence of Sustainability on Adaptive Reuse." *ACSA proceedings*. Portland 2009: 510–517.

4 Sheryl Boyle & Federica Goffi sessions titled: "The Sustenance of Architecture: Making as Re-making." *ACSA proceedings*. Portland 2009: 485–539.

5 Pevsner, Nikolaus. "Time and Le Corbusier," in *Architectural Review*, v. 125, n. 746, March 1959, pp. 159–165.

6 Wigley, Mark. *White Walls, Designer Dresses*, (MIT Press, 2001) quoting from Le Corbusier. *When the Cathedrals Were White*. This is the consequence of the application of the 'Law of Ripolin' in which Le Corbusier explicitly stated that "Whitewash is extremely moral. Suppose there were a decree requiring all rooms in Paris to be given a coat of whitewash. I maintain that that would be a police task of real stature and a manifestation of high morality, the sign of great people." Le Corbusier, *The Decorative Art of Today*. Cambridge, MA. MIT Press: 1987, pp. 192, 185. (Transl. of *L'art decoratif d'aujourd'hui*, 1925).

7 Frascari, Marco. "Drafting Knife and Pen." In *Implementing Architecture*, Atlanta: Nexus Press, 1988.

8 In 1450 Alberti receives the commission by the tyrant of Rimini Sigismondo Malatesta to celebrate his family by marking their presence in the temple of the city, the church of San Franceso. The commission of the Tempio Malatestiano comes at the same time when his *De re Aedificatoria* is first published and it represents a perfect opportunity to practice his architectonic principles.

9 The same phenomena can be appreciated in the Holy House of Loreto, designed by Donato Bramante, for Julius II. The Holy House, preceding the Tempio Malatestiano, might be the paradigmatic precedent for this intervention. The building that housed the mother of Jesus is treated as a relic and is preserved through multiple wrappings. One body contains another, where the inner one concealed from sight is the most precious one. This is also analogous to what American Architect John Russell Pope did when wrapping Abraham Lincoln's birth cabin in 1909–1911, enshrining it within a stone temple.

10 (Alberti, 1988: 10.12. 349–351 [194v–197]).

11 For a thorough understanding of the concept of sempiternity see Ernst Kantorowitcz, *The King's Two Bodies*, Princeton Architectural Press, 1957. The stress that can be found in architectural treatises such as Francesco di Giorgio's *Trattato di Architettura, Ingegneria e Arte Militare*, Edizione Il Polifilo [1474–1482] on the duration of these fabrics underlines that their projected life-span was modeled after sempiternity. See also a paper on "Francesco Di Giorgio Martini's Time-Cosmology: The Sempiternity of Architecture" by Federica Goffi, presented at the 2006 Renaissance Society of America conference held in Chicago.

12 1 Corinthians 15:53 makes this even more clear: "this corruptible must be clothed with incorruption, and this mortal must be clothed with immortality." Three in fact were the modes of salvation and reclothing is one of them. Relics were the last remains of saintly bodies on earth and a pre-figuration of the resurrected body. Holy bodily bits were believed to be 'imperishable matter', empowered with all of the saintly attributes. Their immortal clothing is the reliquary.

13 The etymology of the word habit from the Oxford English Dictionary gives the following definition: [...] The sense development, as seen in Latin and the modern languages taken together, is thus: Holding, having, 'havour'; hence the way in which one holds or has oneself, i.e. the mode or condition in which one is, exists, or exhibits oneself.

14 Icons were gates open into eternity. For a discussion of this idea see Florensky, *Pavel. Iconostasis*, St Vladimir's Seminary Press, New York, 2000.

15 Crystal or gold reliquaries associate body bits with permanence, paintings in which body parts are assimilated to reliquaries or statues... treat the body as permanent locus of person. See Walker Bynum, Caroline. *The Resurrection of the Body in Western Christianity, 200–1336*, Columbia University Press, New York, 1995.

16 By 1300 burial ad sanctum was common practice. Nobles and clergy members alike would want to be buried near the burial places of saints (Walker Bynum, 1992). This would allow them to be together with the blessed ones during the day of resurrection. The operation of the Malatesta family reflects this desire. They propose themselves as devotees and protectors of the church and its saints. The building therefore incorporates the existing church like the faithful incorporate the body of Jesus during the miracle of the Eucharist.

17 The burial places of Sigismondo and his wife Isotta were likely meant to be placed under those arches. See Rykwert, Joseph. *Theory as rhetoric: Leon Battista Alberti in theory and in practice*, in Vaughan Hart and Peter Hicks, *Paper Palaces*, Yale University Press, New Haven and London, 1998.

18 Alberti, 1988: 2.8.

19 Alberti, 1988: 6.2.

20 Andreas Huyssen provides an interesting discussion on what he calls the "voids of Berlin" in *Present Pasts*, 2003.

21 Goffi, Federica. "Architecture's Twinned Body: Building and Drawing", in *From Models to Drawing*, edited by Marco Frascari, Jonathan Hale, Bradley Starkey, Routledge, New York, 2007.

22 Numerous drawings of St. Peter's Basilica (Bramante, U 20 A, Tiberio Alfarano's 1590 print) show New St. Peter's body wrapped around Old St. Peter's. New St. Peter's becomes a reliquary of the old one.

L.U.X. Nightclub, Kreuzberg, Berlin

COUNTER-PRESERVATION

BETWEEN GRIMY BUILDINGS AND RENOVATION RAGE

by DANIELA SANDLER

Prologue: Why is urban decay such a vital part of the city's fabric, connecting social and physical tissues instead of disrupting them? Why do groups and individuals choose to live and work in semi-ruinous buildings when they could afford to be in renovated structures? While in other contexts, such as North and Latin American cities, urban dilapidation is associated with economic and ethnic discrimination and lack of alternatives, in Berlin it is creatively transformed into alternative ways of inhabiting and producing the city. Decrepitude is a way to resist gentrification concretely and symbolically, carving out affordable living and workspaces.

At first sight, to incorporate dilapidation intentionally in the treatment of historical buildings might run counter to the precepts of preservation, restoration, and adaptive reuse. Grime and ruination often mean the destruction of materials and forms, and also—symbolically—the destruction of historical meaning. Here, however, I argue that at least in some cases the conscious appropriation of decay as a strategy in the ongoing life of buildings can represent a more meaningful and rich engagement with history than traditional forms of preservation. Preservation and restoration often run the risk of freezing buildings and urban sites according to fixed ideas of authenticity and originality. When a building is restored to its original design, or to its configuration at a particular point in the past, all of its other multiple and dynamic incarnations are obscured. More than that: what is lost is the dynamic character of history, the passage of time, the gradual accretion of changes (or the radical transformation of spaces), and the interventions of groups and individuals, of designers and users. As an alternative to traditional restoration and preservation, the practice of adaptive reuse opens up old buildings to different forms, materials, and uses, effectively unlocking the "chastity belt" of historical and stylistic cohesiveness. However, most adaptive reuse projects are so minutely designed and carefully planned that they too end up cohering around a fixed spatial solution with little room for present and future interventions.

In contrast, it is possible to occupy and transform the spaces of old structures in a more open-ended way, without trying to clean every sign of history or to submit the structure to an all-encompassing design all at once. This transformation does not happen in a solitary act of creation on the drawing board, but in the collective and everyday experience of space—practice that is as much spatial as it is social. Here I present instances of targeted non-restoration that demonstrate a dynamic and participatory engagement with historical buildings. The examples are not intended as models or as a new paradigm. If anything, they underscore the need for the careful contextual study of structures before any architectural intervention, be it conventional restoration or alternative approaches. Berlin, city of ruins?

More than 50 years after the end of World War II, and a full 20 years since the fall of the Berlin Wall, the German capital is still peppered with signs of decay: pockmarks, grime, and soot cover otherwise restored buildings; decrepit or ruined structures permeate almost every neighborhood; and vacant lots interrupt the urban fabric, exposing raw brick walls and the backside of buildings.

These signs of destruction are historical clues: black soot from war-time fires; pockmarks and missing building parts caused by Allied bombing; puncture wounds left by the Battle of Berlin. But what about the patina, the softly rounded corners that evoke John Ruskin's writings on preservation and beauty in architecture, in *The Stones of Venice* and other books? This patina has covered much of Berlin's historical urban fabric, which is typically made of mixed-use and residential building—the *Mietskasernen* or "rental barracks." The gradual erosion of these buildings, especially in neighborhoods such as Kreuzberg, Prenzlauer Berg, Wedding, Mitte, and Friedrichshain, stems from postwar neglect. Resources both in East and West Berlin went to newer parts of the city, to urban renewal, or to exceptional showpiece restorations. In fact, the urban decay of Berlin has an older precedent in the squalor of the turn of the 20th century, when most Mietskasernen were overcrowded, unsanitary, and dingy.[1]

We can still glimpse these historical threads in the present city—but less and less so. After unification in 1990, public and private investment flowed into the city. This is, after all, the capital of unified Germany, the New Berlin as it has been branded. Renovation, new buildings by "starchitects," urban beautification, gentrification—all of this spread over the city. Private development struck with a vengeance, eating up the old building stock that was so ripe for real state speculation.

The core of the city, the district of Mitte, was the first area to undergo development and restoration—or, in German, *Sanierung*, which means urban or architectural renewal, but implies a process of cleaning and sanitization (the word comes from the Latin *sanare*, meaning "to cure"). Mitte has all the trappings of gentrification: upscale condos, office buildings, trendy establishments devoted to an economy of entertainment and diversion—hotels, bars, restaurants, art galleries, design and clothing shops (fig. 04). It does not hurt that the area has plenty of new and established cultural institutions, and that the architecture itself can be quite spectacular—for instance, the Hackeschen Höfe, a mixed-use complex with a carefully restored Judgendstil courtyard, or the New Synagogue, which had been destroyed in the Kristallnacht and by Allied bombing and has been partly restored in the mid-1990s, including the golden-ribbed dome.

Part of the mystique of the Mitte district was the alternative culture that thrived there immediately after the fall of the Wall. Artists, students, musicians, a whole alternative "scene" coming from East Germany, West Germany and beyond flocked to what was then a derelict area. They squatted empty buildings, some of them in ruins. Gradually, property ownership was determined in court for almost every building. Private developers, many from West Germany, started to buy historical buildings and renovate them, evicting their occupants (who included not only squatters but also students, artists, retirees, and others who lived there because they could afford the very low rents[2]).

For the most part, the developers followed traditional *Sanierung* principles: cleaning and reconstruction according to records of the building's original state, or according to the style of the historical period. These renovations had to comply with the codes of the Berlin Preservation Authority (*Landesdenkmalamt*). Berlin public preservation offices are very active, powerful, and vigilant about the city's historical structures—partly as a reaction to lax policies and neglect in the immediate postwar era, when many sound historical structures were lost to postwar urban renewal. But the restoration of the Mitte area did not follow simply the dictates of preservationists. It also revealed nostalgic, idealized interpretations of the past—the *Mietskasernen* never looked as clean, bright, and airy as they do now! And in many cases, especially with apartment and mixed-use buildings of no particular historical import, developers did not carry out scientific investigations of original colors, materials, and decorations. Rather, they were free to rebuild façades and interior common areas such as hallways and staircases as long as the overall result looked convincingly historical.

As the fresh coats of paint advanced steadily over the cityscape, most of the artist communities and squatters moved elsewhere. Some dilapidation remained, most of it carefully controlled and preserved. For instance, the decayed surfaces of a building on Auguststrasse are sealed off beneath transparent veneer. The Tacheles Cultural Center, which started out as a precarious ruin slated for demolition, has since undergone refurbishments that made it safer for visitors, and it is now protected as a historical landmark. Some of the original sense of the ruin remains in raw or grimy surfaces, and in the back façade, where the abrupt outline of the structure reveals the extant building to be a fragment of a former, larger one. But the ruin was cleaned, secured, and sanitized. Proof of this is not only the increasingly mainstream programming and public nature of the cultural center, but also—most significantly—its incorporation into a New Urbanist scheme by Andres Duany and Elizabeth Plater-Zyberk for upscale condos, shops, and hotels. Before unification, dilapidation had engulfed the Mitte as an integral part of the landscape—from the slums of the Weimar Republic, to the destruction during World War II, to socialist neglect. Now, the vestiges of decay are part of the new urban experience of a city consumed by the tourist-*flâneur*. An exciting touch of roughness subsists, but in an increasingly controlled and planned fashion. This removes not only the element of surprise, discovery, or mystery associated with picturesque settings, but also the possibility for future transformations (planned or not) that could potentially infuse fresh life into the cityscape. The careful preservation of bits and pieces of ruins amidst generalized renovation and gentrification ends up ossifying history—even the evocative, open-ended history of ruins—into a fixed environment.

The widespread *Sanierung* of the Mitte area effaced a complex spatial and social history. While claiming to "restore" the neighborhood, developers provided a new narrative—a sanitized backdrop of a genteel and somewhat generic "historical city." A visitor trying to understand life in socialist East Berlin or during the Weimar Republic would be hard-pressed to visualize these periods in the current landscape. This is not to suggest that the city should have been frozen in its dilapidated state as some kind of open-air museum. Such a congealed scenario is in fact not that different from nostalgic, idealized restoration, as both fossilize the historical fabric in one particular point in history at the expense of all others—including present and future interventions. There are alternatives to both scenarios, as I explain below.

Several art projects, cultural centers, and living communities in Berlin have appropriated states of decay in alternative and creative ways—for example, the Haus Schwarzenberg Cultural Center, and the queer residential community Tuntenhaus (which means Queer House). They incorporate dilapidation to express a more dynamic and layered history, one that tries to account for the multiplicity and conflict of historical narratives and events (the Weimar Republic, the Nazi era, World War II, the years of German division, unification in 1989) rather than subsuming a vision of historical "truth" under a single period or style. These cultural and social projects exemplify what I call "counterpreservation"—a conscious, willful incorporation of decay, of unfinished or incomplete elements, of dilapidation and fragments into the redesign and occupation of historical buildings. The current architectural state of these buildings is determined not by a single designer, architect, or preservationist, but by collective decisions and actions by the building inhabitants. Their spatial interventions often resemble unfinished collages and incorporate found objects, graffiti, posters, and improvised materials. They also take full advantage of the visual and spatial affect of decay: missing architectural elements, soot and grime, exposed masonry, and surfaces softened by gradual weathering.

The intentional framing and display of decrepitude serves a socio-economic purpose by conveying an anti-gentrification message, and a defense of more diverse and inclusive social and urban uses. This social stance is part and parcel of a critique of traditional preservation tenets. The spirit of the Tuntenhaus and the Haus Schwarzenberg is summed up by their critique—explicit and implicit—of *Sanierungswut* (renovation fury). The expression is used pejoratively in

Manteuffelstraße, Kreuzberg, Berlin, 2020. "Ihr dient dem kapital" in the sign translates to "You serve capital."

Near Görlitzer Bahnhof U-Bahn station, Kreuzberg, Berlin, 2020

pamphlets, alternative or local newspapers, blogs, and reviews that express similar views to those of the Haus Schwarzenberg and Tuntenhaus occupants and users. For example, the official website of the city of Berlin characterizes the anti-renovation stance of the Haus Schwarzenberg as "still completely impervious to the renovation rage since unification."[3]

Counterpreservation represents, on the one hand, a departure from conventional restoration and conservation practices. On the other hand, counterpreservation retains a sense of contrivance and intentionality that distinguishes it from neglect. For example, the artists and designers who manage and occupy the Haus Schwarzenberg have carried out necessary renovations to prevent the collapse of the building—from rebuilding the structure of the side wing, to cleaning and securing the street façade. In so doing, they have not only reinstated a socio-political stance, but they have also managed to preserve an ineffable quality of decrepit structures: the romance of glumness, the gripping quality of surfaces slowly carved out by time and use, or violently torn by aggression. These spaces are haunted by the signs of the past even when the memory of events has faded. This gap between physical sign and faded memory contains the seduction, the fog of mystery that invites us to guess, to imagine possible histories, to fill in the missing parts, or simply to dwell in the murky corners.

Counterpreservation mixes the romance of glumness with functional and utilitarian activities such as inhabiting, working, eating, and recreation. But the need to accommodate daily life poses difficulties that most picturesque ruins do not have to address if they function as monuments or open landscape structures. How much dilapidation can a building sustain before it becomes uninhabitable?

There is another limitation. To a great extent, counterpreservation derives its force from the contrast with renovated, conventional surroundings. The Haus Schwarzenberg would lose its effect if all buildings kept the same characteristics. Not only would the aesthetic impression be diluted, but the intentionality behind dilapidation might be mistaken for urban decay. Clearly, counterpreservation cannot be applied as a model for treating historical environments everywhere. But this is not necessarily a shortcoming. Any attempt to universalize architectural designs, functions, and programs instead of carefully considering local needs and circumstances will be doomed to disconnection and inadequacy. In this sense, counterpreservation—both as a theoretical concept in architectural design and as a practice grounded in the specific context of Berlin—can be seen as one possibility among many in the treatment of historical structures, alongside restoration, conservation, reconstruction, adaptive reuse, and radical redesign. Counterpreservation contributes to a larger dialogue among theorists and practitioners in search of a more dynamic, open-ended, and complex approach to the past in the built environment.

NOTES

1 Rudolf Eberstadt's *Handbuch des Wohnungswesens und der Wohnungsfrage* (Jena: G. Fischer, 1909) is an early indictment against the cramped and precarious *Mietskasernen*, or tenement houses. The most traditional source on Berlin Mietskasernen is Werner Hegemann's *Das steinerne Berlin: Geschichte der grössten Mietskasernenstadt der Welt* (Berlin: G. Kiepenheuer, 1930). For a vivid reconstitution of everyday life in a Mietskaserne see Christopher Isherwood's "The Nowaks," in *The Berlin Novels* (London: Vintage, 1999), 362–408.

2 For an explanation of the issue of contested property in East Berlin and its implications for urban planning and renovation, see Elizabeth Strom, *Building the New Berlin: The Politics of Urban Development in Germany's Capital City* (Lanham, Md.: Lexington Books, 2001).

3 In German, "noch gänzlich unbeeindruckt von der Sanierungswut seit der Wende." The text is about the Central Cinema, located in the cultural center Haus Schwarzenberg. See http://www.berlin.de/orte/kulturorte/central_kino/.

The images in this article have been updated since it was published in 2009 to reflect the changing nature of grimy buildings and revolution rage.

CULTURAL AMBASSADORS

ALLOPATRIC ADAPTIVE REUSE AND SECONDARY NARRATIVES OF HUIZHOU ANCIENT DWELLINGS

by HONGJIANG WANG

The Original Narrative of Huizhou Folk Dwellings

Huizhou merchants dominated the Chinese business community for nearly 500 years during the Ming (1368–1644) and Qing (1644–1911) Dynasties, and these merchants, who traveled far from their hometowns, accumulated enormous wealth by selling salt, tea, rice and other commodities. Many successful Huizhou merchants returned to their hometowns, located in today's Huangshan City and Jixi County in Anhui Province, and Wuyuan in Jiangxi Province, where they built many exquisite dwellings and ancestral halls. The process of urbanization in modern China today has led to the shrinking of family units and population migration. Today, few descendants, whose forefathers lived in the 7,000 folk houses of more than 100 ancient villages in Huizhou district, are still willing to live in these dim ancestral houses. In addition to some outstanding dwellings that were protected and repaired by local governments at various levels, some scattered old houses that were not on the protection list in the early years were purchased by outsiders. These neglected houses have benefited from relocation and adaptive reuse. In the era of globalization, some excellent dwellings rebuilt in other places have become cultural ambassadors of spatial narratives through their distinctive architectural and symbolic features.

Architectural narrative endows a place with identifiability and memorability through stories, establishing a connection between people and space. The first narration of Huizhou folk dwellings, which are regarded as the physical shelter and spiritual home of Huizhou merchants, is based on a unique residential culture. In the humid

A Huizhou settlement in the Xixinan town of the Anhui province in China

Wood-carving panels under windows are a feature of Huizhou dwellings

monsoon climate and beautiful hilly environment, the site selection and spatial layout, guided by the Feng Shui theory of Zhouyi, embody the unity of man and nature in traditional Chinese philosophy and its respect for nature. The introverted living philosophy and the spiritual beliefs of Huizhou merchants, also known as Confucian traders, were conveyed through the home's protective inward spatial order, as well as the application of wood, brick and stone carving crafts as symbolic narrative elements. These decorative crafts, which were carved on the beams, pillars, doors, windows, entrance walls, etc, mostly describe animal and plant patterns that symbolize auspiciousness and good luck. Character images from Chinese folklore and literary tales conveyed the owner's desire for a better life by using rhetorical devices such as metaphor, metonymy and synecdoche. They employ a basic narrative method similar to that of the murals and sculpture in Western churches. Generally speaking, the original space narrators of Huizhou housing were not professional architects but homeowners and folk craftsmen. They iteratively developed the architectural style based on local customs and accumulated experience and gradually formed the cultural semantics of Huizhou housing as a unique narrative.

The Secondary Narrative in Relocated Sites

With the development of economic globalization and the rapid dissemination of information, this architecture has gradually become a symbol of politics, capital, and culture, separated from the existing place spirit and life experience.[1] After the original residential space was translocated to public cultural places, such as museums, new stories were implanted from its reconstruction. In the process of demolition, transportation, restoration and adaptive reuse, a secondary narrative is generated, one which merges the migrated Huizhou housing with the local culture. Yin Yu Tang, which opened in the Peabody Essex Museum, Salem, MA, in 2003, is one such example. The story began with American

Yin Yu Tang, Salem, MA

Nancy Berliner's chance encounter with the Ancient House of the Huang Family, located in Xiuning County, Anhui Province. Nancy, who loved Chinese culture, met the Huang family in 1996 as they were preparing to sell their ancestral house. They immediately made a deal. The demolition of the house the following year took four months and 2,735 wooden components, 972 stone pieces, together with the living goods placed in the house, and even the paving stones at the entrance were removed. In the Spring Festival of 1998, nearly 40 containers carrying these articles crossed the Pacific Ocean. This normal ancient dwelling was reborn on the other side of the Pacific Ocean through a careful reconstruction in 2003 and became a sensational story in the Sino-American folk cultural exchanges of that year. Years later, when Qiuhua Huang, the 36th generation descendant of the Huang family, stood in the former ancestral house in Salem, a small town near Boston, USA, listening to Yo-Yo Ma's cello performance in the courtyard, could not help but burst into tears. This sense of sorrow and joy was triggered by the architectural cultural genes that carried the nostalgic memory of the family. As the members of the original family were involved in the migration and reconstruction of the old dwelling, and contributed a large number of precious documents such as daily necessities, genealogy and old photos, the story of the reconstruction was complete and vivid. Because of its relocation and reconstruction, both the original and the secondary narratives of this legendary dwelling were completely represented on the PEM's official website, yinyutang.pem.org.[2]

On the campus of Shanghai Institute of Visual Arts (SIVA), three ancient Huizhou dwellings with a total area of 2,450 square meters have become another case of adaptive reuse. Unlike the Yin Yu Tang Museum in the United States, which preserves the original narrative as much as possible, the reconstruction of Huizhou dwellings at SIVA focuses on dynamic reuse rather than static spatial display, providing a large number of secondary narratives. The three ancient dwellings were all built in the late Qing Dynasty, with a history of nearly 200 years. Two of them were purchased by a private collector in 2005 and transferred to SIVA in 2012. After their reconstruction in Shanghai from 2013 to 2014, the former Lin Family House was transformed into the Double-snug Tea House, the characteristic gathering space of SIVA's teaching staff, and the Ancient House of the Xu Family an inclusive multi-functional academic research center. The Zhuangyuan House, which was newly purchased from Leping county, Jiangxi, in 2014 has been transformed into a teaching building of the School of Cultural Relics Restoration of SIVA. During the three-year process, a team of SIVA leaders and professional architects reconstructed the surrounding environment, spatial form and interior furnishings of the building. A comprehensive design of architecture, landscape and interior has successfully transformed the ancient folk houses from private residence to public space, completely reshaping the spirit of the place. The user acquires a brand-new spatial cognitive experience based on newly inserted functions. "It is the value orientation and goal of architectural narrative to investigate

The Huizhou-style community relocated to the Shanghai Institute of Visual Arts

A Huizhou house with a new use as SIVA's Double–snug Tea House

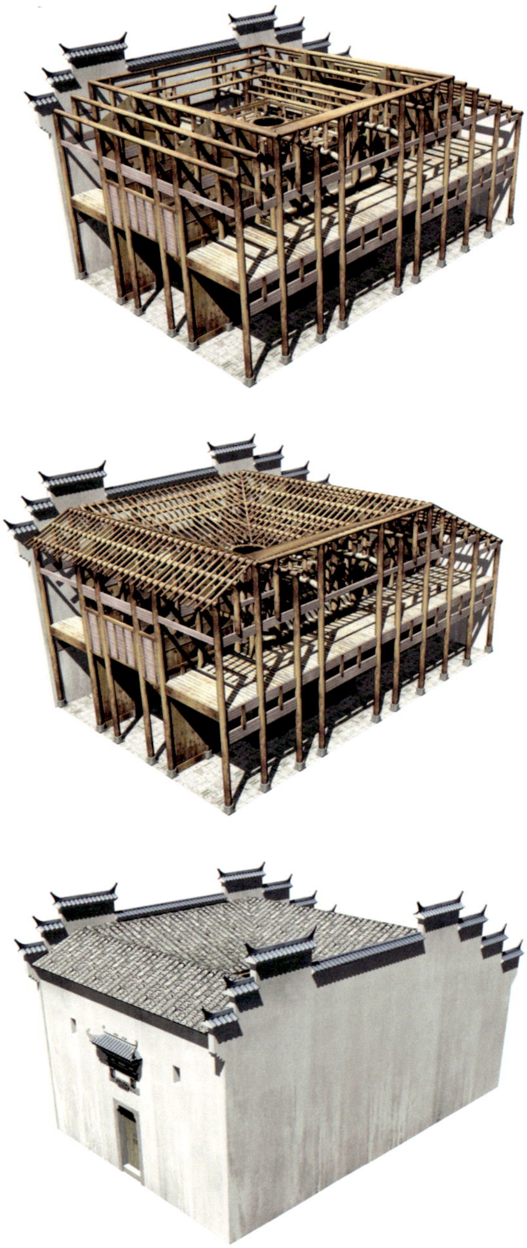

and evaluate the social and cultural significance of spatial construction by considering the built environment and the life it carries as a whole."[3]

The move of the Lin and Xu Family dwellings from Anhui to Shanghai required both the careful preservation of the existing structure and the restoration of missing components. An architectural model of the original was created for their reconstruction on the SIVA campus. The houses were first carefully dismantled from the original place, and the core timber frames numbered and packed one by one. During this process, the timber frame was rebuilt on a newly made reinforced concrete foundation. To guarantee structural safety, the load of all new roofs was taken up by the brick-concrete exterior wall, independent of the original wood-frame system, which greatly reduced the pressure on the aged wooden frame. In addition, the old and new structures were horizontally connected by pre-embedded steel bars. On the interior, new brick floor tiles made in the ancient method replaced the old tiles broken during the dismantlement. Missing wooden components were replaced according to the original building, using a restoration technology for traditional residences.

When the Huizhou ancient dwellings were rebuilt at SIVA, the houses, according to the original characteristics, maintained the north entrance in layout, the iconic Ma Tau Wall and the black-white tone in appearance. Due to changes mandated by both the new site and the new functions, however, the houses differed from the originals in both the exterior and interior. New narrative elements have been implanted. For example, the lotus pond and the curved bridge in the courtyard, together with transplanted trees, were added to the site, constituting a garden landscape that echoed the local Jiangnan culture in Shanghai. In order to enrich the architectural form and the outdoor space experience, the original simple south facades of the Lin and Xu Family dwellings were amended with wooden wind and rain corridors, as well as larger, richly detailed doors and windows. Skylights were introduced to bring more natural light to the second floor. A glass roof was added to the atrium space to provide a sheltered outdoor patio. The original low beams were increased by 300mm to improve the usability of the academic center on the second floor. The old, narrow and steep stairs were widened. Fire protection requirements such as smoke alarms, sprinkler systems, VRV central air conditioners were introduced in inconspicuous locations.

Alumni of the School of Design at SIVA run the Double-snug Tea House. The refreshing tea as well as the gentle background music of the Chinese zither enrich the details of the secondary narrative and spatial cognition of Chinese traditional culture through taste, smell and hearing. These preserved classical spaces with their Chinese traditional cultural temperament offer the faculty and students stories that have traveled through hundreds of years of history. There is a coexistence of past and present lives in what has become the spiritual home of SIVA.

A similar case of adaptive reuse can be found at Singapore University of Technology and Design (SUTD) where four Zhejiang ancient architectural structures were donated in 2015 by Jackie Chan, the famous Chinese kung fu superstar. They have been carefully reconstructed by the university and serve as an immersive space for displaying ancient Chinese architectural culture as well as a host for various performances.

The computer-aided structural analysis of the original Lin ancient dwelling

The sitting room of Xu ancient dwelling, before and after relocation

The two dwellings by a lake, a stage and a pavilion on the lawn are extremely popular on campus and have become the landmarks of SUTD.

Localization via Dynamic Behavioral Expression

In these adaptive reuse cases, the essential architectural narrative symbols, such as wood structures and carved artifacts, can be preserved and passed down through the process of the migration. But these scattered Huizhou houses, far away from their hometown, are like the stray wild geese, having lost the beauty of the village community through their separation from original environments and historical contexts. The original nostalgic cultural memory carried by them will inevitably be lost and partially alienated during the reconstruction process. Sophia Psarra addresses this lack of relationship between spatial structure and social order due to the dissolution of the cultural vein of the place in "[h]ow space and cultural significance are constructed in architecture and communicated to observers."[4] From the perspective of the immovability of architectural relics, the migration of heritage buildings is regrettable. As the rescue of non-protected old houses through relocation and reuse, the unique value lies in the localization of architectural culture in which an original living narrative of the building is integrated with a secondary narrative. Such a story is continued by various designers and users. Its dual narrative semantics reconstruct the new spatial experience of ancient dwellings and reflect human life in both modern and contemporary China. From the perspective of spatial behavior organization, space is not a container of invariable behavior, but a place of dynamic behavioral expression.[5]

Fortunately, the cases of these ancient dwellings at PEM, SIVA and SUTD have all been favorably received and the precious architectural heritage is further appreciated. Innovative migration and reconstruction have endowed traditional dwellings with a new life force, widely spreading the architectural culture originally confined to a certain area. But the three cases are very different. The core value of Yin Yu Tang is the static reappearance of original Chinese countryside home life in the form of a special museum exhibition. This translocation project received strong support from the department of cultural relics protection of Xiuning Count before the migration, with a signed cultural exchange agreement. The Chinese local government hoped to improve the international visibility of the Huizhou architectural culture with the help of American cultural institutions. It turned out to be a big success, with endless streams of visitors and researchers who have gained an immersive experience of the Huizhou culture of China in Yin Yu Tang and a deeper understanding of life in a Chinese village of that time. With Yin Yu Tang as the base, the PEM often conducts a series of Chinese cultural exhibitions.

In the cases of SIVA and SUTD, the relocations fused functional aspects of the traditional dwellings with modern campus life. At SIVA, the Huizhou residential community, which was completed and opened in 2015, has not only become a living sample for teachers and students of Chinese wooden dwellings, but also a window for international visitors to understand Chinese traditional culture. Mrs. Shen Chen, from SIVA's School of New Media, has created a full-digital VR display design for the tea house. The user can realize remote immersive roaming with the help of the VR helmet, thus expanding the performance dimension of spatial cognition of the place. At SUTD, the four ancient structures have infused the modern campus with traditional Chinese customs. At the time of the transaction, there was some resistance to Jackie Chan gifting the houses to Singapore. The controversy dramatically increased the consensus of the importance of in-situ conservation of Chinese ancient buildings. With time, the SUTD case has been gradually accepted as that of a cultural ambassador rather than that of a loss of Chinese heritage. As Jackie Chan stated, "This is helpful to the world of cultural exchanges, it is hard to say only taking things back is patriotic. I have been committed to the promotion of Chinese culture overseas."[6] In both SIVA and SUTD, the vivid life of college staff and students continues the second narration of these ancient dwellings. In order to meet the requirement of teaching and research, both institutions have chosen innovative intervention and adaptive reuse instead of restoration.

An antique Chinese pavilion on the campus of the Singapore University of Technology and Design

As a cultural phenomenon, the allopatric reconstruction of Huizhou ancient dwellings is driven by a number of reasons. While in-situ conservation is recommended for the protection of nostalgic culture, attention should be given to the new cultural value generated by ancient dwellings that have been relocated with the implantation of a secondary narrative. This value is reflected not only in the new spatial experience of the ancient dwellings, reconstructed by double narrative semantics, but also in the external communication of the local architectural culture in the context of globalization. In the life cycle of ancient dwellings, allopatric adaptive reuse has enriched the narrative connotations of the architecture across and in between different dimensions.

NOTES

1 John Dewey, *Art as Experience*, Capricorn Books, NY, 1958.

2 https://yinyutang.pem.org/.

3 Shaoming Lu, "The origin of architectural narratology," *Journal of Tongji University* (social science edition), no.5(2012): 25–31.

4 Sophia Psarra, *Architecture and Narrative: The Formation of Space and Cultural Narrative*, Routledge, 2009.

5 Ropo A, Höykinpuro R, "Narrating Organizational Spaces," *Journal of Organizational Change Management*, no.30 (2017): 357–366.

6 Jackie Chan, Interview by Yansong Bai, *News 1+1*, Talk show of CCTV, Beijing, May 10, 2013.

The dismantled houses in storage at a Shanghai warehouse

ECOLOGY

The recognition in the late 20th century of the effects of climate change and architecture's culpability in global greenhouse gas emissions has cast a new light on the age-old practice of adaptive reuse. Quantitative evidence indicates that despite two decades of efforts towards sustainable design, a net zero carbon future lies in the reuse of structures. The simultaneity of adaptive reuse in conserving the past while repurposing for the present is a unique characteristic contributing to the social foundations for sustainable ecosystems. Spatial and temporal, adaptive reuse sustains the evolving relationship of humans to their built environment.

130 **Back to the Future: The Spatial Dimension of Water Management [Volume 08]**
Kees Lokman

140 **Between Resiliency and Adaptation [Volume 08]**
Catherine Joseph

148 **(re)Made by Water: Obsolescence, Urban Nomadism and the New World Mall, Bangkok [Volume 08]**
Gregory Marinic

156 **Taking on the Shape of Things | Roberto Collovà: The Spirit of Resilience [Volume 05]**
Liliane Wong

BACK TO THE FUTURE

THE SPATIAL DIMENSION OF WATER MANAGEMENT

by KEES LOKMAN

From the inception of our species, coping with the availability — or unavailability — of water resources has been an essential element of human beings' strategies for survival and well-being. Throughout history human ingenuity was manifest in the means by which water was procured, transported and allocated to various uses. The quality, distribution, seasonality and amount of water have been key determinants of subsistence, health and settlement potentials.
(Hassan 2011: 14)

Water management is essential to human development. Throughout history, reciprocal relationships between water management, human settlement, food production, climatic conditions, and social organization—on both local and regional levels—have produced a range of physical landscapes with a myriad of social-ecological and spatial dynamics. More recently, technological advancements coupled with accelerated processes of urbanization and agricultural production have created new demands for water, as well as new approaches to wastewater management and flood control. As such, today, we are confronted with multiple dimensions of water management—operating across various spatial and temporal scales.

In this context, the 20th century was primarily characterized by a command-and-control attitude towards water management. Often sponsored by state governments through large-scale infrastructure developments (i.e, irrigation works, hydroelectric dams, and so on), these projects have favored the notion of

The Big U is one of the winning projects of Rebuild by Design. It combines a continuous 10-mile, long flood protection infrastructure along Lower Manhattan with new open spaces and public programs to benefit surrounding communities

hydraulics (engineering) over hydrology (ecological processes). Not surprisingly, the cumulative effects of these interventions have triggered drastic changes to (river and coastal) ecologies, built environments, people's livelihoods and geopolitical relationships (Lokman 2016a). With the realities of climate change, ongoing urbanization and environmental degradation, there is an urgent need to develop adaptive planning approaches, policies and spatial strategies to manage water.

In recent decades, several of such new water management concepts have been proposed, including: *integrated water resources management, adaptive management,* and, more recently, the *water–energy–food nexus* (Giupponi and Gain 2016). And while these frameworks certainly help to elevate the debates on water management, they primarily focus on the use of planning tools and policy mechanisms to enact change. The role of design and the inherent spatial dimensions of water, however, remain largely overlooked. Roggema (2009: 59), in discussing climate change and its consequences for water management and energy developments, states: "The adaptation to climate change is well represented in strategies, policies and the media...but integrated designs for adapted spatial plans are hardly available. This is curious, because adaptation to climate change needs to be implemented and realized mainly through spatial patterns and layout." In other words, there should be more emphasis on the translation of policies into spatial design strategies in order to shift people's ways of thinking, and to make visible how the world can look by offering new ideas and formulating physical solutions to complex issues.

Along these lines, Priscoli (1998: 623) argues: "The spatial and functional characteristics of the river basins influenced human settlement and interaction long before the idea of the river basin started to be formalized into legal and administrative terms." Priscoli emphasizes water management has an inherent socio-spatial character which has evolved over time and space. We can learn from history in order to study how spatial, technical, and managerial solutions in the past can inform approaches to contemporary challenges such as sanitation, flood control and irrigation farming. As such, this article will focus on the interdependencies of people, water and space by discussing how we can manage water by actively co-designing with natural processes. How has water management historically informed the spatial configuration of landscapes? In which ways are these approaches incorporated in contemporary water management? Ultimately, how can we combine hard and soft-engineered water management practices to cultivate productive and dynamic social-ecological relationships?

The article begins by exploring three historical examples of water management, including: (1) the *chinampas* in Mexico City (a type of Mesoamerican agriculture which uses small, rectangular plots to grow crops); (2) Major John Wesley Powell's *drainage districts* (a proposal for an alternative hydro-political organization and water democracy for the American West); (3) the Dutch p*older model* (a mixed model of top-down and bottom-up approaches to develop and maintain flood control infrastructure). Each example illustrates an approach to water management that fundamentally responds to local conditions, while embracing dynamic relationships between human agency and natural processes. Finally, the article discusses how these site-specific and culturally informed approaches are influencing contemporary water management projects.

Chinampas: A Co-Evolution of Social and Ecological Processes

One of the most sophisticated ways of manipulating landscapes to manage water and grow food was developed in Mesoamerica, in an area now known as Mexico City. Founded by the Aztecs in 1325, Mexico City (then known as *Tenochtitlán*) is situated in the Basin of Mexico, a highland plateau with no natural drainage outlet. Until the late 19th century the Basin contained a network of shallow lakes, which fluctuated between 0.8 and 3.0m during dry and wet seasons (Sanders 1979). In order to control flooding and to provide access to fresh water and food, the Aztecs developed an ambitious system of dikes, aqueducts, and *chinampas*: rectangular farming plots filled with fertile dredged sediments. This half-natural, half-artificial landscape was based on a dynamic stability between ecological processes, agricultural productivity, economic vitality and specific forms of social organization (Torres-Lima et al. 1994; Nichols et al. 2006, Lokman 2016b).

Chinampas provided the backbone of the Aztec Empire. When the Spanish invaded the region in the 16th century, *chinampas* covered an area over 1000 sq. km (Hassan 2011)—nearly a third of Rhode Island. Originally ranging from 6.0 to 9.0m wide and lengths of up to 100m, *chinampas* were constructed by alternating layers of dredged sediments and "thick mats of decaying vegetation" (Torres-Lima 1994: 38). A wattle fence and a planted row of native willows (*Salix Bomplandiana L.*) helped to retain soil and stabilize the edges. Once matured, the trees helped to block wind and trap warm air, permitting year-round cultivation and providing additional crop protection. The continuous application of animal manure, mud, and water from the drainage and transportation canals enhanced soil fertility and soil humidity, improving the overall growing conditions (Parsons 1991). This recycling of nutrients and waste not only reduced environmental impacts, but increased biological interdependence between crops and pests, and improved crop productivity, creating a highly complex and sustainable agro-ecosystem (Torres-Lima et al. 1994).

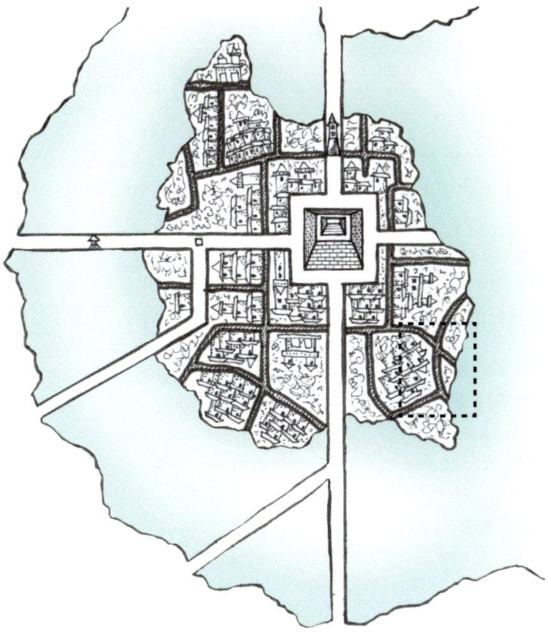

Tenochtitlan & Logo de Texcoco
1500 CE

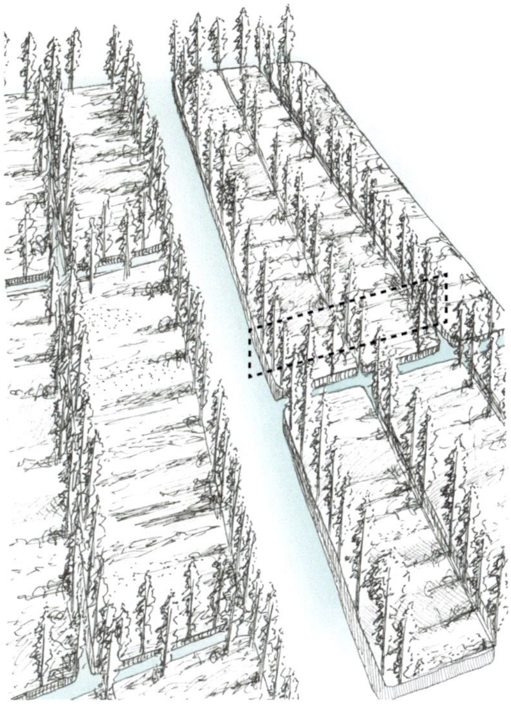

Chinampa Aerial

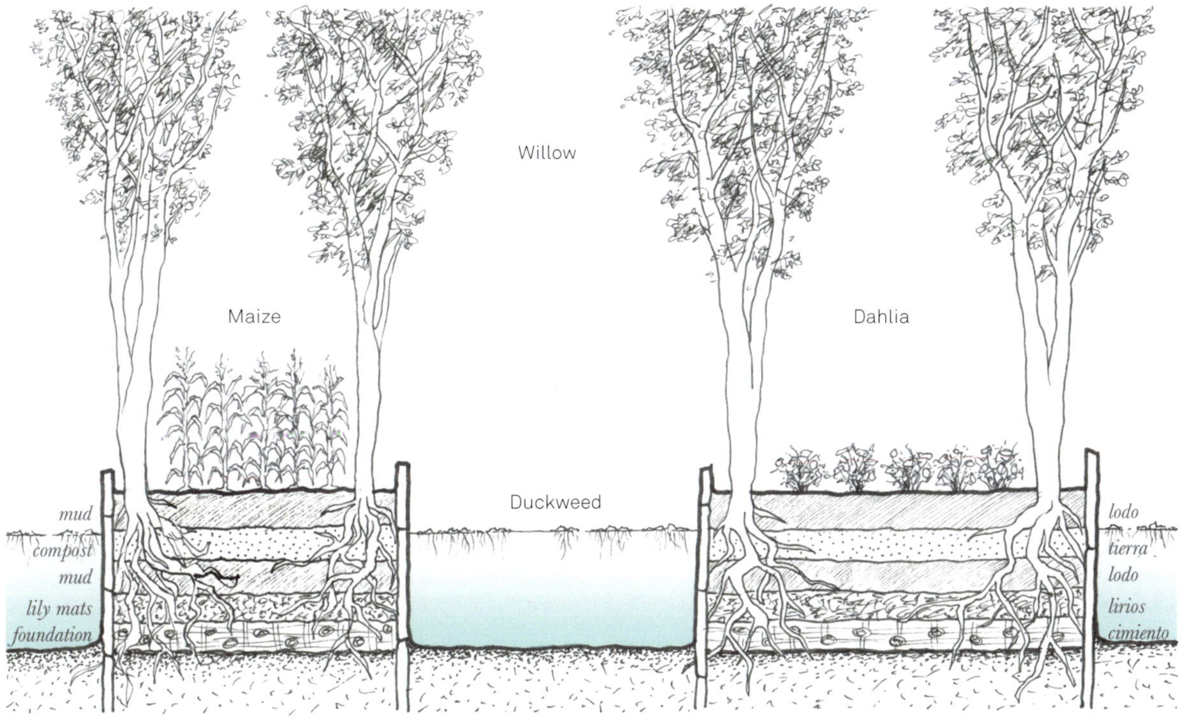

Chinampa Section

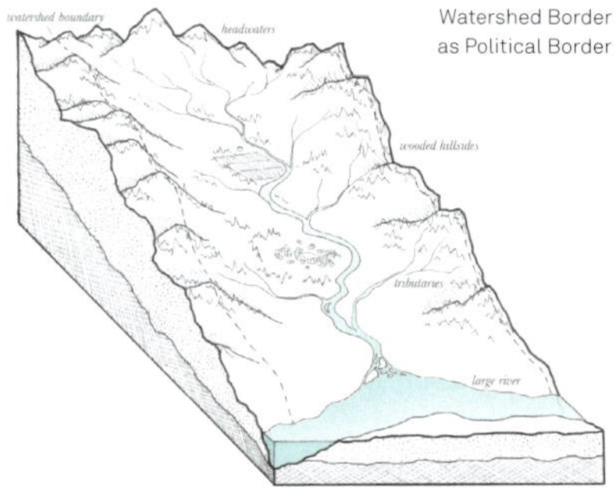

Inherently shaped by the co-evolution of social and ecological processes, the distinct spatial configuration and sectional qualities of *chinampas*, in combination with centuries-long human stewardship, cultivated a heterogeneous landscape with numerous ecosystem services, including food provisioning, aquifer recharge, flood control, carbon storage, climate regulation, as well as providing critical habitat for numerous endemic and migratory species (Merlin-Uribe et al. 2013). Due to their spatial and functional complexity, *chinampas* were able to adjust to many different environmental and socio-economic pressures over time (Torres-Lima et al. 1994). In contrast to contemporary farming practices, which are mechanized and require large inputs of water and fertilizers, *chinampas* represent a low-tech and scalable form of agriculture based on closed-loop systems attuned to local ecological conditions. Moreover, they provided a diverse set of uses—from agriculture to housing, livestock keeping and recreation. And while only a few pockets of this pre-colonial agro-ecosystem remain today, the *chinampas* remain an inspiration in terms of developing sustainable methods of water management centered on the co-evolution of human systems and ecological processes.

Watershed Democracy: A Communal Way of Water Management

The next example focuses on John Wesley Powell's proposal for establishing *hydrographic basins*—political units defined by climate, topography and the natural flow of water. This idea not only promoted a communal way of managing water on a regional scale but also introduced a radically different way of organizing the territory of the American West—both spatially and politically.

Powell (1834–1901) was a geologist, explorer and conservationist. Through his many expeditions of the West, which is characterized by limited rainfall, high temperatures and poor soils, he understood that the political and jurisdictional systems governing water rights and natural resources in this part of the continent could not follow the conventional logic at the time. In 1878, he published the "Report on the Arid Lands of the United States," which recommended that none of the water should be privatized; it belonged to everyone within a specific "hydrographic basin," or what we now call a *watershed*. According to Powell, water rights should be tied to the land, and not be sold except along with deeds to the land.

Counter to the 19th century frontier mentality, Powell opposed common practices that allocated parcel, county and state boundaries based on Euclidean geometry. Instead, he suggested dividing the land based on topographic features, thereby establishing "irrigation districts"; small tracts of irrigable lands in the lower lying areas, and "pasture districts"; larger livestock ranches for grazing nearby springs and small streams (Powell 1878). From the forests on the upper slopes, the grazing lands at mid elevations, and the arable bottomlands, residents were to work together across the basin to establish regulations for the use of water for irrigation and subdividing the land. Privileges to mineral rights (and the use of water and timber for mining) would be managed by the United States in order to prevent powerful individuals to obtain single control over these resources. Beyond this, government had no role: communities should be left to control their own water resources and production.

Moreover, as second director of the US Geologic Survey (1881–1894), Powell also developed important new knowledge and spatial information. His team created an extensive inventory of maps in order to visualize America's geography—its watersheds and the inherent relationships between climate, physiography, soils and hydrology (Worster 2009). Using these scientific assessments, along with detailed studies of indigenous and Mormon irrigation systems (Lewis and Torbenson 1990), Powell estimated that only a fraction of the West could ever be effectively irrigated. He predicted that misalignment of socio-political boundaries and hydrographic regions would result in geopolitical conflict and unsustainable water management. Powell said: "I tell you, gentlemen, you are piling up a heritage of conflict and litigation over water rights, for there is not sufficient water to supply these lands."

Illustrations of political border following the regional watershed boundaries

In an era that encouraged expansionism and individualism, Powell advocated for cooperative stewardship, conservation and environmental planning. The *watershed* would serve as the foundation for a resilient sociopolitical and place-based organization of the West by instilling uniquely democratic principles and Jeffersonian ideals. Unfortunately, Powell's recommendations were never adopted, and today his words could not be more true. California, after witnessing the worst drought in its history, is currently facing extreme rainfall and flooding. The recent failure of Oroville Dam highlights the challenges of America's aging flood control infrastructure. At the same time, the West is facing increased tension and disputes among municipalities, governments, farmers, environmental groups, industries and Native Americans over water allocation and management. With the implications of climate change, ongoing urbanization and environmental decline, now more than ever, it is important to revisit Powell's ideas and envision new socio-spatial frameworks for managing water.

The Dutch Polder Model: Designing with Water

The final precedent concerns the Netherlands, where a long-standing relationship with water has informed innovative adaptation strategies and a distinct socio-political attitude characterized by consultation, compromise and consensus, also known as the Dutch '*polder model*' (de Vries 2014).

With nearly a third of the country situated below sea level, integrated solutions to water management have always been important to the Netherlands (Lokman 2016c). Dating back as far as the 9th century, the Dutch began building dams, dikes and other flood control measures to protect settlements, agricultural areas, and reclaimed areas of land. While initially a primarily local matter, with the growth of cities and their hinterlands it became increasingly important to coordinate flood control among various stakeholders (de Mul and van den Berg 2011). This meant people and social classes living in the same '*polder*' (a reclaimed area of land protected by dikes) had to work together to fund, build and manage appropriate flood control infrastructures (van Tielhof 2015). Over time, they established 'water boards' (regional water authorities) to coordinate flood protection, preserve water quality, and manage the general water economy of their respective regions. These water boards are one of the first forms of public administration, and the oldest form of democratic government in the Netherlands (Dutch Water Authorities 2015).

Since water-related tasks are of existential importance to the Netherlands, the organizational structure of water boards is decoupled from the political structure—they have their own administration, governing body and financial structure. As such, the budget for water management is not balanced against that of health care, education, defense spending, and so on (Dutch Water Authorities 2015). Water boards also maintain an *interest-say-pay* principle: the higher the interest of a stakeholder, the more tax is raised. In return, these stakeholders will have more influence on decision-making. As such, taxes differ substantially across the country.

In line with the emergence of a new ecological paradigm, including notions of complexity and resilience, the Dutch have recently changed their water management approach from focusing primarily on protection *against* flooding to working together with water. After major floods in 1993 and 1995, the government initiated the Room for the River program (2006–2015). The project focuses on increased flood storage and enhancement of the spatial quality. It consists of 39 distinct but interconnected local projects, which deploy numerous

Ruimte voor de Waal
Rendering of the new bypass channel at Nijmegen and Lent

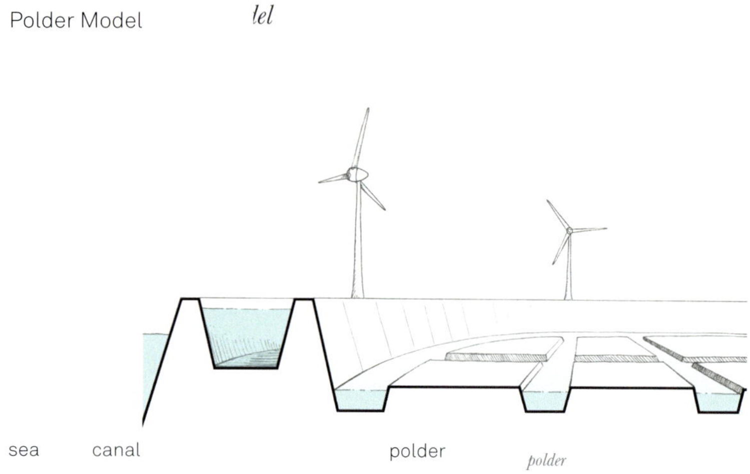

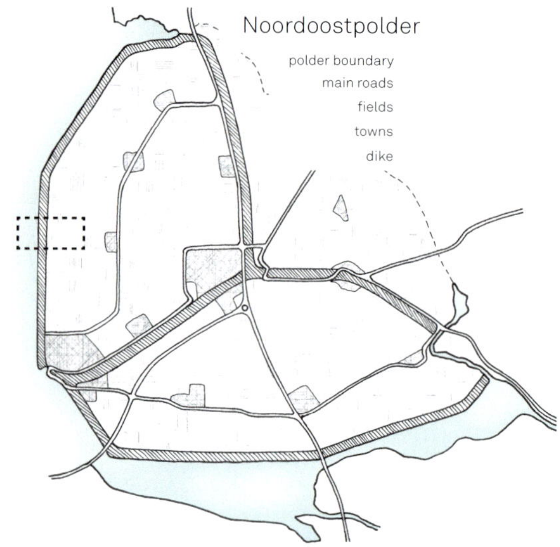

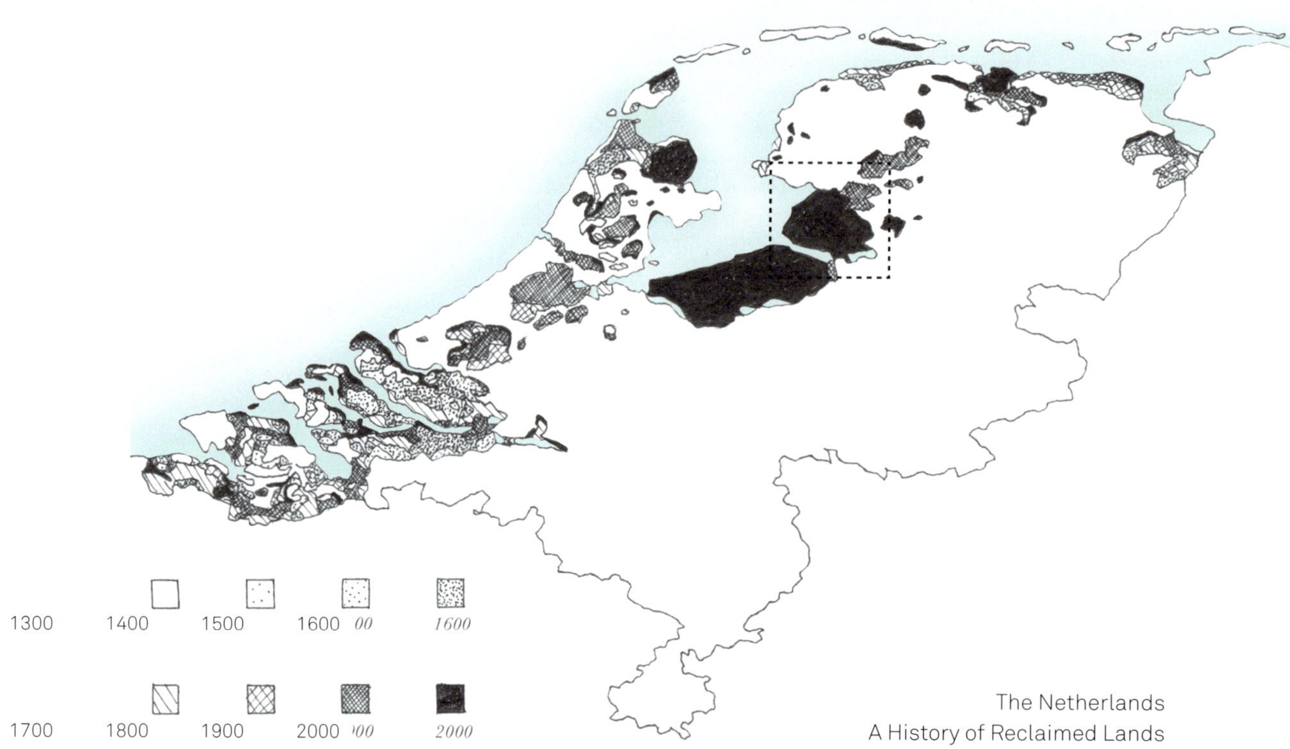

Illustrations of the contemporary Dutch Polder landscape

adaptation strategies and approaches, including depoldering (allowing water back into a polder), flood bypasses, dike setbacks and relocation of buildings to higher grounds. In addition to establishing extensive public participation platforms, the government also worked with various water institutes to develop a digital hydrologic model to calculate, coordinate and assess the overall effectiveness of all 39 projects.

Among the more visible projects is Ruimte voor de Waal, where a new bypass channel not only increased flood storage and provided habitat for fish and wildlife, it also created a new island with unique opportunities for recreation and urban development. Climate change and flooding are no longer seen as a risk but rather as a possibility to unlock new social, ecological and economic opportunities. As suggested by Veerman (2008: 7), "Changing the way our country is managed creates new options; working with water may improve the quality of the environment and offers excellent opportunities for innovative ideas and applications. Where there is water, new forms of nature can arise. Water can be used to produce food and generate energy. Flood defenses can be used for roads."

Moreover, these complex and multi-scalar spatial planning projects call for planning approaches that combine top-down policies with bottom-up participation. According to Jeroen Rijke et al., it is exactly "through application of a mixed centralized–decentralized governance approach [Room for the River] has tackled governance pitfalls related to centralized planning approaches that previously impeded integrated water management" (Rijke et al. 2012: 379). Thus, while climate change is a serious challenge it is also provides preconditions for testing new planning frameworks, and for the design of dynamic, multifunctional landscapes.

Back to the Future

The examples discussed above illustrate sustainable water management that involve adopting practices capable of dealing with dynamic and ever-changing social-ecological conditions. They are based on notions of *co-designing* and *co-evolving* social and biophysical systems. As pointed out by Priscoli (1998: 623): "Increased interdependence through water sharing plans and infrastructure networks can be seen as increases of our flexibility and capacity to respond to exigencies of nature and reduce our vulnerability to events such as droughts and floods and thereby increase security." This also means, rather than holding on to a single approach to water management, we should develop a multiplicity of strategies and frameworks to solve issues of water scarcity, flood control, water governance and water ethics (Schmidt and Shrubsole 2013). This requires collaborative efforts and concerted action by all stakeholders in order to integrate knowledge and coordinate cross-boundary planning approaches.

Looking to the future, there are some reasons to be optimistic. The practice of landscape architects SCAPE, for instance, provides a good example of how mutualistic interactions between people, animals and plants (such were inherent to the *chinampas*) can be designed to create productive and resilient urban environments. In particular, SCAPE's Oyster-tecture project, which was commissioned by the Museum of Modern Art in 2009 for the *Rising Currents* exhibition, shows how humans, natural processes and marine animals can work together to create an ecological infrastructure that provides flood protection, habitat restoration, food, and recreation.

Located in Brooklyn, New York, the proposal harnesses the various qualities of oysters and other shellfish to construct new cultural and environmental relationships. Using a low-tech FLUPSY system (floating upwelling system), the oysters are nurtured in postindustrial Gowanus Bay, where they help filter and clean the water. Once matured, they are transferred to the intertidal zone of the Bay Ridge Flats. Here, the artificially seeded shellfish species are attached to an armature of fuzzy rope and old wharf piles to create a reef for aquatic species, birds and people. Over time, as sediment, plants and shellfish inhabit this constructed landscape, the reef becomes a living breakwater that simultaneously acts as a unique ecosystem and wave-attenuating armature to protect against storm surges and rising sea levels. The design-research for Oyster-tecture has informed multiple ongoing projects, including the proposal Living Breakwaters, which envisions a series of ecological infrastructures along the shores of Staten Island. The project recently received $60M from the U.S. Department of Housing and Urban Development (HUD) and is currently being implemented by the NY Governor's Office of Storm Recovery.

With respect to communal water management, the *acequias* in New Mexico present an alternative to current water-intensive and highly mechanized forms of agriculture in arid regions. While not a new invention (*acequias* have been around for centuries), both the social and spatial practices of the *acequia* culture can inspire novel ways of water management. Originally introduced by the Moors (North Africa) and further developed in Spain and former Spanish colonies, the term '*acequias*' refers not only to the physical irrigation channels but also to the social and organizational structure of a water-sharing network (Santistevan 2016). Construction and maintenance of the *acequia* system (canals, ditches, reservoirs) is done collectively (Lewis and Torbenson 1990). Engineered to use gravity and natural contours of the land, *acequias* divert snow runoff from a main river into an artificial network of channels to irrigate farming plots. The mother ditch (*acequia madre*) distributes water to lateral ditches (*linderos*) and secondary laterals (sangrias) to irrigate

specific fields. These ditches also help to restore aquifers and enhance habitats along riparian areas.

Acequia members (*parciantes*) elect a 'ditch boss' (*mayordomo*) who is in charge of managing the water and settling disputes. Together with the *acequia* community, the *mayordomo* is responsible for making sure all members meet their water needs for agricultural production throughout the season. As a non-capitalist form of farming and social relations, the *acequias* "call attention to alternatives in how societies can reproduce themselves materially, from households to the broader economy" (Gunn 2016: 91). The emphasis is on cooperation and sharing in order for each *acequia* member to leverage a certain level of material independence. Instead of seeking to generate profit, the motivation is to maintain a regenerative way of life between people and the land. The fact that water is still flowing through the *acequias* speaks to their socio-economic and spatial resiliency. With economic uncertainties and the implications of climate change (variation in available water supplies and crop yields), *acequias* provide an adaptive, resilient and democratic model to support small-scale agricultural practices in semi-arid and arid regions.

The area of water management which is perhaps most rapidly evolving concerns regional flood risk mapping as well as the development of new spatial planning and design strategies for sea level rise adaptation. After Hurricane Sandy hit the New York Region in 2012, HUD launched the Rebuild by Design initiative to facilitate collaborations between transdisciplinary design teams and local communities in order to develop strategies that promote socio-economic opportunities within a framework of ecological resilience. With a focus on using a research-based and design-driven approach to problem solving, Rebuild by Design provided funding for 10 teams to develop innovative approaches for those areas in the region most vulnerable to flooding. These teams then worked, several months with experts, community and local government stakeholders to develop strategies that were both realistic and replicable. In 2014, HUD announced six winners—SCAPE's Living Breakwater being one of the winning proposals—which have received additional funding to further develop and implement their projects.

Rebuild by Design has been a big success, both in terms of raising public awareness and in developing cutting-edge spatial strategies to combat climate change. At the same time, it has inspired similar initiatives across the United States, including Changing Course (2013), which challenged interdisciplinary design teams to develop strategies for the future of the Lower Mississippi River Delta, and ongoing projects in Miami and the San Francisco Bay Area. In each of these initiatives, adaptation to climate change is approached first and foremost as a *spatial* opportunity: by focusing on hybrid approaches that combine hard and soft engineering strategies, we can design landscapes that are dynamic and productive while cultivating new nature-culture relationships (Rojas et al 2015: 188).

The 1799 dike breach at Bemmel in the Netherlands by Christian Josi

Alongside developing new approaches to water management, there is a need to preserve cultural landscapes of traditional water management. As illustrated in this article, these landscapes have evolved over extended periods of time. They are key sources of knowledge concerning appropriate governance structures, social relations, spatial strategies and economic incentives essential to developing long-term sustainable water management. As pointed out by Kate Orff (2017): "Looking back reminds us that dramatic change in place, environment, and ecosystem is part of understanding current urban ecology, and critical in projecting forward newly modified cohabitats and communities." In the same way a site's history can inform future landscape proposals, historical water management approaches and techniques can guide us in developing new mechanisms moving forward. To do so we must develop solutions that neither over-romanticize the past nor simply revert to a 'technological fix' (Priscoli 1998). Instead, we should embrace the myriad of interactions among the human, non-human, and abiotic components of (urban) landscapes to develop a diversity of spatial models of water management.

REFERENCES

J. De Vries, "The Netherlands and the polder model: Questioning the polder model concept." *BMGN-the Low Countries Historical Review*, 129, no. 1, (2014), pp. 99–111.

Dutch Water Authorities. 2015. *Water Governance: The Dutch Water Authority Model*. URL: http://www.dutchwaterauthorities.com/wp-content/uploads/2015/05/Water-Governance-The-Dutch-Water-Authority-Model1.pdf (accessed August 30, 2016).

A. Graber and R. Junge, "Aquaponic Systems: Nutrient Recycling from Fish Wastewater by Vegetable Production." *Desalination*, 246, (2009), pp. 147–156.

Carlo Giupponi and Animesh K. Gain, "Integrated Spatial Assessment of the Water, Energy and Food Dimensions of the Sustainable Development Goals." *Regional Environmental Change* (2016).

C. Gunn, "Acequias as Commons: Lessons for a Post-Capitalist World." *Review of Radical Political Economics*, 48: 1, (2016), pp. 81–89.

F. Hassan, *Water History for Our Times: IHP Essays On Water History* (United Nations Educational, Scientific and Cultural Organization, Paris: France), 2011.

M. E. Lewis and Craig L. Torbenson, "Cultural Antecedents of J. W. Powell's Arid Lands Report." *Journal of Geography*, 89, 2, (1990), pp. 74–80.

K. Lokman, "Dam[ned] landscapes: Envisioning fluid geographies." *Journal of Architectural Education* 70, 1, (2016), pp. 6–12.

K. Lokman, "Exploring a New Paradigm: Water Management in Mexico City." *Topos: European Landscape Magazine*, 96, (2016), pp. 44–50.

K. Lokman, "Progressive Pragmatism: The Next Generation of Dutch Landscape Design Practices." *Proceedings of the Cracow Landscape Conference*, 2016, pp. 19–28. ISSN 2451-1692 http://www.clc.edu.pl/wp-content/uploads/2016/09/VOL_1_CLC2016.pdf.

Yair Merlín-Uribe, et al. "Environmental and Socio-Economic Sustainability of Chinampas (Raised Beds) in Xochimilco, Mexico City." *International Journal of Agricultural Sustainability*, 11, 3, (2013), p. 216.

F. D. L. Nichols, et al. "Water management and political economy in formative period central Mexico." *Precolumbian Water Management: Ideology, Ritual, and Power* (2006), pp. 51–66.

K. Orff, "Ideas." http://www.scapestudio.com/ideas/ (accessed February 8, 2017).

J. R. Parsons, "Political implications of prehispanic chinampas agriculture in the Valley of Mexico." *Land and politics in the Valley of Mexico. A two thousand year perspective.* (1991).

J. W. Powell, Report on the lands of the arid region of the United States: With a more detailed account of the lands of Utah with maps (Government Printing Office: Washington, DC, 1878).

C. Rojas, B. De Meulder, and K. Shannon, "Water Urbanism in Bogota. Exploring the Potentials of an Interplay between Settlement Patterns and Water Management." *Habitat International*, 48, (2015), pp. 177–187.

N. Raheem, "A Common-Pool Resource Experiment in Acequia Communities." *International Journal of the Commons*, 9, 1, (2015), pp. 306–321.

R. Roggema, *Adaptation to Climate Change: A Spatial Challenge*, Springer Science + Business Media, 2009: 59–111.

C. Salewski, *Dutch new worlds: Scenarios in physical planning and design in the Netherlands, 1970–2000* (Rotterdam: 010 Publishers, 2012).

W. T. Sanders, Robert S. Santley, and Jeffrey R. Parsons, *The Basin of Mexico: The Ecological Processes in the Evolution of a Civilization* (Academic Press: New York, 1979).

M. Santistevan, "Acequia Culture and the Regional Food System." https://coyotegulch.blog/2016/10/16/acequia-culture-and-the-regional-food-system-miguel-santistevan/ (accessed November 15, 2016).

J.J. Schmidt and D. Shrubsole, "Modern Water Ethics: Implications for Shared Governance." *Environmental Values*, 22, 3, (2013), pp. 359–379.

P. B. Torres Lima, Canabal-Cristiani, and G. Burela-Rueda "Urban Sustainable Agriculture: The Paradox of the Chinampa System in Mexico City." *Agriculture and Human Values*, 11, 1, (1994), pp. 37–46.

M. Van Tielhof, "Forced Solidarity: Maintenance of Coastal Defences Along the North Sea Coast in the Early Modern Period." *Environment and History*, 21, 3, (2015), pp. 319–350.

C.P. Veerman, "Foreword." In *Working together with water: A living land builds for its future.* Delta Committee: Hollandia Printing, 2008.

D. Worster, "A River Running West: Reflections on John Wesley Powell." *Journal of Cultural Geography*, 26, 2, (2009), pp. 113–126.

C. Zevenbergen, et al. "Taming Global Flood Disasters. Lessons Learned from Dutch Experience." *Natural Hazards*, 65, 3, (2013), pp. 1217–1225.

BETWEEN RESILIENCY AND ADAPTATION

by CATHERINE JOSEPH

Each time there is a coastal storm event, architecture's position becomes that of a militaristic, tactical defense system. The storm is the opposing military; the high winds are the artillery fire; the storm surge is the cavalry; and the flooding is the infantry, swarming the ranks of architecture for one final defeat. Humans have been trained to see buildings as safe spaces: safe from climatic variations, both daily and seasonal; safe from most of the forces that nature repetitively exerts; safe from perceived dangers that roam our immediate referential universe. It is easy to envision architecture's position as victim of a militaristic climatic attack. What is more difficult to imagine are the ways that architecture can truly defend itself against such forces.[1]

Contemporary visions of architecture maintain the perspective, for the most part, that our buildings are designed and constructed to be eternal. As architects, we rarely visualize their demise, or the situation in which our design will meet its end. Demise for the sake of a philosophical architectural death is not the intent, nor is it a necessary outcome. Rather, the loss of a structure can be the result of a latent function that is designed to provide some benefit in its demise or its transformation.

In coastal scenarios — particularly those with threat of tropical storm damage — this might be a useful tactic to employ. Visualizing a building's end of life and anticipating potential modes of failure allows architects to design the building to either withstand the assault or, in a more incongruous case, to fail functionally in order to serve some protective purpose.

Just as one might interrogate material and elevation strategies in studies of flood mitigation and recovery, here too, the underlying cause for destruction must be identified and addressed. To understand the waterborne forces of tropical storms, one must first understand the basics of the destructive energy in water.

[destructive energy in water]

The National Oceanic and Atmospheric Administration defines a storm surge as an "abnormal rise of water generated by a storm, over and above the predicted astronomical tide." The atypical rise above standard tidal levels is an effect of both offshore meteorological conditions and localized winds.[2] To understand the potentially destructive capabilities of storm surges, it is useful to consider the conveyance and transference of energy within a storm system. Typically, waves are the result of wind passing over the surface of the water, transferring energy from air to water. Wave height is determined by the speed and duration of the wind, and the bathymetry of the water body. The water-borne forces that can cause architectural damage are a direct result of the energy input from the wind that is transferred first to surface waves, then to land. The energy that a wave contains is directly proportional to the square of the wave height. Thus, as wave height grows, as during a tropical storm, the energy contained in those waves grows exponentially. Significantly, although the storm surge undoubtedly brings a great deal of water mass with it, it is the transmission of energy, not mass, which is the focus here.[3]

[stronger is safer]

The destructive capacity of tropical storms is a given. Often, the most significant damage is caused by massive flooding. However, when Hurricanes Katrina and Sandy devastated New Orleans and New York, respectively, the initial disaster was caused by deadly storm surges. Similarly, when Typhoon Yolanda (Haiyan) struck Tacloban, Philippines, in November 2013, the storm surge was the primary cause of the widespread destruction.[4] Since then, proposed strategies and policies have generally adopted a "stronger is safer" approach to coastal design. A 350-mile ring of protection around New Orleans — consisting of bigger, stronger levees, gigantic flood gates, and massive sea walls — was awarded $14 billion in federal aid.[5]

This effort to divorce architecture from its potentially destructive surroundings seems, at first, to be a logical solution. But what happens when these constructions fail, as during Hurricane Katrina? What happens where protective infrastructure is not a likely investment, as in Tacloban? Or when people have no option except to build exactly as before, with the poorest living over water because they cannot afford to own land? Architecture consistently falls victim to such events, amplifying the hardship and victimization of the people who see that architecture as safe space. Bulking up the coastline is an impulsive response that seeks to dominate nature and keep its dangers, and its many benefits, away from society.

[the sacrificial mindset]

The sacrificial mindset seems rather grotesque, but buildings are not living beings. Understanding their sacrifice means understanding the ways that we can alter our design process in order to accommodate an adaptive strategy. Although buildings themselves are not living beings, it is important to consider them to be part of a living ecological system. Achieving this means considering them as more than a one-time construction whose life-span is eternal and unchanging. Change is intrinsic to living systems; uncertainty, dynamism, and perceived imbalances are necessary characteristics of these systems.[6] If a system's response to a stimulant maintains a level of uncertainty, this implies an uncertainty in the effects that response will then provoke. In short, fluctuations within a system will occur, and it is this uncertainty that is typically neglected by architects.

Félix Guattari, in *The Three Ecologies*, discusses three complementary domains of ecology: social, mental, and environmental. Of great importance is Guattari's rejection of the notion that the psyche, the socius, and the environment are three separate entities that are acted on separately. Nature, he says, is inseparable from culture, and the relationship of anthroposystems, ecosystems, and referential universes must be considered transversely. This method of thinking across ecologies instead of within each allows contemporary designers to reconsider and reorient their strategies. It allows design to focus on the relationship of different entities instead of their individual, isolated functions.[7] This reorientation might also be categorized as systems thinking, as one is designing for anticipated events based on known relationship characteristics.

Ecological and systems thinking do not permit absolute control of the relationships among disparate systems and the events these relationships cause. Instead, they allow the considered analysis of interactions and permit speculative strategies that accommodate likely occurrences regarding potential reactions and affects. In adopting this mode of thought, we find that theories of resilience in ecology accept fluctuations and change as part of the process of equilibrium, not as an exception to it. Inherent in the acceptance and embodiment of this type of ecological thinking, and within any subsequent design strategy, is the acknowledgment of processes of constant change and adaptation within a system.

In acknowledging the dynamism of ecological systems, we see that the demise of certain components is inevitable. One might then question if that anticipated demise might be designed for, that the inevitable failure might be made functional. Designing for functional demise goes beyond the typical engineering design strategy of "design for failure." In designing *for* failure, engineers anticipate the multiple potential failure modes and the design accounts for each so that the design does *not* fail in that mode. There are a few engineers, however, who design their work to strategically fail. More specifically, failure here means that the design intelligently succumbs to applied forces instead of withstanding them.

[crumple zones]

Crumple zones of automobiles represent one type of design in which failure is embedded in the everyday function of the component or system. The components of the crumple zone of the car are staged such that the failure is a result of a certain event. More specifically, their demise is a function of the amount of force that is applied, and that they absorb. This embedded protection is a latent feature of automobiles. Most of us have likely owned automobiles in which this latent potential was never utilized (happily so). Although this latent potential exists silently for the life of the automobile, a more thorough thought exercise reveals that in order to design for the potential of a devastating collision, engineers must acknowledge fully that such an event could occur. The existence and considered design of the crumple zone itself acknowledges the grave danger that humans accept when they travel at high speeds in automobiles.

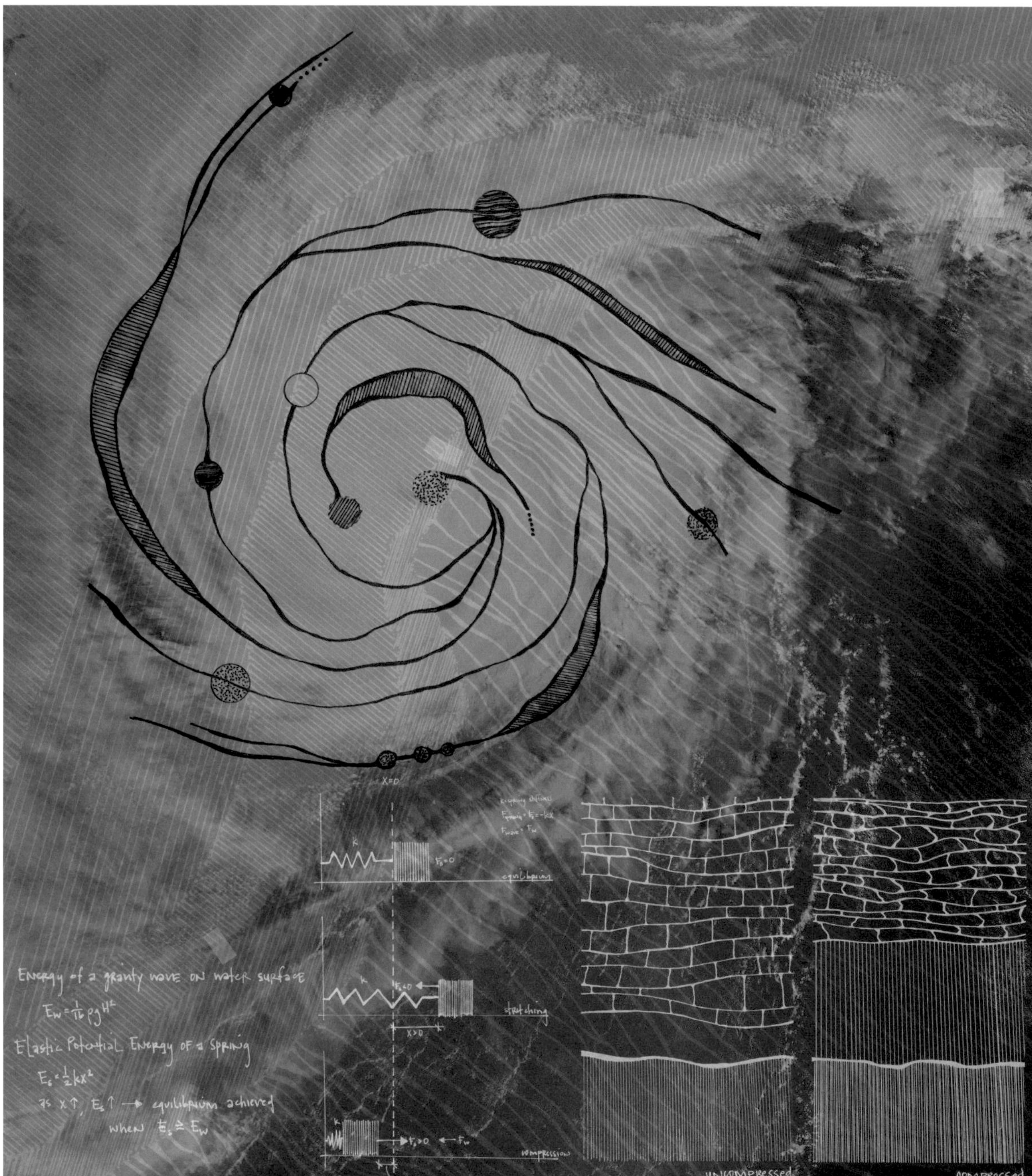

Consider an automobile moving at a constant rate toward a stationary object — another car, a tree, a telephone pole. In the time before the collision, there are no physical warning signs or indications that the body is moving towards demise (the human occupants, of course, can foresee the collision, but the automobile cannot). At some point, however, those moving bodies will collide and incur significant damage. This damage, in the form of kinetic energy, is ideally absorbed by the crumple zone. The folding of the crumple zone releases the energy of the collision as both heat and sound, decelerating the objects in the collision and protecting the human occupants. In this instance, the transfer of energy between the colliding bodies destroys the designed element but activates its latent protective function.[8]

Architects might adopt a similar approach in rethinking designs for coastal protection, particularly in regions where the threat of waterborne destruction is a known, anticipated entity. In such an instance, however, the crumple zone strategy might be applied to the stationary object (in this case, architecture) as protection from the moving body (here, storm surge). One might first consider designing for energy exchanges that can be predicted and calculated. Two such conditions have been identified and assigned the preliminary monikers of *Conversion* and *Absorption* for the sake of this text. In one, the force applied is absorbed through resistive measures that are somewhat more refined than a wall. In the other, kinetic energy is converted to potential energy and expended in a controlled manner during the storm event.

[conversion systems]

Conversion systems include those in which the transformation of energy is a means of dissipation and coastal protection. These might include water turbines or alterations to the bathymetry of the sea floor in order to affect the potential of a surge forming. Architecture may also provide some level of protection if these alterations or energy-harvesting technologies are not viable. In its simplest form, the Conversion system might consider the conversion of kinetic energy to potential energy, which can then be expended in a controlled, intentional manner. The most basic example of this, one of the four simple machines, is the Inclined Plane. Very simply, as the wave front moves in, the wave's kinetic energy is expended as it moves up the inclined plane. The energy is converted to potential energy, which can be expended as the water moves back out to sea, or when the water drops over the upper edge of the inclined plane.

[absorption systems]

Absorption systems of protection operate via designs that integrate resistive constructions in which force can be absorbed. Consider a spring. Just as the energy contained in a wave is proportional to the square of the wave height, the energy contained in the spring, or the spring-loaded construction, is proportional to the square of the displacement distance. This energy, produced when the wave or storm surge causes displacement of the construction, is potential energy. Thus, the kinetic energy of the wave is converted to potential energy in the spring that can then be expended calmly. Given the rhythmic nature of the waves within a storm event, one can imagine a similar rhythm to the build-up and expenditure of potential energy within the Absorption system. As a wave front moves in, the kinetic energy is converted to potential energy within the system, and in the time between the wave fronts, the energy is expended in a controlled manner, allowing the system to recharge for the next incoming wave front.

The Conversion and Absorption systems of protection might take any number of forms. Only a few very literal, preliminary iterations have been shared here. The two Absorption systems are a spring-loaded hinge and a compressible/expandable cellular structure.
The Conversion system is the integration of inclined plane characteristics into architectural designs. These systems have been sketched in the accompanying images. To describe them further would require a presentation of the physics that characterizes them. This has been discussed previously. The integration of energy conversion and energy absorption into coastal architectural design warrants further consideration as a method of ensuring safety.[9]

[design for functional demise]

Design for functional demise raises the question of social adaptation and social resilience. Social resilience is defined by Wu and Wu as the ability of a community to withstand, and to recover from, external environmental, socioeconomic, and political shocks or perturbations.[10] Perhaps the most pertinent question regarding social adaptation with regards to architecture is: can social resilience be designed? Or must adaptive cities and architectural reinvention be deployed strategically within communities that already exhibit social resilience? If the composition of our built environment were to change, would it be necessary to teach humans to adapt, or would we innately adapt to the new spaces?

In this regard, again, Félix Guattari provides insight. His essay "The Three Ecologies" highlights the importance of consistent and perpetual reinvention, seeming to encourage reinvention based on varying rhythms of repetition, the cadence of which will deter an entrapment in deathly repetition (which, of course, is different from the repetitive nature of reinvention). He discusses emergence and re-emergence, seeming to encourage reinvention based on varying rhythms of repetition, the cadence of which will also deter "deathly entrapment." He describes the effort of repetition as 'mechanical,'

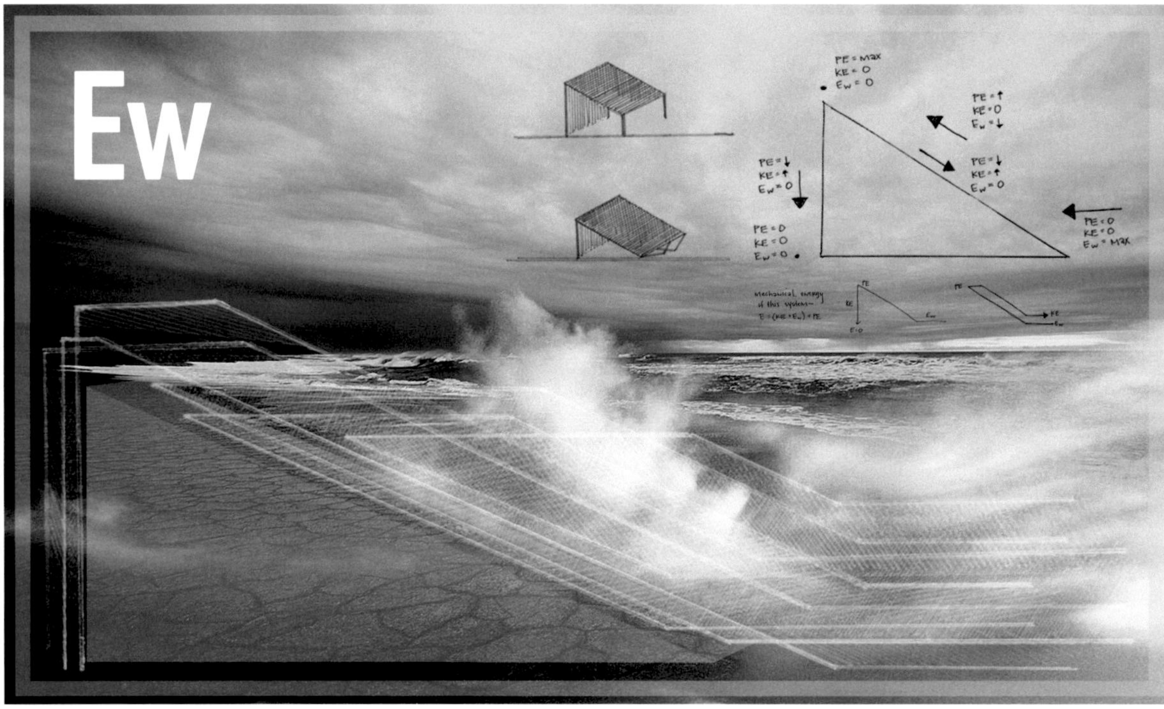

TOP
Inclined Plane
BOTTOM
Hinge

bringing to mind visions of tedious but repetitive and effective mechanistic processes. He vocalizes support for continued inventiveness and the perpetuation of innovative practices. It is this alternative experimentation that can both respect the singular nature of the psyche and work towards the proliferation of an agency that can exist simultaneously as autonomous and collective.[11]

More significantly, however, Guattari presents a philosophy that relies on a level of social and cultural resilience that is unique to specific regions. This resilience is necessary for an amplified, perpetual reorganization and reinvention of our built environment. It is a repetition that is wholly different than Guattari's mechanical repetition, as it is a repeated reinvention of the built environment according to the conditions that exist at the time of rebuilding. The level of resilience and reinvention is a social expectation. One might consider that Guattari's mechanical repetition is currently how we engage in architecture, and is furthermore relevant when we design for coastal habitation. The question becomes, what sort of reinvention must architecture undertake to adapt to the changing regional characteristics and the needs of people who inhabit our buildings?

Guattari's idea of repetitive rebuilding suggests the potential for a projective and progressive regeneration through the reconfiguration and development of what existed before. This way of thinking, reflecting the previously discussed ecological and systems thinking, amplifies the ideas that processes of disorganization and reorganization help society to move towards social order. This sort of thinking lies outside of what we currently think of as resilient architecture or coastal storm protection.

To say that architects must face the impending (and current) effects of a slowly shifting climate and the storm events that accompany the phenomenon is a statement that clearly underscores the potential of the field and the designers and practitioners that compose it. Architects, urban planners, and designers have an opportunity to rethink the way that our built environment functions, and the ways that we can further it to serve the people who inhabit and care for it. Anticipating and accepting potential damage and demise is necessary to design in anticipatory and conscientious ways. It requires understanding that damage or destruction cannot always be prevented, but that architects can design ways to transform the energy inputs and to mitigate the effect of the destructive forces. It hints at a design strategy that embeds latent adaptive and reactive performance into architecture. It speculates on an architectural design strategy that challenges notions of permanence, function, and safety.

NOTES

1 The topics presented here do not ignore policy and economic strategies, although this paper does. Instead, the ideas is to look beyond to tactical design methods that might provide additional protection during storm surge events, particularly in areas where retreat is not an economic or culturally viable option.

2 NOAA. "Storm Surge Overview," *National Hurricane Center | National Oceanic and Atmospheric Administration*. <http://www.nhc.noaa.gov/surge/>. (August 27, 2015).

3 Note that flooding as a destructive event is not addressed here. Rather, it is the forces associated with moving water (i.e, storm surges) that will be addressed.

4 "Mapping the Destruction of Typhoon Haiyan", *The New York Times*. November 11, 2013. <http://www.nytimes.com/interactive/2013/11/11/world/asia/typhoon-haiyan-map.html>.

5 John Schwartz, "How to Save a Sinking Coast? Katrina Created a Laboratory," *The New York Times | Science*. August 7, 2015. <http://www.nytimes.com/2015/08/08/science/louisiana-10-years-after-hurricane-katrina.html?_r=0>.

6 Chris Reed and N. Lister, "Parallel Genealogie," *Projective Ecologies*. (2014).

7 Félix Guattari, *The Three Ecologies*. 1989, Trans. Ian Pindar and Paul Sutton (New Brunswick, NJ: Athlone, 2000).

8 Christopher Erickson, "Crumple Zones in Automobiles," sourced through the American Institute of Physics (accessed July 28, 2015).

9 Note that these proposals are for temporary structures, not for residential or other more permanent structures. Also note that the proposed temporary structures assume that all people have been evacuated to a secure, inland evacuation center at the time the storm event reaches the coast.

10 Jianguo Wu and Tong Wu, "Ecological resilience as a foundation for urban design and sustainability." *Resilience in Ecology and Urban Design*, 2013, pp. 211–229.

11 Félix Guattari, *The Three Ecologies*. 1989, Trans. Ian Pindar and Paul Sutton. (New Brunswick, NJ: Athlone P 2000)

(re) MADE BY WATER

OBSOLESCENCE, URBAN NOMADISM AND THE NEW WORLD MALL, BANGKOK

by GREGORY MARINIC

In 1997, an extension to the New World Mall in central Bangkok was ordered to cease operations by the Supreme Court of Thailand due to an unlawful addition. To conform with the court order, owners responded by demolishing the top stories of the annex and abandoning it. The deserted structure attracted vandals who set fires that further exposed the interior to the elements. Monsoon rains slowly flooded the ground floor into a pool of water which came to host tropical fish and aquatic plants. Over the next 20 years, this 'dead' mall incrementally evolved into an ecology connecting the local community to the global backpacker circuit. Here, water radically remade a conventional space of consumption into a place of rogue tourism.

This essay engages my ongoing research of retail architecture and urban obsolescence. It examines how corrupt development practices and partial destruction transformed an ordinary shopping mall into an extraordinary aquatic landscape. This essay acknowledges informal methods of adaptive reuse mobilized by ecology, people, and everyday actions. It begins with an overview of the historical interface of water and architecture in Southeast Asia to provide context for this blended building-landscape. The writing aims to construct a broader narrative surrounding the New World Mall in relation to the spatial theories of Walter

The New World Mall, Bangkok

Benjamin, Guy Debord, Henri Lefebvre, and Anthony Vidler, as well as practices of urban nomadism across time and cultures. Further, the essay frames a socio-cultural perspective on retail architecture unintentionally remade with water, adapted through everyday practices and rediscovered by global wanderers—a new flânerie.

Water and Architecture in Southeast Asia: A Brief Overview

Across the geographically and culturally diverse region of Southeast Asia, water has historically served as a primary feature in both sacred architecture and urbanism. Beginning in the third century BCE, the Hindu and Buddhist religions expanded from India into the Indochinese Peninsula via sea trading and overland migration. At the beginning of the Common Era, Indian merchants brought Hindu Brahmins and Buddhist priests to settle in the region.[1] By the end of the first century, many of the kingdoms of Southeast Asia had adopted Hindu and Buddhist traditions suited to their needs. Since then, both faiths have imparted significant influences on social organization, literature, art, architecture, and urbanism in the region.

Water is revered in the Hindu and Buddhist traditions for its purity, cleansing powers, and spiritual properties. Ancient Sanskrit texts advise that temple sites should include water features that support the growth of lotus, water fowl, songbirds, and fish.[2] Vedic scripture states that such characteristics were meant to engender nirvana and the idyllic realm of deities. As such, the holiest Hindu pilgrimage sites are located along rivers and lakes, while temple compounds in urban environments incorporate constructed pools used for ritual bathing. Similarly, Buddhism employs water as reflecting pools, ponds, and lakes in the landscape design of temple complexes. Monumental Hindu temples to Vishnu and Shiva, for example, were built during the ancient Khmer empire along major bodies of water.[3] Among the most impressive, Angkor Wat was conceived during the 12th century as a Hindu temple and later converted to Buddhist use. Surrounded by ramparts and a moat teeming with lotus and koi, it demonstrates a strong connection between sacred architecture and water, as well as a spatial fluidity linking the Buddhist and Hindu traditions. Today, the nations of Southeast Asia share water aesthetics informed by these hybrid influences.

In contemporary Bangkok, water is an omnipresent and atmospheric condition in the city. Known as 'The Venice of the East,' the Thai capital was historically defined by a vast network of *khlongs* (canals) which connected the Chao Phraya River with districts and neighborhoods throughout the urban core. From the 14th through the 19th centuries, floating markets served as nodes which spawned the growth of mercantile, social, and cultural activities.[4] Floating markets allowed farmers and merchants to sell agricultural products, prepared foods, textiles, and other goods directly from their boats. By the 20th century, however, road and rail networks began to supplant many of the *khlongs*, while at the same time, others were eliminated due to public health and sanitation concerns.[5] Today, the Chao Phraya River continues to serve as a primary commuter artery in Bangkok, while floating markets remain active in Wat Sai, Taling Chan, and Khlong Lat Mayom.

Theoretical Framework: Consumption, Obsolescence, and Flânerie

It is important to situate the lifecycle of the New World Mall within a broader social, historical, and theoretical context. Since the early 20th century, theorists have routinely critiqued the impact of capitalism on buildings and urban space. It is widely acknowledged that the consumptive origins of contemporary society may be traced to the whims, desires, and projections of the 19th century. As evidenced by the 20th century transition from arcades to department stores and, later, by 21st century shifts from a physical world of shopping malls to the virtual world of internet commerce, retail environments have become increasingly obsolete. Continual changes in production, communication, and connectivity have radically transformed the rules of retail, as well as the future of retail building typologies around the world.

Over the course of the 20th century, theorists Walter Benjamin, Guy Debord, Henri Lefebvre, and Anthony Vidler analyzed the influence of consumption on urbanism and architectural form. Beginning in the 1930s, Walter Benjamin studied the Parisian arcades to discern the social, architectural, and phenomenological conditions of a declining 19th century retail typology. In his seminal work "The Arcades Project," Benjamin viewed the arcades as a visual device, or space frame, that provided the bourgeoisie a curated view on life. Within the confines of these interior worlds, expectations changed and contemporary consumerism emerged.[6] Benjamin alluded to dreams and fantasies—of the simultaneity of the literal world contrasting with an alternative, controlled, and sublime one existing within the sky-lit arcades. Alongside retailing, the Parisian arcades supported an underworld of illegal and illicit activities. Vices such as gambling and prostitution were beyond direct police jurisdiction, spawning a broader bohemian culture of transients, artists, and gays which challenged racial, ethnic, and socio-economic boundaries.

Benjamin's research on the Parisian arcades was influenced by the poetry of Charles Baudelaire and his characterization of the 19th century flâneur as a gentleman stroller of the streets.[7] For Baudelaire, the flâneur represented the sophisticated urban aficionado who was recast by Benjamin as both a dandy and connoisseur of the modern metropolitan experience. The flâneur was an object of significant scholarly analysis, critique, and understanding of 20th century urbanity and social conditions. Flâneurs revealed class tensions and gender divisions of the 19th century city while their behaviors shed light on a broader sense of alienation with modernity, mass production, consumer culture, and societal expectations. In this sense, the flânerie was not simply limited to the physical act of strolling in the Baudelairian sense, but also implied an enlightened way of thinking, living, and navigating the world.

Representing a hybrid social type, flâneurs were at once a product of the bourgeoisie and the bohème.[8] Benjamin framed the flâneur as the definitive figure of the modern era however, it was the habitats of the male flâneur in which he was primarily interested. As an urban stroller and loiterer, perhaps without an ostensible purpose, the flâneur was intuitively invested in the history of the city. In search of the sublime, delightful, or erotic — he wandered the boulevards, parks, cafés, and arcades. The urban forms which gave rise to flâneur culture simultaneously conveyed both aspirational largesse and zones of alienation in the city.[9] Although the flâneurs met their demise with the triumph of consumerism, other forms of this socio-cultural phenomenon reemerged in the contemporary era. Today, urban nomads and global backpackers seek out authentic experiences in a similar manner to the flâneurs, yet on a transcontinental scale.

Urban Nomadism and Everyday Forgotten Space in Bangkok

The impact of human activities on cities and within buildings makes the study of the everyday a compelling filter for designers. Unlike the formalized rituals of design, everyday manipulations are anonymous, layered, and unstructured actions likened to social needs and cultural traditions.[10] Independent from the formal hand of professional architects and designers, everyday manipulations — ranging from post-occupancy changes to ground-up adaptations — significantly shape the functional, aesthetic, and qualitative aspects of the built environment. Henri Lefebvre acknowledged the everyday impact of production, consumption, and multiplicity of authorship in the built environment. He asserted that cities, buildings, and interiors are hybrid productions authored not only by designers, but also through cultural traditions, social practices, and autonomous interventions.[11] As a Marxist theorist who was critical of economic structuralism, Lefebvre proposed that the everyday manipulation of space is fundamental to the growth of society and the shape of the city.[12] He posits a theoretical perspective that distrusts the heroic, formal, and fashionable, while condemning design practices that operate as agents of commodification. Reframing the design of the built environment with the inverse — the everyday impact of people reshaping space — he celebrates the ordinary actions that cities, buildings, and interiors receive apart from the top-down hand of designers. Lefebvre fixes his gaze on the lives of designed spaces well beyond the moment of their completion.

The abandoned mall filled with rainwater

In 1956, Guy Debord defined the term *dérive* as "a mode of experimental behavior linked to the conditions of urban society, a technique of rapid passage through varied ambiances." As a founding member of Situationist International, he contributed to shaping a mid-20th century discourse of urban drifting which embraced playfulness, constructive exploration, and awareness of psycho-geographical effects.[13] The *dérive*, a form of urban exploration, demonstrated a significantly alternative engagement with the city than the typical journey or stroll more akin to the studied encounters of the flâneur. Debord and his Situationist collaborators sought to identify fissures in cities, distinct neighborhoods with no correlation to administrative boundaries, the role of urban micro-climates, and the character of places of attraction. As political revolutionaries and provocateurs of the 1960s counterculture, Situationists proposed a different way to read, analyze, and critique cities. They acknowledged the inherent value of marginalized urban spaces.

The counterculture of the 1960s emerged from the earlier Beat Generation as an anti-establishment social, cultural, and political movement. Its origins may be traced to European bohemianism and a rising awareness of Eastern religions and spirituality.[14] The "hippie" subculture found significant inspiration in non-western cultural traditions and was defined by an ethos of communal living, creative experimentation, ecological balance, and recreational drug usage. From the mid-1960s to the late 1970s, young people from North America and Europe incrementally forged an overland route to the East.[15] The "hippie trail" began in London, moved across continental Europe to Istanbul, and then traversed the Middle East and Indian subcontinent to Bangkok. This alternative, modest, and interactive form of tourism contrasted sharply with the bourgeois tastes of the jet set. The trail was defined by hostels, cafés, and shops that catered almost exclusively to Westerners as they journeyed both east and west.[16] Much like the 19th century flâneurs, these global wanderers sought out the sublime, delightful, and erotic by wandering the bazaars, temples, and markets of the East. Although the hippie trail ended by the late 1970s due to political upheaval in Iran and Afghanistan, its influence on contemporary backpacker culture endures along fragments of the original route.

As Westerners migrated east in pursuit of authentic experiences, the East was developmentally moving west in pursuit of urban modernization and economic expansion. By the early 1970s, a first generation of shopping malls were built in the national capitals of Southeast Asia, joining a retail landscape historically defined by shophouses, open-air markets, hawker stalls, and department stores.[17] Traditional commercial types

were violently displaced in a wave of urban renewal that forged broader streets, infrastructure, and office towers.[18] Retail activities were increasingly relocated and encapsulated within the earliest shopping malls. In 1973, Siam Center opened as the first climate-controlled mall in Bangkok achieving an international standard. Housing 60 shops and the offices of Pan American World Airways and Chase Manhattan Bank, it set a new precedent for retailing in the central business district.[19] By the early 1980s, enclosed shopping malls became increasingly commonplace, and later, overbuilding throughout the 1990s and early 2000s resulted in notable levels of underuse and abandonment.[20] Today, many of the oldest malls in Bangkok have migrated toward remarkably alternative uses.

Located in the Bang Lamphu district, the New World Mall opened in 1982 during the second wave of shopping mall construction. In 1997, a court order filed by the Bangkok Metropolitan Administration claimed that an extension to the mall had been built seven stories taller than approved.[21] In response to the court order, the owners of New World Mall haphazardly demolished its outlawed floors. The compromised structure attracted arsonists who attempted to burn it down in retaliation for being taller than the Grand Palace.[22] Meanwhile, the abandoned mall filled with rainwater, while the exposed floor plates slowly came to host vegetation. Since its closure, litigation between municipal authorities and the owners has focused on who should fully demolish the building or rebuild its roof.

In 2003, residents of the surrounding community released koi, tilapia, and catfish into the waterscape to combat the mosquito nuisance.[23] Locals introduced tourists to the space and began selling food to feed the fish.[24] In 2013, 30-year-old American backpacker Jesse Rockwell stumbled across New World Mall and wrote a blog post to document his visit.[25] By mid-2014, Rockwell's blog was discovered by a popular website, The Verge, and interest in the New World Mall went viral.[26] Cyberspace has transformed the mall into a popular stop along the global backpacker trail, while proximity to the Khao San Road hostel district made it accessible to the masses. With increased foot traffic, the narrow alleys surrounding New World Mall spawned mom-and-pop shops and cafés serving a rogue tourist industry.

In an ironic twist of fate — embedded within a city known for its floating markets — the New World Mall represents a radical inversion of retail and water. Blending the vastness of a temple complex with the spatial ambiance of walled aquatic gardens, New World Mall has recast the sacred relationship of water, koi, building, and landscape. Although this unplanned "aquarium" remains extremely popular with tourists, as well as economically beneficial to its surrounding community, municipal authorities view it as a public hazard. In January 2015, fishermen were dispatched by municipal authorities to net the fish for transport to the Thai Department of Fisheries and various bodies of water throughout Thailand.[27] Although entering the former shopping mall remains illegal, urban explorers continue to find their way into the condemned structure. Haunted by a recent past much like the dying arcades of Benjamin's Paris in the 1930s, the New World Mall rests in limbo between politics and the people awaiting an uncertain future.

Reflection

Urban theorist Anthony Vidler uses the term "uncanny" as a metaphor for unplanned influences. In his book *The Architectural Uncanny*, he analyzes obsolescence in everyday buildings of the recent past — abandoned shopping malls — as the aftereffects of consumerism, corporate disinvestment, and post-industrial culture.[28] Like Benjamin's analysis of the arcades, Vidler considers the trajectory of buildings that lose their purpose and fade to host alternative uses. He proposes a future vision of retail environments built upon their advancing obsolescence. In a similar manner, the New World Mall has been detached from its intended uses and appropriated by others. It documents a recent past embedded within the dense urban fabric of central Bangkok. As both a public interior and an aquatic landscape, New World Mall exists along the undefined margins of the built environment by means of incremental, parasitic, and illegal actions. Furthermore, the appropriated mall demonstrates subtle similarities with the walled, water-oriented sacred spaces common to both the Hindu and Buddhist traditions of Southeast Asia. Here, water became a force of spatial appropriation and cultural expression that motivated communal responses. Water represents an informal occupancy that has reshaped the larger built environment, from the inside-out, via natural processes of adaptive reuse. Water became a catalyst for human actions ranging from community mobilization to mercantilism and rogue tourism.

Through an uncommon convergence of circumstances, New World Mall demonstrates how ecology and people transformed an obsolete shopping mall into a place of delight for the 21st century flâneur. Intentionally destabilized by government-sanctioned demolition, this structure also offers a perspective on the transformative forces impacting retail infrastructure worldwide. While internet-based retail threatens the worldwide viability of sustaining overbuilt physical environments, aging shopping malls also fall prey to shifting urban-suburban redevelopment strategies. In the case of New World Mall, the marriage of physical destruction and water allowed an interior urban space to organically grow within the ruins of a failed space of consumption.

From a design perspective, the temporal nature of retail buildings coupled with shifting socio-economic conditions fuels a vast interior territory of worldwide obsolescence, abandonment, and potential for regeneration. Viewed through the structuralist theoretical perspective of Lefebvre, this de-programmed mall has never been empty — it resonates with subtle traces of the past, fosters social interaction, and draws tourism with links to the Situationist *dérive*. Today, however, the mall exists within a markedly different era defined by the immediacy of social media connectivity to the masses.

It is critical that architects, landscape architects, and interior designers, as makers of the built environment, intentionally anticipate non-conforming future uses in their work. As evidenced here, disruptive and destructive forces can informally reactivate underused buildings and infrastructures. Design scholars and educators should critically engage the ways in which informal occupancies spawn adaptation and consider advocating for occupancies that organically grow and change over time. Likewise, it is important for designers to understand narratives of places and users as they seek effective ways to contextualize design problems[29] and embrace more nuanced, porous, and adaptive ways of intervening in the built environment. They will need to better anticipate diverse forms of appropriation that take root within the buildings and spaces that they design. By celebrating the inherent value of informal adaptions in an era of diminishing resources, designers can recalibrate their agency by supporting regenerative, emergent forms of urbanism.

NOTES

1 Christopher V. Hill, *South Asia: An Environmental History* (Santa Barbara: ABC-CLIO Publishing, 2008), pp. 35–38.

2 Vinayak Bharne and Krupali Krusche, *Rediscovering the Hindu Temple: The Sacred Architecture and Urbanism of India* (Newcastle-upon-Tyne: Cambridge Scholars Publishing, 2012), p. 19.

3 Alison Behnke, *Angkor Wat* (Minneapolis:Twenty-First Century Books, 2008), pp. 24–25.

4 Lauren C. Heberle and Susan M. Opp, *Local Sustainable Urban Development in a Globalized World* (London: Routledge, 2008), p. 177.

5 Vinayak Bharne, *The Emerging Asian City* (London: Routledge, 2013), pp. 86–89.

6 Esther Leslie, "Ruin and Rubble in the Arcades," *Walter Benjamin and the Arcades Project* (2006), pp. 87–89.

7 Walter Benjamin and Michael W. Jennings, *The Writer of Modern Life: Essays on Charles Baudelaire* (Cambridge, MA: Belknap Press, 2006) pp. 2–8.

8 Hsiao-yen Peng, *Dandyism and Transcultural Modernity: The Dandy, the Flâneur, and the Translator in 1930s Shanghai, Tokyo, and Paris* (London: Routledge, 2015), pp. 6–8.

9 Anna Budziak, *Text, Body and Indeterminacy: The Doppelganger Selves in Pater and Wilde* (Newcastle-upon-Tyne: Cambridge Scholars, 2008), pp. 47–52.

10 Michel Foucault and Jay Miskowiec, "Of Other Spaces." *Diacritics* 16, no. 1 (1986): 22–27. doi:10.2307/464648.

11 Ibid.

12 Henri Lefebvre, *Critique of Everyday Life*, Volume II (Brooklyn: Verso, 2002), pp. 309–312.

13 Tom McDonough, *Guy Debord and the Situationist International: Texts and Documents* (Cambridge: The MIT Press, 2004), pp. 255–257.

14 Peter Burke, *The New Cambridge Modern History: Volume 13* (Cambridge: Cambridge University Press, 1979), pp. 357.

15 Agnieszka Sobocinska, "The Expedition's Afterlives: Echoes of Empire in Travel to Asia," *Expedition into Empire: Exploratory Journeys and the Making of the Modern World* (2015), pp. 227–228.

16 Ibid.

17 David Turnbull, "Soc. Culture: Singapore," *The Architecture of Fear*, (1997), pp. 229.

18 Ibid.

19 Nicholas Grossman, *Chronicle of Thailand: Headline News Since 1946* (Paris: Editions Didier Millet, 2009), pp. 194.

20 Boonying Kongarchapatara and Randall Shannon, "Transformations in Thailand's Retailing Landscape: Public Policies, Regulations, and Strategies," *Retailing in Emerging Markets: A Policy and Strategy Perspective*, pp. 7–9.

21 Mark Byrnes, "Removing Fish from a Surreal Abandoned Shopping Mall," *The Atlantic*, January 16, 2015.

22 Chris Pleasance, "Splashing out at the shops: Hundreds of fish take over abandoned Thai mall after it's flooded," *Daily Mail*, June 26, 2014.

23 Terry Fredrickson, "Bangkok's hidden fish pond," *Bangkok Post*, July 1, 2014.

24 Supoj Wancharoen, "A New World fish pond," *Bangkok Post*, June 30, 2014.

25 Sasha Goldstein, "Abandoned Bangkok shopping mall becomes incredible koi pond after years of neglect," *New York Daily News*, July 1, 2014.

26 Ibid.

27 Supoj Wancharoen, "Fish pulled from New World pond," *Bangkok Post*, January 13, 2015.

28 Anthony Vidler, *The Architectural Uncanny: Essays in the Modern Unhomely* (Cambridge: The MIT Press, 1994), pp. 3–5.

29 Tasoulla Hadjiyanni, "Rethinking Culture in Interior Design Pedagogy: The Potential Beyond CIDA Standard 2g," *Journal of Interior Design*, Volume 38, Number 3 (2013), pp. viii–xi.

New steps, Salemi

TAKING ON THE SHAPE OF THINGS

ROBERTO COLLOVÀ: THE SPIRIT OF RESILIENCE

EXCERPTS FROM AN INTERVIEW WITH AND TRANSLATED FROM ITALIAN BY INT/AR EDITOR LILIANE WONG

The text of the full interview is available in its entirely as a PDF http://intar-journal.risd.edu

For centuries, Sicily was the crossroad of western civilization. With a rich heritage that includes the Phoenicians, Greeks, Romans, Arabs, Normans, French, and Germans, the history of Sicily and its many different inhabitants is a quintessential example of social resilience. As an island, it has demonstrated a remarkable ability for continuity, recovery and change. The work of architect Roberto Collovà in Sicily comprises architecture, urban design, landscape design, furniture design and photography. His projects, writing and photographs capture the resilient spirit of Sicily, from the bustle of Palermo to Gela, a historic town on the southern coast, transformed by industry and violence, and the western towns of Salemi and Gibellina, destroyed by an earthquake and rebuilt. In its spare and poetic simplicity his work speaks of an endurance that is at the heart of Sicily and its peoples. I had the great fortune to meet and speak with him at his studio in Palermo.

Int|AR: What characterizes Sicily and its peoples that enables them to adjust, survive and thrive under different circumstances?

RC: Sicily is rich in artistic and literary patrimony, but each is relative to a colonization, and therefore the beauty of art and architecture corresponds to different forms of domination. Often, justly intoxicated by beauty, we forget that the most impressive manifestations of human work in history correspond to periods where power resides in the hands of a group or of a single person: a king, an emperor, the pope... and this is not so for Sicily. I think that this condition of subjection to different rulers – from the Spaniards to the Piedmontese, the unification of Italy to the Republic – has trained the inhabitants of Sicily to adapt to language and customs, behavior, practices, and even psychological disposition.

Int|AR: Today we have invaders of a different nature. What are the elements that pose the greatest threat to present-day Sicily?

RC: Unfortunately, it is largely internal invaders. The condition of subjection and millennia of adaptation to colonization have simultaneously developed in Sicilians different aptitudes and skills, both good and bad, and, at times, seemingly contrasting: hospitality towards a stranger as nothing more than a "get rich" scheme, kindness vs. distrust; submission vs. contempt; inferiority vs. arrogance; roughness vs. refinement; generosity as a form of seduction that creates a kind of double bond, a circular one: 'my gift in any way belongs to me.' These qualities and characteristics, at times extreme, distinguish different individuals from delicate to terrible, and can coexist in the same person or the same social groups. For certain, today the Sicilian capacity to adapt is evident from the absence of any form of discrimination, a disposition that certainly comes from mixed social customs and a certain proportion of ethnic hybridization of ancient origins. The adaptation, I think, took place in passing with mistrust, accession, intermarriage, and autodidactic skills. A true exercise of an intermediate ground that urges the attitude to "take the shape of things."

Many of these interesting and perverse contradictions can explain, I think, the phenomenon of the mafia, proudly separatist and stupidly antiprogressive, bloodthirsty and religious, traditional and unscrupulous, like an invader that is, at the same time, part of an invasive body; and not only as a society, but at times as individuals, though in varying degrees, through deep cultural structures that are stratified within us, like the jarring and fascinating co-presences of our architectures, that like spaceships, seem to come from different worlds, both near and far.

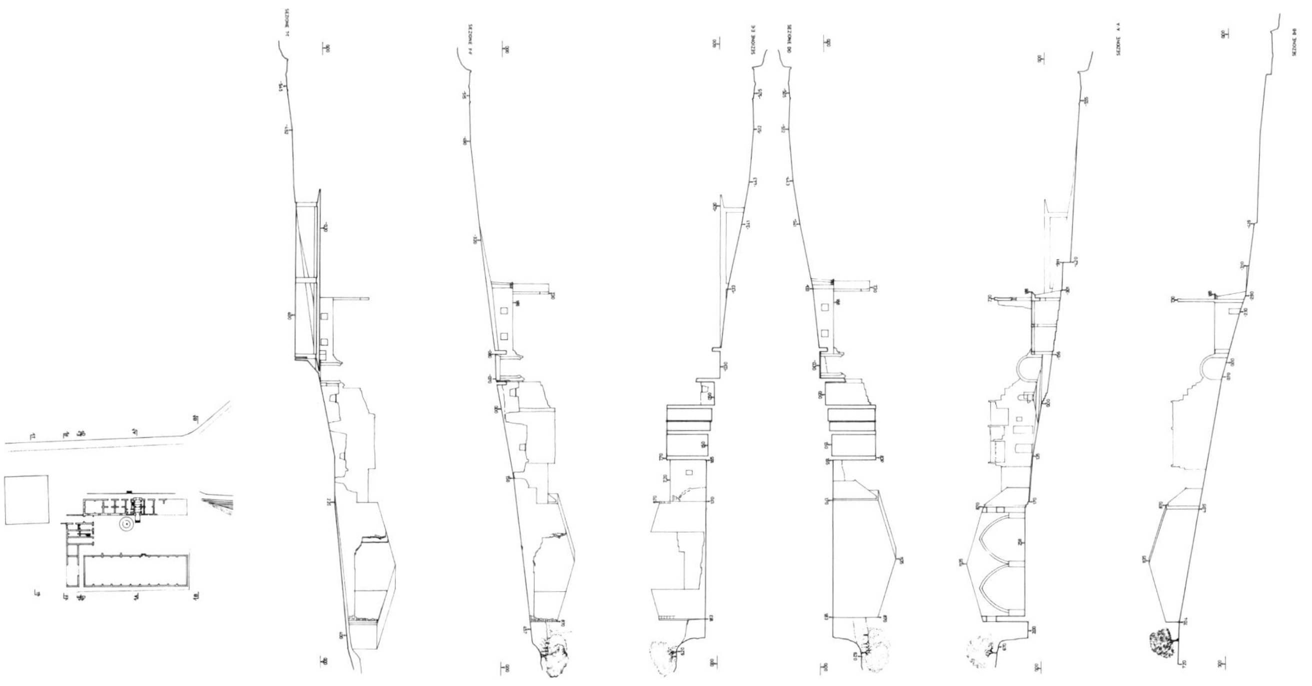

Sections through Case di Stefano, a new museum incorporating the ruins of an old farmhouse destroyed by earthquake, Gibellina

This and all subsequent illustrations are the work of Roberto Collovà

Case di Stefano, Gibellina

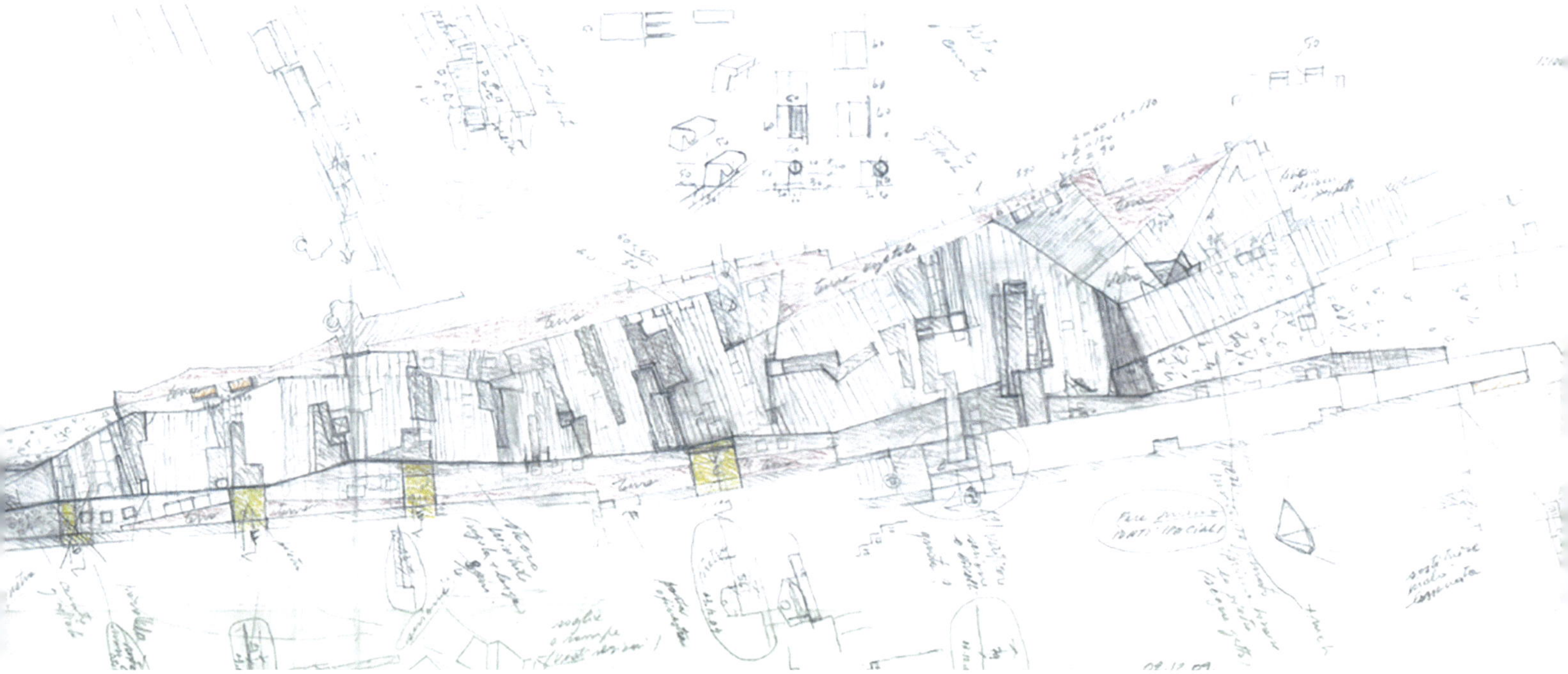

Int|AR: What of Sicily's architectural resilience? Did Sicily's architecture adapt itself to the styles of its many different inhabitants – Greeks, Romans, Normans, Arabs? How did each period adapt to the last to arrive at the coherent whole that is present today in Sicilian cities? What characterizes the present-day architecture of Sicily? How does modern-day architecture coexist with the past, both in adaptive reuse projects and in new construction?

RC: The coexistence of architecture from different eras was very natural until the early decades of the last century. But modern thought, with the myth of progress, at first blush has made it seem impossible to accept each hypothetical coexistence, theorizing and urging a certain erasure of the past, replacing it with the 'new.'

In Italy the question of coexistence between modern and historic architecture takes on special characteristics in view of the enormous consistency of our heritage, with a fatal production of false conscience. After the end of the war, an initial period of excessive boldness in confronting the past, characterized by reckless destruction, was followed by the development of a true and proper ideology of preservation that produced devastating and anachronistic para-picturesque forms. It is a matter of two extreme visions, two attitudes placed obtusely in opposition. The need to safeguard the works of the past operationally overturns new construction through mimetic practices—especially in historic city centres—that make them resemble ancient ones, at times grotesque and always inauthentic. I believe the only way to preserve, in the sense of "passing down the care of the object and its meaning," is to continue to transform it; naturally, the extent of the transformation depends on the object, which in many cases must remain intact, as a precious document of itself for the world, while others ask to be transformed to an adequate extent, if only to survive and continue to have a sense of the old and the current. And this is especially true for architecture and for the city.

A way of being modern or, more humbly, adequate to the times, it seems to me is not to necessarily and demonstratively contrast every new building with the past, but to look for forms and conditions specific to each problem, to recognize a sort of DNA to modify it profoundly if this also gives it a new sense.

Int|AR: The city of Gela is an example of a city that has evolved, for better or worse, since its founding by the Greeks. It has a long history of survival; Roman, Byzantine and Arabic domination, its re-emergence under Federico II, its survival through warfare and its lamentable fate in the modern era with the violence imposed upon it in the 1980s. What defines Gela in the 21st century? Your winning competition entry *Una via tre piazze* was a long time in the making. What is the history of the commission? What were the city's goals? What were your goals? How does the design mediate between the historic layers?

Sketch of the winning competition proposal, Gela

RC: I believe Gela is a 20th century hybrid city. It has 80,000 inhabitants and suffers the typical contradictions of a modernization without growth.
At Gela illegal and wild building coexists, the interesting effects of the synergy between "enterprise and culture" and the idea of 'social condition,' theorized by Adriano Olivetti, experimented on the rationalist neighborhood of Macchitella (see website for full discussion on Macchitella).

As for the time for the completion of the first intervention ...? In Sicily, time takes on a metaphysical dimension and actions seem to be independent of their ends. I won the competition in 1993. There were immediate public presentations and enthusiastic reactions. It seemed that everyone wished the projects realized, as soon as possible. In 1998, I was commissioned to do the design of the first intervention, the Piazza Roma, the most complex and interesting part that was tied to the creation of a public building with small shops; there would have been an upper square with a garden and a low one which overlooked a long 'urban room.'

The project was delivered on time but by then, the municipal administration was so fragile that, primarily due to a lack of organization, it did not succeed in getting approved by the municipal council. Political factions, not necessarily in opposition, provoked these useless and self-destructive incidents.

Finally, in 2000, a strong-willed official from the City Planning Office succeeded in getting the entire competition project approved as a general urban project, and beginning the commission from the other square at the opposite end of historic center, that is now realized.

The work began in 2006, but the contractor was not up to the task and it took more time to appoint another. Meanwhile, in 2005, at the behest of the new mayor they entrusted me with the second part of the project: 3/4 of the Corso and the other three piazzas, excluding the Piazza Roma, now definitively compromised.

The new mayor, in fact, a fierce opponent of the competition while he was municipal Councillor-purely

Pavement from the realized part of the *Una via tre piazze* competition, Gela

 Pavement construction, Gela

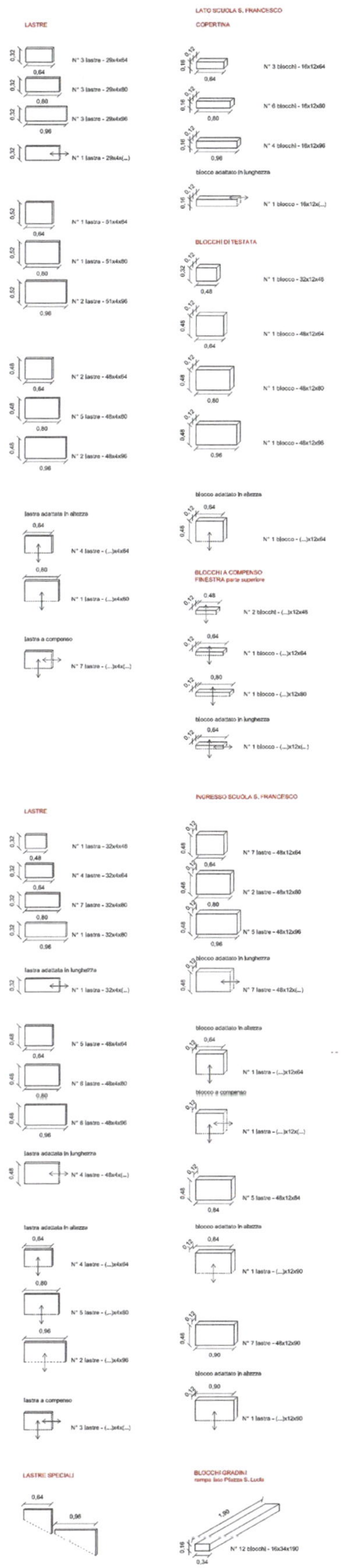

Pavement unit types at Gela

for the sake of political rivalry – as soon as he took office attacked it as he had before, but without succeeding in reviving the dissent of the previous years. So far, my '1° Prize', unanimously selected by a competent and strong jury, has built only a square and a solo section of the Corso; to do this it took about six years. A paradoxical situation!

From time to time, lazy and inefficient civil servants and citizen groups opposed to any transformation have sought to slow down the second part of the project. The executive project was approved more than two years after the other four due to a stretch bristling with obstacles and boycotts. Up to now, the administration has not taken any effective financing initiative-about eight million euros-to complete the construction.

The municipal administration had entrusted the architects, organisers of the competition, with the elaboration of the theme; from the wording of the notice, one was aware that the competition was designed to transform public spaces in a modernist direction; it solicited an exercise in design, as there was neither a real program, clear themes nor precise objectives. In the absence of a program, the design of the pavement became almost the only theme, so the risk of an excess of graphics was great.

For my part, it was clear right from the beginning that I had to critically face the philosophy of the notice; to bring to life everything that was not said in the notice and the latent and specific question of that area of work and its geographical and urban condition. We worked against any form making and beautification of the historic centre, to some precise urban changes that could start a concrete integration between the degraded historic center, degraded but still of some interest, and the outskirts, the product of wild speculative building, microscopic, widespread and extensive.

Attention to the structure of the urban spaces and the buildings that define them allows one to experiment with forms and relationships laden with new meanings; the areas of my work are naturally the urban transformations that face the new needs of the historic city and especially the various relationships with the 'city without qualities' that has grown disproportionately around it.

> **Int|AR:** What threatens cities today and what is necessary in city planning to develop capacities to absorb future shocks and stresses?

RC: The cities today risk a vital and self-destructive chaos of no specific interest, the opposite of rich, cultured and vital chaos that comes from the city's

history. I am skeptical of the urban planning discipline and its ability to predict and plan. Of course I am referring especially to urban planning in Italy. Italy has, I think, the most complex and articulated system of town planning in the world; notwithstanding that, it is a country with a high incidence of illegal building and a persistent ineffectiveness. This happens for a collection of reasons: untimeliness, the lack of checks and controls; the complicated rules and practices of approval and authorization, referencing a 19th-century bureaucracy; finally, the slow processing of plans, their lack of simplicity, an overly long validation in relation to the rapidly changing phenomena of transformation.

Int|AR: One key aspect of resilience theory relates to disaster, disaster recovery and strategies for avoiding disaster. Your projects at Salemi and Gibellina are a direct result of natural disaster, the devastating earthquake of 1968, Terremoto del Belìce. Historically one of western Sicily's largest seismic events, this earthquake destroyed 14 towns, including Gibellina and parts of Salemi. Disaster relief was hindered by the lack of preparation, excessive bureaucracy and, as noted in Leonardo Sciascia's January 1968 articles in *L'Ora*, a lack of trust on the part of the refugees of help from outside the island, a result of the social differences between the north and south of Italy. Do you think these issues have any relevance today?

RC: From the age-old problem of the 'Southern question,' which was already present at the end of the 19th century and of which Antonio Gramsci accurately wrote in the 20s, one can say that its results are still visible in the jarring presence of the signs of modernity such as, for example, highways and obvious states of marginalization and neglect, natural beauty and inefficient services. It is a paradox, seeing that Sicily was the first Italian region to have a statute of regional autonomy approved in 1946, a year before the Constitution of the Italian Republic; even if the advanced concessions were the obstacles to the constituent government and the fragile separatist movement of Finocchiaro Aprile. With respect to the refugees' distrust of State intervention, I can say that it was justly founded.

"Witness the jarring discrepancy between the state intentions and the local situation, written by Ludovico Corrao, (introduction to the book *I maestri di Gibellina* by Davide Camarrone, for editions Sellerio 2011) in which he tells that the Government of those years had not even raised the issue of reconstruction, to the extent of making available boats to send the families of the earthquake to South America or Australia. Later, in the vision of the State, the issue of Belìce, became

The Belice region after the earthquake, from the exhibition *Belice '80*

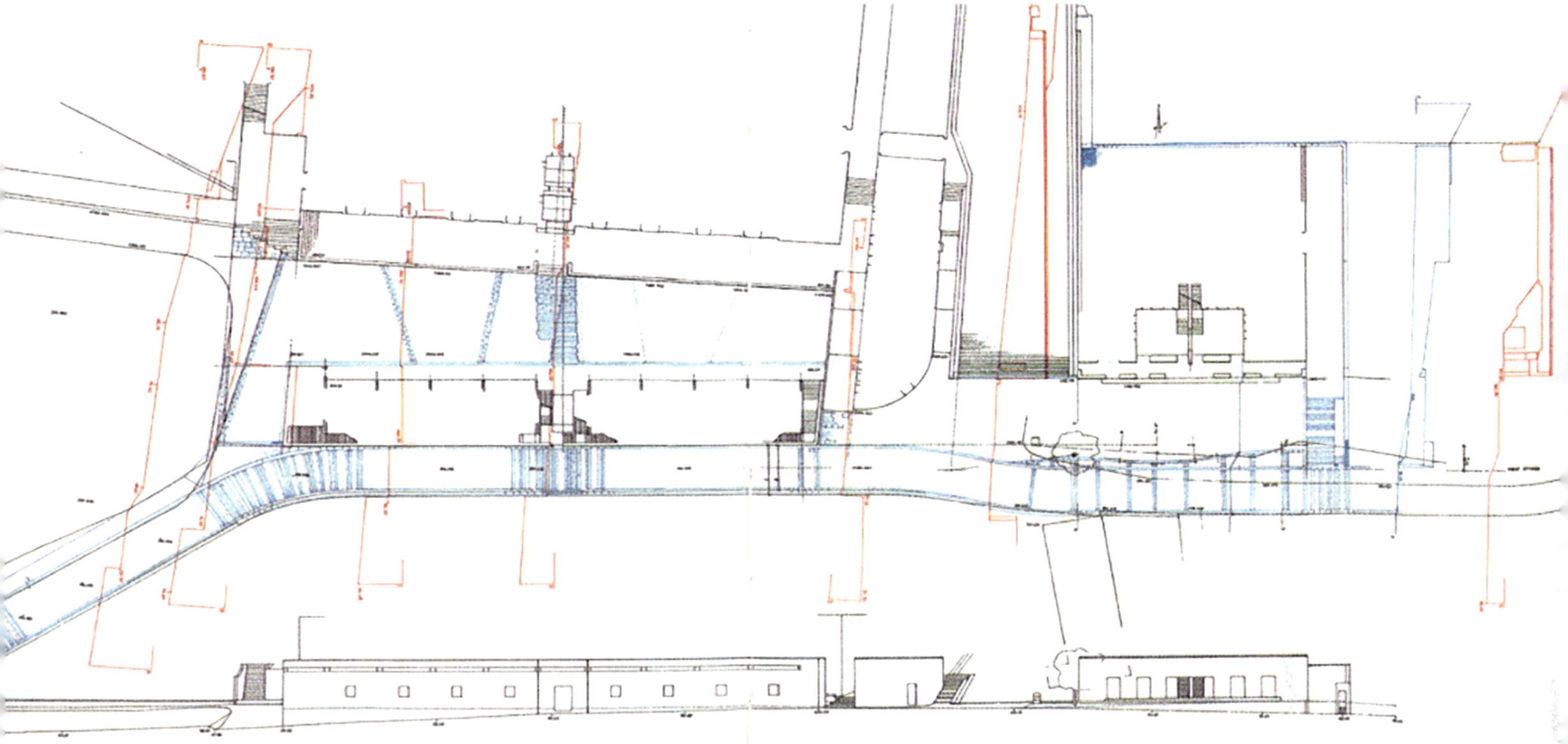

an almost exclusive problem of physical reconstruction and this involved not so much an investment for the construction of new infrastructure, public buildings and homes, as applications of an automatic model, a pure transfer of money without the production of wealth...' (From "Utopia di Gibellina," in Roberto Collovà, *Piccole figure che passano*, "22 publishing," Milan, 2012).

Int|AR: Recovery efforts were extremely slow and took more than a decade to materialize. Your project with Álvaro Siza to rebuild parts of the historic center of Salomi did not take place until the 1980s. What were the reasons for this lengthy delay of recovery efforts?

RC: Immediately after 68 concrete platforms were constructed almost exclusively to accommodate barracks for the earthquake victims. A great deal was demolished, much of it avoidable, in the emotion of the emergency, with the goal of a more consistent reconstruction.

'... .The earthquake of 1968 in the Valley of Belìce left ruined a poor but often erudite architecture. With reconstruction, each city gave rise to three cities: the ancient city, at times only in ruins; the shantytown, cement terraces for the installation of prefabricated houses; the new town, built often with an urban model

TOP
Plan, Case di Stefano, Gibellina

BOTTOM
Temporary housing after the earthquake, from the exhibition *Belice '80*

unsuitable for responding to specific issues and to the complexity of the issues posed by the disaster. The completely destroyed ancient cities had been abandoned. When the destruction was partial it was rebuilt over or next to them. In the shantytown, over time, wood and plates have been replaced or supplemented by new masonry walls; footings and tanks have improved their functioning with protection against the climate; the individual vegetation began to merge and take on an urban consistency; the slums became resistant and stable for decades, integrated by poor signage and street furniture. Self-organizational processes, developed in the shantytown from the 70s to present day, have created forms of resistance to urban systems and certain essential public and domestic qualities of real places, creating a strong identity. (from "Utopia di Gibellina," in *Piccole figure che passano*, Roberto Collovà, 22 publishing, Milan, 2012).

Álvaro Siza and I were in charge of the restoration project for the Mother Church of Salemi in 1982, after the Belice '80 Workshops, organized by the initiative of Pierluigi Nicolin and a bunch of us young architects who taught at the Faculty of Architecture in Palermo.

In the 12 years that elapsed between the earthquake (1968) and the workshops (1980), the mother church that had not collapsed but was badly damaged was demolished for the sake of public safety; no one thought that it could be put back safely.

Int|AR: The severe damage to the historic 17th century Chiesa Madre in the Piazza Alicia destroyed its ability to function as a church. It however presented an opportunity for a reuse of the site for a new purpose. The work is twofold; the visible design interventions are often structural and purposefully minimal, with a distinct architectural vocabulary, while the invisible ones change the urban plan and historic use of Piazza Alicia and the Chiesa Madre.

RC: I would say there are structural interventions both invisible and visible. The construction was very poor, in spite of its erudite architecture; the mortar of the walls was pulverized and the interventions consisted of preventive repair of the external stone walls in 'stone sacks' with the technique of 'stitch and unstitch' ; the wall was later injected with cement mortar after having been reinforced with steel bars inserted in a quincunx every 60 cm. Even the operations on the ruins are visible and structural. The walls had been cut at different heights according to their shape, and the top of the wall was completed by a band of white limestone blocks, trapped on sheets of lead to protect the cut; final forms showed the anatomical features of the construction, accentuated by interior stucco, now exterior, to reinforce the trans-

TOP
Plan of Piazza Alicia and the Mother Church, Salemi
BOTTOM
Mother Church after the earthquake, Salemi

formation of the church into a public open space. Other visible changes within the internal perimeter of the church are sustained by the continuous use of material from the pavement that is of the same white limestone, 'bush-hammered' in part from the old town square and cut by a wire 'saw.'

Int|AR: How do the two types of interventions relate to each other? What role do the new materials (steel struts, new paving) play in the new use? Are there any lessons here for seismic interventions to other surrounding buildings for future prevention?

RC: We made a thorough survey of thresholds, stairs, ramps, parapets, cornices, balconies, plates ... by making very precise typological indications for all these minute elements, adapting historical typologies and devising new ones in reference to new requirements as, for example, in making the ground floor of the houses by the steep streets accessible for car parking. The solutions studied are recurring and thus applicable throughout the rest of the historic center, as from a manual. With regard to prevention in relation to seismic events, we did not experiment, not so much due to the lack of technological solutions, as to resistant regulations.

To reduce risks and to limit the damages, it sufficed that the stone and wood constructions were made to the 'rule of art.' Many of the collapses in Salemi were due to damage from poor construction often associated with the improper use of reinforced concrete that produces mixed structural systems with inconsistent levels of stiffness; the ability to adapt was diminished and the fragility grew in relation to earthquakes, of course within certain limits.

Int|AR: As an outdoor plaza/monument how does your design intervention change the historic center with its important position at the top of the hillside and in juxtaposition with the Castello? How does this change in the urban plan impact the future growth and development of the town itself?

RC: This project has given the city a modern square and at the same time it has regenerated the old piazza, profiting from the phenomenon of the catastrophic earthquake, like a transforming energy for the future. It has made some new open and semi-public spaces available for leisure and cultural activities as well as for meeting places.

We have done our job. It is now for the Administration to profit from these new possibilities that, in fact, have radically changed the structure and image of the city, without betraying its identity. Now it's just a matter of initiative and organization. By now at Salemi and

Piazza Alicia, the new urban space from the ruins of the Mother Church, Salemi

Gibellina there is even a special tourism from architects and students coming from schools of architecture in Europe and other places, typically, Swiss and German.

Int|AR: While the city has continued to thrive for 45 years since the earthquake, many neighborhoods of Salemi remain ruined as in 1968. The Carmine neighborhood is one such area with many condemned, roofless structures of half walls. Your project with Marcella Aprile and Francesco Venezia, Il Teatro all'aperto del Carmine, is set amongst these ruins. Built on the old footprint of the Carmine convent, the concept of a community garden and an outdoor theater is a healing one. The serene nature of the architecture supports such a program with the backdrop of the valley beyond. However, this poetic space with its amazing views of the Belìce region stands vacant, strangled by weeds. What stands in the way of recovery for these areas? How do these damaged areas affect the life of the city itself as it evolves?

RC: I am sorry to continually return to issues of management and politics, but this is the real problem. Unfortunately, each Administration tends to ignore the actions and achievements of the previous. This irresponsible distraction influences the citizens, becomes a true delegitimizing of works that causes them to be unused, scorned, and indirectly reduced to ruin. A self-destructive form of extremely expensive administrative discontinuity. The Sgarbi administration in Salemi not only ignored the value of the new works (mother church, squares and streets, open-air theater, the Cascio draft plan of the subdivision behind the church, designed in detail by us but unfulfilled, historic centre of U. Riva) but tended to characterize them as a caricature in the eyes of the citizens, urging a form of vulgarity through somewhat picturesque uses. Once a Secretary of the Sgarbi party said to me with respect to the Teatro del Carmine:' This work is interesting, pity we don't know what to do with it ... 'I answered: '...make it a theater... just prepare a program, very economically created by the students and teachers of schools ...' Some time after they waterproofed the central part of the theater, forming a 60 cm deep tub filled with red wine. Dancers in bathing suits went in and out of this pool at a wine tasting. I went to the tasting and I met Sgarbi who was very polite and complimentary: I told him I was very satisfied, if the theater worked well for that scene, then it would work for any other representa-

LEFT
View from the town looking up towards Piazza Alicia

RIGHT
The ruins of the Mother Church as a new urban space

tion, it was truly a theater, it could continue. But nothing happened.

A weak point of the theater is its isolation; before the project was executed we drafted a masterplan of the Carmine neighborhood, in which the theater is just the first of the interventions. The theater is among the ruins in the area because you cannot rebuild homes for geological reasons. Therefore, the plan assumed, as a guiding concept, the recovery and conversion of each portion of ruins as a typological urban transformation of the neighborhood of Carmine in the park, with the use of the ruins of destroyed houses and estates like an open quarry of naked architectural elements. The lack of realization of the other interventions of the plan is, together with the absence of a program, the main reason for abandonment and decay.

Int|AR: Your photographs exhibited this past summer at the Museo d'arte contemporanea "Ludovico Corrao" in Gibellina (***Belìce '80***) portray Gibellina, new and old, as it remakes itself after the earthquake. The images capture a spirit of silent endurance and, at times, resignation. What are your thoughts today in looking at these images, so many years after you captured those moments?

RC: During these months I have been working on a new report on the Belìce, after more than 30 years since those black-and-white photographs, with the idea of putting the two stories together. It's hard work, a lot has changed for better or for worse. The countryside has irrevocably changed and, as a result, the new report will produce a different landscape.

For example, in the 80s travel on the highways that were rarely used was like moving in a low flight over the territory, the highway almost disappeared and one perceived a poor but essential country, with isolated farms-like the Case di Stefano; one saw small homes and *pagghiari*, the agricultural warehouses consisting of only one very small room. Now, along the highways, huge eucalyptus trees impede the view of that countryside now, consolidated in memory, and compel one's attention of the stretch as a blind corridor.

Int|AR: In *Il Gattopardo* (The Leopard), Tomasi di Lampedusa's famed novel of Sicily in the Risorgimento, Tancredi, the last in a line of nobility, says, "Se vogliamo che tutto rimanga come è, bisogna che tutto cambi." (If we want everything to remain as is, everything must change.) Sicily has

TOP
Interventions behind the Mother Church, Salemi

BOTTOM
Plan at the pergola adjacent to the Mother Church, Salemi

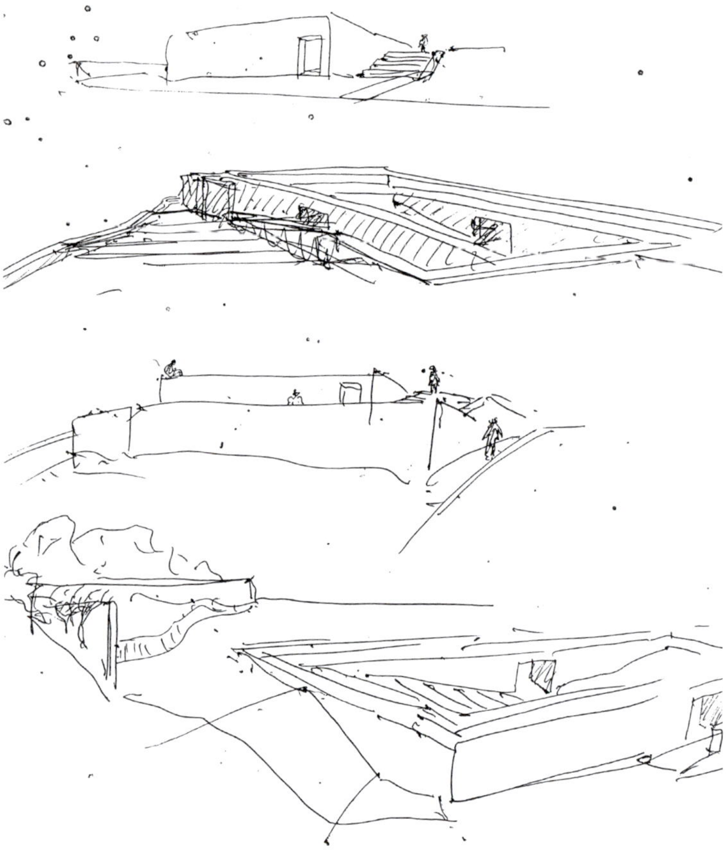

changed dramatically in the last decade with development of the coastal towns for tourism – for example, the arrival of Prada on one of the remote Egadi islands. Is this necessary for Sicily to remain as it is?

RC: I imagine you refer to the island of Levanzo, a delightful place where I go on vacation once or twice a year. Prada has solely aquired a beautiful and large house in the centre of Cala Dogana and il Baglio, property of the Florio family, on the plateau above the village. I don't think there is any intention of producing one of their boutiques on the island, as it would be the end of one's holidays with friends. However, this recent event could solicit some interesting reflections on the life of the inhabitants of Levanzo, on the tourists that frequent the place, though almost exclusively in July and August, on the economy of the island, but also on some likely curious denials of tardy, progressive ideas of history in the globalized post-modern world. The economy provided by new visitors seems certainly stronger than that of the approximately 226 inhabitants of the island, two- thirds of whom, on the other hand, winter in Trapani. The prospect, in its anachronism, could be of great interest ... say ... ecologically: the fish are not wanting, it is possible that the inhabitants are pushed to dedicate themselves to an essential production and even more refined fare instead of importing almost everything from Trapani including bread, vegetables and fruits, as they do now, waiting to sell everything at a higher price to tourists for two months of the year. It is possible that they will plant fruit orchards and engage in organic farming and then everything remains as it is; indeed, one can conserve development while improving the environment. Would this hypothesis be a fascinating form of resilience? But the new buyers, for their part, seem to want to use the 40 hectares of land around il Baglio to plant a large vineyard, just as the Florios had done. And it is presumably that, in addition to vineyards, there will be vegetable gardens and orchards and maybe even olive trees. And one can't exclude the possibility that this production would immediately have a brand.

Then Levanzo could transform itself into a kind of medieval castle, a little kingdom, where the inhabitants, like those of the villages at the foot of the Castle, will have to orient their attitudes towards the needs of the new rulers and return to being farmers and fishermen, but in service? Would this less fascinating hypothesis be a form of resilience?

TOP
Sketches of open-air theater, Salemi

BOTTOM
Open-air theater, Carmine neighborhood, Salemi

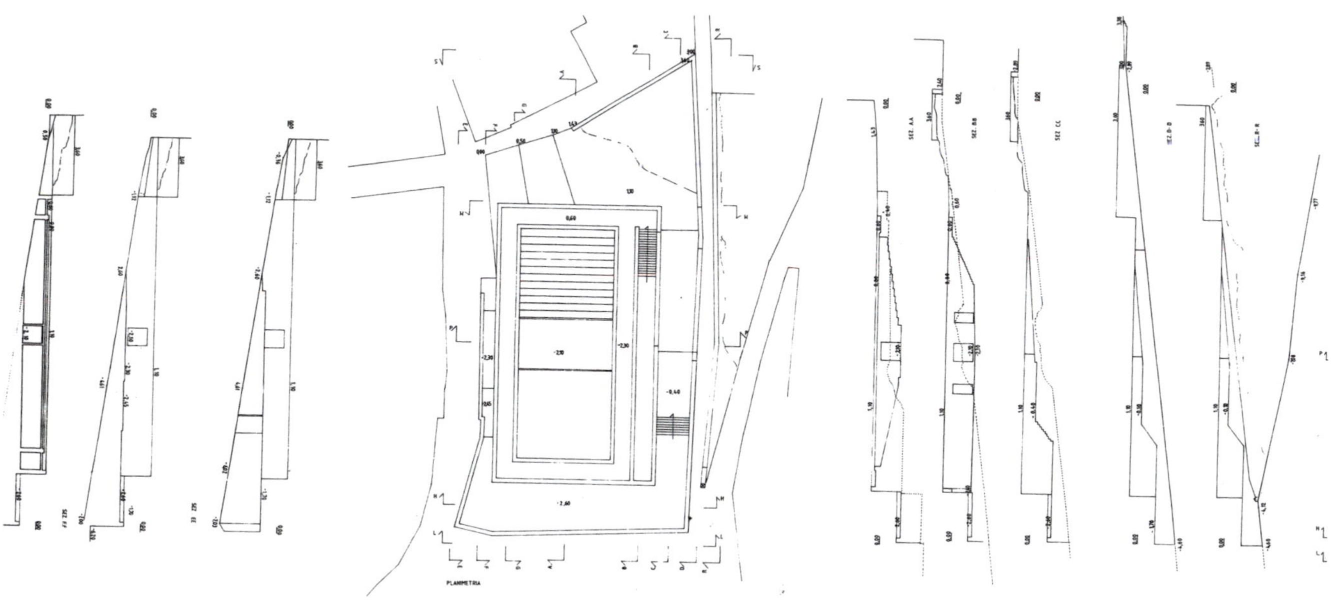

TOP

View looking through open-air theater, Salemi

BOTTOM

Sections through open-air theater, Salemi

Roberto Collovà is an Italian architect whose expansive body of work includes urban design, landscape design, furniture and photography. He is the author of *Piccole figure che passano*. He also writes for different journals in Italy and elsewhere. He has taught at the Facoltà di Architettura di Palermo and at the Academia di Architettura of Mendrisio in Switzerland as well as in institutions that include Barcelona, Lisbon, Las Palmas, Venice.

His work was exhibited at the Venice Biennale and the Milan Triennale. His many awards include the Premio IN_ARCH for Design, the Premio Gubbio for architecture in historic centers, finalist in the Mies van der Rohe Award in 1990, finalist in the Italian Architectural Gold Medal Award 2003, winner of the Competition internazionale Diagonal, Barcellona 1989, winner of the Competition *Una via, tre piazza*, Gela 1993, winner of the Competition for the Masterplan at S. Cesarea Terme, 2007.

He was on the jury for the Mies van der Rohe Award 2005, BSI Swiss Architectural Award 2008 and for the Young Architects Program MAXXI / MoMa Ps 2011–2013. He lives and works in Palermo, Sicily.

The Belice region after the earthquake, from the exhibition *Belice '80*

EQUITY

With roots based in economy, the practice of adaptive reuse has evolved over the centuries from notions of thrift to those of craft. In the millennium, it is a social practice that is reliant on the inherent wealth in the context of built environments laden with architectural, historical, political and environmental treasures. What of those places and peoples of other environments? Who benefits from adaptive reuse? Does it hold a universal value? If spatial justice exists, can adaptive reuse be a means to achieving it or redressing the inequity of the past?

176 **Tactical Urbanism Where It Matters: Small-Scale Interventions in Underserved Communities [Volume 09]**
Sally Harrison

184 **Luanda's New Frontier: The Peri-Urban Growth in Angola [Volume 03]**
Célia Macedo

192 **Empowering Actions: The Participatory Renovation of a Shelter [Volume 09]**
Cristian Campagnaro and Nicolò Di Prima

Play Lancaster is a project of Public Workshop that teaches local youth design-build skills and gathers community volunteers to construct street-front play space on a struggling commercial corridor

TACTICAL URBANISM WHERE IT MATTERS

SMALL-SCALE INTERVENTIONS IN UNDERSERVED COMMUNITIES

by SALLY HARRISON

Tactical Urbanism and the Creative Class

In 2005 a collaborative of artists and designers paid for two hours at a parking meter and installed turf, chairs and a potted tree. Inspired by stealth interventions of artists like Banksy and the Situationists, the parking space installation by the San Francisco group Rebar posed a critique of cultural values embedded in the use of urban space.[1] The idea of natural and human elements invading a space designated for car storage, and visitors finding a pleasurable respite in a parking space, became iconic. Images went viral.

Two years later, this spatial détournement had become an international event: Park(ing) Day became an opportunity for young designers to express their creativity and assert the right to claim public space, if only for an afternoon. Rebar's instant global success is often cited as the beginning of the movement now called "tactical urbanism."[2] Employing small-scale, short term interventions to return vibrancy to city life and "seed structural environmental change," tactical urbanism tapped into the estrangement of the common citizen from having a role in shaping cities.[3] Though various iterations have retained a seriousness of intent with a view to addressing critical, environmental and

social issues, the once subversive Park(ing) Day is now an annual staple of celebratory, "fun urban design." As the leading edge of the tactical urbanist movement, Park(ing) Day has engendered a cascade of novel, engaging interventions made and enjoyed by members of the young creative class. Pop-up markets and beer gardens, chair-bombing, hand-made wayfinding tactics, downtown beaches and unsanctioned bikelanes are hallmarks of casual-chic tactical urbanism in cities worldwide – a brand in itself.

Begun as spontaneous, community-generated activism, tactical urbanism – with the tag line "lighter, quicker, cheaper," or "LQC" in the parlance of the Project for Public Places – has been popularized in various media and exhibited in prestigious venues, guaranteeing mainstream acceptance. [4] Almost as quickly, tactical urbanism has attracted city leaders and the development community, seeking opportunities to promote gentrifying neighborhoods with an allure of hipness. Installations become nothing more than a marketing tool, stealthily reversing the grass-roots ethos of the movement. [5] A favorite of young urbanites is the much replicated pop-up-beer-garden-in-vacant-lot. Vaguely reminiscent of a suburban backyard barbecue with its picnic tables, kegs and Adirondack chairs, the beer garden tactic has been seized by the development community to promote so-called emerging neighborhoods by creating a familiar, nonthreatening scene – a strategy for attracting young, white gentrifiers into poor, strategically located neighborhoods where they might otherwise feel uncomfortable living, and for the unwitting neighbors, a kind of pacification through lot clean-up.[6] Sadly, these techniques have been remarkably successful.

Informality and Urban Space

Urban tactics have been around as long as there have been cities: the street vendor, the sidewalk lounger, the child at play, the graffiti artist, the squatter, the guerrilla gardener – all have taken their corner of the city and appropriated it for individual or collective use.[7] Historically urban tactics have been open to all. Those without privilege survive through creative inventions and have utilized the city opportunistically: finding unclaimed space, using available materials, bending the rules to accommodate needs unmet by the powerful entities that plan and organize their environment. Without self-celebration these urban tacticians operate in what de Certeau calls the drifts and ellipses of the urban order – by-passing or overwriting with lived experience the formal strategies of the top-down city.[8] While tactical urbanism has deep roots in age-old

Designed and built by PhilaNOMA (Philadelphia Chapter of the National Organization of Minority Architects), this seasonal installation extends the library's literacy mission into the neighborhood

informal practices of urban dwellers, its contemporary iteration can be traced to mid-century resistance against modernist planning and bureaucracy – articulated at length by Lefebvre, Rudofsky, Alexander, Jacobs, Team Ten and others. Van Eyck of Team Ten decried postwar redevelopment as "mile upon mile of organized nowhere, and nobody feeling he is 'somebody living somewhere.' No microbes left – yet each citizen a disinfected pawn on a chessboard, but no chessmen – hence no challenge, no duel, no dialogue. ... Architects have left no cracks and crevices this time. They expelled all sense of place. Fearful as they are of the wrong occasion, the unpremeditated event, the spontaneous act…" [9]

The call to human-centered design provoked study of everyday spatial practices. These were undertaken in non-western contexts such as Rudolfsky's 1964–65 groundbreaking exhibition at MoMA and subsequent book, *Architecture Without Architects*, but also in the epicenter of corporate power, by William Whyte in his famous New York City plaza studies. Partly due to his accessible language and non-threatening tone, and partly to the rigor of his observational methods, Whyte's contributions have helped to popularize an understanding of urban dynamics. His observations astutely (though often hilariously dated) point out simple truths about informal, spontaneous use of highly formal space: access to food, movable seating and "triangulation." It is not surprising that Whyte has become the godfather of the current tactical urbanism/placemaking movement.[10]

Though Whyte's work is important, it is apolitical. He opens his film "The Social Life of Small Urban Spaces" with scenes of street life in Harlem (circa 1969), but it is a sentimental depiction of otherness, with "no challenge, no duel" that would address the larger inequities of urban space.

Tactical Urbanism for Whom? Stories from Two Sides of the Same River[11]

Tactical urbanism and placemaking projects have chiefly concerned themselves with activating underutilized space in almost-healthy, well-served environments.[12] Indeed, prerequisite conditions are cited in the *Project for Public Spaces* website: "Once components like accessibility, safety, and overall comfort have been addressed, it may be the right moment to think about some LQC strategies." [13] That excess of caution certainly contradicts the movement's stated desire to seed structural environmental change; it precludes those places that may most urgently need well-designed catalytic interventions – in underserved urban neighborhoods accessibility, safety and overall comfort are among the chief issues that undermine active social spaces that build community. Add to this high household poverty levels and inadequate public funding and the result is that lighter, quicker and cheaper is most often the only option. In view of this, a discussion about a new iteration of tactical urbanism in places where it really matters is important and timely.

Despite being known for its recovery from postindustrial depopulation through the ascendancy of its creative class, Philadelphia has another narrative. Its 26 percent poverty rate exceeds that of the 10 largest cities in the US, and directly across the river Camden, New Jersey, is the poorest city in the country. Citizens of both Philadelphia and Camden suffer deep unemployment, a predominance of single-parent households with high numbers of children, low educational attainment and poor health. Consistently, residents report the isolating impact of drug culture and criminal activity and the erosive effects that the concentration of vacant lots have in their neighborhoods.[14] These are not conditions in which small, temporary acts of design intervention can easily ignite significant change. Nevertheless, design centered in a deep understanding of place provides a more hopeful perspective. Even – and especially – in these most profoundly underserved neighborhoods there are patterns of citizen action that are creative and pragmatic spatial responses both to need and to opportunity; here, as in impoverished neighborhoods around the world, in Cathy Lang Ho's words, "what we call tactical urbanism is simply a way of life." [15] Designers with a commitment to broader social impact might find ways to collaborate with communities who know their own landscape, and together develop urban tactics to tap veins of unrealized possibility.

How can a new version of tactical urbanism be employed to advance a social justice agenda and reclaim democratizing effects of the movement? How, outside the centers and contested gentrifying periphery, can small-scale design interventions address the multi-layered quality-of-life issues born of poverty and public underinvestment? What must be added to the "spontaneous" act of intervention to make sure that it knowingly engages larger spatial, socio-economic and temporal contexts? Who participates, and how do designers, who are mostly outsiders, operate?

Play, Tactics in the Interstices

On Lancaster Avenue, a struggling commercial corridor in West Philadelphia, play is a vehicle for social and physical health. Play Lancaster, led by the design collaborative Public Workshop, teaches youth within the local neighborhood skills in building and designing urban space. Eschewing the guerilla-designer-as-Robin-Hood role, Public Workshop draws enthusiasts and skeptics alike into a collective ethos of placemaking. The group has an established collaborative history with the local CDC that has been at work on revitalization strategies for the Avenue, and Public Workshop has demonstrated long-term commitment to the neighborhood and evolution of the project by co-inhabiting a storefront near the play site.

The neighborhood-generated idea for Play Lancaster began with an empty lot that called out to be a playground. However, the 80' by 100' lot on the Avenue defied the security principles of natural surveillance: no surprise that it was soon revealed as a nighttime drug hangout. Undeterred, Public Workshop and its young crew first enclosed the deep back of the lot with a decorative fence and lockable gate, reducing the play area to a ten-foot band along the Avenue. Not exactly expelling the intermittent drug users, the enclosed off-street space was gradually colonized by youth activities, becoming a seasonal workshop for future community design-build projects.

The street-front play scape is owned by the neighborhood. Fun and informal, this strip merges with the public space of Lancaster Avenue. Public Workshop furnished it with a community chalkboard, a platform with table for eating and relaxing, a "switchback play bench," a mini-fort and simple exercise equipment. Counter to the traditional design of playgrounds as unique bounded areas, the play space spills out on to the street for hopscotch and other pavement games. It operates in the spirit of Christopher Alexander's observation, "Play takes place in the interstices of adult life. As they play children become full of their surroundings..."[16] Indeed, the sidewalk is where city kids, instinctive tacticians, have always played – out in the carnival of street life, but also under the watchful eye of parents and neighbors.

Understanding the ecosystem of the neighborhood, Public Workshop saw the potential for this tactical intervention to both thrive and to have a critical impact at a larger scale. Despite the lot's reputation as a tough corner, it is directly adjacent to a popular deli; across the street are a daycare and after-school center, and around the corner a charter school, all filled with kids who gravitate to the site.

The founder of Public Workshop says he wants to "rewire the community engagement process" by making it tangible, visible and animated by the creative energy of youth. While at work on Lancaster Avenue, the crew drew wide participation from diverse members of the community: some helped build, some set up chessboards, some gave advice. Some were part of the very drug culture whose space the project had appropriated, but as is common, many were related to participants and became invaluable as guardians of the site.[17]

Test Before You Invest: Reimagining the Public Realm in Camden

Nowhere are the challenges to the public realm as evident as, Camden, New Jersey, the poorest city in

Street games are age-old urban tactics. Children engage and re-create the world on their own terms but "in the interstices of the adult world"

the country. Directly across the Delaware River from Philadelphia, Camden claims distinction as an active port city as well the home of an important university and hospital, but these assets cannot compensate for the depth of its poverty. The crisis of identity, of truly belonging neither to Philadelphia nor New Jersey, is painfully clear in its active recreational waterfront whose public spaces and amenities unapologetically turn their backs on the city. By contrast, in the experimental interventions within Roosevelt Plaza Park at the heart of Camden, democratic access to public space is the driver. The two-acre park replaced a demolished parking garage, but was only a wind-swept walk-through with few amenities that could build community and civic identity. Led by a public-private partnership and designed by landscape architects and planners Sikora Wells Appel and Group Melvin Design, the seasonal installation is ambitious and innovative in terms of design, program and research. Its tactics serve the placemaking principle of "test before you invest" famously used in the Times Square project, but now in a very different context: Roosevelt Plaza Park is bordered by City Hall, a large methadone clinic, a Rutgers academic building and small-scale commercial uses. [18]

Over three years of iterative placemaking – designing, building, studying, revising– the designers have been able to experiment freely with low-cost, high-impact interventions, and observe how they engage the public. Sourced from the nearby port, Intermediate Bulk Containers (IBCs) are stacked to form towers as the centerpiece of the plaza where jazz concerts and other public events are held. Off to the side is the Grove, a node with movable tables and chairs and brightly colored umbrellas interspersed with plantings. It serves as the "social room" of the site where the exceptionally diverse population in the area comes to lunch and hangs out with friends – city workers, outpatients from the methadone clinic, Rutgers students, neighborhood children. Here the social-bonding agent is a simple upright piano where people from every walk of life love to perform. This small but compelling intervention creates what William Whyte has famously called "triangulation," an urban event stimulating complete strangers to interact as if they know one another. [19]

The park is a work in progress. During the first year the IBC towers supported canopies, and the towers were lit from within to create a nighttime spectacle. Motion sensors changed the light color from cool to warm as people passed. In the second year the same cubes were reinstalled as vertical planters topped with rainwater-capturing saucers. These green towers and a rain curtain set the stage for a lively, interactive teaching demonstration about the water-based environmental problems facing Camden. And in the third year the green towers were reinstalled and concerts expanded; health was introduced as a theme, with new food stands, play space, and exercise programming.

During each six-month installation the park was documented using time-lapse photography, video interviews, ground observations and postcard surveys. This documentation identified and mapped how the park was used and by whom, what worked and did not – methods straight from William Whyte. New ideas surfaced – more music events, more family-centered space, a playground, food carts, and, interestingly, an often-voiced concern over the excessive presence of "police" (potentially the uniformed park "ambassadors").[20] An overwhelming sense of satisfaction and pride infuses feedback from visitors. Says one: "Camden has been neglected for so long...and to have somebody just care enough to give this – it's the smallest thing but the biggest thing."[21] This is a poignant remark, at once validating the project's success and revealing a flaw. Perhaps the intensity of surveillance for research and safety has had the unintended consequence of distancing placemaking from the users. For all its generosity and focus on activity, the park is "given," rather than co-created with this hugely underserved community.

Night guardians. With broad support and engagement of the community, the playground is informally protected by older siblings of the primary users

The interviewee's gratitude shimmers with awareness of endemic powerlessness, a recognition that others choose the agenda to serve the interests of the populace.

Rules of Engagement: Context, Commitment, and Collaboration

These very different cases speak to how a tactical urbanism might be used to advance social justice goals in underserved communities. However well-meant or cleverly conceived, designer-generated tactical urbanism applied in struggling neighborhoods is challenging; we cannot simply draw on the now-predictable social-space tropes to transform quality of life. While the ethic of unfettered pro-active intervention tempts designers to decide what is in the interest of the common good, in order to carry social impact, a design intervention – even one quite small – should evolve from a deep recognition of how the neighborhood works.

Thoughtful designers do have much to offer. Trained as we are in multi-scale research, representation, and making, we can help a community to create a

Light towers. The stacked IBC cubes from a local shipyard are the building blocks of the site, their verticality organizing the large open plaza. Lit from within, they provide changing ambience at night

simultaneous reading of larger systems and locally practiced tactics, suggesting how and where intervention would be most effective. We understand that the tactical project itself cannot be a no-risk proposition. However much it may be lighter, quicker and cheaper, it is a commitment of some significance. It must be well designed because what is temporary often becomes permanent.

A commitment to continued involvement further distinguishes these cases from the typical tactical urbanism project. Whereas in healthy environments, simply "seeding" might reasonably yield new and sustainable growth, in underserved communities the rough terrain presents significant obstacles to survival and continuity. At Roosevelt Park, it has taken years of vigorous programming, evaluation, redesign and reprogramming for patterns of human-centered civic expression to take root. Notwithstanding the disconcerting excess of oversight, the annual experiments in placemaking in this once bereft plaza have succeeded. And though the "LQC" tactics employed by the designers were meant to minimize risk for future capital expense, it may be that the vibrancy of change is the most valuable contribution to the long-term identity of the place.

Play Lancaster has also undergone constant change since its inception. Less about a fully-formed future vision than about a process that takes full advantage of trial and error, it has become a space that learns and teaches. Intentionally educative, the program challenges its young builders to balance the discipline of making with the porosity of creative thought. Inviting collaboration from all corners of the neighborhood, it also challenges the community to commit to its children. The seeming paradox of play, front and center in the public realm, literally spilling out on the sidewalk of a shopping corridor, tells us something important about what our society should value. Is this not what tactical urbanism is meant to do?

NOTES

1 Blaine Merker, "Taking Place: Rebar's absurd tactics in generous urbanism," in *Insurgent Public Space: Guerrilla Urbanism and the Remaking of Contemporary Cities*, ed. Jeffrey Hou (New York: Routledge, 2010): 42–51.

2 Mike Lydon and Anthony Garcia, *Tactical Urbanism 2: Short Term Action, Long Term Change* (Washington: Island Press, 2012), and Susan Silberberg, "Places in the Making, How Placemaking Builds Places and Communities", https://dusp.mit.edu/sites/dusp.mit.edu/files/attachments/project/mit-dusp-places-in-the-making.pdf. MIT Department of Urban Studies and Planning, Accessed May 12, 2016.

3 Merker, 49.

4 Three high-profile exhibits were mounted between 2008 and 2013: *Actions: What You Can Do with the City* (Canadian Centre for Architecture); *Uneven Growth: Tactical Urbanisms for Expanding Megacities* (Museum of Modern Art) and *Spontaneous Interventions: design actions for the common good* (American Pavilion at the Venice Architecture Biennale).

5 Oli Mould, "Tactical Urbanism: The New Vernacular of the Creative City," *Geography Compass 8.8* (2014): 529–539.

See also: Gordon Douglas, "The formalities of informal improvement: technical and scholarly knowledge at work in do-it-yourself urban design," *Journal of Urbanism: International Research on Placemaking and Urban Sustainability* (2015): 1–18.

Gordon Douglas, "Do-it-yourself Urban Design in the Help Yourself City," in *Architecture Magazine: Spontaneous Interventions,* (August, 2012): 44.

6 Damon C. Williams, "Gentrification dispute revived," *Philadelphia Tribune*, February 20, 2016, http://www.phillytrib.com/news/gentrification-dispute-revived/article_e3d6f076-6878-5e92-9cb5-d3d94a3cfa8b.html. Accessed 3 June 2016.

7 See John Chase, et al., *Everyday Urbanism*, (New York: Monacelli Press, 1999), and Ananya Roy and Nezzar AlSayyad, *Urban Informality: Transnation Perspectives from the Middle East, Latin America and South Asia*, (Oxford: Latham Press, 2004).

8 Michel de Certeau, "Spatial Practices: Walking in the City," in *Michel de Certeau*, trans. Steven F. Rendell (Berkeley: University of California Press, 1988), 91–110.

9 Aldo Van Eyck, "The Role of the Architect," in *Team 10 Primer*, ed. Alison Smithson (Cambridge, MA: MIT Press, 1968), 44.

10 William Whyte, *The Social Life of Small Urban Spaces* (New York: The Conservation Foundation, 1980). I use placemaking and tactical urbanism as co-related terms that both refer to iterative processes that support human-centered use of public space. Generally, the spatial tactic is a (smaller) tool for (larger) placemaking.

11 Portions of the case studies of "Play Lancaster" and Roosevelt Plaza Park have been published in my article "Innovation: Tactical Urbanism in Underserved Communities," in *Context, the Journal of AIA Philadelphia* (Spring 2016).

12 Notable exceptions are Corona Plaza in Queens, NY; the Detroit Alleys Project; the Rebuild Foundation in St. Louis; the Village of Arts and Humanities in Philadelphia.

13 "The Lighter, Cheaper, Quicker Transformation of Public Spaces," *Project for Public Places*, http://www.pps.org/reference/lighter-quicker-cheaper/ Accessed 2 June, 2016.

14 Nila Luiz et al., "Quality of Life Plan," unpublished report by Asociacion Peurtorriquenos en Marcha, 2010.

15 Cathy Ho, "Spontaneous Interventions: Design Actions for the Common Good," in *Architecture Magazine: Spontaneous Interventions* (August, 2012): 24.

16 Christopher Alexander, "A City Is Not a Tree," in *Architectural Design*, 206 (1966): 12.

17 Alex Giliam, Personal interview, January 22, 2016.

18 Lydon and Garcia, 36.

19 Whyte, 94–101.

20 Joseph Sikora, Personal Interview, Feb. 3, 2016.

21 Sikora Wells Appel and Melvin Group Design, Unpublished report, "Activating Roosevelt Plaza Park, Placemaking in Camden's Public Spaces," 2015.

LUANDA'S NEW FRONTIER

THE PERI-URBAN GROWTH IN ANGOLA

by CÉLIA MACEDO

Angola currently faces an almost impossible mission of healing its territory and people from the wounds left behind by nearly three decades of violent conflict. Since peace was first installed in 2002, Angola and its entire population has been under the world's gaze, a fact that has highlighted the many issues and obstacles facing this sub-Saharan country. In order to address such challenges a general reconstruction strategy, which particularly emphasizes the need to mitigate the lack of housing and related social problems, has been put in place. Understanding and rehabilitating the country's built environment, particularly within urban areas, represents a paramount but much needed task to rebuild Angola as a whole. The complexity of this task is further enhanced by the many difficulties currently affecting the poorer fringe of the population—those who have been failing to sustainably accompany the emerging economic development of Angola.

As far as the evolution of the urban built environment is concerned, Angola's background does not differ significantly from that of other former colonies in sub-Saharan Africa. Whilst under a colonial rule which endured for roughly five centuries, Angola was subject to a profound reinterpretation of the essence of its built environment, regardless of the country's established architectural traditions. New concepts of space, mainly influenced by acclaimed European models, were gradually introduced all over the country but especially in urban areas. Entire cities were thus designed and built from scratch, composed of massive buildings framed by large avenues and orthogonally organized streets, as opposed to the earlier confusing arrangement of apparently fragile settlements. Over the years, these thriving cities became points of attraction to many thousands of people arriving from Europe as well as from different parts of Angola, generally seeking a better life. The demographic patterns, mainly characterized by rural-urban movements, were further enhanced during civil war, subsequent to the independence from Portugal in 1975. This caused further densification in the existing urban fabric and the physical expansion of Angola's major cities until exhaustion. Today Angola is a country of deep social inequalities, where one of the most expensive cities in the world is built side by side with endless sprawl of informal occupation and extreme poverty. With urban development not showing signs of stabilizing, the issues associated with lack of housing and urban poverty are a difficult reality for many. In a time when sustainable development is a global issue, the question of how Angola will be able to mitigate the acute housing shortage arises as one in urgent need of an answer.

AAA

Peri-urban Growth in Angola, the Example of Luanda

The capital of Angola—Luanda—embodies the typical example of the demographic patterns and urban development described above. Following its creation in the mid-16th century, up until the mid-20th century, Luanda was characterized by a reduced resident population and low economic activity. As described by Amaral (1983), the environment of 19th century Luanda was one of a city well adapted to its context, displaying a morphological and functional balance with its surroundings. The built environment was mostly composed of an array of adobe and wattle-and-daub houses, often built side by side with Baroque churches.

The explosive growth of Luanda would only take place after the Second World War to then gain further momentum with the industrialization of Angola. In subsequent years the growing development of Luanda would sustain a continuous rising trend, thus contributing to the redefinition of the city's identity. The cityscape of Luanda quickly revealed all the signs of a common western modern city where high-rise buildings, concrete, steel, and glazing emerged to play the principal role.

This prosperous period, however, also had its shortcomings. One of the obvious consequences of the growing prosperity was the rapid increase of the inhabitant population. Despite lack of current census data, this rising trend was registered until the last general population census carried out in Angola in 1970, where Luanda's resident population increased dramatically from 50,588 in 1930 to 475,328 people in 1970 (Amaral,1983). Today, although numbers are solely based on estimates, Luanda's population already reached approximately 3.2 million. This results in a high demand for housing, services and infrastructure.

As Fonte (2007) explains, during the colonial period of Angola, architecture and urbanism generally reflected the policies in place at the time, a fact that clearly influenced the early planning and laying out of Luanda. The city revealed distinct layers or types of occupation, in which location and morphology of buildings were fundamental variables. Given that these were mostly determined by occupants' social status, one could find, for example, the planned area made by Europeans for Europeans to occupy, other planned areas of the city occupied by a mixed-race population, and finally the indigenous *bairros*, planned by Europeans but to be occupied by the indigenous population.

Most of the unqualified work force of Luanda, however, was sourced from one area that was not contemplated in urban plans: the informal *bairros* surrounding the main city. These areas, also designated as *musseques*, housed those who either could not afford, or were not considered sufficiently civilized, to inhabit any of the planned areas of the "cement city."

The existence of areas of informal huts scattered throughout the outskirts of Luanda dates back to its origins, and their physical expansion has been developing in parallel with the growth of the city, up until the present date. The massive growth of peri-urban Luanda is mainly attributed to continuous fluxes of rural-urban internal migrations or displacements of African population; nevertheless, over the years the musseques also provided shelter for poor populations with different origins and backgrounds. This meant that having a weak economic condition became the main feature of the musseques' resident population, rather than a racial one.

A 19th century view of Luanda

Building and Inhabiting the Musseques: Adapting to a Life of Uncertainty

The built environment in the musseques has developed under unique circumstances. Up until the 19th century the outskirts of Luanda were mostly used as agricultural land. However, as the city expanded, clusters of settlements developed in stages to accommodate the various waves of migrants seeking a better life in Luanda. With respect to the nature of the dwellings, unlike the main city, in which European concepts of architectural and urban space were gradually introduced, construction activities in the musseques during the 20th century tended to be associated with absence of planning and infrastructure and, therefore, with self-building activities. These were areas frequently described as dense labyrinths of wattle-and-daub huts which spontaneously occupied any piece of land available. Moreover, given the diverse ethnic backgrounds of its inhabitants, the buildings frequently resembled traditional rural dwellings found elsewhere in Angola.

The proximity to the cement city, coupled with a later influx of a poor Portuguese population, eventually provided the perfect environment for the metamorphosis of the musseques' fabric. This assimilation of European architectural features extended not only to the building form of the dwellings but also to the building materials and technologies adopted. As illustrated in Redinha (1964) and Thyssen's (1966) studies of the Angolan indigenous house, the single-room circular plan house, for example, was abandoned in favour of the multiple room rectangular house, and the façades began to incorporate more windows than previously. Overall, the building envelope was altered into something that accommodated elements of both modern and indigenous forms of construction. Therefore, despite the growing use of materials such as metal sheets or asbestos for the roofs; concrete blocks, fired bricks or timber for the walls, and cement for the floor, one could still find references to indigenous construction in the musseques. This view is further supported by the data provided by the 1970s census which reveal that the majority of houses in the musseques had wattle-and-daub walls (Monteiro,1973).

The complicity between the main city and its spatial surroundings where the musseques developed was, and still is, a major decision factor in choosing the building technology for one's dwelling. As Trindade (2000) remarks, at times it was difficult to distinguish accurately where the city ended and the musseque started. The constant swelling of the city limits put extra pressure on the musseques' population, who reacted to the authorities' claim of land for urban development by moving and rapidly building shelter elsewhere, usually further away from the city. In this respect, Monteiro (1973) concludes that the preference for certain construction techniques and building materials in the musseques would depend on various aspects, namely cost, availability and flexibility of use. Further to this, the temporary or permanent occupation, as well as the dynamic social structure of the household—which repeatedly required additions and/or modifications to the core structure of the building—would also define the type of dwelling to be constructed. This could, for example, make the difference between using stone, cement blocks (permanent materials) or earth and timber (temporary and/or demountable structures).

The uncertainty with regard to the ownership of land, combined with the precarious nature of the dwellings, lack of infrastructures and urban management, meant that the musseques have always been very susceptible to disasters. Fires, floods, landslides and other naturally occurring disasters frequently wiped out considerable areas of houses. For this reason, the design and implementation of a rehabilitation strategy of such areas is currently considered to be an absolute priority, as shall be explained in due course.

Life in the Musseques Today: Building a Sustainable Future for the Musseques and its Inhabitants

According to the UN-HABITAT more than 80% of Angola's population lives in slum areas, many of those based in the peripheries of Luanda. Moreover, the capital has grown to more than four times the second-largest city in Angola, and estimates indicate that it accounts for about a quarter of the country's total population (UN-HABITAT, 2010). The poor conditions experienced in the musseques today have not undergone dramatic improvements over the last years. In fact, apart from the few musseques existing inside the actual city, which did not have further room to grow, the settlements in the periphery continue to expand outwards, increasing the distance between the city and the musseques. In addition to the spreading out of existing areas, new musseques were even created after the independence. This is the case with the musseque Rocha Pinto which, as stated in Trindade (2000), has a population of roughly 900,000 people and, due to the distance to the city, has achieved near self-sufficiency by incorporating basic services within its limits.

Since the colonial period, efforts have been made towards finding the most adequate solution to tackle both the acute housing shortage as well as the problems resulting from the almost total lack of infrastructure in the musseques. Nevertheless, according to Amaral (1968), these urban planning experiments were not always very successful, since they often failed to consider natural and human environments. An example provided by the same author was the inadequacy of the buildings' design to people's cultural context, ignoring for example the importance of the outside space to cook or socialize. Furthermore, many of the buildings were structurally unsound and formed monotonous streets where landscape was scarce. As a result, valuable lessons were learnt regarding the need to have an in-depth knowledge, of both the site and the inhabitants, in potential upgrading programmes. Spaces where communities can thrive and live harmoniously, where family life can evolve and be respected, creation of a diversity of spaces and houses which can be flexible and adaptable enough to accommodate different needs in different periods of people's lives, were aspects recommended as primary for any successful urban intervention in the musseques.

Currently, probably more than ever, there seems to exist an agreement on the urgency of providing the Angolan population with the right to housing and a decent quality of life. In 2004, extreme poverty was acknowledged by the government as a serious issue in Angola, as can be found in the document "Strategy for Combating Poverty" (República de Angola, 2004). Herein, the reduction of poverty and improvement of people's quality of life is set as a goal to achieve in the near future, which necessarily entails action at the level of the building sector. Thus, the government hopes to improve the overall conditions of the musseques and degraded buildings of urban areas, mainly through urban requalification programmes. Such programmes would range from providing infrastructures to existing degraded areas, to designing and building whole new parts of the city. The latter would include construction of social housing to accommodate and relocate the poorest fringe of population—particularly the homeless and displaced. In line with this target, in 2008, the government launched the National Urbanism and Housing Programme, with a very ambitious goal of building one million houses before the end of 2012, of which 115,000 will be provided by the government, 120,000 by the private sector, 80,000 by cooperatives and 685,000 will be constructed through self-help building activities.

The programme is still ongoing and, therefore, the amount of information available remains rather scarce. Nevertheless, questions have been raised regarding how the one million houses goal is being pursued and, especially, as to its effectiveness amongst the poor population of the informal settlements. International organizations such as Amnesty International have reported that, in order to clear land for the construction of new housing developments, continuous evictions of thousands of families have been taking place in the periphery of Angolan cities. Furthermore, as Amnesty International adds, this has been done without any

Wide availability of prefabricated building materials in the musseques

'prior notification, information or consultation, legal protection, adequate alternative accommodation or an effective remedy' (Amnesty International, 2008, p.1) which, in the view of the organization, constitutes a clear violation of human rights. In order to highlight such issues, during the celebrations of the World Habitat Day in 2008, which took place in Luanda, Amnesty International directed an open letter to the Executive Director of the UN-HABITAT, condemning the choice of Luanda as the location for the celebrations, arguing that it constituted an 'insult to the injury committed against Angola's thousand affected by forced evictions' (Amnesty International, 2008, p.3).

Nonetheless, the progress on the construction of houses since the launch of the National Urbanism and Housing Programme has been frequently reported as successful through local and international news agencies. Additionally, despite the accusations of forced evictions, the rehousing process of some of the people whose houses had been demolished between 2004 and 2006 is expected to start in September 2011, as recently announced by the government. The intention of eliminating the musseques entails, yet again, profound changes and adaptations from the

Kids playing in musseque Chicala

low-income population, who so many times throughout Angola's history had to readjust to new realities and paradigms, building new homes, livelihoods, social and economic structures from scratch. Reusing existing housing does not seem to be included in any plan or strategy, which rather prefer looking at more radical solutions, whereby eliminating the musseques is the main objective. However, while such plans do not come into practice, people have been developing creative solutions to adapt existing dwellings to meet constantly changing needs. A building in a restrained plot of land can easily change configuration to accommodate a growing family, create private areas to rent out, or incorporate a small business accessible through the elevation facing the road. Houses in the musseques thus grow organically, expand horizontally and/or vertically, usually according to people's financial means. This dynamics has been possible partially thanks to the wide availability of prefabricated building materials such as cement blocks or metal sheet roofing, which have clearly outgrown traditional building practices in popularity and appear to be the way forward when it comes to informal settlements in Luanda.

The Constitutional Law of Angola's article 85 states that 'every citizen has the right to appropriate housing and to a decent quality of life.' It carries on by declaring that the state has the responsibility to 'promote the social and economic conditions to ensure the right to housing and quality of life' (Assembleia Nacional—Comissão Constitucional, 2010). Although, apparently, the country is heading towards this direction, it is clear that there is still much work to be carried out, in order to sustainably mitigate the housing shortages in Angola. In this respect, the way that built environment is conceptualized may indeed play a significant role in assisting the poor population to achieve a better quality of life. The familiarity with self-help building of the informal settlements seems to have been picked up and is now being utilised as an important tool of the National Housing Programme. Self-building kits have been made available for the low-income population, who, according to the government, will also be able to benefit from special financial schemes to buy or rent houses. As stated above, the programme is still ongoing; however, according to recent statements that consider the possibility of surpassing the goal of one million houses, the country's reconstruction process mentioned in the beginning of this paper appears to be taking place in Angola. One will have to wait until 2012 to determine the immediate success as well as the sustainability of the programme. More importantly, it is fundamental to assess its effects in areas such as the musseques, where the most pressing issues exist.

In 1983, we were reminded by Amaral (1983) that the research focused on the evolution of the musseques' environment is very scarce. He further adds that the urban periphery is an incredibly complex reality and, therefore, any intervention or proposed upgrading programme necessarily requires the action of studies, which should be conducted by a multidisciplinary team, given the different nature of the many issues inherent to the periphery of Luanda (economic, social, technical, juridical, financial, etc). Regrettably, this situation has not changed over the last years and the musseques still lack thorough studies and research.

Considering all the aforementioned, if on the one hand it is a reality that the musseques are lacking even the most basic infrastructures and are therefore in urgent need of an intervention; on the other hand one has to wonder whether a radical solution based on demolishing the existing to rebuild according to western models is the most adequate one for this particular context. The flexibility and adaptability which characterizes these informal settlements, despite reflecting a sustainable practice, are also often regarded as a sign of insecurity. For this reason, it is likely that people are open to embrace a new style of living which will necessarily include a new approach towards the built environment.

A deep understanding of the social characteristics of these informal settlements as well as of their social, economic and environmental contexts may prove to be a fundamental tool to orient towards a sustainability agenda of any future policy or upgrading plan for the informal peri-urban settlements in Luanda.

REFERENCES

Amaral, I. (1968). *Luanda: (estudo de geografia urbana)*. Lisboa: Ministério do Ultramar.

Amaral, I. (1983). Luanda e os seus "muccques" problemas da geografia urbana. Finisterra – *Centro de Estudos Geográficos Portugal XVIII* (36), pp.293–325.

Amnesty International (2008). Joint letter for Executive Director of UN-HABIAT. London: Amnesty International International Secretariat. Available at: http://www.amnesty.org

Assembleia Nacional Comissão Constitucional (2010). Constituição da República de Angola – Projecto Final. Luanda: Assembleia Nacional Comissão Constitucional.

Fonte, M. M. (2007). *Unpublished PhD thesis – Urbanismo e arquitectura em Angola – de Norton de Matos à Revolução. Faculdade de Arquitectura*. Lisbon: Universidade Técnica de Lisboa.

Monteiro, R. L. (1973). *A família nos musseques de Luanda: subsídios para o seu estudo*. Luanda, Fundo de Acção Social no Trabalho em Angola.

Redinha, J. (1964). A *habitação tradicional angolana; aspectos da sua evolução*. Luanda: Centro de Informação e Turismo de Angola.

República de Angola (2004). Estratégia de combate à pobreza – *Reinserção Social, Reabilitação e Reconstrução e Estabilização Económica*. Luanda: Ministério do Planeamento Direcção de Estudos e Planeamento.

Thissen, L. (1966). *A habitação entre alguns povos do médio-Cuango (Angola)*. Luanda: Instituto de Investigacão Científica de Angola.

Trindade, A. J. P. (2000). *O fenómeno urbano na Africa subsahariana: o caso de Luanda*. Lisboa: Instituto Superior de Ciências Sociais e Políticas.

UN-HABITAT (2003). *Slums of the world: the face of urban poverty in the new millennium?* Nairobi, Kenya, United Nations Human Settlements Programme (UN-HABITAT).

UN-HABITAT & UNEP (2010). *The state of African cities 2010 governance, inequality and urban land markets*. Nairobi: UN-HABITAT.

Eliminating the musseques entails profound changes for the low-income population

EMPOWERING ACTIONS

THE PARTICIPATORY RENOVATION OF A SHELTER

by CRISTIAN CAMPAGNARO AND NICOLÒ DI PRIMA

Action and Spatiality

What does it mean to act within a space? And acting on a space with the clear intent of transforming it? We should firstly consider that not only subjects act on spaces but, in turn, spaces act on those subjects that traverse and inhabit them. "The meaning of a space lies in its effect on any objects that come into contact with it and which, while trying to alter the space, end up being transformed themselves." [1] As semiologist Gianfranco Marrone states, spaces and subjects share an indissolubly reciprocal relationship: space-object connection is always characterized by a need for narrative, meaning that – on the connotation level – both the space and the object may function alternatively as subject and object.[2] Thus, a space, far from being static and unchangeable, must in fact be considered an actor, able to control the behaviour of any objects that interact with it. When considering a space, we must think of it not merely as a physical entity, but also – and above all – as a conveyor of meaning. Understanding a space means "rediscovering the human intervention behind the objects of the world that has in fact given them sense." [3] In other words, the sense of a place is not given unequivocally (though it may be foreseen and planned) but rather it is continually ascribed by the very subject or subjects inhabiting it; furthermore, it can also change over time. We can therefore affirm that not only does a subject produce (both physically and semantically) the space– and the physical objects that constitute it – but also that spaces produce subjects.

In our everyday lives, this process occurs silently and imperceptibly. Referring to Goffman's frames theory,[4] anthropologist Daniel Miller states that "material objects are a setting. They make us aware of what is

The 1st floor hall after the collaborative renovation process

appropriate and inappropriate [...] They work most effectively when we don't actually look at them." [5] He defines this property as the humility of things: their silent presence produces a normalising (and normative) effect on the context. In this consists the very subjectivising power of the space. Simply by staying in place, its constituting objects produce in individuals a sense of familiarity with their surroundings, a sense of habitual normality which helps the living being to define, decipher and recognise the environment around them.

This mechanism is generally reassuring and reduces cognitive overload; it produces that feeling of "home" which allows individuals to inhabit a space "naturally," somewhere they can carry out their activities without feeling continuously out of place. Since the physical stability of a space is directly linked to the stability of its connotation, the "humility of things" also suggests that places function the more static and unchangeable they are.

But when the connotation ascribed to a space by an individual is unclear or not shared, he feels out of his element, uncomfortable in his surroundings. He feels excluded from the context, immobilised or perhaps he even has a desire to escape. In these cases, the "humble" immobility of spaces partly inhibits the idea of acting on a space, in order to transform and align it more with the connotation desired by the individual or the community inhabiting it. This means that the individual ends up suffering in the space around him.

The humility of objects (and, we could add, of places) is therefore concurrently reassuring – in regard to our more habitual daily activities – and inhibiting, compared to more transformative actions.

The Shelter: a Space with No Action

This theoretical introduction will help us interpret the case study we present herein, referring to a particular type of space in which the freedom of its inhabitants' actions (daily and transformative) is particularly inhibited.

Since 2009 our interdisciplinary research-group, composed of designers from Polytechnic of Turin and anthropologists from University of Turin, works in the field of homelessness in several Italian cities.[6] The research reflects on the power of places to define the wellness of people that inhabit them and looks at the way in which spaces and objects interact with the stories of users and with the educational actions of social workers.[7]

From the very beginning, the research aimed at interlinking analysis with concrete actions that could have tangible effects on the spaces for the guests and those working therein as social workers, therefore establishing itself as an action research.

Concrete actions are, in fact, a useful analytical tool in reaching more in-depth understanding of the institutional policies and mechanisms that regulate housing systems as well as stimulating immediate improvement within the contexts of study. They are also a way of understanding if and how such contexts and their inhabitants are able to take on board, or even sustain, the transformations generated by the interventions.

On the conceptual level shelters seem to correspond with those that Michel Foucault defines as heterotopias.[8] The shelter is a heterotopic space; though in appearance it resolves the issue of someone who has lost a home (due to economic, health and/or migratory issues), at the same time it contributes to labeling him as deviant. The function of the shelter in our society is strongly influenced by the fact that the housing crisis is interpreted as deviant but also as an emergency, leading welfare institutions to think (and hope) that the situation may be as temporary as possible.

Access to these structures is not based on the desire of individuals but is regulated by our welfare system, through strict institutional procedures. Those inhabiting these places are, in a certain sense, banned.[9] The shelter is, therefore, an "other space," one that enjoys a marginal (and often marginalising) relationship with the "normality" into which it is inserted, thus generating extreme physical and psychological suffering among inhabitants. They are places which, despite having a specific raison d'être (to accommodate those in difficulty), produce an inflexion that may prove destabilising for inhabitants: "I'm here (because I have no other choice), but I wish not to be here." Inhabited only by 'guests,' these are places that generate a sense of perennial exclusion and permanent temporariness.[10] These factors greatly inhibit the individuals' freedom of action within the space, not only how they use it but – even more so – in that they cannot make even the slightest alteration to their environment.

The space of the shelter, furthermore, produces exclusion, marginality and a sense of temporariness not only due to its functional systems (rules, curfews, and rights of access) but also through its physical characteristics. Buildings that host shelters are rarely designed for that function. Generally speaking, they are buildings constructed for specific purposes (schools, offices, factories) which, once their original function ceases, are temporarily transformed into housing. In other cases, due to the presumed temporariness and state of emergency of the service, basic prefabs are used. Furthermore, on the topographic level, buildings that are identified for this use tend to be found in the suburbs of cities and/or in so-called social districts which often are already populated by low-income or poor inhabitants and by a high percentage of immigrant residents. Finally, these buildings are often in a state of almost-complete abandonment and manifest rather serious structural problems and yet, despite this, they are used for housing purposes.

In these cases, reuse would appear to be counterproductive, as renovations can prove extremely costly (due to the evident structural incompatibility between the old and new functions) but also because, given the urgency, rarely are the renovations completed before the inhabitants move in. Often, in fact, renovations are carried out when the service has already started and further complications inevitably arise.

Finally, there is also the risk that effective renovation works cannot be fully completed either because the (council or state-owned) building is protected by architectural regulations aimed at preserving the historical authenticity thereof, or because they are not considered to be a sufficiently profitable investment for the (non-state) organisation granted the contract for the short-term housing service and commissioned to manage the premises. Additionally, we cannot ignore the effect that this option has on public expenditure in terms of added costs. Management of a service supplied in places that are inefficient, from the perspective of the provision of welfare services, implies an extraordinary consumption of personal and material resources that could otherwise be avoided.

All these aspects basically allude to the fact that any chance of modifying and renovating these spaces is, though vital, in no way aided.

Action as a Relationship

Based on the theoretical scenario briefly introduced in the first part of the article (which looks in-depth at the functioning of reciprocity in the space-subject connection) and the empirical observation of housing carried out by the Turin research group (of which we have highlighted some elements of analysis emerging from both the semantic and physical-spatial level), we can understand how the transformative processes may appear simultaneously delicate and complicated.

In order to better understand these processes, we hereby present the case study of a collaborative project to renovate a Milanese shelter in which our research

The making of one of the benches that will be installed in Via Mambretti 33, during the workshop goBENCHING, attended also by a group of design students from the Polytechnic of Turin

Some of the corridors at the end of the collaborative renovation process, with a co-constructed bench in foreground

group has been involved for over two years now. In December 2013, the Council of Milan granted Fondazione Progetto ARCA Onlus a 20-year lease without charge of the former school building in Via Mambretti 33. Immediately, the building housed more than 250 people, including homeless adults and asylum seekers. The lease included all systems to be updated, and the structure to be renovated and furnished for housing purposes. Located in the Quarto Oggiaro district, the building was constructed in the early 1900s and stands out for its neo-Classical style typical of early-20th century public buildings in Italy. The structure extends over three floors, each of around 1,200 m^2 and its unusual "C" shape gives it a courtyard of around 760 m^2. Its façades have, by now, completely eroded. The marble entrance hall contains a majestic central double stairway. Each floor contains a number of spacious, well-illuminated rooms opening onto straight, naturally lit corridors which have since been set up as bedrooms for its current function. It is an enormous and imposing

building whose initial magnificence only emphasizes today's decline, partly the natural effect of the decades that have passed since it was built, but also due to a more gradual decay.

In order to transform the former school into housing, in 2015 the foundation commissioned our research group to scientifically supervise the overall development of the renovations project. The project was called "Cantiere Mambretti."[11]
As with the other experiments carried out by our group in other Italian cities, the idea was that any renovation work was to be undertaken in close collaboration with and including the building's inhabitants (both beneficiaries and providers of the service) in all procedures, from selection and planning all the way through to execution.

We used the need to transform the spaces as a chance to activate the occupants. The collaborative approach emerged from the idea that, in order to be effective and recognised by the inhabitants themselves, the planning or re-planning of housing should involve them directly. The interventions undertaken, therefore, do not merely aim towards the realisation of the same but rather to encourage the users to act, taking on board the aspirations, needs and abilities of each individual. From consultation to co-planning to the co-production of the service, the project has involved the expertise of current and future inhabitants – guests, social operators, Foundation managers and, in future, the inhabitants of the district – in designing suitable forms of housing and the effective processes and tools for putting them into practice.

Preparations were characterised by the use of some qualitative research tools, such as ethnography, in-depth interviews, semi-structured interviews, focus groups, "guided" tours of some of the Foundation's housing and a comparative analysis thereof. During this phase, we surveyed the living and working needs of the various people affected by the project and also their knowledge and skills, so that the final project may utilise the practical and theoretical contribution of all and be subscribed to and recognised by as many of the group as possible. This analysis brought us to the strategies for renovating the spaces, mitigating as many living and working difficulties as possible which increasingly distinguish the very intent of the project.

The objectives of the collaborative activities are:

- To re-interpret: re-read and re-configure the spaces of the structure, best utilising the building's most characteristic structural features, while in line with whatever constraints have been placed on its transformation. Experimentations consisted in reinforcing the communal areas aimed at socialising and daily activities.

- To equip: furnish the spaces with equipment that is (both in quality and quantity) suitable for the functions assigned to them. Flexible seating systems, multiple mobile phone recharging points, way-finding systems and waste disposal systems of suitable capacity.

- To involve: experiment in cooperation with the operators and guests, utilising people's skills and aspirations, in order to promote care and attention to the spaces and equipment.

- To bring together: involve citizens in activities, promoting a non-stigmatised approach to and knowledge of the residents.

The Workshop as a Tool of Collective Action

Collaborative planning as a process includes moments of analysis and research and is characterised by scrupulous moments of observation and inspection. These are alternated with other briefer and more intense moments in which reflection and planning pave the way for on-site experimentation, inspection and collective action.

One of the most effective devices that action-research has used is the temporary workshop, an experience of union and reciprocity. As we have verified in this and previous case studies, the idea of transforming space struggles to be consistent with the ordinary time of daily life. Yet the context of workshop, thanks to its extraordinary nature, can enable this idea. According to this, workshops become extraordinary events in which the entire group of inhabitants is ideally and practically invited to participate in the transformation. They are events that create "spaces" of participation and collaborative reflection between all interested parties, generating a dimension of enthusiasm, curiosity and creativity.

The workshop itself is preceded by tangible planning proposals which are, in fact, elaborated by the research group interlinking the data acquired from the qualitative research (bottom-up) with the needs of the managing organisation (top-down). The technical designs and study models are discussed with the service operators and with the building's most permanent inhabitants, aimed at gradually refining the proposals. Once the project has been negotiated and defined, we pass on to the experimental dimension of the workshop, collectively and collaboratively undertaking the enterprise together with the beneficiaries of the service. In this context, we focus on the execution and preparatory techniques: quick, simple activities to involve all those who wish to participate, whether or not they have any experience of the theme in question; however, it should be clarified that this does not mean that the final result is of poor quality. Indeed, all the co-design and co-construction processes are strongly managed by designer and researcher from the point of view of outputs and outcomes.

The images of the workshop give the idea of how the execution of every project – from wall painting to production of benches – is the result of this rich and dynamic cooperation between designers and guests. It is a process of mutual learning in which sometimes guests learn from designers and conversely guests teach designers and other participants.

Action and Housing

The collaborative experience is still ongoing and has not been without risks. Firstly, we have witnessed how the occupants have to be continually stimulated to participate in discussing the themes in question. The very complexity of the place and the social relationships

A moment from the "ColorFULL Workshop": a series of workshops aimed at repainting common spaces of the building

that are generated therein slow the transformative process. One serious problem consists in the (real and perceived) temporariness that reverberates not only in the management and transformation of the spaces, but which also characterises the perspective of the individual in regard to the (again, real or perceived) permanence of stay in the shelter. The workshop is able to arouse curiosity and cooperation, but this tends to remain circumscribed within the workshop as a singular event.

With respect to the social workers, on the other hand, our challenge is keeping them focused on the management and transformation of the spaces. Burdened as they are by the arduous educational work that they are required to provide, they demonstrate a propensity to delegate to the research group for anything non-educational.

If it is so that this situation determines a modest decline in transformative effectiveness (in terms of time rather than quality), it must however be noted to what extent the collaborative transformation process increases its effectiveness: by understanding that concrete action immediately and perceptively influences the place in which they live, an individual's focus on elements that are of direct interest to him is catalysed and renewed regularly. And it is precisely this matter that we should use as a launch-pad to create moments of inclusion characterised by debate, discussion and a sharing of knowledge and to some way encourage direct action by the occupants themselves.

We have observed that reusing spaces for housing purposes poses some specific problems regarding the setup and effectiveness of transformative actions. But through this case study we have been able to verify that only through collaboration, invitation and the possibility to act is it also possible to give these spaces a certain sense of dignity, triggering new visions of change and progress in the daily temporariness of the functions carried out in these spaces.

We run the risk of not being able to significantly influence certain marginalising mechanisms of housing that trace back to the very policies on housing itself. These mechanisms prove fossilised, but it is only thanks to this collaborative method of action that we have been able to experience these mechanisms, understand them and experiment with new, more democratic and inclusive housing strategies. Moreover, the experience is not limited to the specific case in point. Within a "research through design" [12] perspective, action highlights some elements of focus which, when linked to many reports of similar experiences in other contexts, allows us to constantly return to discussing and updating the methods and aims of research on processes to humanise housing areas for the homeless and to promote a policy of this transformation that is both necessary and possible.

NOTES

1 Gianfranco Marrone, *Corpi sociali. Processi comunicativi e semiotica del testo* (Torino: Einaudi, 2001), 323. Translated by the authors.

2 Ibid.

3 Ibid., 320. Translated by the authors.

4 According to which "much of our behaviour is cued by expectations, determined by the frames which constitute the context of action." [Daniel Miller, *Stuff* (Cambridge, UK – Malden, USA: Polity Press, 2010), chap. 2.1, ePub.]

5 Miller, chap. 2.1.

6 The research "Living in the dorm" is managed by Professor Cristian Campagnaro (Department of Architecture and Design of Polytechnic of Turin) and anthropologist Valentina Porcellana (Department of Philosophy and Educational Sciences of University of Turin) within the cities of Torino, Verona, Agrigento and Milano, with the patronage of fio.PSD (Italian Federation of Organisations for Homeless people).

7 Cfr. Cristian Campagnaro, Valentina Porcellana, "Beauty, Participation and Inclusion," in *Art and Intercultural Dialogue. Comparative and International Education (A Diversity of Voices)* ed. Susana Gonçalves, Suzanne Majhanovich (Rotterdam: SensePublishers, 2016), 217–31.

8 Michel Foucault states that heterotopias are: "real places— places that do exist and that are formed in the very founding of society— which are something like counter-sites, a kind of effectively enacted utopia in which the real sites, all the other real sites that can be found within the culture, are simultaneously represented, contested, and inverted. Places of this kind are outside of all places, even though it may be possible to indicate their location in reality. [...]In the so-called primitive societies, there is a certain form of heterotopia that I would call crisis heterotopias, i.e., there are privileged or sacred or forbidden places, reserved for individuals who are, in relation to society and to the human environment in which they live, in a state of crisis [...] These heterotopias of crisis [in our society] are disappearing today and are being replaced, I believe, by what we might call heterotopias of deviation: those in which individuals whose behavior is deviant in relation to the required mean or norm are placed" (Michel Foucault, "Of Other Spaces," trans. Jay Miskowiec, *Diacritics* 16, No. 1 (Spring 1986): 22–27.

9 Agamben states that "what has been banned is delivered over to its own separateness and, at the same time, consigned to the mercy of the one who abandons it – at once excluded and included, removed and at the same time captured" [Giorgio Agamben, *Homo Sacer. Sovereign Power and Bare Life*, trans. Daniel Heller-Roazen (Stanford: Stanford University Press, 1998), 109–10].

10 See Mauro Van Aken, "Introduzione," in *Antropologia: Annuario* 5, No. 5 (Roma: Meltemi, 2005): 5–13.

11 "Cantiere" in English means "construction site".

12 See Wolfgang Jonas, "Design Research and Its Meaning to the Methodological Development of the Discipline", in *Design Research Now. Board of International Research in Design*, ed. Ralf Michel (Basel: Birkhäuser, 2007), 187–206.

IDENTITY

Political change, secularization, shifting demographics, economic advancements, technological innovations are developments that render existing structures outmoded and obsolete. Resurrection and reincarnation, the hallmarks of adaptive reuse in extending the lives of buildings, proffer new use as their means. Distinguishing characteristics of structures are often threatened, if not entirely obliterated, in the action of accommodating new purpose. Mirroring the search for personal identity in a fluid millennium, buildings, too, grapple with new identities in their adapted existence.

202 **Flying Tea Rooms: On Search for Identity in Saudi Arabia**
[Volume 03]
Caroline Jäger-Klein

212 **A Sacred Translation: Holy Trinity Church to Jesus Son of Mary Mosque**
[Volume 07]
Dennis Earle

218 **Figural Identity in Adaptive Reuse: Preserved, New, and Hybrid**
[Volume 07]
Marie S. A. Sorensen

224 **Looking from the Voids In-Between**
[Volume 10]
Géraldine Borio

234 **Learning from Old Xining: The Adaptation of Urban Form**
[Volume 03]
James Patterson-Waterston

Roashan, Historical Area of Jeddah

FLYING TEA ROOMS

ON SEARCH FOR IDENTITY IN SAUDI ARABIA

by CAROLINE JAEGER-KLEIN

All started with an invitation for an academic field trip to explore the vernacular architecture of Hedjaz and Asir, the Red Sea regions of the Arabic peninsula in 2008. Meanwhile, a multidisciplinary research project on documentation and analysis of domestic building traditions has been signed by representatives of the King Abdul Aziz University of Jeddah and the Vienna University of Technology under the patronage of the Minister of Higher Education of the Kingdom of Saudi Arabia. The intense working phase of the Austrian experts with their Saudi Arabian students began in October 2011 and will last for three years.[1] *The proclaimed result of this first working phase is to get sufficient information through survey and inventory of the building stock of the country. Hence the most intriguing aspects of the project will arise afterwards in avoiding the creation of inanimate museums and national monuments but proving the traditional building stock's potential for rehabilitation and adaptive reuse. Let me outline a first vision after a brief glimpse on three completely different sites, each separated by 700 kilometres and therefore based on dissimilar social, economic and ecological parameters.*

Old al-Ulah: Mud-cluster Town of Oriental-Antique Atrium Houses

Old al-Ulah, more than 300 kilometres north of Medinah, once an important caravan town on the trading route connecting Yemen with the Mediterranean shore, still represents itself as an organic mud-cluster with basic court-houses on two levels. Extreme temperatures of the surrounding arid desert dictated exterior and interior space qualities for centuries. Nevertheless, its population moved out completely half a generation ago when the government provided them with fine new houses, grander than the old ones, of course, with the latest sanitary standards and each accessible by car. Besides the general contentment about the amelioration of comfort, some sentimental comments from former inhabitants reached us on our visit in 2008. Mostly the loss of communicative qualities of public space was mentioned. Modern al-Ulah lacks the shadowed corners within the narrow alleys, originally connecting the private living quarters with the busy main road, where the caravans passed through and commercial life took place under perimeter street arcades. Exploring the site ourselves we quickly found out what the natives meant. The old lanes were narrow, close and meandering in order to shelter the grounds from direct sunlight. They were partially covered by apartments linking one side of the street with the other. The inhabitants name these structures "flying tearooms," thus further unwrapping their function. Especially the female members of a family sat up there, above the lane, invisibly controlling the social life of the neighbourhood. They noticed exactly who passed by or claimed entry into their private sphere, a design configured to serve basic issues of Islamic culture. The newer generation of private houses transferred the court-type on two levels but the urban context was forgotten. Therefore, social life and interaction between the families is recently somewhat reduced.

Due to the arid climate, the physical condition of the probably pre-Islamic site stayed more or less intact. Thanks to modest repair based on traditional craftsmen's knowledge, the place is still inhabitable. Obviously, modern comforts would have to be provided such as the supply of drinking water for each house, electricity and sewage systems. More difficult questions included the issue of the somewhat weak ceiling structures—traditional wickerwork between brittle palm trunks—hence the distinct feature of this specific architecture. Still applicable are the ground plans of the smaller and larger housing units, all composed around a well-proportioned, planted courtyard in the antique atrium tradition including a great open double-height niche for protected and unsheltered living outdoors. The major question nowadays is for whom to rehabilitate these buildings? Will the former inhabitants move back into their now technically improved houses if they already upgraded themselves with bigger modern houses? European experience in urban rehabilitation projects shows that, instead, a different social class is more likely willing to move in, depending on various factors. Either the creative, young avant-garde is attracted by the atmosphere of living as well as modest rates for housing, or the location is developed to a touristic place of interest. Al-Ulah shows great potential for the latter through a fantastic natural landscape of spectacular rock formations in its close surroundings, remains and remembrances of Thomas E. Lawrence's destruction of the Hedjaz railway during the First World War, and the close vicinity of Hegra (now Al-Hijr),[2] the second capital of the Nabatean empire after Petra, Jordan. Gentle tourism concepts have to be installed quickly by the already established Saudi Commission for Tourism and Antiquities (SCTA), banning destructive mass-tourism at its roots. Al-Ulah shows great potential for individual tourism, strengthening local services as well as local crafts. In May 2010, the first International Conference for Urban Heritage in the Islamic Countries stated useful recommendations for both optional developments—to force (private) "investment in heritage hotels" as well as "encourage reverse migration from crowded urban areas to heritage villages and towns with the necessity of providing sustainable incentives and finance tools and investment in infrastructure for this purpose."[3]

Historical Area of Jeddah: Multiple Storey Urban Palaces from Coral Stone and Lattice Work

Jeddah, the international pilgrimage port of the holy Islamic sites, had to react in its building tradition to far more humid conditions by wind-catching wooden bay-window structures (roashan) on multiple-storey buildings of fragile coral stone, which stem mainly from the 19th century. As el-Balad, this old domestic building structure in Mecca and Medinah, is already completely lost, there is an urgency to save and protect

the historic city center of Jeddah as the last trace of this great cultural epoch. A distinct feature of its urban fabric is the wooden lattice work, irregularly spreading over the northern and western façades where the cooling winds come from the sea. Every panel has its own dimension as well as its singular pattern carved out of teak wood, shaping unique scenery for every street section. Indonesian pilgrims brought the panels to pay for their hajj expenses, startling evidence of dislocated prefabrication within pre-modern building processes. Local building masters provided blank openings within the vertical wall of quarry stone. The bay-windows projecting into the street space were then completely configured after the conveniences of those most valuable wooden panels. Even the "floor" of the bay-window, situated on a height practical to sit on, was made of wood, so that the cooling air stream of the shaded alley reached the resting person within the lattice work. However, the sun-lit enclosure walls of the eastern and southern elevations are made of massive masonry without openings. Approximately every three feet slim horizontal beams of wood subdivide the masonry, helping to avoid cracks within the coral stone material. The quarry stone freshly cut from the sea still shrinks during the drying process. Additionally, the houses are based on rather weak foundation systems, causing spectacularly twisted structures. The use of that specific material might be tribute to a shortage of high-quality building material within the region. Nevertheless, the porous stone could very well provide surprising, yet undiscovered, physical features.

In general, the building plan wraps rooms around a middle staircase, thereby forming a stable core for the rather high raised structure as well as enabling efficient natural vertical ventilation. The bottle-neck effect of the window grating helps cool down the incoming air stream, which will warm up inside and finally leave the house using the staircase as chimney. For the hottest periods of the year roof terraces with an open pavilion of latticework help with sleep. The whole fabric manifests pure human intelligence enabling one to live in comfort, even luxury, despite an absolutely unfriendly climate. Recently their intriguing design concepts gained attention through some architects of the region. Dr. Adas, director of the department for developing and renovating buildings in the historic district, as well as Dr. Angawi, former collaborator of Frei Otto in Stuttgart, have both constructed their private residences in the suburbs of Jeddah after those traditional principles and adapted to up-to-date building technology and current lifestyles. Nevertheless Dr. Angawi's house is said to be the only modern building within the peninsula not addicted to energy-annihilating air-conditioning.

Dr. Adas is also fighting heroically for the preservation of Jeddah's urban heritage,[4] seriously threatened by fire through electrical short-circuit and condensing water dripping from air-conditioning units into the valuable woodwork. The disaster originated with the rental of old buildings to large numbers of Saudi and expatriate tenants without the capability to maintain them.[5] The functioning ventilation system is now blocked by new subdividing walls and additional ceilings, a shocking example of destructive intervention. A turn in that development could either be provoked by strict preservation orders or, what would be more sustainable, by changing the social structure of the neighborhood. Recent interventions to break the palace structures into smaller units would be superfluous if the old noble families, in most cases still the owners of the property, could, by a bundle of actions ranging from tax relief to creation of hip urban qualities, be convinced to move back themselves. Family structures within that segment of society would allow the restoration of the old, generous space within the houses. If this well-educated and proud clientele manages to match its search for identity with this fantastic precursor of the "urban loft," with its architectural and artistic features that form a homogeneous fabric, along with the paths, quads and souks still intact within the quarter, a living example of a genuine Arab Islamic city would be easily installed for the future. Hence it has to be made clear from the very beginning that hereditary urban qualities of the Arab town cannot be bought on the Western

Wickerwork, Old al-Ulah

TOP
Hedjaz railway, Old al-Ulah
BOTTOM
Court, Old al-Ulah

Roashan, historical area of Jeddah

market, but have to be courageously discovered, developed and autonomously experienced, throwing overboard current imported patterns of behavior.

Asir-farmhouses: Rural Palaces of Clay with Protecting Layers of Stone

Towards Yemen the highlands of Asir suffer under sudden heavy rainfall through monsoon clouds as well as under the ever present martial attitude of their tribal clans. Impressive farmhouses with freestanding watchtowers sprinkled in between determine the nearly inaccessible, rough landscape. Social anthropologists as well as the Saudi youth itself tend to emphasize the defensive character of that specific vernacular architecture.[6] However, our first impressions of those distinct rural palaces with their tamped clay layers striped through rows of overhanging stone plates strengthened the vision of a role model for regional sustainable building patterns. Meeting the first so-called old palace in Abha, we were immediately attracted by the modernity of the concept—stone plates to protect the mud walls from being washed away in heavy rainfalls as well as shading the surface of the building permanently during the heat of the days. A rather high, plain and sloped basement holds some sparse, lower hipped, miniscule openings—another strategy to keep out the hot air of the surrounding deserted exterior. Exploring the region the next days we saw that such is the typical building structure of the region, which is still very much in use, mostly in connection with modern extensions. The biggest problem by far seems to be the maintenance of the mud walls. Many farmers set a new "crown" of corrugated iron sheets on top of the walls to save the existing substance. The interiors offer an amazing richness of plasticity. Again the staircase forms the central element winding itself around the two-storey kitchen stove. Wooden window shutters and vertical slots within the tamped clay layers allow a charming albeit gloomy atmosphere together with the colored walls and ceilings resembling rich carpet patterns.

A propensity for decoration is present everywhere, yet completely without trumping the harmonious beauty of simplicity. The rare resources—bizarre pieces of juniper wood serve as lintels, slim plates of slate stone form the walls outside the mud-building areas— force a stunning truth of material, which could finally cure the region from its depravity of senseless luxury. As Asir is a major inland destination for tourism due to its modest climate it might meet those challenges successfully by alternative vacation concepts like "living temporarily within the rural heritage" or "adopt a farmhouse" campaigns.

As an educational side effect, the temporary urban users would quickly learn the message about sustainability and resource-saving building concepts from the vernacular heritage. The proclaimed goal of the Austrian researchers is to analyze and exploit exactly those features with the knowledge and expertise of our "passive-house" concepts, but transferred into opposite effects. Austrian vernacular architecture tried to "build with the sun" whereas Arab vernacular architecture tries to build "against the sun." How effective are the overlapping and overhanging stone plates for cooling the exterior of the house by shading the sun-heated façades during the day, especially in the fabric of a village where the farmhouses in the vicinity are not close

Urban fabric, historical area of Jeddah

enough to shade their neighbor? How long can the stone plates protect the mud walls from a downpour of rain? How can the heat of the day be stored sufficiently to warm the rooms during the cool desert nights? How much cross-ventilation do the vertical wall lots allow? Those are the major scientific questions of interest, not only concerning features of the urban and rural palaces of the Arab region but in a global context. They play an important role in finding clever future design strategies for energy saving, "blue" building concepts, as we are convinced, for example in reestablishing mud as ecologically beneficial building material within the region. Another step is simply to enhance the awareness of clients as well as architects that palaces of glass are not the right answer to the climate of the desert. The traditional massive house concepts of the region show already how to save heating or cooling energy.

Outlook

The potential of domestic building traditions within the west of Saudi Arabia cover a wide range of options for future architectural designs reusing existing structures and infrastructures. The concept of intervention and adaptive reuse, however, is not yet known at all within the region. To force its impact we recommend to our partner institutions two major strategies following models that we developed and practiced for some years with our academic program at the Vienna University of Technology. Public documentation of the regional building stock convinces its population of the value of the substance as another kind of historical memory. Parallel to those activities, university professors and their architecture students conduct politically and economically neutral consulting campaigns for the communities concerning their opportunities through preservation and maintenance of this heritage.

Of ultimate importance for the Arab region today is the ability to strengthen the current tendencies to find its own profile. Exploring the unique local building tradition and adapting it to future models will help it to avoid a trend of using "imported" architecture as well as unfitting Western urban patterns and scales. Therefore, our project should successfully contribute to a fresh regional identity created by new architecture in and out of the historical context. Our Arabic students, learning together with us the lessons of their own traditional architecture through the project, will hopefully be the future generation of architects to transform this knowledge into sustainable design strategies.

NOTES

1 The interdisciplinary team consists of the following researchers: Dr. Vittoria Capresi (Urban Analysis), Dr. Petra Gruber (Building Structure and Bionics), Dr. Ulrike Herbig (Photogrammetry and Recordings of Architecture), Prof. Caroline Jäger-Klein (History of Architecture), Prof. Erich Lehner (Architecture of non-Western traditions), DI. Irmengard Mayer (Building Research and 3D-Laserscanning), Prof. Hermann Mückler (Social Anthropology) and Arch. DI. Gudrun Styhler-Aydin (Building Research).

2 The Al-Hijr Archaeological Site (Madâin Sâlih) was the first Saudi Arabian site inscribed on the World Heritage List, in 2008. Compare UNESCO edited journal, *World Heritage* No. 60, June 2011, pp.54–59.

3 Recommendations of the first International Urban Heritage Conference held in Riyadh during the period from May 23–28, 2010, were published on http://www.scta.gov.sa/sites/english/news, dated on 5/30/2010 9:34 AM.

4 The latest *World Heritage Journal* No.60 from June 2011 reports on the historical area of Jeddah in its "Tentative Lists." See p.75f.

5 To illustrate by figures: "There are about 550 historical buildings in the district. ...During the last 25 years some 60 buildings have collapsed. The last two years have seen some 10 to 13 buildings in the district either collapsed or burned." *Arab News*, Tuesday, February 5, 2008, p.3 (kingdom).

6 See Alexander Sieghardsleitner, Traditionelle Bauformen im Westen Saudi Arabiens, Diploma thesis, Vienna University of Technology 2010, pp.95–101.

A SACRED TRANSLATION

HOLY TRINITY CHURCH TO JESUS SON OF MARY MOSQUE

by DENNIS EARLE

The role of art in the psychic and social functioning of spaces or places devoted to the sacred can be critical. Perhaps the primary role of material, non-ephemeral art in such spatial contexts is to provide a sign of identity, both of the space as the proper realm for the experience of the sacred, and of the identity of the tradition, culture, or community of belief using the space. A second role, distinguishable from, but interrelated with that of identification, is 'mediation,' wherein art modulates and generally creates conditions conducive to the particular kind of spiritual experience intended. Sacred art in sacred spaces often plays both roles, but understanding how or why it does so can reveal a great deal about visual culture, cultural space, and the sacred as it is conceived in various traditions. In this article, I examine a situation of the adaptive reuse of a sacred space for a similarly sacred function within a larger context of inter-cultural conflict. But as the new use supports a different spiritual and cultural tradition, it brought into pointed dialogue quite different approaches to, and readings of, sacred art in sacred spaces.

The project involves the translation of a sacred space with one particular cultural and religious identity– a German-American Roman Catholic church–into one that could embody and support quite another such identity, an Islamic-American one. The story of this translation involves an encounter between two very different notions of the role of art in sacred space or in the sacred in general – an encounter that reflects, but also illuminates, the nature of a much larger conflict unfolding across our society and the wider world between (one strand of) a substantially Judeo-Christian culture and Islam. The implications of this wider conflict have created a unique context for the transformation sought by the Muslim community – the 'client' for the design of the Masjid Isa Ibn Mariam (the Mosque of Jesus Son of Mary) at the site of the former Holy Trinity Church at 501 Park Street, in Syracuse, New York. The project began as an undergraduate interior design studio assignment at Syracuse University's School of Design in January of 2014, and it provided the opportunity for relevant research and exploration of issues and solutions, with substantial community input, before design actually began. I created the new design, which is still being implemented, in the summer of 2014.

The story of this transformation began with the closing, decommissioning, and sale of the church building to a local non-profit community development organization, which in turn leased the building on a long-term basis to an Islamic community group for use as a place of worship. The non-profit, according to its mission, had been devoting an ever-larger portion of its work to serve the struggling immigrant community on the north side of the city that has in recent years become predominantly Muslim. At 501 Park Street, societal trend lines crossed: attendance at the city's Catholic churches has been declining for several years as Islam became the city's, and the nation's, fastest growing faith. Many members of the local community around upper Park Street grew up with the church as an active neighborhood institution

Prayer hall, Masjid Isa Ibn Mariam, Syracuse, NY

and symbol of faith, community, and heritage. More than a few mourned and even complained about its closure and, with the sale and lease of the building, real anger became apparent at the prospect of turning over the building to a Muslim immigrant community. At one point in the process of preparing for renovation, it became necessary to hold a neighborhood meeting, sponsored, mediated, and staffed with security personnel by the city, to air complaints, quell rumors, and promote tolerance and understanding between the building's new occupants and some of their non-Muslim neighbors.
As the architect for the renovation project, I was charged with the implementation of the adaptation according to a certain few key principles beyond building codes and permit criteria. The Muslim faith community (*ummah*) wanted to observe specific traditions in the design, but not too strictly or ostentatiously – in part out of a sense that the powerful ideological and ethical underpinnings of American civic life should in some way color this 21st century and unusually situated *masjid* (mosque). (A minimal budget played a constraining role as well.) The fundamental architectural operation to be achieved was the reorientation of the main space to face toward the holy city of Mecca – meaning that the key focal elements of sacred niche (*mihrab*) and sermon platform (*minbar*), presumably supported and tied together by an

Original nave windows in the early stages of renovation

enveloping screen wall, would need to be designed so that the focal axis of the space was rotated some 240 degrees. As part of this reorientation, the location of the twin focal points (*mihrab* and *minbar*) and identifying components needed to be conceived, scaled, and placed for their primary functions, but in accord with the main conceit suggested by the unusual circumstances: that the intervention as a whole should be designed to seem at home with the still-visible features and overall character of the existing interior environment. The third design imperative, after re-orientation and appropriate design of main new components, was to either remove or cover all of the a figurative and b explicitly or emphatically Christian art or iconography. This practice was in keeping with Islam's traditional strictures against figurative art and related iconography, and for rectifying the inappropriateness of the most sacred iconography of another faith in one's own sacred space. Here is where the challenge, the conflict, and the need for both creativity and tolerance were greatest. Since the City of Syracuse's Landmarks Preservation Board deemed the stained-glass windows to be of significant cultural value to the neighborhood and wider community, they mandated that these not be removed in any renovation of the building. The leadership of the Muslim *ummah* decided to take the notion of preserving existing features for the benefit of the wider community and broaden it to include almost all of the art found there. So, much of the Christian art was to remain a part of the building– but masked, ultimately in a permanent way, though in a manner that allowed for periodic viewing. This circumstance created a design and budgetary challenge that has not yet been fully met. Beyond the technical and aesthetic challenge, the continued presence of the windows also brought into sharp relief the contrast of approaches taken within the two traditions – Christian and Muslim – toward sacred art.

In the *masjid* design, the reorientation of the main space was accomplished with the imposition of a screen wall not unlike examples to be found, in various forms, in traditional Islamic interiors – but detailed in certain ways to match the existing church interior. The design of the decorative screen-panels comprising much of the main screen wall is based on a motif which appears in the Al-Aqsa *masjid* in Jerusalem, albeit much simplified to satisfy the budget and to effect a more contemporary, restrained interpretation of the original. This motif is repeated in a simple, regular way to form the perforated portion of the main partitions separating key spaces. The motif as executed – the decorative module, laser-cut into wood – would in itself hardly seem to suggest an autonomous work of art, but it became both a signal of a heritage and an aid to a mode of spiritual experience in its repeated form as the typically 'Islamic' screen. Its environmental or perceptual effect is to articulate light and shadow in a way both familiar ('Islamic') and appropriate to the spiritual focus and self-submersion demanded by Muslim worship. In this important dual role and in its visual appeal, the screens could arguably be deemed Islamic-inspired art.

Taken together, the screens seem in some ways the opposite of the stained-glass windows in nature and effect; they are composed of an abstract, uniformly repeated and geometrically ordered device for modulating light and view, that facilitates a meditative surrender to the will of the divine. The stained-glass windows, each a unique composition and scene that is illustrative and didactic, figurative and narrative, teach and remind, as they convert white light into colors to stimulate exultation and wonder at the divine. While the windows are additive and more autonomously contribute to a Christian notion of the sacred, the decorative screen walls are spatially integral and tend to disappear into the setting. The screens are what Islamic art scholar Oleg Grabar called "intermediary" ornament; they are neither focal objects/images – perhaps presenting spiritual axioms or entities – nor are they mute architectural planes merely defining the limits of sacred space. They are in between foreground subject matter and background boundary, ambiguous and multivalent. They are subordinate and adorn rather than create, but they adorn *space* more than mass or surface, and they qualify the delimitations of space that they impose.

In the former church, the forms and images that could be understood as sacred art were either figural images, as in the crucifix, saint and angel images, or body-related symbols, such as crosses and bleeding hearts. This body-focused 'iconism' has historically dominated the Christian ideal of sacred art and its function. In most Christian settings, spaces are made sacred most obviously and importantly by the presence of such art, which signals the identity and function of the space. Islam does not permit the presence of images of living beings or figural iconography. For Islam, the creation of an image of a being is an imitation of the divine creator and therefore an act of arrogance. The absence of the Christian concept of the divine incarnated in humankind, combined with the emphasis on the incomprehensibly infinite nature of Allah, means that the attempt to capture divine essence in an image or icon would contradict the Prophet's teachings. So, in the creation of Islamic sacred space, the relationship between art and space or place is basically reversed; art or potential art is made sacred, and made art, more clearly by its deployment in a space, which is understood as sacred by its explicit orientation, organization for sacred function, and environmental conditioning in a perceptual sense. The paradigm for imagery – so often what we think of as art – becomes one more of absence, of representation, or of figuration, rather than its presence in rendering the space sacred. Empty space, architectural surface, or detail uninhabited by all but the most purely deco-rative

and stylized representational images, if any, are meaningful, even representational in an abstract way, and conducive to a meditative spirituality.

For the city, represented in this project by the Landmarks Preservation Board, the important art in this situation was first, the building itself as a sculptural whole and iconic landmark, and second, the stained-glass windows, not fully visible from the outside of the building. The Board adopted the stance that although the windows could only be properly viewed and appreciated from the main space of the building's interior – the only space suitable for a new Muslim worship space, these locally familiar, admired, and 'historic' works of art are cultural resources worth preserving and keeping available to the community. This reflects a civic perspective according to which art is, in effect, a secular community resource of presumed cultural value to the citizenry. The generally understood philosophy underlying the preservation of historic and cultural resources formed the justifications for imposing this art on the new occupants, and insisting that while the stone crosses mounted on the church exterior could be removed, they must be stored inside the building and made available to the public, or for some future display or use.

Some in the local neighborhood (according to their own informal testimony) had once sensed that the neighborhood had something of special value and meaning in its midst in the building and its grand windows. Now they saw in quick glimpses, and heard about in descriptive rumors, the supposed stripping of

LEFT
Temporary coverings for cherub heads

RIGHT
Plaster cherub head ornament before covering

the once beautiful interior as a kind of assault on that value and meaning by a largely Islamic immigrant population. For the most upset among them, the need to cover or remove iconography with which they could culturally identify seemed more an act of negation than one of faith. The very grace and nobility they saw in the saintly personages, rendered with a skill and a richness now too expensive to be employed, invoked a lost, hallowed past. The feeling of loss and negation was only heightened by the visual drama of the removal of stone crosses from steeples and gables – even though those crosses were eventually replaced with non-iconographic ornaments.

On the other hand, for the Islamic *ummah*, there was some frustration and resentment expressed over the mandate to retain the windows (and the ongoing delays in covering them). In contrast to the perspective of the Landmarks Preservation Board, the belief of many in the *ummah* was that the presence of the stained glass windows was an indication that the powers could not accept their full possession of this hallowed ground and a reminder that they must deal with being Muslim (and 'immigrant') in a not entirely Muslim-friendly or immigrant-friendly society. Meanwhile, according to deeply felt tradition, any viewing of the image of the Virgin Mary holding the Christ child, to cite one example, quite apart from historic or present-day social or cultural relations between faiths, will strike the devout Muslim as an inappropriate display of human beauty and importance, or of human artistic skill and illusionistic 'powers' before Allah. While the devout Christian willingly suspends disbelief and finds herself in the presence of a personified transcendence, the traditional Muslim sees a celebration of humans and their capacities as being at the expense of praise for and submission to God.

Ultimately, the modest but adaptable ornamental screen form, based on a type and motif from a rich ornamental tradition, proved to be the "art" essential to solving the challenges of the project – essential as a mediator of aesthetic and cultural roles, as part of the major partitions in the main space, and as part of the permanent solution to masking the windows in an operable way. While these screens are not comparable in some ways to the evocative and magical windows, they are representative, in a modest way, of something especially Islamic: in their conceptual purity and adaptability, their aniconic abstraction, their reliance on multiplicity for a sense of richness, and the way they blend together their part in supporting a focused, sacred experience with their more generic appeal as a simple, almost homely decoration. This was the key to this sacred translation: to create an intermediary and modulating, rather than overly assertive or exclusive, sort of design. It is this aspect of much of Islamic art and architecture that will serve the faith well in its attempt to negotiate its place in the American cultural landscape.

Decorative screen at rear of main prayer area

FIGURAL IDENTITY IN ADAPTIVE REUSE

PRESERVED, NEW, AND HYBRID

by MARIE S. A. SORENSEN

Experimental Ambitions and Legacy – Architecture as Art in the Modern Period
Why is it useful to explore the apparently semantic discussion of art and its categorical difference from architecture? Architecture's aspirations to achieve 'artistic' merit are endemic to the discipline – appearing in recorded history as early as Vitruvius' first century BCE platform of 'firmitas,' 'utilitas,' and 'venustas' (strength, utility, and beauty). However, the 'beauty' of early architecture was a classical and symmetrical undertaking, and a majority of the work of architects during and since Vitruvius' time fell within a mode of 'fabric' buildings, structures with height, bulk, proportions, and detailing based on the existing construction and stylistic traditions of a given city, town, or rural region.

Departing from the 'fabric' building tradition, formal inventiveness in architecture flourished at the turn of the 20th century in the horizontal and vertical expansiveness, volumetric drama, and sculptural freedom of residences for professors by Bernard Maybeck in the Berkeley Hills of California and in Frank Lloyd Wright's Prairie School compositions for Chicago's elite. On the eve of the First World War, Henry van de Velde and Bruno Taut celebrated the excitement of the new spatial possibilities engendered by steel, reinforced concrete, and glass in temporary exposition buildings for the Werkbund Exhibition in Cologne. While regular in their symmetry, these buildings and Erich Mendelsohn's post-war Einstein Tower near Berlin are highly stylized, geometric formal departures from the metered vocabulary of the earlier regional and classical traditions. But in the post-World War II building boom, the 'fabric' building returned, now taller. Chicago's first skyscrapers, quickly adopted in New York City and other dense cities, set the trend for the regular shape of urban buildings from the turn of the 20th century.

In the past 40 years, only the most virtuosic architects who created advertising value through formal distinctiveness – employing visually memorable silhouettes; dramatic use of sculptural relief and cladding color and texture; strongly contoured horizontals, verticals, and curves; and/or shapes with form references easily understood by reference to familiar objects (such as 'the washboard,' as the Boston Fed is known)[1] managed to break the developers' pro-forma of maximum leasable space and achieve divergent artistic form in urban settings: Jorn Utzon with the Sydney Opera House (1973); Philip Johnson and John Burgee at Pennzoil Place in Houston (1975); Hugh Stubbins with the Boston Federal Reserve Bank (1977); Dominique Perrault at the National Library of France (1995); Frank Gehry with the Guggenheim Museum Bilbao (1997); OMA with the Beijing CCTV Headquarters (2012); and others – but few.

Building or Complex as *Objet Trouvé* – 'Found Object'
Architects and artists seeking large-scale formal experimentation outside of this commercial setting looked to factory complexes as territory. Writing reflectively in 1990 on the prior two decades of industrial decline and prospectively on the continuing economic need to revitalize districts left vacant with offshoring, theorist Kevin Lynch envisioned vacant urban factories as places

An informal exterior composition in red, turquoise and white as a 'topographical artwork', 50 Moganshan Road, Shanghai

of unbounded possibility.[2] The low economic value of these purpose-built structures and complexes at city edges made them ideal sites for low-risk experimentation within their large volumes. Upon their surfaces, and through additions, the architects or artists worked with the existing structure as a large-scale *objet trouvé*. This term describes an artist incorporating a 'found' object with culturally specific meaning into a new context wherein its meaning is transformed by the perception of the artist's work of art. Marcel Duchamp's *Fountain* (1917) – the display of a urinal as art – is the iconic example, though the descriptive term *objet trouvé* came into use in 1937. Artists 'find' buildings designed for manufacturing, science, engineering, offices, and housing in districts that have been eclipsed by new developments fulfilling related needs. Upon securing access—through cooperative and/or governmentally financed means, through direct arrangement with the owner, or, in unfortunate cases, illegally – artist occupants respond to the megalithic form with three overarching purposes: (1) to shelter themselves and their art-making; (2) to create at an unprecedented scale in terms of 'numerousness' or sheer size; and (3) to alter our understanding of the building's signification as a shelter. Developers and owners often encourage and facilitate artist occupancy and alteration of vacant industrial buildings and complexes, as their creative culture has been shown to precipitate district regeneration in cities around the world, including New York, Boston, San Francisco, Basel, and Copenhagen.

We look here at two spatial expressions of adaptive reuse within the *objet trouvé* typology – *the complex as topographical artwork* and *the building as hybrid figure* – to describe those qualities that make them 'art.' Illustrating *the complex as topographical artwork* are two projects that create a morphological play between the existing complex and the new forms or surface treatments: Richard Meier's Westbeth Arts live-work housing in New York City and the informally developed arts complex 50 Moganshan Road (M50) in Shanghai. Describing *the building as hybrid figure* are two projects separated by nearly 50 years in time: a pair of Paris townhouses in Les Halles altered by artist Gordon Matta-Clark for the 1975 Biennale (now demolished) and Herzog & de Meuron's Elbphilharmonie in Hamburg. These are discrete, singular structures changed by a significant addition or subtraction of form. Derelict or otherwise underutilized buildings have long been locations of expansive creativity for artists – and in fact, the four examples given are programs for artists and the arts.

Art's Critique of Architecture and the Built Environment

In the 1970s, art reacted to architecture, and the ensuing experiments in turn influenced architects. Sculptors Donald Judd, Robert Smithson, Richard Long, Gordon Matta-Clark, and others carried art practice into the built environment. Robert Rauschenberg criticized the archetypal sterile white gallery by breaking the edge of the frame in mixed-media collages he called 'combines.' Smithson created *Spiral Jetty*, a large rock formation in the landscape; Richard Long documented long lines walked across desert territory and allowed only recordings of the ephemeral actions to be curated; and Donald Judd made geometric vertical and horizontal forms with deep voids breaking masses. The architecture world almost claims Judd – and he confirmed the presumed affinity with his purchase of a former army base in Marfa, Texas, as *objet trouvé*. These experiments, briefly mentioned here, have detailed histories beyond the scope of this analysis and impacted art in additional ways.

As Smithson and Long drew the art world's attention to the environment, historians J.B. Jackson and Dolores Hayden contemporaneously penned critiques of the new look of the American landscape: the sprawling cities, redeveloped downtowns, proliferating highway interchanges, and increasingly abandoned factories. Landscape photographers Robert Adams and Lewis Baltz – members of a group of large-format photographers referred to as New Topographics – photographed the dystopia of residential and industrial sprawl. In their images, clusters of dwellings read as topographical aberrations on scraped sites.

Complex as Topographical Artwork

This 'topographic' trend in art surely influenced architects such as Richard Meier, also based in New York City, a major center of the 1970s art world. Today, we know Meier as an architect of major commercial works of new construction – luxury apartment buildings, academic centers, and government offices with clean lines and bold white humanistically scaled facades. But Meier's first large commission, completed in the 1970s, was a renovation project for the J. D. Kaplan Fund and the National Council on the Arts: Westbeth Arts. This 384-unit complex in New York City's Greenwich Village was the first publicly funded live-work housing project in the United States. The existing buildings, Bell Telephone Laboratories' late 19th and early 20th-century office and research and development complex, were an agglomeration of robust brick structures assembled to utilitarian ends. The multiple structures on the large block had diverse footprints and heights, though several strong rectilinear axes brought drama and coherence to the assemblage.

Subtracting two existing timber-framed structures, selectively painting facades, and adding geometric elements like fire escapes, concrete park benches, and a fountain, Meier developed a new language of form to be read at an urban scale simultaneously with the existing historic volumes. The resulting Escher-esque

composition of white on brick showcased new geometrically defined gathering spaces while allowing the formal identity of the existing office and lab building complex to remain visually whole.

Today, the website of the architect, to whom Ada Louise Huxtable referred in 1969 as "…one of the city's more conspicuously talented and stylish younger architects,"[3] lands on a sizable life sciences research building at Cornell University, clad in white. Headlines move along the website with the text of Meier's 1984 Pritzker Prize acceptance speech:

> White is the most wonderful color because within it you can see all the colors of the rainbow. The whiteness of white is never just white; it is almost always transformed by light and that which is changing; the sky, the clouds, the sun and the moon.[4]

Meier's use of white paint to alter the urban presence of the former Bell Labs complex is elemental to its resonance as a large-scale work of art. It brings the former office and test facility buildings into the modern spatial idiom of solid and void by amplifying the presence of certain facades. This use of white on such a large scale is the earliest expression of Meier's later oeuvre.

Westbeth's Executive Director, Steven Neil, understands the importance of the white paint to the historic significance of the modern period of this complex and the work of Meier. He is currently supervising the restoration of the complex as part of a $7 million renovation project that includes deferred maintenance left off the project in 1970, like fixing roofs and other envelope issues. The New York City Landmarks Preservation Commission, which designated the complex in 2011, men-

Complex as Topographical Artwork – Richard Meier's 1970 topography of white paint on brick exteriors at New York City's Westbeth Arts can be understood as a megalithic artwork at the scale of an urban block

Westbeth Arts, the first publicly funded live-work artist loft project in the United States, is an Escher-esque composition of white on brick by Richard Meier, showcasing geometric additions like these park benches

tions Meier's alteration work but attributes Westbeth's contemporary significance primarily to the building's social history as a community of significant artists.[5] As early work by Meier and other members of the New York Five – an avant-garde group of architects featured in a 1969 exposition at the Museum of Modern Art – increasingly requires substantial renovation, preservation tides will surely shift. Docomomo, the international preservation organization for modern movement heritage, and *Metropolis Magazine*[6] are at the head of this trend, building the case for the significance of noteworthy works of architecture built since 1970.

As at Westbeth, exterior paint is the primary element of change in the adaptive reuse of 50 Moganshan Road (M50), a studio, dwelling, and gallery complex developed in the late 1990s in a multi-structure 1930s-era former textile mill complex owned by Shangtex, the state textile company, in the Putuo District of Shanghai, China. Over 100 artists' studios are located here and merge with the adjacent residential and industrial neighborhoods. The underutilized factory buildings in this area are quickly being converted to residential, office, and artist studios such as the nearby Creek Art Center. Located near the downtown of the Jing'an District, the area is a part of Shanghai's Suzhou Creek Renewal District and has been improved through public park amenities and infrastructure replacement over the last decade.

The M50 buildings are an assortment of tile-roofed one-to-four-story concrete, brick, and stucco structures with dark gray, white, and red brick weathered exteriors, alternately advancing and receding at irregular intervals. The varied topography of façades and roofs is connected on the ground plane by broken asphalt access drives from which furniture-scale water, sewage, and fire protection piping access points protrude and cluster, and large pipes occasionally pass overhead from building to building, making informal thresholds.

Within this discordant setting – reminiscent of the dystopic 1979 Russian film *Stalker* by Andrei Tarkovsky that initiated the 'landscape urbanism' trend, in which abandoned industrial landscapes are reclaimed as parks – the artists have built empathy with their surroundings by framing doorways, installing studio signs, and graphically altering entire sections of the exterior as informal site-specific artworks. One of these works, in red, white, and iridescent blue paint, colonizes a metal stairwell, a grouping of human-scale pipes, and the adjoining two building exterior walls.

Art enacted on the existing structures is an empathy-generating design mode, setting in play a new formal way of looking at the building forms and the experience of the space within. While the episodic alterations of M50's exteriors are small-scale topographic interventions, the interiors are claimed and altered in their entirety by the artists whose gear, workbenches, and framed works occupy the lower third to half of the 15 to 30-foot-high spaces. The upper two-thirds of the walls, the figurally-expressive rectangular columns with four-sided trapezoid-faced capitals, and the flat and saw-tooth ceilings are a topographic artwork of whitewashed planes. Within one of these radiant white volumes stands a 20-foot-high plaster figure of Mao Tse-tung with sculptures of children prostrate at his feet. As at Westbeth, the *complex as topographical artwork* is created through the amplification of latent spatial geometries.

Building as Hybrid Figure

In the 1970s, art reacted to architecture not only at the scale of the complex, but also in disputing the culturally prescribed meanings of individual structures. Artist Gordon Matta-Clark is arguably the initiator of *the building as hybrid figure* mode of adaptive reuse within the *object trouvé* typology—in which existing buildings are dramatically transformed through the addition or subtraction of large-scale elements with distinct figural identities.

Splitting (1974) and *Conical Intersect* (1975), two of Gordon Matta-Clark's works of 'anarchitecture,' exemplify the alteration of a 'found' building whose signification as a sheltering structure is dramatically ruptured by a counter-posing figural gesture. Bruce Jenkins, biographer of Matta-Clark, chronicles the emotional impact of Matta-Clark's first building-scale works. He describes the New Jersey tract house that Matta-Clark split by making two vertical cuts one inch apart with power hand tools and by chiseling the foundation to cause its settlement to one side of the house. Matta-Clark had invited a group of friends to come see the work, but even right before the intended exhibit, Matta-Clark told interviewer Liza Bear, "there was a terrific suspense, not really knowing what would hold or shift." In the end, the cut building's two halves settled outwardly, creating a wedge of light that destabilized the solidity of the structure and carried the social commentary of that rupture with it.[7]

The geometric play of *Splitting* relies partly on an equivalency between the rectangular proportions of the original house and that of the two halves, which are proportionally identical to the house. *Conical Intersect* is a temporary work that Matta-Clark constructed in two Les Halles townhouses on the edge of the Pompidou Center construction site during the 1974 Paris Biennale. Matta-Clark's geometric dialogue with the existing structures similarly destabilizes their original meaning, in this case through the cutting away of a telescope-shaped form on the third, fourth, and fifth floors of the structure, its roughly 10 to 15-foot diameter opening, and several additional circular cuts beyond visible to passersby below. The drama of *Conical Section* is clear in Marc Petitjean's photographs taken inside the structure during the construction of the artwork, in which the brick, timber, and plaster of the floor and wall construction make a rough contour for the conical volume of intersecting circular cuts.

Equally dramatic is Herzog & de Meuron's alteration of Werner Kallmorgen's 1966 Kaispeicher A in Hamburg into a hybrid form with a brick base and soaring glass crown for the Elbphilharmonie symphony, hotel, and condominium complex (completion expected in 2017). As in *Splitting* and *Conical Intersect*, the historic form, the new form, and the compositional whole are uniquely identifiable. The distinctiveness of the historic form within the architects' hybrid composition stems from both its unique appearance and the geometric parity set up by the adaptation.

Kaispeicher A, rising 98 feet above a 25-foot-high pier in the Elbe River, appears like a fortification, with three roughly 80-foot-wide brick piers interspersed with the dark slots of vertical loading bays.[8] Small, square, regularly spaced openings evoke gun emplacements in a castle wall and have a similar aspect to the now classic postmodern façade of Michael Graves' 1980 Portland Building.

Above the brick base, trapezoidal in plan and used now for parking, a one-story high recess, perhaps 15 feet in height, separates the brick volume from a soaring glass crown above that the architects refer to as a 'crystal.' This joint is the structure's main circulation node, the arrival point from the sweeping grand escalator and the entrance lobby to the two symphony halls. With the exception of the sky-reaching fore and aft portions of the 'crystal,' the heights of the brick volume and the glass volume are identical. The proportional balance strengthens the identity of the historic structure.

Herzog & de Meuron intended the glass addition to look like "an immense crystal, whose appearance keeps changing as it captures and combines reflections from the sky, the water and the city..." and also "like a tent," bringing a vertical "accent" to the formerly planar pier.[9] The operable apertures in the building's skin – precision-formed and coated slumped-glass panels of variable profile roughly 11 feet high and 16 feet wide on standard floors[10] – might be interpreted as a riff on the small, regular openings of the warehouse façade, whose "abstract" beauty the architects admired.[11]

The Elbphilharmonie's *hybrid figure* resonates as a compositional whole through proportional equivalency, the language of its apertures, and through the dramatic and abstract deployment of classical forms. In the glass crown, these forms resonate with the traditional language of the brick base: both the vaulted openings at lobby level and the arced forms of the 'crystal' play on the Gothic arch.

Experimental Ambitions — Formal Distinctiveness in Urban Settings

The successful and coherent transformation of complexes and buildings into *topographical artworks* and *hybrid figures* argues for acceptance of the progressive approach outlined here, in which added elements have voice, historic works maintain material and formal integrity, and the resulting hybrid building or complex is itself a new work of art. These strategies are not simple or proscriptive, and any proposed development aspiring to artistic merit should be held to strict standards of review. But formal distinctiveness is a value we have neglected in the design of urban buildings, and we can and should use adaptive reuse as a vehicle for experimental ambitions.

NOTES

1 Katherine Solomonson. *Design for Advertising* from *The Chicago Tribune Tower Competition*. University of Chicago Press, 2003.

2 Kevin Lynch. *Wasting Away*. Sierra Club Books, 1990.

3 These words were included in the National Register of Historic Places Nomination for the former Bell Laboratories complex, penned shortly after the alteration work in 1975 (though, unfortunately, perhaps due to the stigmatization of modernism in some preservation circles, not in its *Statement of Significance*). James Sheire. *National Register of Historic Places Inventory – Nomination Form for Bell Telephone Laboratories (common name Westbeth)*. March 5, 1975.

4 Richard Meier & Partners Architects LLP, www.richardmeier.com, accessed October 16, 2015.

5 Jay Schockley. Landmarks Preservation Commission, Designation List 449 LP-2391. October 25, 2011.

6 Paul Makovsky and Michael Gotkin. *The Postmodern Watchlist*. November 2014.

7 Bruce Jenkins. *Gordon Matta-Clark Conical Intersect*. MIT Press, Cambridge MA, 2011. 54, 59, 63.

8 "A Crystal in the Harbour – The Glass Façade of the Elbphilharmonie." *Detail*. 2010-5. 498–508.

9 Herzog & de Meuron, www.herzogdemeuron.com/index/projects/complete-works/226-250/230-elbphilharmonie-hamburg.html, accessed October 16, 2015.

10 *"A Crystal in the Harbour"*, 498–508.

11 Herzog & de Meuron, www.herzogdemeuron.com/index/projects/complete-works/226-250/230-elbphilharmonie-hamburg.html, accessed October 16, 2015.

LOOKING FROM THE VOIDS IN-BETWEEN

by GÉRALDINE BORIO

Behind the legitimate city, for which we can easily draw the outlines, lies the city of "in-betweens," a city in a constant state of transformation, but which inspires precisely because it has not been finished or defined, leaving room for the imagining of a future or a past. At a macro scale, morphological "in-betweens" are identified as industrial wastelands, infrastructure surroundings, vacant plots, waste grounds; so-called urban diseases resulting from deindustrialisation or territorial fragmentation pushed by economic agendas. At a micro scale, they are small gaps and recesses, resulting from the mutational process of the built environment.

For users, these areas in transition, abandoned, offer a momentary space to appropriate. Motivated more by pragmatism than sentimentalism or nostalgia, users of in-betweens find a space that answers a need. Activities taking place in these vacant lands are more or less legal, but always temporary. The intensity of the appropriation of voids is tightly linked to the extent of the repression felt in the built, the planned, and the official surrounding them. Yet, devoid of systematic functions, programmes, and rules, in-betweens bring a feeling of liberation. We feel free to interpret them.

A shoemaker located at the entrance of a back lane in Sham Shui Po

For an architect in search of a territory for action, these sites represent an opportunity to intervene. Without the need to leave a physical imprint, one can imagine strategies for recreating relationships—between people, between sites, between people and sites—turning the negative connotation of these sites into new potential. Perhaps they can reveal another part of the city's identity.

Observing and analyzing the residual spaces raises awareness of the need for emptiness, a fundamental component in the process of making space. Recalling Rem Koolhaas' "strategy of the void," [1] the study of the city through the gaps, we are tempted to question an architecture that deals only with the solid and the tangible; that tries to fill in every space it encounters. How do those spaces in-between inform the way we build and use the city? This article intends to provide an overview of how contemporary architectural discourses use the term "void" as a theoretical concept, and how observation of two Hong Kong types of in-betweens has helped to broaden architectural knowledge and practice.

Genealogy

At an urban scale, voids that were not planned but appeared as scars resulting in urban transformation were starting to interest architects by the mid-20th century. Alison and Peter Smithson, from Team X, for example, categorized the voids as holes in the city, "made by the abandonment of sites and city centres, industrial dereliction, clearance by planners of historic centres, new connective systems that cut great swathes into the urban fabric."[2] A few decades later, in the book *Mutations*[3], Rem Koolhaas highlighted the transformation of urban territories under the pressure of global economic restructuring. Socioeconomic changes have struck everywhere: neoliberal rationales have pervaded urban spaces and brought about a functional specification of all spaces, with the ascent of the two notions of "programme" and "event."[4] Both are in fact essential for Bernard Tschumi, who conceptualises the inbetween as a residual – an interstice where unexpected events can happen.[5] Such a place doesn't result from a formal or aesthetic composition of space, but instead comes out of a programmatic logic. Instead of looking for coherence, for Tschumi the role of the architect is to compose with the undefined and allow the mismatch to exist: "This extraordinary space derived from the concept [of in-between] appears as a "gift" or "supplement": a space where anything might happen; a place of experimentation; a place located on the margins."[6]

By the 2000s, a new generation of architects had expanded upon these visions and revealed a growing interest in understanding the city from what it rejects. In 2003, the Group E2 published *E2: exploring the urban condition*[7] and coined the term "in-between" after studying and working on the presence of "void spaces" in suburban areas of Paris. Their ideas were framed by a time of intensified globalisation, which led to the relocation of industries and the reorganisation of territories, guided by economic rationales. As a result, new unidentified shapes disseminated throughout territories imprinted on the urban fabric.[8] E2 explained that these spaces "generate ideas of instability, unadjustment, strangeness, imprecision, diversion, disorganisation, polymorphism, indeterminacy, complexity, trouble, incoherence. These ideas that create the conditions of uncertainty may lead to a feeling of discomfort, or to a form of curiosity."[9] For them, identifying such sites is before all else an opportunity to intervene, and the in-between a condition that triggers imagination.

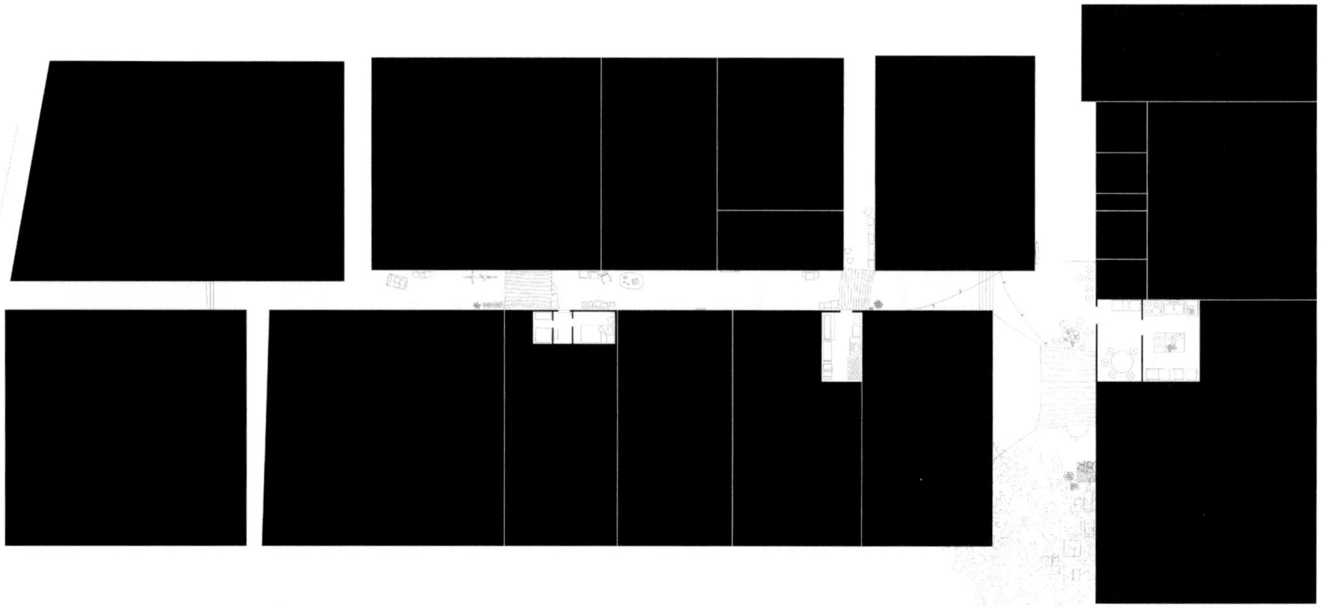

Back lane from above. Location: Tin Hau

Illegal activities in Tin Hau. Playing such games is forbidden in Hong Kong's official public space

A similar phenomenon of resultant voices can be observed in the contemporary Asian context. As Atelier Bow Wow explains in *Bow Wow from Post-Bubble City*, the mutually reinforcing densification and fragmentation of the urban fabric in Tokyo has dramatically reduced the size of land plots.[10] Banal by-products of this contemporary architectural practice in Japan, interstitial spaces are simply called 隙 間 – "sukima" (literally "gap space.")[11] Their morphological, legal, and temporal ambiguousness make them prime objects of interest for Yoshiharu Tsukamoto and Momoyo Kaijima of Atelier Bow Wow, who include "gap spaces" within the development of their architecture. As they compose with these spaces, they manage to transform spatial constraints into an opportunity to make the inside spaces of their architecture interact with the contemporary urban context. "The fact that gap spaces will emerge in any case should be treated as feedback at the start of the design process, which I think is a strategy for designing small buildings that only form a part of the metabolism of the existing city," states Tsukamoto.[12] Once identified, they are quickly adopted by architects who want to approach buildings in relation to their environment.[13]

In betweens are also a programmatic expression of a transitional state. For example, in Japan, the idea of "in-betweenness" is embedded in architectural and cultural traditions. The programmatic thresholds, or transitional spaces, are accentuated by a search for materiality. This is notably illustrated by the omnipresence of the key concept of 間 – "ma," literally "a ray of moon passingww through a gate" and commonly translated as "Japanese sense of place."[14]

The architectural components of the traditional Japanese house are developed and spatially arranged to reflect on a perception of space tightly connected to time and movement as expressed by the ma.[15] As a result, some spaces are conceived to bear the functions of both border and bond: the "engawa"(縁側 —veranda),

Transversal section through Hong Kong with landmarks in the background

the "genkan" (玄関 – entrance) and the "shoji" (障子 – screen panels) will present the porous quality of elements that create transitions, as they are expected to "separate without completely cutting off the view."[16] In other words, the transformational condition of the space (or the capacity to create a total merging of inside and outside spaces) was primordial in the traditional Japanese house, and furniture elements were designed with the paramount purpose of permeability.[17]

However, the post-WWII urban dynamic gradually erased this layering of porosity. Kazuhiro Kojima and Kazuko Akamatsu[18] point out that at this time, a new model of dwelling became massively adopted, namely the nLDK model (literally Living, Dining and Kitchen added to n number of bedrooms). While in traditional houses, rooms hosted a variety of activities, allowing for an overlap of functions, the nLDK's fixed program imposed a specific function on each space. In other words, overprogramming limited individual interpretation of place.

Interestingly, as transitional spaces disappeared in the realm of the private house, interstitial spaces seemed to concomitantly appear in between houses. These outdoor thresholds are therefore a useful material for the development of an architecture deeply embedded in the urban.

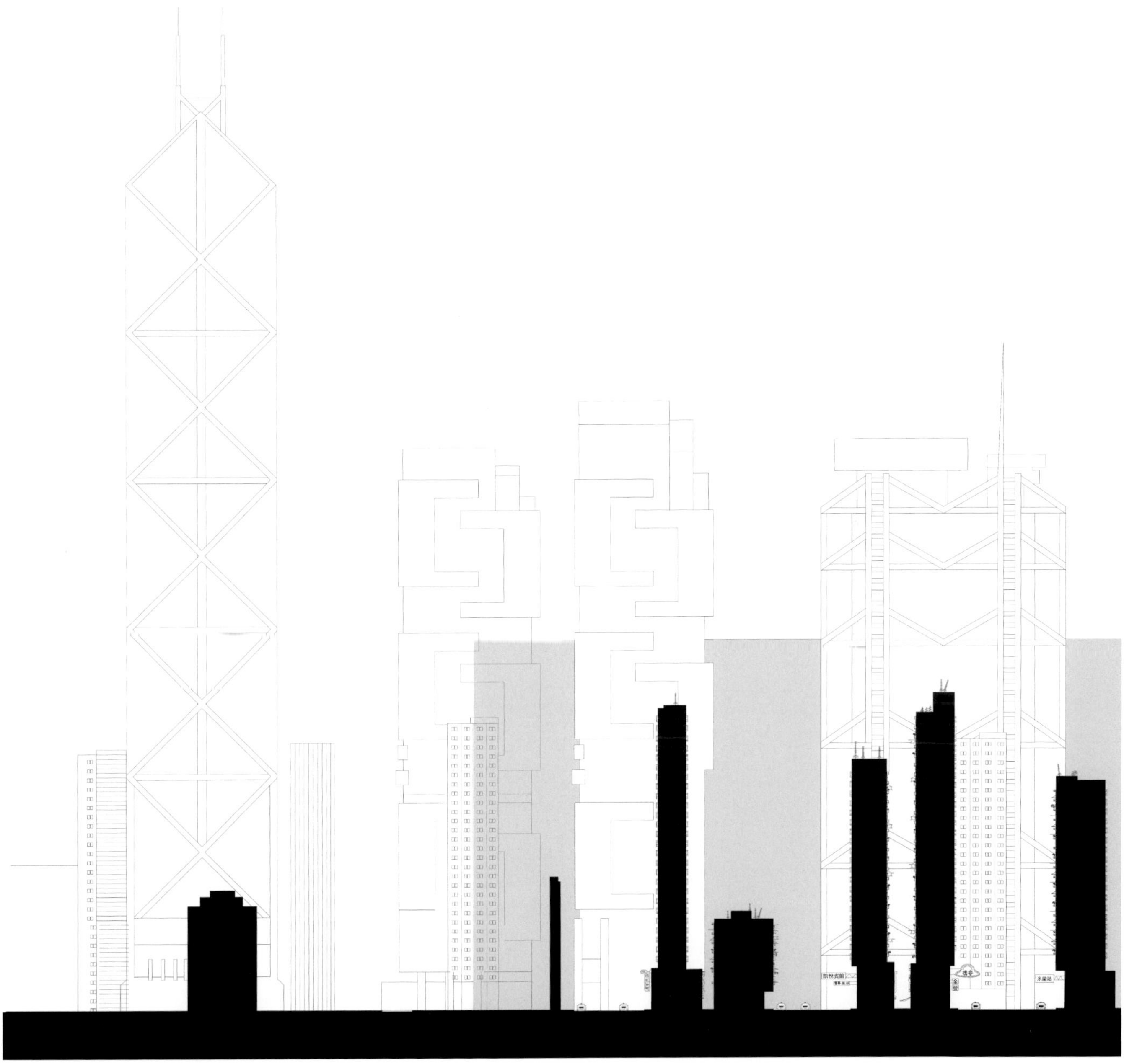

Transversal section through Wan Chai with Hong Kong landmark in the background

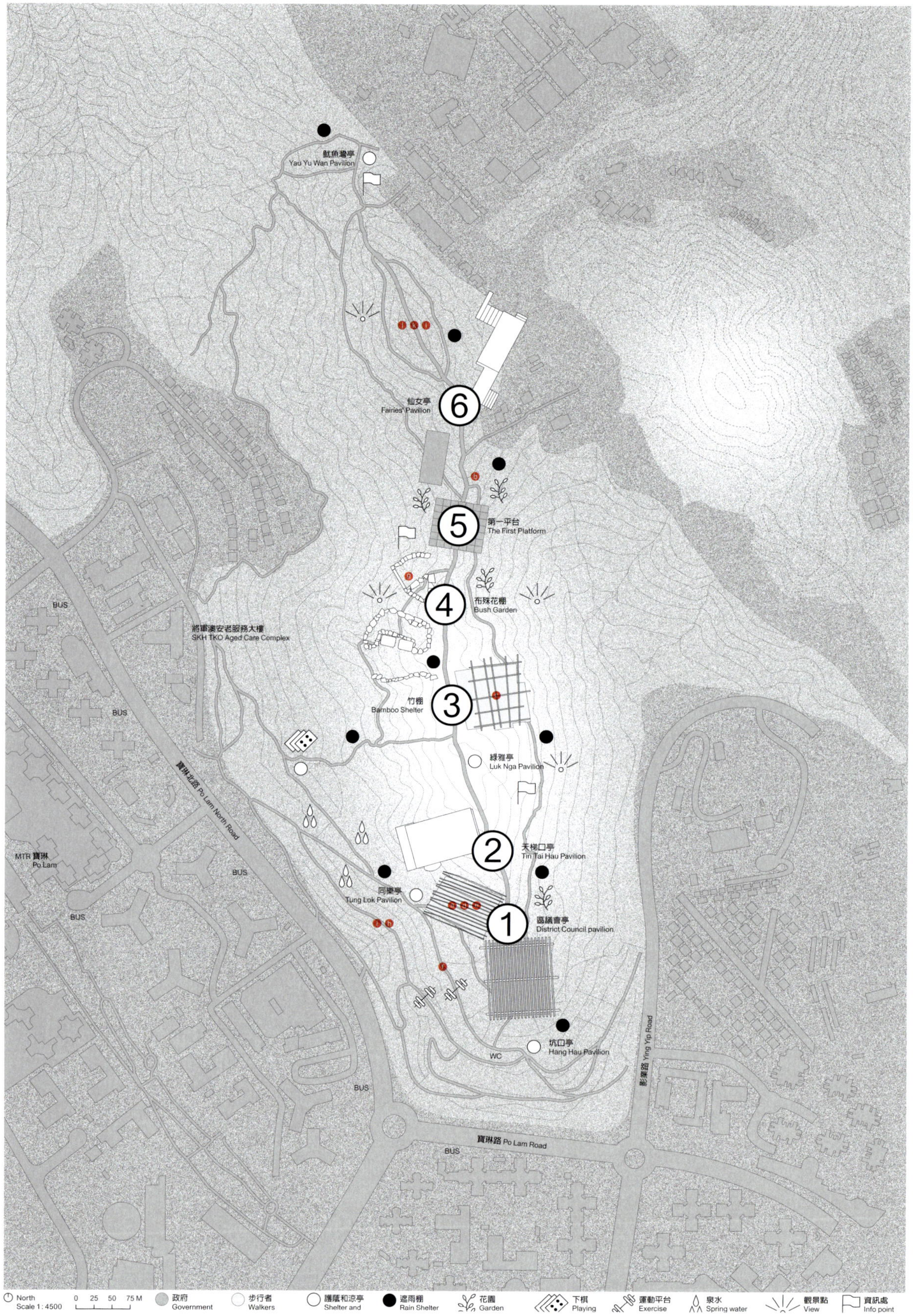

Duckling Hill site map

Hong Kong In–Betweens

During the last decade, the focus of Géraldine Borio's research has been on understanding Asian cities' development mechanisms through the lenses of urban voids. Instead of looking at built forms, she studied the residual buffer zones and nonplanned spaces within the dense urban context of Hong Kong. These peculiar spaces forced curiosity and led to the development of analytical and design tools within her architecture office Parallel Lab. The tools, named the STAG project and the Duckling Hill newspaper, became agents to enquire into and navigate the in-betweens.

In-betweens in Hong Kong are narrow back lanes that form a network of interstitial spaces in the dense urban morphology. These narrow back streets are not registered on official maps, however, put together, they represent an area of 150 square kilometers, four times the area of the recently reclaimed land that makes up the West Kowloon Cultural District. Although tiny in size, their recurrence in many urban areas has a strong impact on the way we perceive and experience the city. Less regulated and sterile than official public spaces (where one is welcomed by an arm long list of interdictions), these residual spaces – unplanned and appropriated by their inhabitants – function as important buffer zones across the city. When lack of space is an issue, these morphological in-betweens collect the overflow of life.

Inherent in the in–between condition is the ambiguity of ownership. In Hong Kong's back lanes, private activities overlap with public ground. A secondhand couch, potted plants, a mirror on a wall or t-shirts on hangers are indicators of a whole living system. Making the most out of the ambiguity of ownership, the network appears as a giant urban living room, configured to react to instant needs. Compared to official public spaces that are over-regulated, the back lanes offer ground to all kinds of activities that would not usually be allowed in them: "and because the spaces are not saturated with function, there is room for appropriation."[19]

Within this territory of unwritten rules, space-appropriators and passersby are shifting the lines of their personal boundaries. Because their forms are in constant negotiation between different users[20] the lack of clarity of ownership seems to call for consensus.

From these observations, it is possible to understand the connections between the different programs and to realise that in such a dense and harsh city, the types of interactions observed are similar to those you would expect to witness in a small village.

To further enquire into this ambiguous aspect of ownership, the observer had to become an actor. The STAG project, which included the design of a portable stool combined with a backpack, emerged as a type of experimentation with these ambiguities of time and ownership. The stool was the tool to reveal the unwritten rules. By organizing events (a tea ceremony, open-air cinema, DJ party) in the interstices, temporary occupation led to negotiations with the neighbors and, occasionally, with the police, both scenarios prompting a recognition of the legitimacy of semiprivate uses on semipublic ground.

This unexpected outcome was an incentive to seek other ambiguous situations. The next case was that of a group of elderly people who, acting at another territorial scale, were engaged in a similar, subtle negotiation for domestication.

At the edge of Hong Kong's urban territory, the green slopes of Duckling Hill (鴨仔山) offer a natural buffer zone in which to escape from the standardised new town of Tseung Kwan O (將軍澳). Over the years, the local residents have gradually appropriated the hill and turned these slopes into their own public space. To facilitate access and enable a wide range of activities, they have built with great care a series of light interventions: stairs, resting spaces, flower gardens, self-made benches, pavilions and rubbish bins.

Once more, it is a matter of negotiation. Alleging safety concerns, the government of Hong Kong, uncomfortable with the idea of losing control, regularly makes claims on the land by eradicating the facilities. Yet, expecting this type of reaction from the authorities, the people of Duckling Hill have developed all sorts of strategies to circumvent the law. Among them: to mimic the appearance of official installations, and to dismantle and reassemble the pavilions, benches and staircases according to government warnings of destruction.

This situation shows another case of private use overlapping public ground. Behind the manicured flower garden, the set of hanging brooms, or the polished ground cleared of all leaves, we can sense a strong feeling of home, and the intimate relationship elders have with the hill. Their innate knowledge of the place's ecology puts them ahead of any team of experts. The question here is not "what to do?" or "can we do it?", but "how?" With direct testing on-site, the design is never fixed and there is always room, in between the laws, for adaptation.

In their negotiation process with the authorities, the group of elders resorted to using a research team to convey their concerns. From researcher and designer, their role shifted to an agent inbetween the negotiating parties. Yet, rather than responding to their proposal to design a pavilion, the creation of a publication in the form of a newspaper, "The People of Duckling Hill"[21] aimed to voice every party's view on the Duckling Hill case.

Towards Architecture

The term "inbetween" appears as a useful tool to refer to the residual and ambiguous buffer spaces found in the dense urban context. Interestingly, the level of uncertainty associated with this concept of in-between

illustrates a situation that seems difficult for architects to depict: in-betweens do not fall into the common categories of public/private, legal/illegal, indoor/outdoor, interior/exterior, and although they can be identified, they are often "given neither name nor shape"[22] and are not represented on official maps. Consequently, under one term, very different situations seem to cohabit. This ambiguity reflects how these spaces question the way we use and build the city.

From a user's perspective, over-programming and regulations upon public spaces mirror the authorities' need to control, and of non–definiteness. Thanks to their ambiguous status, these spaces provide multiple ways of interpretations and enable more intuitive forms of usage to emerge. Far from being a threat, this sense of domestication in a dense city encourages social coherence and stability: indeed, "who would want to destroy one's own living room?"[23]

Researchers are often expected to take a clear position. The question of whether to be for or against, to preserve or fix the spaces, is often asked. Once again, we cannot bear to live with ambiguity. In these cases, the researcher's role was to be an observer, acknowledging in-between spaces' existence as a city component

Six Duckling Hill walkers

The core of regular Duckling Hill walkers, Tseung Kwan O residents aged between 60 and 90 years old, numbers around 200 people.

that speaks about its status and needs. However, by revealing them the concomitant risk is to annihilate their in-between qualities. When the marginal begins to interest the authority — the planners and the developers — it immediately loses its allure as a refugee zone, while the legitimate city simply soaks it up.

We must therefore understand this notion of in-between as a condition that thrives within the city, rather than one that adopts the superficial appearance of a leftover.

For an architect, observing these spaces is a rich source of inspiration that can lead to the reinvention of one's practice. In this overbuilt context, the role of the architect, designer, and planner is challenged; couldn't we be doing more than just filling gaps? Exploring this potential territory at different scales and scopes forces us to realise that no guidelines or designs would be able to reproduce the qualities held by such spaces. In essence, they cannot be planned.

Yet, if we should not intervene within them, and not try to create them, what should we do? Withdraw from any decision-making process and encourage a "laissez-faire" standpoint? Only by observing and understanding the city's mechanisms, can one truly evaluate where and where not to act, and allow this conversation to perpetuate.

NOTES

1 Rem Koolhaas, 'Strategy of the Void', in *S,M,L,XL* (New York: Monacelli Press, 1995), 602–62.

2 Alison Margaret Smithson and Peter Smithson, *The Charged Void: Urbanism* (New York: Monacelli Press, 2005).

3 Rem Koolhaas et al., *Mutations: Rem Koolhaas, Harvard Project on the City. Stefano Boeri, Multiplicity*, ed. Arc en rêve Centre d'Architecture (Barcelona: ACTAR, 2000).

4 Bernard Tschumi, *Bernard Tschumi: Architecture: Concept & Notation*, ed. Frédéric Migayrou and Aurélien Lemonier (Paris: Centre Georges Pompidou, 2014).

5 Bernard Tschumi and Joseph Abram, *Tschumi Le Fresnoy: Architecture In/Between* (New York: Monacelli Press, 1999).

6 Tschumi and Abram.

7 Groupe E2, ed., *E2: Exploring the Urban Condition* (Barcelona: ACTAR, 2003).

8 I bid.

9 Ibid.

10 Atelier Bow Wow, *Bow Wow from PostBubble City* (Tokyo: INAX, 2006).

11 Ibid.

12 Tsukamoto, p.210 in Atelier Bow Wow.

13 Kitayama Koh, Architectural Work. *InBetween* (Tokyo: ADP, 2014).

14 Günter Nitschke, "'MA' The Japanese Sense of Place in Old and New Architecture and Planning," *Architectural Design*, March 1966, 113–56; and Arata Isozaki, *JapanNess in Architecture* (Cambridge, Mass: The MIT Press, 2006).

15 Mitsuo Inoue, *Space in Japan* (New York: Weatherhill, 1985).

16 Adrian Snodgrass, "Thinking Through the Gap: The Space of Japanese Architecture," *Architectural Theory Review* 2, no. 16 (2011): 136–56.

17 Nohirito Nakatani, ed., Transition of Kikugetsutei, *Equipment In Between*, Window Research Institute (Tokyo: YKK AP Inc., 2016).

18 Kazuhiro Kojima and Kazuko Akamatsu, *Essence Behind*, Contemporary Architects' Concept Series 21 (Tokyo: LIXIL, 2016).

19 Géraldine Borio and Caroline Wüthrich, *Hong Kong InBetween*, Bilingual edition (Zürich: Park Books; Hong Kong: MCCM Creations, 2015).

20 Ibid

21 Géraldine Borio and Caroline Wüthrich, *The People of Duckling Hill* (Hong Kong: Parallel Lab & Hong Kong Polytechnic University, 2014).

22 Atelier Bow Wow, *Bow Wow from PostBubble City*.

23 Borio and Wüthrich, *Hong Kong InBetween*.

Exterior living room in a temporary illegal shelter located on the hill

LEARNING FROM OLD XINÍNG

THE ADAPTATION OF URBAN FORM

by JAMES PATTERSON-WATERSTON

The rapid urban growth in emerging economies, particularly in China, is profound, and the People's Republic stands at a crossroads in terms of urbanization. The stated goal of reaching parity across the country, although clearly ambitious, is currently underway. The leadership has declared willingness to prioritize environmental and social considerations in the most recent phase of development, which poses an opportunity to preserve cultural identity and memory within a process of mass urbanization and industrialization. The city of Xiníng, the capital of Qinghai Province, is the most cosmopolitan of any provincial capital in China, with a population of 1.8 million people. It is due to almost double in size over the course of the next 20 years, in line with Chinese Western Development Plan objectives. This is possibly the world's largest centrally derived plan for mass urbanization, yet what is to be learned from the urban structure of the city of Xiníng has yet to be defined. As such, there is scope for a design proposition to suggest an alternative path to urban development, one that recognizes value in the existing.

The adaptation of the urban form of the city of Xiníng to meet modern development demands becomes a critical question of whether a new model is required to meet environmental and economic ideals, or whether a solution can be found in the design principles on which the city has developed historically. The city of Xiníng is part of an arc of frontier cities with particular social, demographic and economic problems, encompassing many ethnicities and religious faiths. It has been assigned 'model' status by the central government due to its relatively low occurrences of inter-ethnic and inter-religious violence in comparison with other similar cities, such as Urumqi, Hoh-hot, Lhasa and Golmud.

The city may be described as traditionally 'Chinese' in that the urban plan and form lack the interference of colonial administrators, as opposed to many of the cities on the eastern seaboard. Shanghai, Hong Kong, Guangzhou and Qingdao all have, to varying extents, urban grids laid out by colonial administrators or merchants. These cities have followed a path of western and Chinese hybridization both in architectural and urban form, something that Xiníng, like many other Chinese cities, appears eager to follow.

The question in this instance is therefore, what is meant by 'Chinese' given the ethnic and cultural heterogeneity? The city has grown over many centuries around an 'old city' core of a walled Han Chinese settlement surrounded by later walled areas containing

Xining 'Old City' North-West District Lynch Analysis

Zones of public and private action within the 'old city'

largely Muslim minority populations. This follows a standard form of city development on the frontier. Ethnic and religious minorities were traditionally excluded from the Han walled cities and so instead constructed adjacent parallel cities in order to trade and benefit from the security granted by the garrison. Unlike many cities on the frontier, however, Xiníng was early to allow the mixed residence of ethnic and religious groups. This may be one of the reasons the 'old city' has been able to maintain its form during tumultuous times, given that there were fewer foci for inter-ethnic violence and damage, due to a perceived sense of collective ownership.

Xiníng maintained this traditional form and mixed demographic well until the mid 20th century, when political change in Beijing, thousands of miles away, altered the outlook for the city. The Cultural Revolution acted as a catalyst for change, as did Mao's earlier "Go West" policy of the 1950s. The city saw huge growth during these periods as Han migrants moved from the east into a new modern and expansive area of the city to the west of the 'old city.' During this period some of the 'old city' streets were widened, while street-based communal activities were substituted with those led by the state. The 'old city' remained largely intact due to the perceived 'backwardness' of such areas in the minds of state planners. Attention and care was focused on the newer districts of the city, to the detriment of the area's residents. This has, in hindsight, however, proven a boon.

A unique opportunity exists in the unusual urban grain of Xiníng in that, in the old town, it has maintained the traditional street layout and urban form of a Chinese frontier city. Unlike many historical settlements in the western provinces however, the city was not formed as a military outpost but as a trading centre, signifying the role the city played as crossroads to Han, Mongolian, Uighur and Tibetan peoples. The built form has encompassed these various cultures as they have adapted the Han structure to meet their own needs. Unlike many cities on the Han periphery, Xiníng has developed a mixed residential model, with ethnic groups living aside one another in many districts, particularly in the 'old city.' This pattern has developed over many hundreds of years and may, in part, be due to the mercantile nature of the city. Trade has acted as a bind to the many peoples, forced to interact daily in the street markets and commercial areas. These activities are reflected in the hierarchical urban plan of broken privacy zones.

That is not to suggest that the city does not also conform to traditional Han Chinese ideals of separated zones of public and private action. The analysis of the 'old city' has identified three clear zones; a private inner core of residential uses, surrounded by a semi-private zone of transition where many social activities take place, surrounded by a public retail-led collar.

It is this zone of transition that is peculiar to Xiníng. These spaces, identified as the courtyards and alleys behind the commercial collar, are where different peoples interact. They act as informal trading areas, as zones of social activity (community education and leisure) and as communal access points to residential units. It is this mixed-use, active urban character that is increasingly desirable for user well-being and comfort and suggests a model of spatial use that provides a basis for investigation. It is also particularly interesting that these forms have largely been structured around the needs and wants of the private sphere as opposed to those of the state and are based on retail models of interaction. As such, there is potential in using the existing city framework and the principles that underlie the urban grain to continue the expansion of the city, rather than adopting a regime of demolition and crass interpretations of internationalism, as in many cities throughout Asia.

In China it has become the norm for non-core cities to embrace a now aged ideal of strictly zoned land uses throughout. These structures often take the form of commerce and administration-led urban cores, surrounded by mixed-use suburbs, enveloped by peripheral high-rise residential districts. The consequent urban banality is often a precisely planned attempt at western urbanity. Xiníng has the opportunity to adopt a different path, utilizing its own unique form as a model for modernization and growth.

Initial experiments in commercial property towards the end of the 20th century somewhat damaged the 'old city' grid in an embrace of the 'new' and a rejection of the old. Larger projects closed spaces previously accessible from multiple points. At these points of earlier intervention the existing building footprint may have been retained, but the ambience was lost. Some of the main obstacles to using the existing framework are the limitation on unit size and the demand for larger stores. Modern western-style malls like those located at several intersections in the 'old city' have enveloped existing buildings and blocked access to light and space.

The city is therefore faced with a decision to address the new and the 'foreign' and rework the city form, or to adapt the existing urban grain to its own uses, to create Qinghai modernity. The current state-sanctioned fashion in China is to embrace cultural heritage, authentic or pseudo. There is a real social value to be derived from both maintaining and enhancing existing urban fabric, specifically in the areas of continuity and stability; China's modern mantra.

The danger is in the city adopting a Disney-esque approach to its collective memory in the form of themed districts or built interventions, as has occurred in Shanghai and Beijing, as opposed to developing strong contextual design language. It is suggested that future development apply the principles of multiple access, light-tough footprint and transitional zoning in order to meet environmental, social and cultural objectives.

The mercantile nature of Xiníng lends itself to urban spaces and forms that encourage interaction and communication. It is suggested that these attributes contribute to relatively low levels of inter-community violence in the city. This provides an additional incentive to utilize these existing design strategies in future development.

There is also a limited history of literal reuse in terms of historical sites within the 'old city,' largely due to limited inward investment in the past. The city was forced to reuse and repurpose purely due to lack of funds. This has granted the city a historical core that many others in the region lack. That is not to say that huge numbers of ancient buildings exist; they do not. Buildings do, however, largely continue to follow built environment conditions concerning footprint, height and layout. This built pattern is modeled on centuries of land ownership traditions that prioritized the status quo.

This started to change at the turn of the century when investment began to flood into the city and developers began to demolish sections of the 'old city' to a mixed public response. Many residents were dismayed, but the metropolitan and Party elite largely viewed the process as that of modernization and progress.

Recent developments in Xiníng have, however, begun to adopt a hybrid form, via the reuse of existing building footprints and uses. This has largely been by convention and convenience as opposed to a design-led agenda. These interventions, including shopping arcades and semi-formalized market streets, have followed the same massing and block forms of existing commercial buildings in the 'old city.' These can be found at junctions throughout this area of the city, as redevelopment has focused on transportation and visual nodes—as it has throughout the city's history. These physical junctures are often centers of commercial and social activity in cities throughout the world.

There is, however, a discord between what is viewed as required, essential or even necessary between the municipal authorities and the building users. The city is in a time of transition and needs to set clear objectives as to what defines the city architecturally and culturally; what it wishes to maintain and what it wishes to disregard. It is clear that some elements of the city's structure will have to change to accommodate developments in transportation technologies and household structure. Enhanced guidance on internal environmental conditions, such as improved ventilation, access to natural daylight or increased green space, may act as drivers for change. These user-led drivers act alongside those enforced or encouraged by the public and private spheres. Examples of these top-down drivers include planning guidance from the central government that new or redeveloped districts should include ease of access routes for paramilitary intervention, and the commercial drive for enclosed, ever-larger floor plates to sate Chinese consumers.

In a time of both growing nationalism and resurgence in Confucianism there is a growing reflectance of the historical value of the built environment. There is thus a real potential to commercially utilize the existing built footprint and the principles by which it has been constructed to provide an alternative path to development. There is an opportunity to preserve a cultural heritage that is intrinsically Chinese.

The next stage of research should include a full cataloguing of buildings, spaces and ground-floor uses (including both mercantile and social activities). It is intended that this information provide a basis for design decisions regarding the reuse of existing buildings and the adaptation of the existing urban structure to suit the demands of the city's development program. While the first stage of analysis has focused on the urban form, there are also many environmental as opposed to cultural issues to investigate, prior to implementing a new strategy. In particular, how both the existing buildings and their construction materials are 'of the climatic context' in comparison to other contemporary options.

In furthering the study of the growth and modernization of Xiníng, municipal authorities will be informed as to how to adapt and re-purpose their existing urban structure to the growing needs of their citizens. If these issues are not addressed, as Piper Gaubatz eloquently states, there is a very real danger that Xiníng will "celebrate its past in books and museums, not in its landscape."[1] The current wave of development in the western provinces of China is an opportunity to reflect on the mistakes of the past and investigate further the scope for an architecture and urban form of place and context.

NOTES

1 Gaubatz, Piper. "Commercial Redevelopment and Regional Inequality in Urban China: Xining's Wangfujing." *Eurasian Geography and Economics*, Vol. 49 (2) (2008): 180–199. Print.

MEMORY AND REDEMPTION

Entwined with conservation and preservation practice, adaptive reuse is predicated on the narratives embedded in the structures of the past. As witness to history, adapted and preserved structures were often commemorative. With the changing face of war and the destructive nature of weaponry, the idea of memory has shifted and expanded the idea of memorials. With the introduction and acceptance of the value of 'negative heritage,' the notion of culpability has emerged as a design concept. The reuse of structures offers an opportunity for atonement in a malleable terrain.

240 **Tuol Sleng Museum of Genocide Crimes [Volume 04]**
Barbara Stehle

250 **Malleable Remembrance And the Re-Consolidation of Fragments [Volume 04]**
Victor M. Serrano

254 **Everybody's House: *The Rosa Parks House Project* [Volume 09]**
Ryan and Fabia Mendoza, João José Santos, Diogo Vale

266 **Croydon's Tower: Reconciling Old Traumas and New Hopes [Volume 04]**
Robert Schmidt III, Dan Sage, James Pinder, Charles Holland, Simon Austin

274 **Between Memory and Invention: An Interview with Nieto Sobejano Arquitectos [Volume 06]**
Luis Sacristán Murga

Remains of the security prison

ANTERIOR SPACES AT S.21

TUOL SLENG MUSEUM OF GENOCIDE CRIMES

The author acknowledges William Greaves, Youk Chang, Lindsay French, Oumneang Moul for their contribution to the article.

by BARBARA STEHLE

Some places function on another plane of time: a walk through them takes us into an anterior space. When the place has been the actual site of atrocities, the memories it holds are often terrifying to face. The place is feared for the spaces it held. In certain historical contexts, during wars, under oppressive regimes, architecture has been usurped, kidnapped for a perverse usage. This is the case of a group of buildings in Phnom Penh, a manifestation of Khmer late modernist style, designed as a high school. After 13 years in their original function, the buildings were used as an instrument of oppression. Their name was changed, their appearance affected, their plans modified. They were transformed into a machine for killing under the code name S.21.[1]

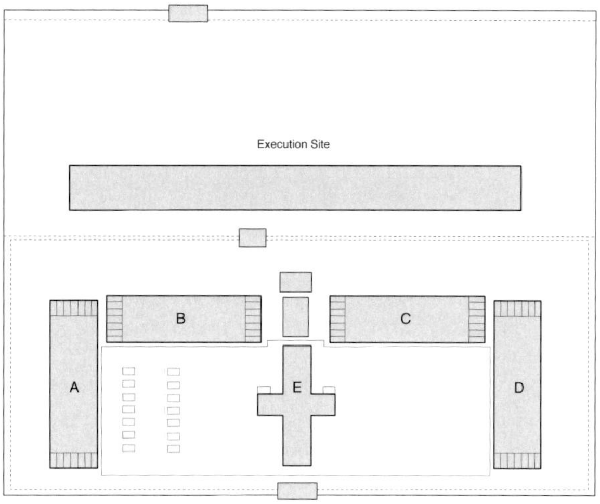

In Phnom Penh, last February 2012, the ex-director of S.21, Kaing Guek Eav, alias "Duch," was condemned to a life sentence for crimes against humanity.[2] The United Nations Court qualified his "death factory", "amongst the worst humanity has known."[3] Over 12,380 men, women and children accused of counterrevolutionary crimes came to be prisoners at S.21 and only seven survived.[4] When the Vietnamese forces entered Phnom Penh on January 7, 1979, they discovered the site with 14 freshly killed prisoners shackled to their beds and thousands dead in the killing fields nearby. The staff had fled, abandoning documents.[5] In a year, cleaned and organized, it reopened as the Tuol Sleng Museum of Genocide Crimes.[6]

Neither inhospitable nor oppressive, how did the architecture of a modern high school turn into an instrument of crimes against humanity? How do the anterior spaces express themselves in the present built fabric? This article investigates the different layers of the history and politics of the site as a socio-political subject and the radical adaptive reuse it endured as an object bearing the unbearable.

Adapting the Name, Reusing the Site

Tuol Sleng Museum of Genocide Crimes is the last of a series of names given successively to the site. When a site has had multiple names, each of them corresponds to a segment of life and functions as a portal into the respective space/time. Lycée Preah Chao Ponhea Yath, Lycée Tuol Svay Prey, S.21, Tuol Sleng Museum of Genocide Crimes; the succession points to a shift in socio-political identity. They illustrate the unstable quality of the architecture, the writing and reading of which are at the mercy of a different discourse.

The name of a primary school on the western flank of the compound, Tuol Sleng in Khmer means the hillock of the Sleng, a poisonous tree.[7] It refers directly to the vegetation of the area and is now the name of the museum. Judy Ledgerwood writes: "Genocide and death, as displayed at Tuol Sleng, have become the national narrative, the biography of Cambodia as a nation."[8] However contested because of its Vietnamese foundation, the museum has become the symbol of contemporary Cambodia's agency to write its history and engage in the politics of space.[9]

To fully understand the history of the site, one must look back to 1953, when Cambodia gained its independence from the French. In the following years, Prince Sihanouk started an intense building campaign to create a strong national image. Manipulating geopolitical powers, Sihanouk found partnership both in the western and eastern block for his country's development.[10] Key to a modern nation, education was allotted 20% of the national budget. Between 1955 and 1968, over 3000 primary schools and 168 high schools (only 12 existed) were built.[11] The urban plan for a New Phnom Penh[12] included five new high schools for the capital, one of them on our site.[13]

The Lycée Preah Chao Ponhea Yath was built in 1962.[14] It took the name of the 15th century Cambodian king who adopted Phnom Penh as its capital.[15] Ponhea Yath, like Sihanouk, desired a strong state capital. The lycée's royal ancestor was a quasi godfather to the new urban plan. Sihanouk personally campaigned for the renewal of architecture,[16] gathering 50 architects and builders to do public work.[17] At the Direction of Urbanism and Habitat, Cambodian architect Vann Molyvann collaborated with seasoned modernists: engineer Vladimir Bodiansky and urbanist Gerald Hanning (both had worked with Le Corbusier).[18]

On March 18· 1970, the US-backed military coup imposed Lon Nol at the head of a Republic.[19] Cambodia's architectural renaissance abruptly ended. Names of official buildings and streets all over the nation were changed. References to kings had to be eliminated. The high school, from royal, became local and was named after its southwestern district: the Lycée Tuol Svay Prey (hillock of the wild mango).[20]

When the Khmer Rouge took control of the country on April 17, 1975, Phnom Penh was evacuated in 48 hours. All residences and businesses were emptied, streets condemned, pagodas burnt, buildings destroyed.[21] The once state capital became a ghost town for the next four years, as few governmental agencies had access to the city. The lycée avoided destruction, the fate of many schools, but was usurped. Tuol Svay Prey turned into S.21: S for Sala (Hall), 21 for the radio frequency of the area (according to Duch), or the code-number for Santebal, the secret police.[22]

Duch, an ex-math teacher, directed S21, a "total institution" where people were detained, tortured and killed.[23] Terrified young men at the age of 13 were taken from their villages to be trained as guards and executioners. Enslaved servants of Angkar, the almighty and

Site Plan at S.21

watchful organization of the regime, they were to work four years at S.21.[24] As the "Khmer Rouge Ministry of Culture and Social Affairs stated: "Only children can purely serve the revolution and eliminate reactionism since they are young, obedient, loyal and active."[25]

A Modern Cambodian High School

The original architectural drawings for the high school have disappeared. Two young Cambodian architects, Pen Sereypagna and Vuth Danith, surveyed the site and created several sets of drawings on which this article relies.[26] The five concrete buildings with flat roofs and a large open garden are typical of Cambodian governmental educational buildings of the time.[27] The architectural program exemplifies the adoption of modern ideals of hygiene, rationality and functionality.

In the sixties, the entire compound of 600 x 400 meters created an imposing sight: the gardenlike playground and gymnastic court formed a setback for the symmetrical order of the buildings. Legacy of the French, urban gardens were important for the capital's embellishment. Van Molyvann found inspiration in Le Corbusier's "Radiant City": "I took this theory and tried to realize it for the very first time in the city of Phnom Penh. In practical terms, the theory meant that when one builds houses, one has to think about how to arrange them so that they are surrounded by gardens and parks."[28] At the school, large trees and grass offered a refreshing haven from the sun, and helped cool the buildings. The administrative center, Building E, a small one-story building with the same aesthetic as the taller ones, split the garden in two.

The four three-story reinforced-concrete buildings- A, B, C and D – were originally of identical design. Set on a concrete platform, they provided 5 wide and airy classrooms per floor, 15 per building, 60 overall. Each floor had an identical plan before its transformation in 1975. The garden façade was designed with a long distributing gallery divided by slender concrete posts. It acted as a weather buffer for the classrooms and protection from

Classrooms divided into cells

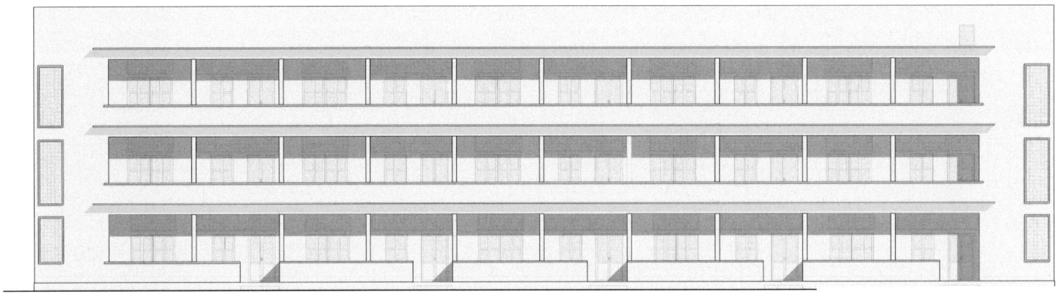

Elevation Building C
Before 1975

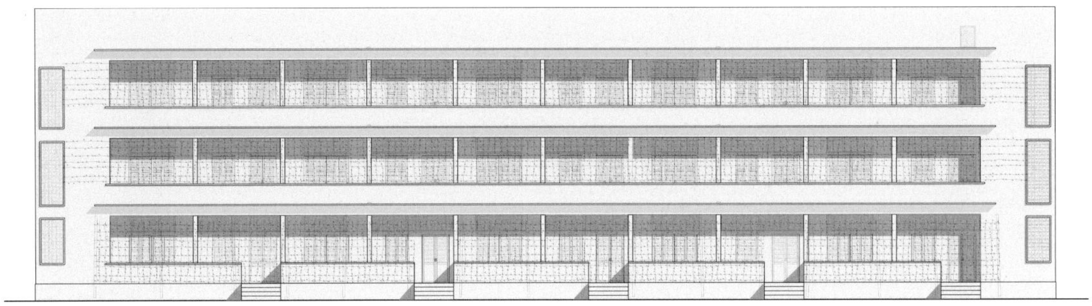

Elevation Building C
1975–1979

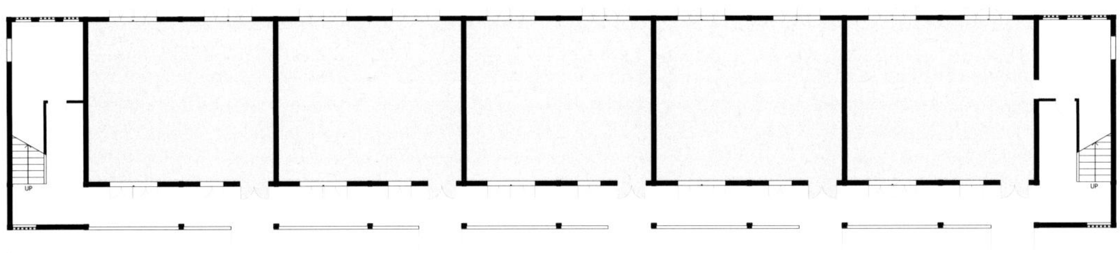

Plan Building C
Before 1975

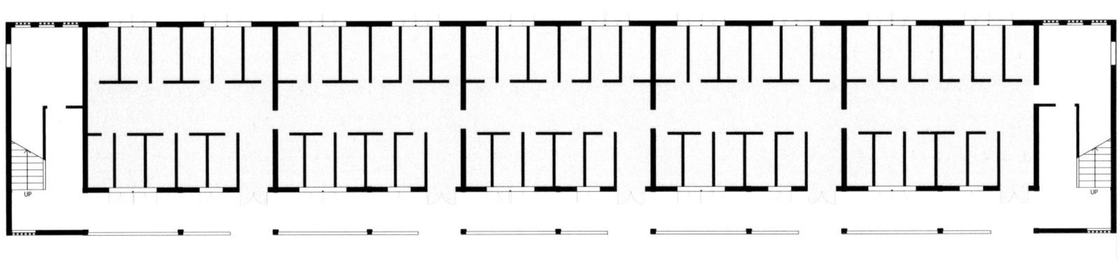

Plan Building C
1975–1979

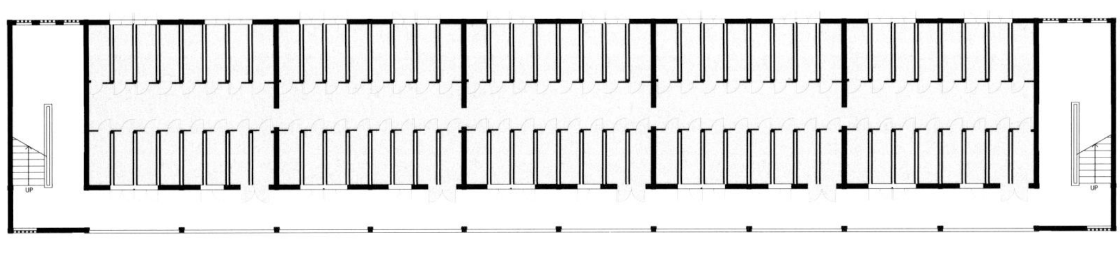

the sun and monsoon with molded concrete parapets. All floors were tiled in ocher and white.

Molded claustra were introduced over key architectural elements. Made of assembled bricks and cement, their geometrical modular ocher pattern matched the color of the floor. A modern ornament, the claustra also prevented water infiltration in the buildings with a square opening, funneled into a small rectangle on the inside. These panels featured in the staircases at each end of the building, providing them with permanent shade, ventilation and lower humidity. Similarly, classrooms had high ceilings and two sets of claustra over the doors and windows. Wood shutters could close on the gallery side during exams, and light and air would come from the other set of openings. [29] The school benefited from a smartly designed structural cooling technique.

Adaptive Reuse, Urbicide and Paranoia

When the Khmer Rouge arrived, the school was ill fitted to lock in people and silence painful screams. But it offered a coherent complex that was easy to divide. The garden set up for physical exercise was easily corrupted. The gym apparatuses were used to hang and tie people. As in the rest of Phnom Penh, fruits and vegetables were planted and animals brought in to sustain the camp staff. Building E in its midst was turned into the managing center of S.21.

Building A, B, C and D were used as detention spaces. The galleries were wrapped in six rows of barbed wire tied to the staircase's claustra. Surrounded by a triple wall of corrugated iron, the camp was rendered off-limits. Houses on the eastern flank of the complex were annexed for interrogation. Screams and accusations resonated throughout the compound, and the entire neighborhood could hear the horrendous pain of the victims.

It is difficult to establish a clear timeline, but structural work must have occurred immediately to adjust the buildings to their new function. A look at Building C gives a good idea of the 1975 early interventions.[30] The open architecture was turned into a closed, fragmented, opaque space. The oppressors had the monopoly of the gaze, of verbal exchange, circulation and space management. Administrative procedures organized the crossing of ingress and egress points.

All measures were taken to prevent prisoners from

committing suicide or escaping. As illustrated in one of the survivor's paintings, one classroom could contain as many as 50 prisoners, 12 at a time shackled to the same metal rod. The rows of prisoners were numbered on the walls.[31] Metals bars closed the windows, chains anchored to the ground. Metal gates prevented access to the staircases. Guards watched every room and escorted prisoners to their interrogation places. Prisoners were blindfolded and shackled, all circulation was controlled by a very strict schedule and silence was the rule.

To maximize all available space, rooms were exploited through fragmentation. Individual cells provided complete isolation for important prisoners. On the first floor, 16 60 cm wide wood cells were fit into one classroom.[32] With a higher level of finish than others, they may have been constructed first. On the ground floor, each classroom was divided into 12 tiny individual brick and cinder cells. The makeshift partitions were sufficient as the starved prisoners were tightly chained to the ground, the only furniture an ammunition box in which to defecate. To facilitate surveillance, corridors were roughly created through the walls to redirect the guard path in between the cell rows.

All mechanisms of an architecture celebrating rationality and hygiene were disrupted. The new cells blocked the cross ventilation resulting in stagnated air. The incarcerated were kept half-naked or poorly dressed, their bodies weak and wounded, infested with parasites and starved. They were beaten with electrical rods and forced to eat feces as routine torture. Waterboarding devices, metal clamps and electrical shock machines were installed. School furniture became attributes of the jailers and blackboards were recycled to post the prison's rules. A decade later the stench is pervasive and the walls and floors remained bloodstained.[33]

After September 30, 1978, buildings A, B and D were re-adapted to create a new typology of detention. Building C solely remained unchanged.[34] An important purge brought in high-ranking Khmer Rouge and troops of soldiers.[35] The new system provided different standards of "comfort" to accommodate this change. The ground floor of Building A was reserved for the high-cadre imprisoned. Each classroom was split in two

Passages cut into walls during Khmer Rouge occupation

to create an individual cell/interrogation room where a bed (for the prisoner to be chained to and rest) and a desk (for the interrogator to sit at) could fit. One of each classroom's windows on the gallery side was changed to a door. Claustra were plastered over, blocking air renewal. Hermetic glass was added to the windows; in some cases metal doors replaced wooden ones.

In contrast, the space upstairs was opened, all partitions destroyed to create communal rooms. The large spaces were used to detain lower-class prisoners, mostly military ones, gathered like cattle. They were killed fast and by the end of 1978, "the special prison" in Building A kept the staff busy.[36]

A Kafka-esque logic with an Orwellian twist defined the institution: one arrived guilty of an unknown crime that was discovered with the help of torture. A confession and full submission to Angkar was necessary before being killed. Confessions were neatly written in school notebooks and annotated by Duch. A photographic record of each prisoner was filed.[37] Close accounts were kept and reported dutifully to the Party. There is no possible fantasy of the sublime in this horror, no lyrical architecture of death, but the production of a terrifying reality with a gruesome administrative look. Architecture at S.21 was reduced to an instrument of paranoiac bureaucratic procedures.

The high school was a victim of urbicide – a technique of urban territorial kidnapping, occupation and destruction, aimed at mass control and terror.[38] Pol Pot and his regime considered cities parasites to the system of production. For the Khmer Rouge, sites of education incarnated a much-despised intellectualism and were breeding farms of counterrevolutionary traitors. Usurping it and adapting it into a prison made logical and symbolical sense.

The killing machine was 100% efficient at S.21, nobody trusted anyone anymore. The Khmer Rouge created a completely paranoiac system of total and circulating mistrust. Of the perfect prison system, Bentham writes in *Panopticon,* "Each comrade becomes an overseer."[39] The power of Angkar exercised its pressure perversely on all: High-ranking cadre of the government could end up in a torture chamber, children denounced their own parents. At S.21, a guard could make a mistake and share the fate of prisoners.[40] S.21 appears to have been an ultimate place of oppression, the iconic space of a destructive totalitarian regime.

Museum, Memories, Mourning

The museum is to date the last incarnation of the site. The effect of peace has moved the site away from its characteristics as S.21 and brought it back to an educational and memorial mission. As in concentration camps, the compound has become a historical monument. Tuol Sleng is a place of collective commemoration and mourning.

Parts of the surrounding walls have been sold and the barbed wire removed (except on Building C). The surrounding interrogation houses were destroyed or reintegrated in the life of the city. Building E, now the museum welcome center, has a new slanted roof. The garden has been restored with ornamental plants, benches surround the well-kept grass. Buildings were cleaned and somewhat repaired and are now occupied by museum display.[41]

Building C has been kept as a witness and stands out in its evocation of S.21 in its worst days. It is the ghostliest space of the site. Also preserved, the ground floor of Building A showcases the "special prison." In some individual cells, along with the furniture, a photograph hangs. It is of the room as it was found in 1979. It offers a reconstitution of the horrific sight it presented with a victim shackled to the bed.

In Buildings B and D passages cut into the walls during S.21 were kept to ease the enfilade circulation on the ground floor of the new museum galleries. Strangely enough, this is the guard path that the visitor traverses. Confessions, photography, clothing, tools and paintings describing the modes of torture and incarceration are exhibited,[42] with a chilling effect.

Some of the upper floors are closed and serve as archives and documentation. The lack of funding has kept scars on the built fabric. Despite the need for restoration, the qualities of the original architecture resurface. The layers of pasts are visible as at an archaeological site. The human experiences are sedimented in the fabric. Inhabited, the museum space reveals and cohabits with its anterior spaces.

"Every story is a travel story – a spatial practice"[43] proposes Michel de Certeau. S.21: *The Khmer Rouge Killing Machine*, a 2003 film by Rithy Panh is a spatial story at S.21. In the documentary, S.21 staff members and survivors are brought together on the site. Decades later, they are able to voice their experiences in a complex exchange. Victims confront the site and denounce the cruelty of the staff. The ex-guards argue with the ex-prisoners that their fate could have been inverted. One is reminded of Foucault's words in *The Eye of Power*: "Do you think it would be much better to have the prisoners operating the Panoptic apparatus and sitting in the central tower, instead of the guards?"[44]

Panh's film contributes as a work of remembering and a work of mourning. If Liberty is a practice, oppression is another, and their acts can seldom be exchanged, they speak of one or the other.[45] Rithy Panh searches the practices of S.21, and he aims to capture their true modalities. The camera follows the men through the place as their movements organize and traverse the interior architecture to reenact their daily activities.[46]

In the empty rooms, their gestures transport us in time: the space of S.21 is "actuated" in the place of the museum.[47] The space as it was in the period of 1975-1979 appears. The bodies of the ex-guard function as vehicles of space and time, their old routines manifest the presence of the passed victims. As Ashley Thomson notes, "There is a strange collapse of time. Watching, we find ourselves in 1976."[48] For the survivors and the ex-guards the experience seems strangely cathartic. Their old selves resurface and animate the space. They are projected in an anterior space. The film represents that anterior space.

In *Point de Folie*, Jacques Derrida notes: "We appear to ourselves only through an experience of spacing which is already marked by architecture. What happens through architecture both constructs and instructs this us." Architecture not only defines our human experience but also informs our identities. Our stories happen in a space that is architecturally framed. Tuol Sleng is a web of narratives from its school days to the dark ones of S.21.

The 14 graves of the last men to die at S.21 lie in front of Building A, where a stupa has been erected for the spirit of all the victims. The reality of death is overwhelming on the site. Tuol Sleng is the architectural proof of a devastating story of national importance.

While Cambodia is still looking for justice and the trial of high-ranking Khmer Rouge continues, the work at Tuol Sleng has brought people closer to the truth and healing: Investigations have been conducted by national and international researchers, creative people and educators, families of victims and survivors. Tuol Sleng has become an epistemological instrument, the most redeeming path one could hope for it.

NOTES

1 David Chandler, *Voices from S.21 Terror and history in Pol Pot secret Prison*, Silkworm books, 2000, p.4. "The code name S21 began to appear on Khmer Rouge documents in September 1975.

2 On Duch, see Rithy Panh's film *Le maître des forges de l'enfer*, 2012 and with Christophe Bataille *L'Élimination* Grasset, 2012. Also David Chandler, 2000, p.20.

3 "Duch, le bourreau khmer rouge, parle," Emmanuel Hecht in *L'Express*, 01/10/2012.

4 Many confessions were lost, used to wrap goods at the local market in the early months after the liberation of Phnom Penh, an estimated 14000 people were tortured at S21. David Chandler, 2000 p. 6. 12 prisoners had been set aside to work for the camp. Only 7 came forward after the liberation. One of the survivors, Van Nath speaks of 4 artists painters and sculptors, including himself. He also mentions 8 workers (electricians, carpenters) with whom he shares a room. Some artists and other workers before them were spared for a time before being executed. Van Nath, *A Cambodian Prison portrait, one year in the Khmer Rouge's S21* trans. Moeun Chhean Nariddh, White Lotus, 1998, p.51–55.

5 See Chandler, 2000 for a full account of the apparatus and activities of S.21.

6 See Chandler, 2000 p.5–7.

7 The primary school was called Bœng Ken Kang School before 1970, its name was changed to Tuol Sleng after 1970, the name of the area which now qualifies the entire site. Interview with Samneang Moul July 2012.

8 Judy Ledgerwood, "The Cambodian Tuol Sleng Museum of Genocidal Crimes: National Narrative" in *Museum Anthropology* 21 (1) 1997, p.95.

9 Ibid. See also Rachel Hughes " Nationalism and Memory at the Tuol Sleng Museum of Genocide Crimes, Phnom Penh, Cambodia" in *Memory, History Nation: Contested Pasts,* edited by Katharine Hodgkin and Susannah Radstone, Transaction Publishers, 2012, p.175–192.

10 "Transformation du mode de vie traditionnel" in *Cambodia d'aujourd'hui* December 1958 reprinted in *Cultures of Independence, An introduction to Cambodian Arts and Culture in the 1950s and 1960s*, Edited by Ly Daravuth and Ingrid Muan, The Reyum Institute of Arts and Culture, Phnom Penh, 2001.

11 Norodom Sihanouk "Le développement de l'instruction publique (Education Nationale), la jeunesse et l'essor extraordinaire des sports sous le Sangkum Reastr Niyum" in *Photo souvenirs du Cambodge Sangkum Reastr Niyum 1955–70,* Education, 1994, n.3, p.2–3. Helen Grant Ross and Darryl Collins, *Building Cambodia: New Khmer architecture*, 2006

12 See *Cultures of Independence, An introduction to Cambodian Arts and Culture in the 1950s and 1960s*, 2001 p.29 and Van Molyvann, *Modern Khmer Cities*, The Reyum Institute of Arts and Culture, Phnom Penh, 2003 p.150–167.

13 Ross and Collins, 2006, p.67. Also *Photo souvenirs du Cambodge Sangkum Reastr Niyum 1955–70*, Education, 1994, n.3.

14 Documentation Center of Cambodia (DC-Cam), *A History of Democratic Kampuchea*, 2007. p. 48–49.

15 Ibid.

16 "A l'école des maîtres angkoriens", interview of Vann Molyvann in *Phnom Penh developpment urbain et patrimoine, Ministère de la Culture et Atelier Parisien d'Urbanisme, Paris,* 1997, p.46.

17 Helen Grant Ross and Darryl Collins, 2006, p.53–55.

18 Ibid p.54.

19 Ibid.

20 Interview with Samneang Moul, ex student at the nearby Tuol Sleng Primary School from 1970 to 1973, July 2012. Michel Igout, *Phnom Penh then and Now*, White Lotus, 1993, p.14.

21 Khieu Kanaharith "Les premiers jours de Phnom Penh" in *Phnom Penh developpment urbain et patrimoine*, 1997, p.50–53.

22 Rithy Panh, Christophe Bataille, 2012 p.165. David Chandler, 2000, p.3–4.

23 Erving Goffman *Asylums* quoted in Chandler, 2000, p.14

24 Huy in Rithy Phan, *S21: the Khmer Rouge Killing Machine*, 2003.

25 Peter Maguire, *Facing Death in Cambodia*, Columbia University Press, 2005, p.51

26 Acknowledgement for the work of Pen Sereypagna and Vuth Danith.

27 *Photo souvenirs du Cambodge Sangkum Reastr Niyum 1955–70*, Education, 1994, n.3, p.17 & p.92.

28 A conversation with Vann Molyvann, Phonm Penh, August 24th, 2001 in *Cultures of Independence, An introduction to Cambodian Arts and Culture in the 1950s and 1960s*, 2001, p.11.

29 Interview with Samneong Moul, July 2012.

30 Ibid , p.83.

31 Ibid, p.41–42.

32 DC-Cam 2007, p.48.

33 See Judy Ledgerwood, "The Cambodian Tuol Sleng Museum of Genocidal Crimes: National Narrative" in *Museum Anthropology* 21 (1) 1997 p.85.

34 Van Nath, 1998, p.83.

35 Van Nath, 1998, p.83–84.

36 Ibid p.85–86.

37 See Lindsay French "Exhibiting Terror" in *Truth claims, representation and human rights*, edited by Philip Bradley and Patrice Petro, Rutgers university, 2002, p.131–155.

38 Urbicide is described by Milan Prodanovic, as the "the intentional, planned destruction of an entire way of life in a city through the killing of its citizens as well as its culture of civility and diversity" *Out of Ground Zero Case studies in Urban reinvention* edited by Joan Ockman Tempel Hoyne Buell Center for the study of American architecture, Columbia University Press 2002 p.139

39 Quoted in "The eye of power" in Michel Foucault, *Power/Knowledge Selected Interviews and Other Writings 1972–1977* Edited by Colin Gordon, Pantheon Books, 1980 p.153.

40 See David Chandler, 2000 Chapter Six "Explaining S21", p.143–155.

41 Ledgewood, p.83–86 describes the curatorial decisions taken.

42 Lindsay French, unpublished recollection of her visit to Tuol Sleng Museum of Genocide on 8/18/1991.

43 Michel de Certeau, *The practice of everyday life*, Steven Rendall, University of California Press, 1984 p.115.

44 Foucault, 1980, p.137

45 "Space Knowledge and Power" Michel Foucault in *Architecture theory since 1968* ed. K. Michael Hays MIT Press Columbia books of architecture 2000, p. 433.

46 On Rithy Panh's films about S.21 see Ashley Thompson, "Mnemotechnical politics: Rithy Panh's cinematic archive and the return of Cambodia's past" in *Modern and Contemporary Southeast Asian Art, An Anthology*, Southeast Asia Program, Cornell University, Ithaca, NY, 2012 p.225–240.

47 *The practice of everyday life*, 1984 De Certeau writes: "space is actuated by the ensemble of movements deployed within it. Space is produced by the operations that orient it, situate it, temporalize it and make it function in a polyvalent unity of conflictual programs or contractual proximities" p.118

48 Thomson, 2012, p.239.

MALLEABLE REMEMBRANCE

AND THE RE-CONSOLIDATION OF FRAGMENTS

by VICTOR M. SERRANO

Life is not what one lived, but what one remembers and how one remembers it in order to recount it.
—Gabriel García Márquez

The experience of Architecture is a construct of the mind where fragments of sensory perceptions are recorded, stored and recalled. When inhabiting a building one senses new materials, textures and sequences of spaces while remembering previously sensed surfaces and spatial compositions. This combination of new and old experiences is evidence of a mental process that allows the memory of a building to become malleable. A recently developed idea surrounding the study of Memory is that of "consolidation"[1] which states that when a memory is retrieved it becomes malleable allowing for it to be altered or even erased.

In a sense, when we remember something, we create a new memory, one that is shaped by the changes that have happened to our brain since the memory last occurred to us.
—Steven Johnson

In his study Johnson explains that within a new associative context, the brain is creating that memory once again instead of activating a memory that has been previously forged. This idea can be extrapolated onto the practice of architectural conservation in order to generate sensitive solutions for interventions in existing buildings. Since the memories of the building are revived by people and not the structure itself, the application of this concept into the architecture realm must be approached from a sensory standpoint purposely ignoring the precision of science. With this understanding, design proposals will not only allow for change in the materiality of a building but will also take into account the immaterial quality of the edifice itself in the continuance of its lifespan.

Architecture is a continuum building model. It is a body with both physical and spiritual qualities; it exists in a given moment and it is affected by time. There is an intrinsic relationship between the body of a living being and the body of a building exemplified in the cycle of birth and decay. This relationship is visible between the skeleton, the skin and the soul of the human body and the structure, finishes and the "Genius Loci"[2]–spirit of the place–in a building. When studying the life of an edifice one must understand the concept of duration,[3] a narrative where surviving pieces of the past coexist in the present. Memories are fragments of those stories intertwined within a complex membrane of associations that act as a structure to hold experiences. Triggering one of these associative elements causes an awakening of a moment in time where both the recollection and the association become alive and juxtaposed in the present instance and context. During this process a new memory is created, a collage of a kind where past and present collide.

This paper proposes that the memory of a building is a malleable physical substance, a part of the body of the building that should, like the building itself, allow for change over time. These ideas are explored through a study of the Murray House[4] in Hong Kong, a building that has witnessed the prosperity of an era, carries the burden of a tormented history and exists as empty stage of a kind on which new experiences will be played.

The Murray House, also known as the Murray Barracks, is one of the early examples of western architecture on the island. It was built to house the British Army quarters in 1846 in the Central District of Hong Kong five years after the British forces took possession of the island. Since its construction in 1846 it has undergone a series of transformations. Its verandas, defined by a sequence of classical columns and openings, are representative of architectural elements that belong to the colonial era in Hong Kong. Its central plan similarly follows a template for British military buildings of that era. This process of change inevitably has and will continue to awaken old experiences, individual and collective, which in turn will allow for new memories to be formed. These changes can be categorized into the following stages: recollection, degeneration, erasure and relocation.

Initial Memory Recollection

Arriving at each new city, the traveler finds again a past of his that he did not know he had: the foreignness of what you no longer are or no longer possess lies in wait for you in foreign, unpossessed places.

—Italo Calvino

The construction of an experience denotes a definite engagement with sensing. To utilize the senses is to understand one's surroundings in relationship to one's own body. This contemplation not only generates images that are processed in the brain but more so constitutes an act of learning. In experiencing the space of the original Murray House, a mental diagram is delineated. This map is a montage of instances that allow memories to be recorded, stored and later recalled and re-shaped.

On approaching the Murray House discernible shapes, such as the classical verandahs, relate to other forms already existing on one's mental map such as other colonial military buildings typical of the time. One finds such similarities in the use of verandas in the Old Tai O Police Station, located in one of the outlying islands in Hong Kong, and in other military-style buildings along the Kowloon District. Traditionally, the site of the building is the generation of design, as the functions of a particular space are often planned according to its placement: the orientation of the building, the relationship between the street and the entry, the location of rooms or the articulation of the fenestrations. In the case of the Murray Barracks, the architecture was rooted in response to the need for such military architecture in the area.

In studying memory, it is important to understand the delineation of character through the building's physical and social context. In the time of the Murray Barracks, the Central District of Hong Kong was mainly dedicated to military and administrative functions within a very important trade port. In this context, the building, along with the Victoria Barracks, the Wellington Barracks and the Admiralty Dock, constituted a fragment of a larger body, a British military compound.

In this sense, the facades of the Murray House were framed by an architecture of like character and function. In viewing the facades more images are processed to form part of the collage of memories. Here it is a unique recall of a Classical style of architecture implemented in the rounded arched openings and the incorporation of orders with verandahs and a Chinese-style roof.

Views of the Murray House

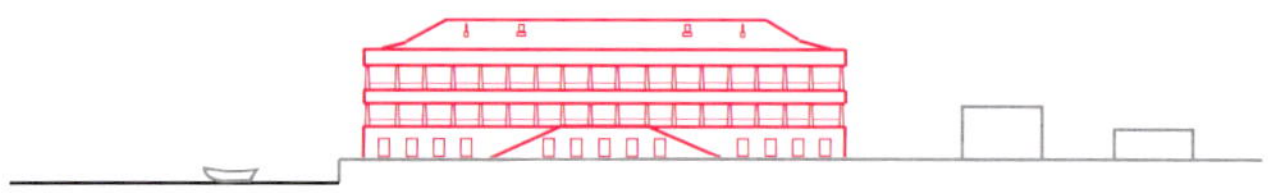

1884: original site

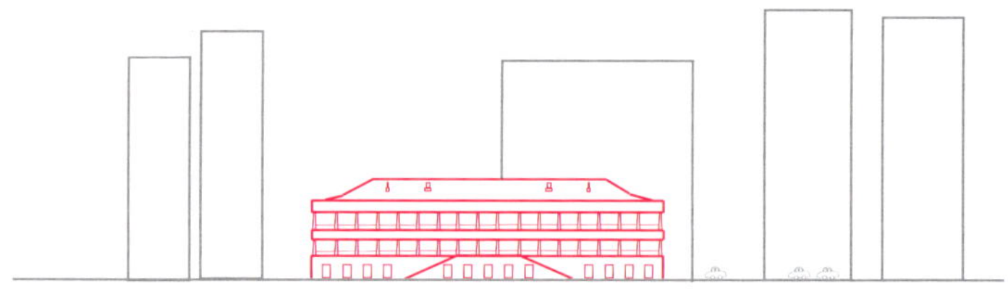

1950: original site

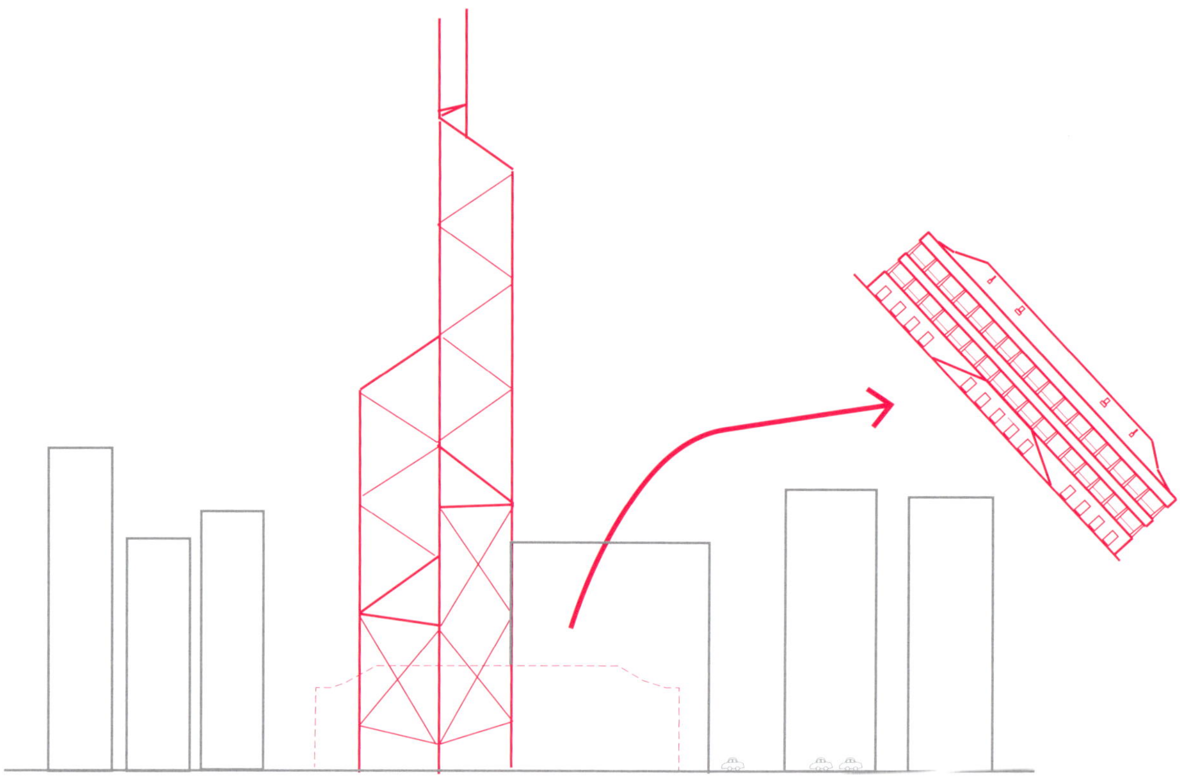

1982: original site

Memory Degeneration and Erasure

Thus there is a visible continuity that creates the image of the city that seems to be lasting and not even needing to change, while the inner workings are always subject to change to its most immediate needs; it is the changeability of the city, that gives it its permanence...

—Koolhaas, 1995

A building ages, the collective memory continues to develop while the contextual fabric of the place becomes deeply rooted in everyone's minds. These images, often depicted in postcards, become the face of the city as presented to the public and are used to recall the past as well as be a starting point for creating new memories. Such depictions of the Murray House qualify as degenerative in that they are used to generate new experiences over a frozen past.

The incorporation of Oriental and Western architectural elements is the first and the most apparent evidence of the memory re-consolidation process present in the building and is at the same time the first sign of this memory degeneration. One can speculate that when the barracks were designed, the British employed a European-styled architecture that conveyed the language of a military building. This transplant of style to the context of Hong Kong became a model of a British military building and, more importantly, defined a British military building in Hong Kong. One can argue that the process of degeneration begins to occur when the building is altered naturally by its decay process;

transformed physically to adapt to new functions; or by the change of its immediate surroundings. In architecture, the set of associative elements inherent to the building-such as materials, colors, the ambiance of the interior space, the program and circulation patterns-is ever changing. Even when a structure is frozen in time by way of constant restoration its permanence will be juxtaposed to time itself and to the context morphed by new generations. All these transformations comprise a degenerative state of memory that will allow for new experiences to be born.

The Murray House was affected in a similar manner during the Japanese occupation from 1941 to 1945, when it was used as quarters for the Japanese soldiers. It became a military center where many Chinese were executed. In this case social changes were responsible for damaging the image of the building. In addition, the Central District underwent a process of metamorphosis that would eventually change the face of the area from a military compound to a center of commercial activity. The Murray House was dismantled in 1982 and its fragments catalogued and stored. The removal of the structure gave way to the construction of the iconic Bank of China Tower designed by I.M. Pei in 1985. The erasure of the building from its site does not necessarily signify an immediate erasure of the spirit of the place. The extent of erasure is directly linked to the level of malleability of the memory. One can keep alive the memory of an object by its association with external elements. If the building is restored, moved or otherwise conserved, the memory, its original state, or parts of it, will remain somewhat intact. This memory is in a malleable state with the change of context. With complete erasure the building and its memory will vanish with time as new generations overlay a new set of experiences onto the place.

Relocation and Re-consolidation

If the Piazza San Marco in Venice were standing with the Doge's Palace in a completely different city, as the Venice of the future might be, and if we found ourselves in the middle of this extraordinary urban artifact, we would not feel less emotion and would be no less participants in the history of Venice.

—Aldo Rossi

The Murray House was re-assembled in 1998 on a new site on the south side of Hong Kong island known today as Stanley. Interestingly, this area was once the administrative region of Hong Kong before these headquarters were moved to the Central District, where the Murray House was originally located. It is a place where East and West meet, architecturally and socially, as Oriental and Western traditions occupy the oceanfront, in the forms of a promenade and a market. The Murray House has been re-located to the main street in the Stanley Market and oriented at an angle, that makes the volume visible from a distance. On approach, familiar shapes such as verandahs are recognized and memories of a colonial period begin to appear. The spaces once dedicated to military training today house a number of restaurants and a museum, patronized by locals and tourists alike. This new context includes fragments of other structures that have also been relocated from other parts of Hong Kong such as the Tong Cheong Pawn's Pillars[5] and the Blake Pier.[6] While the story of those additional fragments will not be addressed here, it is important that they are very much part of the memory of the Murray House. However, its edifice fits seamlessly into its new site by the sea without any evidence of its scars of war. While the body of the building appears intact, its spirit has been transformed to allow it to continue in a new existence.

In its new associative context, old memories of the building as a military and colonial structure blend with the new experiences of the building as a place of leisure. Subconsciously, one can inhabit, discover, feel, understand and re-shape the old memory of the Murray House within that of the new. In this sense, the life of the Murray House is not only composed of the fragments once lost or the torment and sadness once felt but also of the memories of newer generations as it is re-discovered in its new context. These physical and metaphysical changes in the body of the building allow the Murray House not only to communicate its history but also to make it present and part of our times.

NOTES

1 Johnson Steven. (2004). "The Science of Eternal Sunshine: You can't erase your boyfriend from your brain, but the movie gets the rest of it right," *Slate Magazine*. (March 22, 2004)

2 Christian Norberg-Schulz, Christian. *Genius Loci, Towards a Phenomenology of Architecture* Rizzoli, New York. 1980.

3 Bergson, Henri. *The Creative Mind, An Introduction to Metaphysics*. Basingstoke, England (2007)

4 Stanley Market Website. Murray House. http://www.hk-stanley-market.com/Murray-House/ (2012)

5 Hong Kong Stanley Market. http://www.hongkongstanleymarket.com/?p=Murray%20House&i=12 (2011)

6 Wong C.T., Leung M.K., Liu K.M., and Ma, K.Y. (2007), "The Blake Pier Pavilion: Just a Memory?" in *The Structural Engineers*, Vol. 85(20), pp. 38–43.

EVERYBODY'S HOUSE

THE ROSA PARKS HOUSE PROJECT

by RYAN AND FABIA MENDOZA, JOÃO JOSÉ SANTOS, DIOGO VALE

The Rosa Parks House Project *is the result of a series of interactions that began in Detroit, Michigan, where a decaying house on S. Deacon Street was placed on a list for demolition. The home of civil rights activist Rosa Parks from 1957 to 1959, it was saved from demolition in 2016 when her niece, Rhea McCauley, purchased it from the city of Detroit and gave it to artist Ryan Mendoza. It catapulted out of obscurity due to the interventions of Mendoza, who moved the structure, or what was left of it, across the Atlantic Ocean to Berlin, Germany. There, it gained a new identity and notoriety through reconstruction on German soil. Transformed through this act of translocation, the structure would re-cross the ocean, with hopes of a repatriation through Brown University's sponsorship in spring of 2018.*

At Int|AR, we rejoiced that this project—steeped in art, history, preservation, memory and, of course, adaptive reuse – would be in our own backyard. On a late February afternoon, we met the delivery of the shipping containers that crossed the Atlantic with the deconstructed parts of 2672 S. Deacon Street. These were unloaded at its temporary American home: WaterFire Arts Center in Providence, RI, a 37,000 sq ft arts venue that was itself transformed from an abandoned industrial facility for the US Rubber Company. The physical components of the humble structure occupied merely a corner of this vast interior, still marked with traces of its manufacturing past.

In the first days of March, the house slowly began to materialize from the bundles of house parts. We became acquainted with Ryan Mendoza and his team as they began to assemble the Providence rendition of 2672 S. Deacon Street with salvaged parts that comprised facades, partial wood flooring and elements of the internal staircase. Once a simple wood frame structure, the house's structural integrity was undermined

The side facade of 2672 S. Deacon Street in the process of reassembly at WaterFire Arts Center

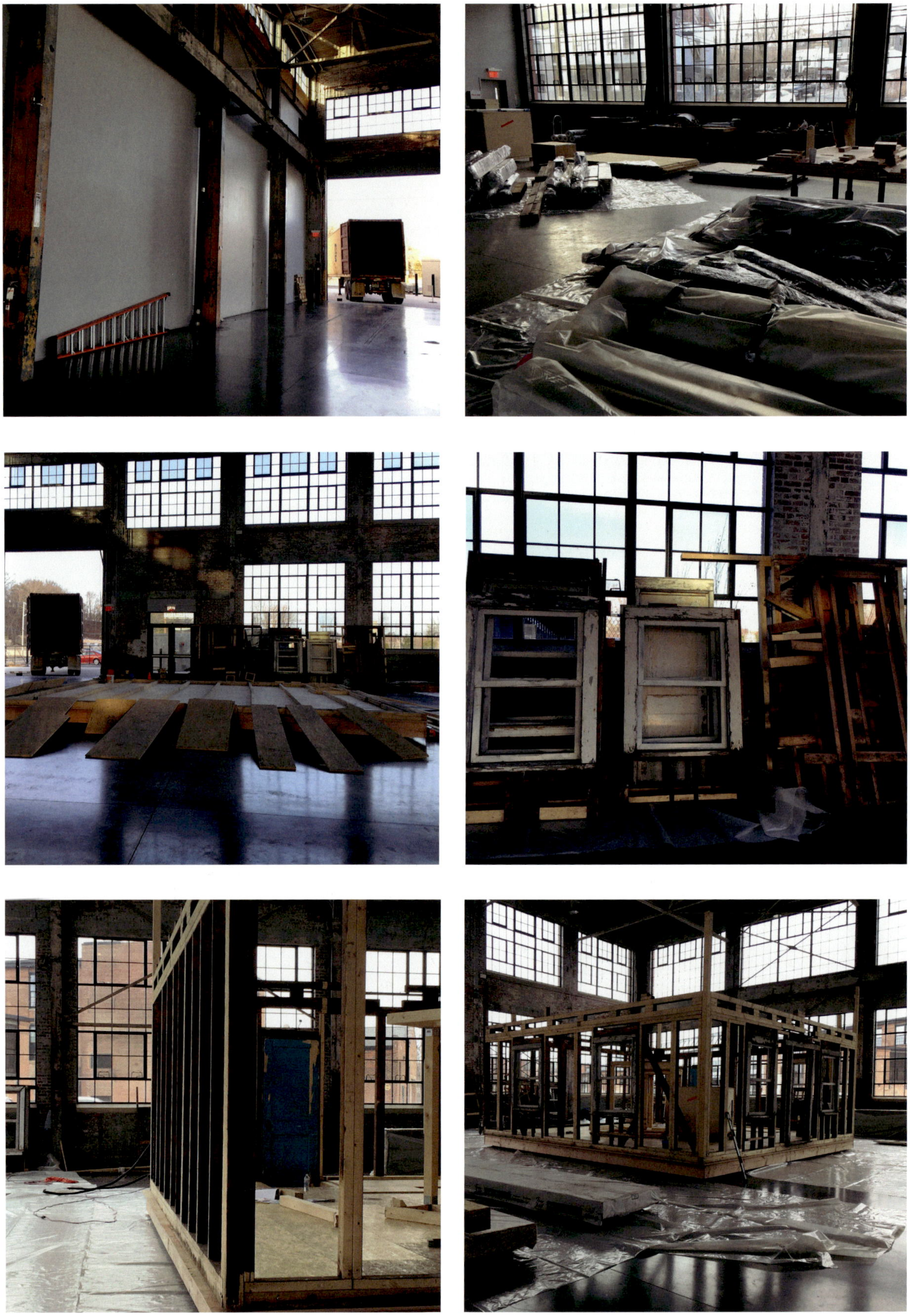

From arrival to construction: the process of reassembly of the *Rosa Parks House Project* at the WaterFire Arts Center

by the deterioration of the second floor. In Berlin, this was resolved by augmenting the undermined structure with new framing. This permitted the presentation of the house as an object in Mendoza's Berlin garden. In Providence, where the house would also be presented as a whole object inside the exhibition hall of WaterFire Arts Center, team architects João José Santos and Diogo Vale designed a new glu-lam structural ring frame to provide additional support from the inside. But the construction was interrupted by the sudden withdrawal of support from Brown University for the project. The house was only a skeletal frame when the work came to an abrupt halt.

The ensuing March days were filled with speculations on the fate of The Rosa Parks House Project *going forward. The barrage of media coverage of this controversial time is easily accessible and, therefore, not the subject of this article. A glance at the headlines would, however, reveal raw emotions, just under the surface, elicited by the return of this simple house to a country that had not come to terms with racism, half a century after the start of the Civil Rights movement. With an imminent deadline for the return of the house to Berlin, WaterFire Arts Center planned a public viewing of the project on the first weekend in April, heralding the 50-year anniversary of the assassination of Dr. Martin Luther King, Jr. Organized with scant time and resources, this celebration of the house was powered by goodwill and volunteerism. The haste to present the project without the previously promised funding placed enormous strain on the team as they attempted to complete the installation in a few days. In the end, the time constraints were insurmountable and the final product included only partially completed facades and roof.*

These circumstances in Providence, however, yielded unprecedented views into the interior, a departure from its previous iterations. In Detroit, where the house was a ruin, the interior had succumbed to mold and rot. In Berlin, as an object in Mendoza's garden, curtains at the windows precluded a view of the nonexistent interior. In Providence, where the house was unwillingly presented in an incomplete state, the interior—or lack thereof—was made visible for the first time, revealing Santos and Vale's intervention of a new internal structure. It also permitted views of two installations: first, the original second-floor doors were suspended in the air where they would have been and, second, the inclusion of three ceramic sculptures by Mendoza, designed in consultation with Rhea McCauley. This incomplete state exposed the scantiness of the original material and, by contrast, emphasized the additions made to support the structure, all previously out of sight in Berlin. While applying conventional standards for heritage to the project may raise questions of authenticity and significance, in an era that includes "experimental preservation," this rendition of 2672 S. Deacon is one that opens a new chapter in the history of the house.

At Int|AR, we were drawn to The Rosa Parks House Project *for its complexity. Once a humble wood home in Detroit, it became an "art object" when placed out of context and, repatriated, has claims as a monument of American civil rights – all through various acts of intervention. What indeed is* The Rosa Parks House Project*? How do we categorize it? Can we define it? What is the process by which it was transformed? What is its legacy and role in history? What constitutes a monument? Who has the right to assign values to monuments?*

Few will have the opportunity to see this project in person and to probe these questions through observation. Herein, we provide the different perspectives on the project from its origins in Detroit to the journeys it has taken to date. We hope that by hearing the voices of not only Ryan Mendoza but that of the team behind the project's realization readers will have an opportunity to claim 2672 S. Deacon Street for themselves. Rosa Parks' civil disobedience on that bus so long ago in Alabama was an act for a collective right; the house that provided her refuge for two years after Alabama and was saved from demolition is one that belongs to more than one person. It is Everybody's House.

Liliane Wong, Int|AR

Ryan Mendoza reassembling the house in Berlin, Germany

It began with ***Ryan Mendoza****, American artist and expatriate living in Germany. In his own words:*

Before getting involved in the 2672 S. Deacon Street, *Rosa Parks House Project*, I was 25 years an expatriate living in Berlin. Having lost touch with my country, I thought, rather than distance myself further from American values, I would embrace them fully in an attempt to epitomize the quintessential American by colonizing Europe with actual American houses. *The White House Project* began thanks to a house donated by a friend of mine, native Detroiter Gregg Johnson. The house was appropriately, though not without controversy, removed from Stoepel Street just off of Eight Mile, the road that divides a segregated Detroit.

Through *The White House Project*—where a house was deconstructed, shipped overseas and rebuilt at the Verbeke Foundation in Belgium—I gained adequate knowledge of how wooden houses could be disassembled and reassembled.

On my trips back and forth to Detroit I met, at a performance at the Charles H. Wright Museum, Gregg Dunmore and Joel Boykin of Pulsebeat.TV. After hearing of my desire to preserve American houses that would otherwise be demolished, they put me into contact with Rosa Parks' niece, Rhea McCauley.

I met Rhea on a wintry day in front of 2672 S. Deacon Street where the 3-bedroom house Rosa Parks had lived in with 15 family members stood in a decaying stoicism. I remember the floors were dipping and the house moved ever so slightly with the wind, the back wall being patched together with the doors of the house itself.

Both projects I had completed in Detroit, *The Invitation* and *The White House*, dealt with the housing crisis, a subtext that is also inextricable from the *Rosa Parks House Project*. Rhea McCauley, who had lived in the house with her aunt, had recently bought it off of a demolition list for 500 dollars. When local government and institutions showed no interest in helping her restore the house as a monument, she approached me and suggested we work together. Our petition for local support was also turned down, so I offered to ship the house to Berlin. It proved essential that the house be extricated from its location for the world to pay attention.

For lack of a more appropriate place, the unassuming house Rosa Parks had taken refuge in after the tumultuous Alabama bus boycott was temporarily relocated to the garden between my studio and my home in Berlin. Last winter, the house arrived to my doorstep as planks of wood in a shipping container and was rebuilt from sketches made during disassembly in Detroit. Reconstructing the house alone, and underfunded during the winter of 2016, was a physically challenging task. Handling the planks, I considered whether the house would one day become the 77th monument to the Civil Rights Movement. I read up on American history where our forefathers were also slave owners

2672 S. Deacon displayed as an object inside the WaterFire Arts Center

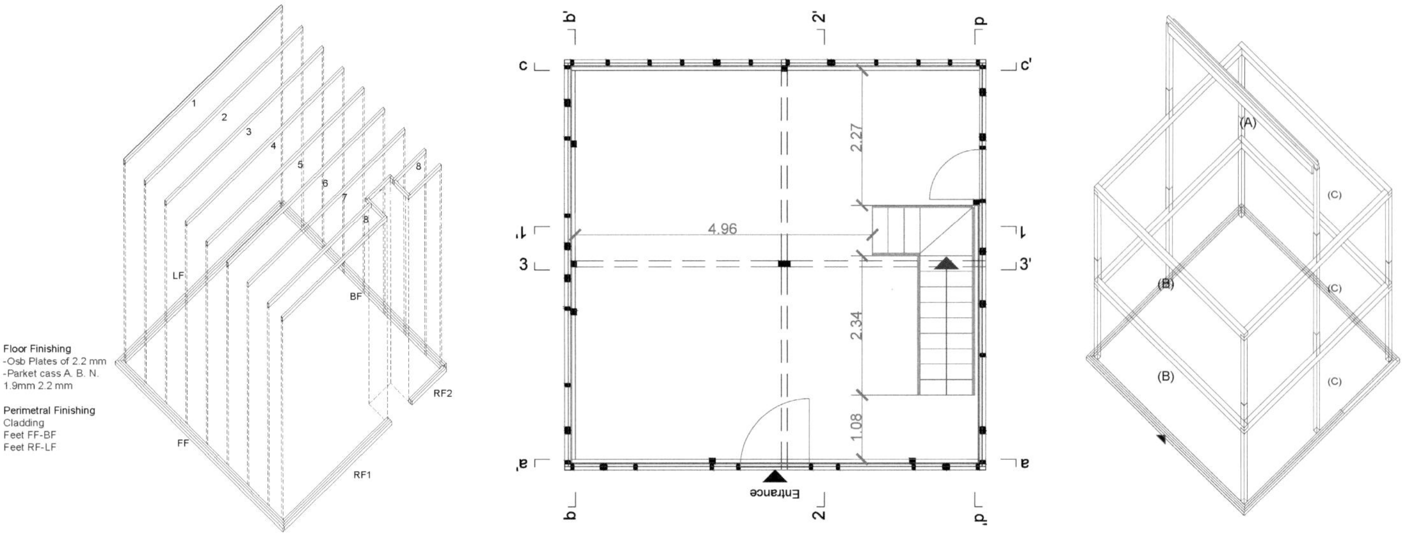

and I struggled with this cognitive dissonance. Thomas Jefferson was undeniably a racist as well as a rather abusive slaveholder, notably punishing his slaves by selling them at auction, willfully breaking families apart. His only plausible solution to the problem of slavery included expatriation:

> *I can say with conscious truth that there is not a man on earth who would sacrifice more than I would, to relieve us from this heavy reproach ... if, in that way, a general emancipation and expatriation could be effected: ... but, as it is, we have the wolf by the ear, and we can neither hold him, nor safely let him go. Justice is in one scale, and self-preservation in the other.*
>
> Letter from Thomas Jefferson to John Holmes, April 22, 1820 [1]

Jefferson worried the flesh would be ripped from the face of the nation, revealing an unsavory truth. Subsequent systematic transfer of enchainment, from slavery itself to segregation through the Jim Crow laws to a privatized prison system, kept the 'wolf' in chains, and the so-called preservation of the face of the nation intact. But with mounting evidence of systemic racism, and with clarity over what the Confederate monuments actually stand for – having been created in a reactionary way to the advancements to civil equality – an opening for the Rosa Parks House to be preserved and possibly celebrated as a monument contrasts with its near demolition at the hands of the local government in Detroit.

During the reconstruction of the house, handling delicately the planks of wood, I wondered: was my mission that of preserving history or was it that of attempting to free the ever-ensnared Jeffersonian wolf, therefore upsetting a national myth? In the end, I realized I am just custodian and messenger. The actual message, I myself, being born white and after the Civil Rights Movement, can only be comprehended in a limited way.

Rosa Parks came to Detroit fleeing death threats, but experienced little refuge in Detroit. After living for two years with her brother, sister-in-law and their 13 children, Parks moved multiple times. She suffered an assault in her home at the age of 81 and was threatened with eviction at 91. While Detroit was briefly renowned as a place where Black residents reached significant levels of homeownership, Rosa Parks never owned a home. She called Detroit 'the Northern promise land that wasn't.' Housing issues, centered around segregation and displacement due to urban renewal, were central to Rosa Parks' activism her entire life. Detroit has ranked among the 10 most segregated metropolitan areas in the United States since the mid-20th century. By the early 1960s, urban renewal and highway construction destroyed 10,000 structures in Detroit, displacing over 40,000 people, 70% of whom were African-American. More recently, since the housing crisis, foreclosure and demolition swept the city, leaving more than 70,000 abandoned buildings and 90,000 vacant lots. [2]

For over 40 years, these four walls and roof were a home. It was the place that Rosa Parks' brother sought to create a better life for his family after returning from World War II, where Rosa Parks' nieces and nephews grew up and where Parks lived for her first two years in Detroit. When the family left in 1982, memories continued to cling to the clapboards, but the home became a house. When it was put on a demolition list in 2013, the meaning attached to the building changed again: it became a number on a list, a statistic in Detroit's decline. In its ensuing incarnations, the structure blurred lines between historic monument and art object.

Santos and Vale's diagrams for the new internal structure supporting the reassembled house

Ultimately, this is a project about memory. By taking the house apart and then piecing it back together, literally 're-membering' it, Rhea McCauley and I invite the American consciousness to remember a house it didn't know it had forgotten. Art often plays with a shift in context to inspire the viewer to look: the house's stay in Berlin leveraged this discordance to get the viewer to pay attention. The house offers a unique opportunity to consider how we remember Rosa Parks, and in doing so, begins to renegotiate how we memorialize American history more broadly.

Recent debate surrounding the dismantling of Confederate monuments indicates the persistent significance of how we inscribe memories into the topography of our surroundings. Seven hundred monuments of Robert E. Lee and other Confederate generals still parade across public squares and school grounds across the United States, despite a recent wave of dismantling. Confederate monuments rely on erasing the context of their construction to foster nostalgia. Confederate monument construction peaked in 1910, a year after the NAACP was founded. Another flurry of building began in the 1950s as the Civil Rights Movement gained momentum. The Little Rock Nine and school integration prompted a disturbing spike of Confederate monuments on school campuses. Many Americans are under the illusion, however, that the monuments were built during Reconstruction. The anachronistic material and design veil the racism that is inextricable from these totems.

I highlight this disconnect in context in order to introduce the way the *Rosa Parks House Project* can offer a mode of memorialization where context is paramount. Of course, the version of Rosa Parks incorporated into the American mythos has also relied on obscured context and idealized narrative. In her biography, *The Rebellious Life of Mrs. Rosa Parks*, Jeanne Theoharis exposes the ways in which the historical narrative surrounding Rosa Parks has reduced her lifelong commitment to activism to one afternoon on a bus, fabricated a story of a quiet seamstress who demurely kept her seat and relegated Parks to be a hero for children. In the introduction of her book, Theoharis emphasizes, "One of the greatest distortions of the Parks fable has been the ways it made her meek.... When Parks died in Detroit in 2005, she was held up as a national heroine but stripped of her lifelong history of activism and anger at American injustice. The Parks who emerged was a self-sacrificing mother figure for a nation who would use her death for a ritual of national redemption." Parks' memorial services also took place in the wake of Hurricane Katrina. In honoring Rosa Parks, the nation was able to glaze over the racial and economic inequality exposed by government negligence during Katrina. The public memorial leveraged a romantic fable of Rosa Parks to quiet contemporary injustice.

My hope is that, by contrast, the dissonant context at play in the *Rosa Parks House Project* will impede nostalgia and obstruct simplification. The house's journey across the sea should inspire questions. Addressing history and the present day with questions, rather than assumptions or generalizations, is a mode of demanding a fuller version of history.

Ryan Mendoza

Team member **Fabia Mendoza***'s film on the project,* The White House Documentary, *received an award at the 18th Beverly Hills Festival in April 2018. She lends her voice to this article with thoughts that provide a cinematic background to the house's place of origin:*

Ryan started his first project, *The White House,* with the intention to reconnect with his home country. It was

Santos and Vale's catalog of parts and their proposal for support elements allowed the house to be reassembled after its relocation from Berlin, Germany

meant as a project about memory. It was serendipity that our friend, Gregg Johnson, who wanted to donate the house for this project, happened to be a Detroiter.

Without the plan to make a political project or one about the Civil Rights Movement, Ryan walked into a battlefield of racial tensions, controversy, political rot and, three years later, he came back to Germany with the Rosa Parks' Family Home donated to him by Rosa Parks' family.

Ryan became the embodiment of the White Savior Complex. And the unsuccessful attempt by Rosa Parks' family members to save the structure and the fact that Ryan was able to do so became proof of a system in which Black oral history is not valued.

The White House Documentary, 75min, 2017, began as a simple documentary about an artist, but the habitants, musicians and friends we collaborated with on the various projects in the city took more and more space in my movie.

I hoped to portray Detroit as a place that can't be reduced to its ruins.

As in fact it is a melting pot of musical talent and wisdom. Living through segregation, the rebellions in 1967, the housing crisis and the downfall of the automobile industry, the Detroiters who resisted the city's depopulation were left with a deep fighting spirit and untouchable pride.

313–One Love, Detroit vs. Everybody, Nothing Stops Detroit tell the story of a city unwilling to surrender.

The image portrayed of Detroit as an abandoned city couldn't be further from the truth.

I learned how the Detroit Techno by Underground Resistance, exported to Berlin in the 1990s, shaped my own city and made it the metropolis it is today.

Experiencing the gentrification of Detroit's downtown area, the progress of projects like the Packard Plant Project on Detroit's East Side, the biggest industrial renovation project in North America, the Berlin – Detroit Connection, a cultural program between both cities, and the new train system are all evidence of Detroit's comeback. I can only hope that city planning and gentrification are being guided correctly in order to positively influence all communities.

Fabia Mendoza

2672 S. Deacon reassembled in the artist's garden in Berlin, Germany

Closeup and through the clapboard to the interior of the *Rosa Parks House Project*

2672 S. Deacon on the demolition list in Detroit, Michigan

Architect Diogo Vale, *team member for disassembling and reassembling the house both in Berlin and in Providence, posits this project by looking backward in history:*

It becomes interesting when one thinks about the power that architecture can physically transmit to society, going back from the opulent and luxurious buildings in the Baroque era to the political and monumental buildings of the Neoclassical period. The weight of authority – as meaning, as modus operandi – is transmitted through the scale and detail of such buildings all over the world.

In the 21st century, in a bankrupt city, the historical heritage of the local community starts to lose meaning for its government and they began to demolish traces of a built history deeply rooted in the city. With this simple house on the verge of being forgotten (demolished) begins a polemic among the community. In a way, its significance increases with no change in scale or detail. In that sense, it is beautiful that a simple word "Unforgotten," unleashes a sequence of socio-political events....

A simple and worn-out house with no architectural signature becomes a curious tool for creating an environment for a debate on different subjects but all with the same goal: an improvement of the quality of life.

The past is revisited as a learning tool to create knowledge, to discuss the future, to move forward, to delete taboos and all because of a simple architectonic maneuver. Detached from the surroundings, the house emanates a different message, on the loss of a country that didn't appreciate the value of its simple but historic monumentality.

And from the strength of one person more layers are added, more people become involved, increasing the value and meaning of this house. Its return to its home country is a perfect moment to discuss, debate about the society and community it has formed.

From a simple, worn-out family house to the house for everybody. Once again architecture serves as messenger of a group of important values, but by the hand of an artist and a house that knows no luxury. Neither palace or political building, this humble little structure holds the same power to transmit messages and inform its people. Rosa Parks House, the house of everybody!

Diogo Vale

Architect João José Santos, *co-producer of the new internal support structure, shares his thoughts on the role of supporting Ryan Mendoza and what it means to add a new layer to history.*

House...as Home, will always be an undisputed symbol of our continuously developing human identity, as we move on and from. As a real-life American hero story, this house of many is then a singular subject, for it had not only been the place of heartful familial gathering but the intimate shelter found later in the storm. Witness of circumstances, molded by them, informing who inhabits it and how it is inhabited, representing at the same time millions in a collective identity. Today the quiet structure of statements from the past still stands and, an inside-out room for collective consideration, it is again formed, readapted, just like Home.

Rosa Louise McCauley Parks, as home for American historic memory and national identity.

There were three main acts to consider for an assembly/disassembly process of this project since it landed in Wedding, Berlin, in 2016; to dissect the one-man job, to re-formulate it, to recreate it.

To Dissect

To learn from the artist and his work as pre-conditions. Acknowledge problems and solutions found upon giving literal and physical shape to this idea, reckoning with little or no assistance from anybody else. Recognize the small assisting construction features created for this purpose and know the new structural system cast in order to make possible this solo "free-style reconstruction."

To Re-formulate

To sum up professional knowledge of the already formed construction for making it a safe, transferable object. Collaborating with both engineering and architectural disciplines as past crutches and innocuous parts are removed, a new sub-structural system is designed and an inventory of the parts and the assembly catalogue are made, all aiming for a final result.

To Recreate

To rescue a kidnapped house when the project finds a 'lasting' new home, when the figure arises from an embodiment of the artist and the personal approach by the building assisting team that, in a collective work, will positively leave new imprints. In a communal accomplishment, the work of art slowly drops authorship to become everybody's work, everybody's house.

João José Santos

EPILOGUE

The Rosa Parks House Project is currently on display at the Palazzo Reale, Naples, Italy.

NOTES

1 Letter of Thomas Jefferson to John Holmes, Library of Congress, https://www.loc.gov/exhibits/jefferson/ 159.html, accessed June 26, 2018.

2 https://www.liveauctioneers.com/item/63230011_the-rosa-parks-family-home, accessed July 2, 2018.

CROYDON'S TOWER

RECONCILING OLD TRAUMAS AND NEW HOPES

by ROBERT SCHMIDT III, DAN SAGE, JAMES PINDER, CHARLES HOLLAND, SIMON AUSTIN

The suburban town of Croydon exists as one of London's 33 boroughs. Located to the south, it has historically been an important gateway bridging central London with southeast England. Croydon has the largest population of all the boroughs, boasts the third largest office stock in London and the largest shopping center in south London.[1] This article examines how Croydon's changing architectural landscapes remember, and rework, urban traumas. It focuses on the adaptive reuse of Croydon's 1960s podium and tower office stock; the iconic Nestlé Tower is discussed as an exemplar.

Croydon's traumatic history is well known: manufacturing industries, transport infrastructure and housing were extensively bombed throughout the Second World War. Bomb damage, slum clearance, London development plans and Croydon's leaders' speculative ambitions then paved the way for modernist, often high-rise, commercial developments in Croydon's center. A once small market town, Croydon became home to several significant public and private sector organisations, developing new office space roughly equivalent to Manchester, Liverpool and Birmingham in the 1960s. However, over the last 30 years the center's modernist legacy has gradually appeared traumatic itself: Croydon will soon lose its largest employer when, at the end of 2012, Nestlé moves its UK headquarters out of the borough, taking nearly 1,000 jobs with it. St. George's House (or Nestlé Tower) has a 47-year history in Croydon—how will the loss of jobs, and potential shift in residents, affect Croydon?

The 2011 riots in Croydon offer a troubling portent in this regard. This vacant landmark building, and others nearby, invite questions about how we define, experience and shape the layers of interwoven architectural memories that record urban traumas, from the exceptional (war, riots) to the quotidian (shifting late-capitalist economies). Moreover, as Croydon's history suggests, traumas may predicate hope—what opportunities exist to reconcile old traumas alongside new hopes, through novel building uses, materials and users? This article sets the stage for understanding how tactical interventions that address trauma can begin to redefine Croydon's built environment.

Defining Trauma

In everyday use trauma usually denotes an immediate experience, a rupture, a moment, an event, in our lives; however, trauma theorists have long acknowledged that trauma is far from an immediate and bounded event; rather, it is a recurring experience bound up with on-going and reshaping memories and histories. The pioneering trauma theorist Cathy Caruth makes this point by defining trauma as "an overwhelming experience of sudden or catastrophic events in which the response to the event occurs in the often delayed, uncontrolled repetitive appearance of hallucinations and other intrusive phenomena."[2] The psychoanalytical emphasis on individual experience, as apparent in early theorizations of trauma,[3] has discernibly widened over the last couple of decades: trauma has been addressed as a collective experience, at the scale of neighbourhoods, towns, cities and nations.[4] While much work along this vein has considered how human collectives experience trauma,[5] we must also bear in mind that at the scale of any community, trauma is always materially mediated, not least by the built environment.[6]

Architecture works through trauma: it invites us to bear witness to trauma; to reconsider collective trauma and our relation to it; or simply to forget. All too often the latter is the *modus operandi* of contemporary urbanisms: our built environments continually rise again phoenix-like out of the ashes of past traumas. Modernist architecture's insistence on discovering and celebrating 'the new,' architectures whose pure geometrical forms and novel materials and construction intentionally eviscerate their historical contexts and traumas, are exemplary in this regard. Notable examples include: the Soviet modernisation of Dresden (and other Eastern

Aerial view of Croydon today

Bloc cities) after Allied bombing during World War II; the rapid rebuilding of Kobe after the destructive 1995 earthquake; the on-going re-development of 'slums' in Shanghai; and the shining ascent of Manhattan's One World Trade Center on the site of the Twin Towers. However, across such revitalization of urban sites, this modern search for the new, this distancing of past traumas, is increasingly itself viewed as traumatic. Our built environments are replete with examples of the 'death of the modern', from 'post-modern' office blocks, whose facades self-consciously parody the absence of industrial pasts, such as Make Architects' Cube in the English City of Birmingham, to the proliferation of sustainable eco-homes within the world's cities that embody rather than deny the trauma of contemporary existence – anthropocentric climate change. Even across the above-cited modern renewals, trauma persisted, or persists, as an excessive reminder of the futility (and perhaps fate) of the modernist project: Dresden's 18th century Frauenkirche Baroque church stood in a state of wartime ruin in the city center for over 50 years; Kobe's city government have intentionally preserved a section of earthquake-damaged waterfront; Shanghai's slums endure and grow; and memorial pools in Manhattan bear witness to the absent presence of the Twin Towers.

The recent experience of modernist architecture suggests that efforts to erase trauma through the built environment may be considered even more traumatic. Such effacing projects must also be understood alongside Marx's famous slogan for capitalism: "all that is solid melts into air."[7] The Marxist view that capitalism is hardwired for creative destruction is hard to ignore when considering trauma and the built environment.

Croydon c1930 (Pre-postwar growth)

Marx famously suggested that capitalism demands new sources of surplus value, more efficient means of production, and greater innovation. If an office building cannot accommodate the latest highly efficient working practices or technologies, capitalism may require that it is destroyed and rebuilt anew. The only defence against capital appears to be capital: a traumatized building can be protected if new sources of capital can be extracted from it; if not, then it is redundant and ripe for destruction. This zero-sum game of creative destruction of course only partially resembles the world beyond Marxist dystopian thought, not least because the State, as well as charities and other similar-minded organisations, can ensure that some traumatized and essentially economically obsolete buildings remain protected. Nevertheless, Marx suggests the possibility that the simultaneous aggrandizement and effacement of trauma – the phoenix mentality – is to some extent beneficial to particular groups and their largely commercial interests, from speculative property investors or even public bodies looking to promote urban competitiveness. Viewed in this way, trauma is not simply an individual or collective experience; it can also be viewed as a social construction replete with political and economic significance.

If, as appears to be the case, the mediation of memories of trauma through the built environment is common to human experience, then we can still argue that our responses to trauma are far from universal. For some, any diagnosis of trauma in the built environment appears to invite opportunities for creative destruction, yet for others past traumas can never be aggrandized then erased because they are actively involved in the reproduction of communities:

Traumatized communities are something distinct from assemblies of traumatized persons [whereby] traumatic wounds inflicted on individuals can combine to create a mood, an ethos – a group culture.[8]

LaCapra suggests that for communities and individuals alike, trauma demands 'working through,' which can be a positive act:

Working through does not mean avoidance, harmonization, simply forgetting the past, or submerging oneself in the present. It means coming to terms with trauma, including its details, and critically engaging the tendency to act out the past and even to recognize why it be necessary and even in certain respects desirable or at least compelling.[9]

As hopefully is now apparent, the palimpsest of past traumas recorded in our built environments is at least as compelling a platform to 'work through' the complexities of trauma as is a novel or historical testimony. In accepting this layered understanding of trauma, memory and architecture, we might then ask how might 'accommodation,' 'adaptation' and 'negotiation' – rather than 'renewal,' 'regeneration,' 'renaissance' – become the development mantra for future urbanisms? These issues will now be considered in the context of Croydon, a town with interwoven layers of trauma.

Croydon

Croydon exists outside of the traditional urban growth model, seemingly akin to an American 'Edge City,' perhaps 'popping up' overnight as a result of post-war growth.[10] Yet such a view neglects its long history, mixing adaptations and renewals. The earliest records of Croydon date back to the Anglo Saxon period, a time of Germanic invasions, with the Archbishops of Canterbury settling a large estate (Croydon Palace) in 960 in what is now considered the old town. While the old palace was abandoned by the archbishops in 1780, it later became a bleaching factory and remains today as a collection of buildings accommodating a school for girls (Old Palace School of John Whitgift).

Prior to the 20th century Croydon existed as a thriving market town (it has the oldest street market in London) and became the first town serviced by rail and canal (Surrey Iron Railway and Croydon Canal). It was at the end of the 19th century when Croydon changed to a County Borough in 1889 that marks its earliest transformation into a suburban town with an initial round of slum clearance and widening of its high street. The early 20th century development in Croydon came with industrial growth in metal working, car manufacture and aerospace technologies. As a result of the First World War, the Beddington Aerodrome was constructed in 1915 to counter the Zeppelin raids and was expanded and served as London's passenger and parcel airport between the world wars until it was again enlisted by the Royal Air Force during the Second World War. German air raids in the Second World War damaged thousands of homes and killed more than 750 civilians. In the summer of 1944, Croydon was bombed more than any other London borough. After the war, the airport was deemed a less attractive location to Heathrow due to its limited scale, and it eventually closed in 1959. Most of the area has been erased, providing parkland and a residential estate, but the control tower and terminal building remain, embracing the memories of Croydon's role and are used as a business center today.

After the Second World War a combination of events – London planners wanting to move office development outside the congested center (A Plan to Combat Congestion in Central London) and Croydon council putting forth the Croydon Corporation Act – ignited the large-scale tabula rasa approach that allowed the town center to transform faster than any other location in England at the time. While the former policy recommended areas for development outside the center, the latter allowed the council to acquire a large amount of land necessary to upgrade infrastructure and release the remaining parcels to private developers to construct new office blocks. Croydon quickly became known as a 'mini-Manhattan' with 45 buildings towering over 25 metres in height.[11] A prime example is Taberner House, a 19-storey tower sitting on a three storey podium. Opened in 1967, the top deck functioned as a viewing platform until it was closed due to the rising number of suicides occurring from it. After 45 years, it appears the life of the Taberner House has run its course, with the council constructing a new building across the street. Taberner House is scheduled for demolition, with the site to be redeveloped as a mixed use residential-led scheme.

In addition to the bundle of modernist office blocks, shopping and civic buildings were also constructed during the 1960s. Fairfield Halls, an arts center with a large auditorium, theatre, cinema and gallery, opened in 1962 on top of a portion of the disused railway. Refurbishment plans by the council for the building have continually fallen through, while at the same time the council has in the past sought new hope in the construction of an arena (albeit failing multiple times) which would have competed as a venue. A new £27m refurbishment project is going ahead and the architects are now being appointed. Whitgift shopping center opened in 1968 on the site previously occupied by Whitgift Middle School for four centuries, until it was forced to move three miles outside the town center. Today, the

Map of buildings promoted by Croydon Council for conversion

1. Prospect First
2. Delta Point
3. Lunar House
4. Sunley House
5. Apollo House
6. Whitgift Blocks A, B+C
7. Emerable House
8. Carolyn House
9. Southern House
10. Centre Tower
11. Amp House
12. Nestle Tower
13. Ryland House
14. Davis House
15. Taberner House
16. Impact House
17. Direct Line Building
18. Grosvenor House
19. Leon House

shopping center is in severe need of redevelopment and has drawn interest from two developers – one proposing comprehensive redevelopment, erasing all recollection of the previous shopping center, and the other suggesting incremental renewal and a return to the open streets and squares atmosphere that existed when the center thrived – offering the council an interesting choice of regeneration or adaptation.

While Croydon has continually attempted to promote its image, it has been turned down for city status on numerous occasions from the 1950s onward – a reminder perhaps of a negative view towards its mono-functional architectural landscape. It has struggled to attract major development since the mid-1980s, when attempts to create a 'visual coherence' through new development were implemented through reflective glass, cladding materials and increased landscaping. These developments, however, are generally viewed as no better (if not worse) than those of the 1960s and can be understood as failed attempts to reconcile meaning through renewal. Thus, Croydon is left primarily with a legacy of 1960s modernist office buildings – a negative image which was exacerbated during the London Riots in 2011, given the prominent coverage by the media of the 144-year-old, five-generational family-owned furniture store, House of Reeves, burning to the ground. The building has since been removed and the family currently trades out of a nearby refurbished building. As Croydon continues to struggle with its traumatic past and its modern legacy of post-war towers and buildings, the council looks to again promote change, but how will meaning be reconciled for this cycle – through adaptation or redevelopment? How will Croydon's architectural landscape remember and rework these urban traumas? It is this theme which is the focus of the next section.

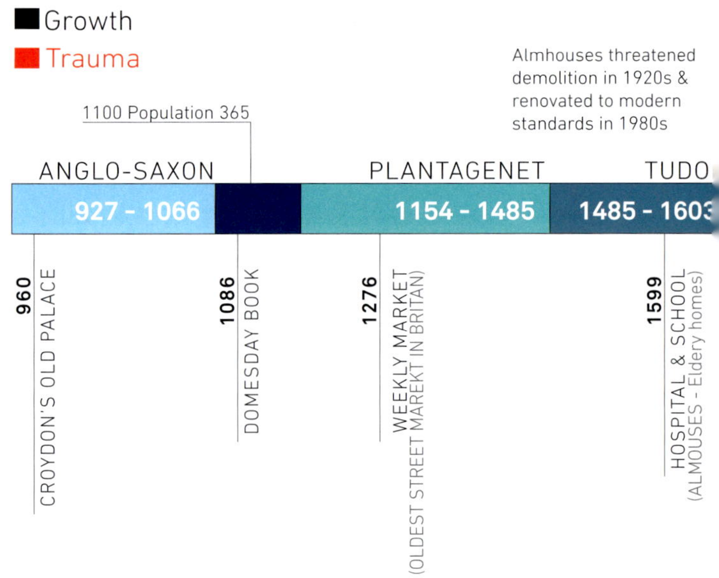

Redefining Croydon Today

There is nothing here that has been built after 1950 of any aesthetic or architectural merit. The urban environment isn't even interestingly bad.

—Deyan Sudjic, *The Guardian*, September 1993

Croydon boasts 550,000m² of office space, 30% of which is currently vacant (the national average is 18%). This equates to 165,000m² of floor space, a conservative number according to some estimates. The large public and private sector organisations that once filled the towering office buildings either no longer exist, have shrunk dramatically or have moved to another area with more modern facilities. In addition, one-third of the remaining occupied office space consists of shrinking government agencies.[12] New tenants tend to be smaller and look for more flexible leasing arrangements to reflect the dynamic nature of today's office market; for instance, 80% of companies relocating to Croydon between 2009 and 2010 were small, consisting of between 1 and 10 people.[13] Croydon's poor economic situation is mirrored by the quality of its town center's physical environment, which suffers from poorly defined and unpleasant places (with decreasing land values), insufficient open spaces, poor maintenance (dated buildings) and a decline in social and cultural assets[14] – all of which contribute to 22% of its streets having dead building frontages.[15]

Today's localism and private development context[16] do not allow for the same clean sweeping and top-down approach to public planning that existed in the post-war era. The current planning context can be described as a 'carrot and stick' game, with local authorities attempting to provide enough of an incentive to nudge developers in the 'right' direction to satisfy their immediate goals in a way that is conducive to long-term development goals. An example of this is Croydon's Opportunity Area Planning Framework (OAPF), a planning document produced by the Greater London Authority (GLA), with Croydon Council, that informs and influences development decisions and is a SPD (Supplemental Planning Document) to the London Plan. The OAPF promotes the conversion of abandoned and under-utilised buildings – 16 of the 19 buildings identified in the OAPF fit the 1960s office block typology. The rationale behind converting the buildings is to increase rental values by decreasing vacancy rates. Conversion of the buildings is the preferred option, and the GLA and Croydon council are considering providing incentives to encourage this, for instance by offering the possibility of adding additional floors to the existing buildings, additional blocks or extensions at lower levels to infill unused space, 100% residential conversions, lower affordable housing requirements (5% on or off site), looser design standards (single aspect units are permissible) and

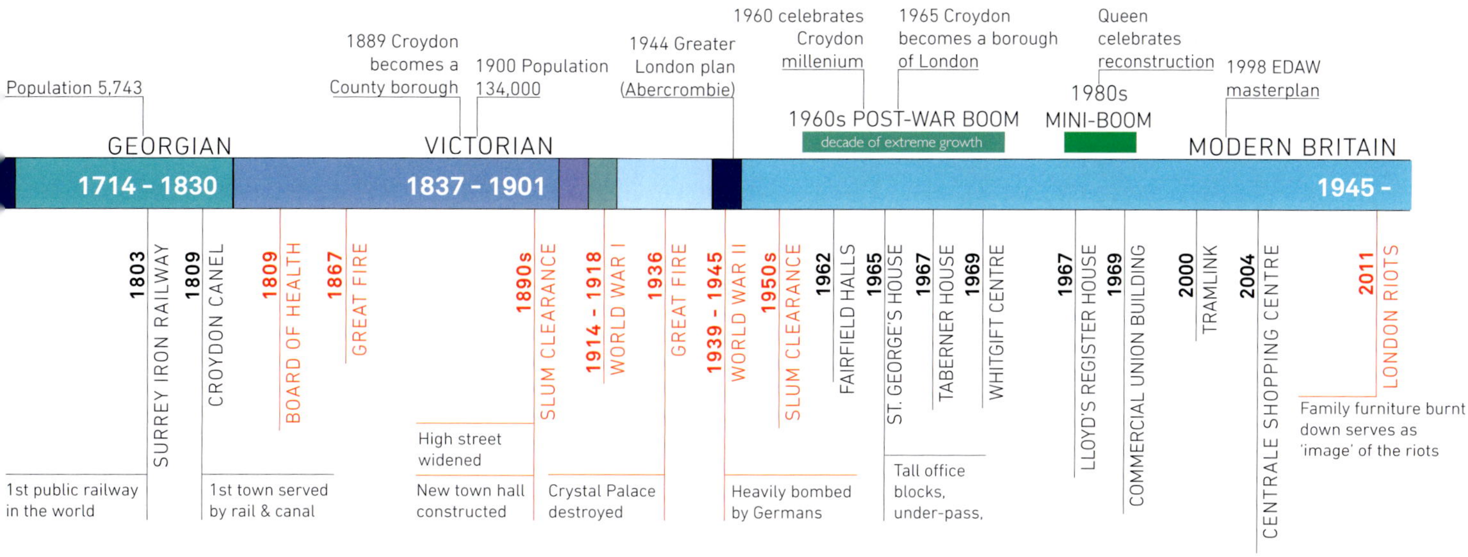

relaxation on renewable energy requirements.[17]

As well as encouraging the conversion of existing buildings, one of the major aims of the OAPF is to provide 7,300 new homes for 17,000 residents. Hence, converting vacant office buildings to residential use offers the potential for a 'win win' situation. Although the cost advantages are somewhat marginal, the potential returns are not – the value of residential space per hectare is currently more than double that of commercial space in the UK.[18] However, while converting office space to apartments is appealing, previous studies have highlighted the technical challenges involved in such conversions.[19] Most buildings will need facade upgrades (recladding, window replacement) to satisfy new energy performance standards, and services will need to be upgraded and laid out according to the new use. An exterior space will be needed for units along with communal amenity spaces. What is more, the technical challenges are only part of the problem: such conversions need to overcome social barriers, not least the stigma that is often attached to 1960s office buildings. The council has won £23m funding from the GLA post-riot to spend on infrastructure enhancement, public realm and business support and has been engaged with the community to find imaginative solutions which can supplement the reactivation of these buildings for residential use.

The tower and podium typology from the 1960s, which makes up a large portion of Croydon's building stock, offers a particular set of conditions – generally a concrete framed structure, shallow plan depth (10–14m), tall floor heights (3m), poor energy efficiency and floor loading standards for modern offices.[20] The typology offers two spatial configurations with the larger, generally more public podium base typically ranging between 2 and 3 stories and the more narrow towers between 10 and 20 stories of ubiquitous floor plates. The two spatial compositions suggest a mixed-use approach allowing the towers to be used for more cellular functions (e.g., residential, hotel, incubator offices) and the podium for social infrastructure (e.g., school, library, leisure center). The Nestlé Tower in Croydon is an exemplar of this typology, but how do the contextual contingencies define the transformation process?

The Nestlé Tower

While most of the surrounding office blocks were developed speculatively, St. George's House was always intended to be the headquarters of Nestlé UK. It was slated to be a landmark in the new Croydon skyline not only because of its large scale (nearly 80m tall), but due to its use of higher-quality materials, high-tech features and design considerations that many of its neighbors lacked. The building opened in 1965 with cavity floors to handle computer cabling, a mechanical mail distribution system and the latest IBM computer occupying most of the second floor.[21] The tower and podium building was accompanied with a linear shopping promenade (St. George's walk) which has had trouble succeeding as an uncomfortable and disintegrated part of Croydon's shopping experience.

After 47 years, Nestlé has decided to leave Croydon, stating the difficulty of redeveloping its current building to meet its modern demands and the lack of redevelopment in the surrounding area, particularly that of St. George's walk. Nestlé, with its approximately 1,000 jobs, is (was) the town's largest private sector employer. How will this dramatic event reshape Croydon's architectural landscape? Financial services company Legal & General have purchased the building and have discussed three possible options: upgrading the office building to meet

Timeline of Croydon's history

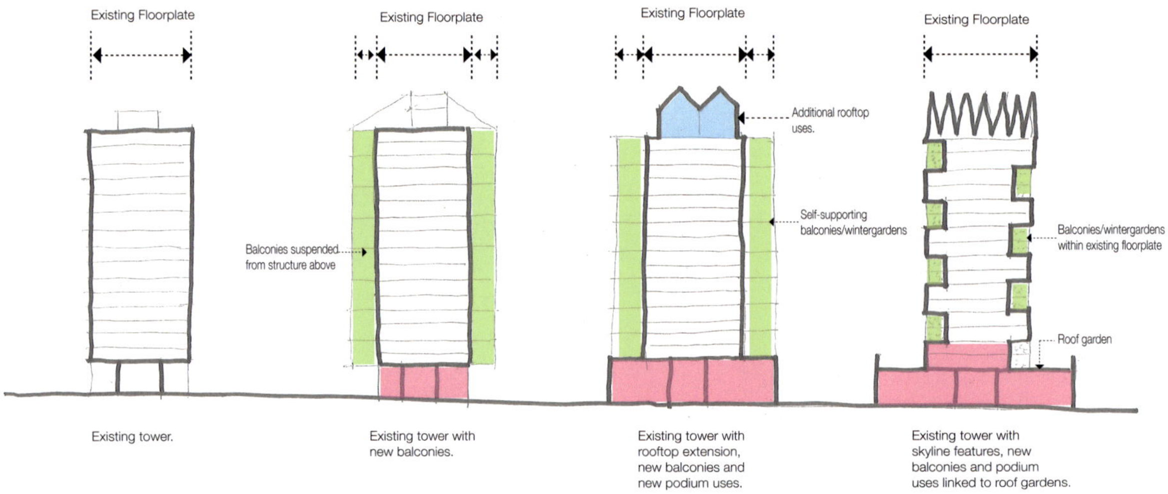

contemporary requirements; converting the building to residential units; or knocking it down and redeveloping the site. With the council clearly in favor of using the opportunity to promote its conversion and residential agenda, Legal & General have recently proposed a scheme of 288 apartments offering a mix of studio, one, two and three bedroom flats. The 3m floor to floor height would be difficult to accommodate modern office needs,- but works well for a residential 2.5m floor-to-ceiling height. The 15m narrow plan depth with a 6m structural grid (2m central zone) lends itself well to a double-stacked residential corridor plan. Reducing the loading criteria from office to residential along with being able to remove the screed means additional floors can be added without expensive foundation reinforcement. The number of lifts in the building is redundant for residential use and can be used as risers for services. On the other hand, trying to fit the plant into the basement and achieve the required air remains a challenge.

The proposal in its early stages would add six floors to the building and would use the ground and first floors for commercial purposes (e.g., retail, medical, gym and cinema). The proposal clearly looks to maximize the incentives offered by the OAPF as a mechanism to support the economic viability of adaptation over renewal. Physically, the transformation is certainly viable, but how will the new use and desired perception be considered as part of Croydon's architectural landscape – will the re-invention of the building and the injection of residential units be the catalyst to revitalize the surrounding area, or will it fall victim to its traumatic surroundings? In the next section we consider how these obstacles might be overcome.

Creative Construction

The Adaptable Futures (AF) research unit at Loughborough University and FAT architects, based in London, have developed proposals that suggest a pragmatic overlaying of program, symbolism and use, rather than yet another erasure of Croydon's history. In line with the OAPF's objectives, they accept the legacy of Croydon's 1960s boom as both an opportunity and a (productive) constraint. In this sense, such projects can be seen as a (partial) critique of the tabula-rasa approach of modernist spatial planning, which, ironically, arose at least partially from the trauma of Second World War destruction.

Instead of disavowal or demolition, it suggests a 'hacking' of the existing condition, on the level of both symbol and use. Not simply in the physical transformation of the office blocks (complete with bolt-on balconies, additional signage and new facades) but at the level of the city – pop-up stores, pocket parks and urban wind farms. Smaller-scale tactical interventions suggest a more incremental and organic transformation of urban form promoting a community role. The building's appropriation as housing and other social infrastructure rejects the purely mono-commercial vision of Croydon's town center and the notion of a central business district without residential use, while embracing the need to generate capital quicker.

The nimble tactics of appropriation involved, as well as a concern for social use and personal territory, draw on an alternative history of modernism, one that includes the surrealist and dada movements of the pre-war era, as well as Arte Povera, pop art and Conceptualism from after it. These gentler, subversive tactics are part of modernism too, and by utilizing them we might avoid the further trauma of rejecting modernism wholesale. Adaptation, negotiation and accommodation critically engage with problematic and even unloved structures and offer a way for us to avoid the sublimated trauma of demolition. Adaptation in architecture is an effort to 'work through' the trauma of our abjection by capitalist creative destruction. New groups, identities and communities can be forged through creative construction, offering us an alternative to capitalist heavy, time-intensive and large-scale new

Possible interventions for 1960s podium/tower office block

build projects which often weaken our fragile social relations.

Reflections and Conclusions

Whereas in the past Croydon (like many other towns and cities in countries around the world) may have looked to rewrite its architectural palimpsest by demolishing what was already there, economic and political constraints mean that the council is looking for more creative solutions involving the adaptive reuse of buildings, particularly for residential use. The council's approach is somewhat novel and refreshing because as While and Short point out, "urban leaders in most cities have been eager to remove or remodel what remains of 1950s/1960s planning."[22] While its approach of reconciling meaning with what is already there might be one of economic pragmatism, it might also be a reflection that wholesale redevelopment of urban areas has often not worked in the past and is not the answer for coming to terms with trauma. Moreover, there is growing recognition that such examples of creative destruction are not particularly sustainable, in social, environmental or economic terms, and are often merely 'bandaids' for short-term problems. Indeed, one of the ironies of the current situation is that the social infrastructure (e.g., schools) that existed prior to the modernist regeneration of the town center is now in high demand as the Council aims to bring families back to the town center.

Whilst the OAPF explicitly promotes the commercial viability of adaptive reuse, via a series of concessions from current sustainability and planning constraints, the reuse of office space for community and civic uses offers a wider level of potential public benefit. Although such reuse must clearly be guided by opportunities for commercial development, its potential complicates what Marx defined as capitalism's traumatic requirement for obsolescence through creative destruction. Adapting and reusing the existing stock of modernist office buildings might therefore help local communities and identities to be sustained through bearing witness to trauma[23], while at the same time recognizing openness and hope towards the future.

NOTES

1 Greater London Authority. (2012) "Croydon Opportunity Area Planning Framework" (OAPF), Consultation Draft: July 2012.

2 Caruth, C. "Unclaimed Experience: Trauma and the Possibility of History," *Yale French Studies*, No. 79, Literature and the Ethical Question. (1991), pp. 181–192.

3 Caruth,1991.

4 Edkins, J. (2003), *Trauma and the memory of politics*, Cambridge University Press: Cambridge and Erikson, K (1995). "Notes on trauma and community". In C. Caruth (Ed.), *Trauma: Explorations in memory* (pp. 183–199). Baltimore: Johns Hopkins University Press.

5 Erikson, 1995.

6 Edkins, 2003. and Lahoud, A., Rice, C. Burke, E. (eds) et al., (2010) *Posttraumatic urbanism: architectural design*, Wiley: New York.

7 Marx, 2002

8 Erikson, 1995.

9 La Capra, Dominick. (2001), *Writing History, Writing Trauma*, John Hopkins University Press, Baltimore, MD.

10 Phelps, N.A. and Parsons, N. (2003) "Edge Urban Geographies: Notes from the Margins of Europe's Capital Cities," *Urban Studies*, 40 (9), pp. 1725–1749.

11 OAPF, 2012.

12 URS Corporation, Ltd. (2010) London Borough of Croydon Office, Industrial and Warehousing Land/ Premises Market Assessment. http://www.croydon.gov.uk/contents/departments/planningandregeneration/pdf/912686/912811/983582/indwarehouselandassessup, Accessed 8.02.12.

13 URS, 2010.

14 Mid Croydon Masterplan, 2011. http://www.croydon.gov.uk/planningandregen-eration/regeneration-vision-croydon/enabling-regeneration-croydon-masterplan, Accessed 6.15.12.

15 Space Syntax. (2007) Baseline Analysis of Urban Structure, Layout and Public Spaces

http://www.croydon.gov.uk/contents/departments/planningandregeneration/pdf/912686/912841/1121679/ch1execsummarybaselineanalysisurbanstructurespublicspaces, Accessed 3.14.12.

16 OAPF, 2012.

17 Ibid.

18 Child Graddon Lewis Ltd., Nathaniel Lichfield & Partners, Robinson Lowe Francis, Gifford. (2011) Departments to Apartments: converting office buildings to residential, e-book. http://nlpplanning.com/nlp-insight/departments-to-apartments-october-2011 Accessed 6.15.12

19 Gann, D.M. and Barlow, J. (1996) "Flexibility in building use: the technical feasibility of converting redundant offices into flats," *Construction Management & Economics*, 14(1), pp.55–66.

20 CGL Architects, 2011.

21 Lacovara, Vincent. London: Croydon's other City. Dissertation for King's, 1999. http://supercroydon.net/downloads/croy-don_dissertation_low-2/.

22 While, A. and Short, M. (2011) "Place narratives and heritage management: the modernist legacy in Manchester," *Area*, 43(1), pp.4–13.

23 Erikson, 1995 and La Capra, 2001.

F. Català-Roca. *Eduardo Chillida en el Peine del Viento. San Sebastián. 1976* – © Photographic Archive F. Català-Roca – Arxiu Fotogràfic de l'Arxiu Històric del Collegi d'Arquitectes de Catalunya (AHCOAC). With the collaboration of the Collegi d'Arquitectes de Catalunya

BETWEEN MEMORY AND INVENTION

AN INTERVIEW WITH NIETO SOBEJANO ARQUITECTOS

by LUIS SACRISTÁN MURGA

Beyond entertainment, culture, or tourism, aspects of the "experience economy" that have evolved since Pine and Gilmore's seminal 1998 definition, recent concepts focus instead on the role of place as experience.[1] Int|AR author Luis Sacristán Murga explores this idea with architects Fuensanta Nieto and Enrique Sobejano, whose projects are exemplary of architectural interventions that contribute to a new and different experience. Beginning with their project for the Museum of San Telmo that is very much a product of "place" in San Sebastián, the designated European Capital of Culture 2016 to key projects of reuse and heritage in Europe, we are offered a unique glimpse into the critical thinking behind their approach to experience and adaptation.

There are few places in the world as San Sebastián, the quintessential picturesque city, where the natural and artificial merge in the absolute. The dialogue with the place generates every action and architectural experience. With a deeply rooted culture and identity, architects and artists have always dealt with its tradition, nature and materials while incorporating the language of the artistic vanguard.

One of its many poetic corners and possibly the most known place in the city, the Comb of the Wind, was created by sculptor Eduardo Chillida in the middle of the 20th century, on the rocks at one end of the bay. As a prelude to these steel sculptures rusted by the sea, the architect Peña Ganchegui built a platform adapted to the topography through a pixelated landscape of cobbles, creating a public space on the edge between the city, the mountains and the absolute ocean.

This place is the origin of everything. It is the real author of the work of art (...). My sculpture is the solution to an equation which, instead of numbers, has elements: the sea, the wind, the cliffs, the horizon and the light. The steel forms are mixed with the forces of nature, they converse with them, they are questions and statements.[2]
– Eduardo Chillida, sculptor and poet

The city appears from the landscape, interlaced with it, in a deep dialogue between epochs and materials, between the natural and the transformed, in which both parts are enhanced to form a new unit, more complete and beautiful.

At the other end of the bay stands the Dominican convent dedicated to San Telmo, saint of sailors, sited at the foot of Mount Urgull and facing the Urumea River. It was built in the mid-16th century, under the patronage of the Secretary of State of Emperor Charles V. This ancient building is a reflection of the city's history, and therefore, it has undergone various transformations and changes of use throughout its lifetime.

After the War of Independence against the French in the 19th century, the city of San Sebastián was razed and the convent of San Telmo, left in ruins, was subsequently transformed into military barracks in 1836. Due to its progressive degradation and neglect, the convent was finally purchased by the city council in 1928, to house the Museum of San Telmo, the oldest museum institution of the Basque Country, founded in 1902.

Following the celebration of its centenary in 2002, the city council launched a public competition for the extension of the museum. The architectural office Nieto+Sobejano won first prize with a proposal based on the recovery of the original volumes of the convent (chapel, church, cloister and tower), and the extension of the museum through an addition embedded in the topography of Mount Urgull and connected to the historic building in specific places. The work began in 2007 with the rehabilitation project that included the demolition of the volumes added in the 20th century, in order to recover the original spaces and materials of the historic building. During the work, ancient crypts,

TOP
Plaza del Tenis, 2015
BOTTOM
Old postcard of the aerial view of La Concha beach and historic city

paintings and archaeological remains appeared, becoming part of the museum.

The new extension of San Telmo Museum opened in 2011 and became a key element of the recent strategy promoted by the city council for the recovery of historic urban spaces, which fosters the modernization of the city through the integration of its memory. This philosophy is one of many essential reasons that led to San Sebastián's selection as the European Capital of Culture in 2016.

In addition to providing splendid natural scenery and a refined urban and artistic heritage, the central strategy of the city towards its candidacy for the European Capital of Culture 2016 was to propose a new type of experience economy by way of the concept "Culture to overcome violence." The Basque Country is currently experiencing a key moment in its recent history, leaving behind decades of social conflict and violence and initiating an era of peace and coexistence. This strategy aims to create spaces for reflection and collective creation, in order to convert European cities into spaces for coexistence. Under a model of respect for human rights, it promotes a culture of peace and education in values and in cultural diversity. This innovative approach promotes tourism as an experience that produces personal enrichment to visitors, allowing them to share an experience of coexistence rather than one of mere cultural spectatorship. In addition, the proposal fosters a new kind of creative tourism, linked to the city's cultural professionals and creative industries.

This philosophy could become the paradigm of a new experience economy, one more socially committed and involved in the transformation of society through the cultural and human values of integration.

In this context, Architecture is responsible for hosting the experiences of creation and coexistence, becoming an active element in the process of exchange and social transformation, as in the case of the Museum of San Telmo. Besides representing the spirit of innovation through the interpretation of memory, during 2016 the museum will also become an essential open space for reflection, creation and experimentation for citizens of San Sebastián and those who come from afar.

Museums can serve as elements for social transformation, based on their mission to provide a service to the community. Increasingly, and with the recent social movements where citizens are demanding more empowerment and participation, museums have the opportunity to become spaces for confluence, and therefore must be conceived as "by people and for people."[3]

The memory of a city, its ability to reinvent itself and look into the future without losing its unique and singular personality, reflects the identity of a culture, and that dual concept – local and global – of the human being, which Chillida imagines "as a tree, with the roots in one place, and with the branches open to the world."[4]

Site plan of the San Telmo Museum

This and all illustrations from here on are the work of the firm Nieto Sobejano Arquitectos

CONTEXT AND PLACE AS A TRIGGER OF THE PROJECT

LSM: When intervening in a special context such as San Sebastián, where tradition, nature and the vanguard have always been interlaced, leading to an urban fabric adapted to the landscape, to sculptures and public spaces in the boundaries of the city such as those of Chillida or Peña Ganchegui, and to a contemporary architecture as sensitive and iconic as Rafael Moneo's Kursaal, what was your initial approach to the project for the extension of the Museum of San Telmo?

N+S: Clearly those three concepts —tradition, nature and avant-garde—define the circumstances that came together in the project of the Museum of San Telmo: in the boundary between Mount Urgull and the Old Town, in the confluence of nature and city, the horizontal plane and the topographic elevation, land and sea, historic and recent buildings. In that sense, the project suggested an architecture conscious of its role in relation to the landscape and history, which does not contradict the will of innovation and transformation. Perhaps for this reason the work was conceived not only to fulfill the needs of the program and its adaptation to the place, but as a response to the boundary condition. We could say that this is an inhabited building / edge, which responds to the complex relationship between the natural landscape and the cityscape.

LSM: How do you understand the 'spirit of the place,' the Genius Loci, in San Sebastián and generally in your projects? Why is the deep understanding of the context so essential for you?

In San Telmo the new building reacts to a succession of urban spaces: the Plaza de Zuloaga and the connection with Mount Urgull, the Plaza de la Trinidad and the interstitial spaces between the historic building and the extension. We understand the context through the sensations received from the site, but also from the images that subconsciously live in our memory and trigger a series of associations from which the project starts.

LSM: How is it possible to reinterpret a unique context and culture such as the Basque one? How does one produce an identity through architecture? How does architecture create experiences that represent a place and culture?

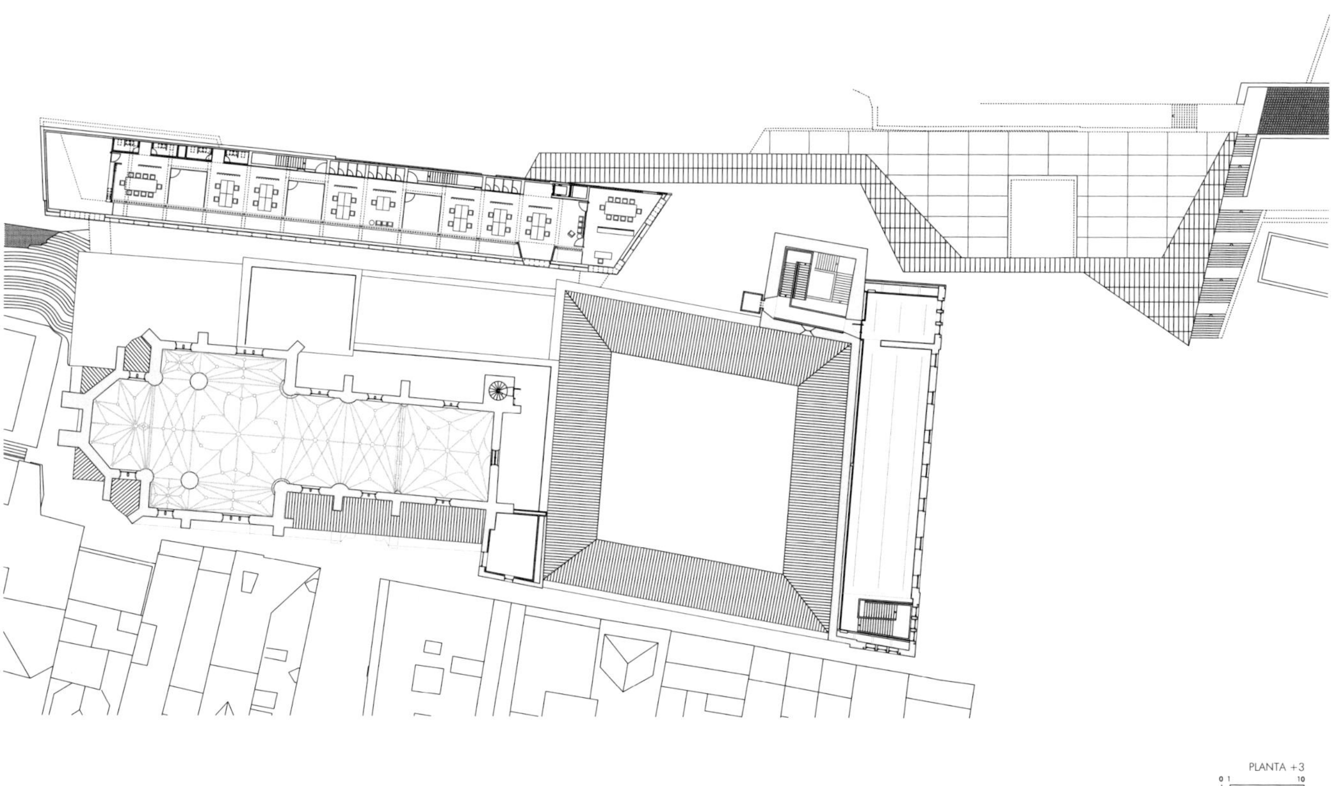

Plan at level 3, San Telmo Museum

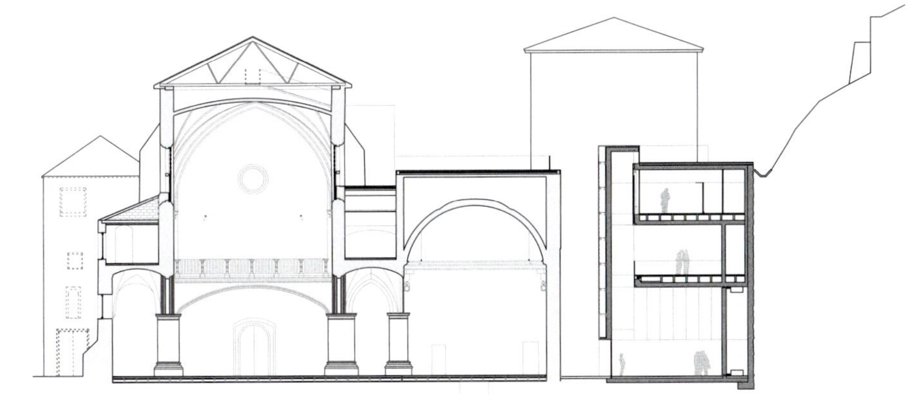

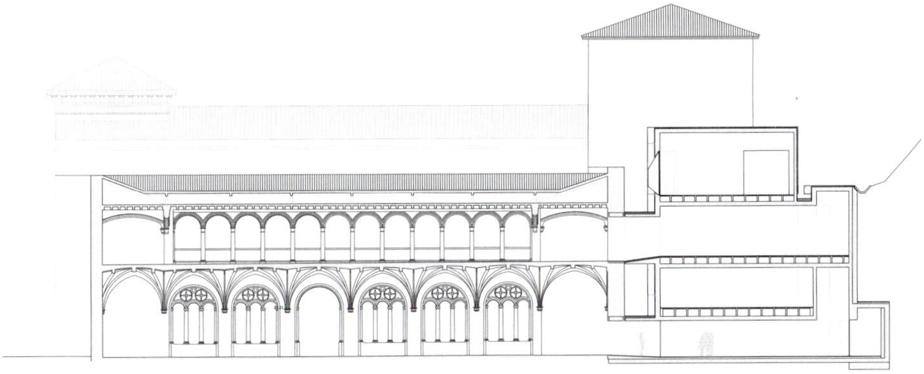

TOP

Sections cutting through the church, monastery and the extension of the museum

BOTTOM

View of plaza at entry to San Telmo Museum

N+S: We do not support generalizations, for example when terms such as "identity," "Basque" architecture or other similar definitions are used. We are interested, on the contrary, in architecture that is able to establish specific connections with a place and a culture through the experience. In this sense, our job is to ultimately uncover the principles or instructions that the context transmits and transform them into new architectural spaces. More than a generic reinterpretation of Basque culture, we understand the extension of San Telmo as a specific intervention, which reacts to the physical conditions and to the memory of a place.

LSM: Our societies have changed from consuming products, then services to recently consuming experiences, in what has been called the Experience Economy. How does this new demand for the consumption of memorable experiences affect architecture?

N+S: The consumption of "memorable" experiences today generates such a wide demand that it paradoxically provokes a rapid oblivion. This happens in almost all areas of culture: blockbuster art exhibitions and performances as well as literary bestsellers. Architecture however, due to its physical reality, constructive and spatial, has different characteristics. Despite suffering a constant overexposure in the media, the direct experience of a building requires time and attention, making it more durable. The so-called Experience Economy has put into its service certain institutions, such as museums, but as opposed to the mere consumption of images, the sensory and spatial experience is the only thing that makes architecture comprehensible.

LSM: Is there a culture of spectacle versus a culture of authenticity in architecture? Is there a division between a stream of global projection of more decontextualized architecture and another one more local and rooted to the context?

N+S: We are conscious that architecture should be experienced directly through the senses. But this phenomenological experience is much more limited than the one which comes through printed or audiovisual media, or through the network. How many of the buildings that are criticized, admired or rejected are a result of a live experience? Facing the global society and its need to consume images, architecture has an advantage over other arts and disciplines: building takes time, it is not immediate, the experience of a building involves traveling, visiting, observing and perceiving with the senses, something that the culture of entertainment cannot substitute with the immediate image. There is no division between decontextualized architecture and "authentic" architecture, since any architectural work is likely to be experienced. But there is a different attitude towards the project: some works are conceived by their authors with a purely iconic will, with the essential purpose of the image, while a very different attitude is the one that is originated in the spatial, material and cultural qualities, which link a building to a place.

Section through the extension of San Telmo Museum

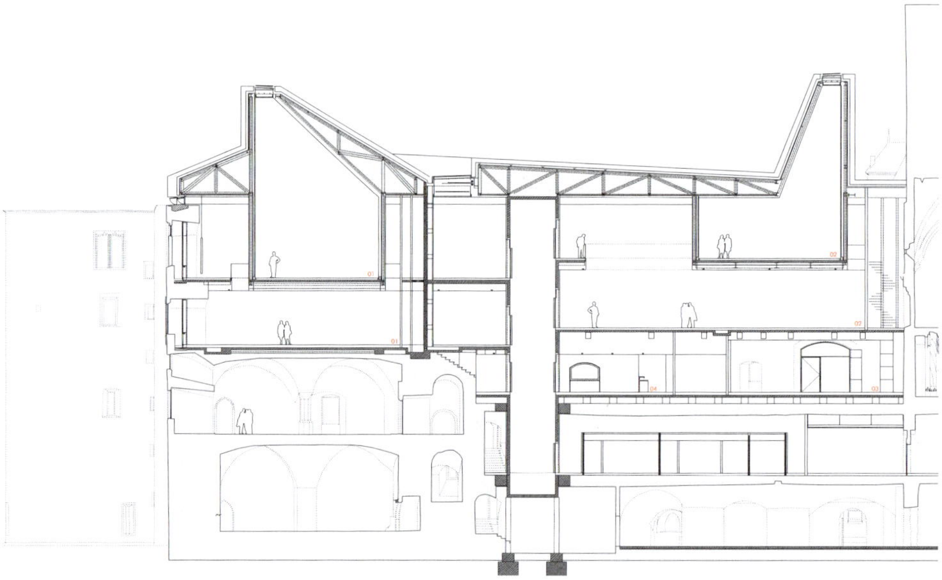

TOP

New roof volumes, Moritzburg Museum

BOTTOM

Section through the galleries, Moritzburg Museum

PUBLIC SPACE, MATERIALS AND MEMORY

LSM: In what way do you think a city like San Sebastián will be affected by being the European Capital of Culture 2016? How important are these events for a city and for its people?

N+S: These events represent the opportunity to carry out works and cultural investments that otherwise would not be launched, or would have been delayed indefinitely in time. In that sense, they are always positive. Our project for San Telmo was, however, prior to the proposed capital, and it was actually a result of a demand for renovation that had existed for many years.

LSM: The public spaces of San Sebastián are one of its wonderful urban experiences. Why should the creation of public space be always present in the background of architectural projects? What is the importance of having a good network of public spaces in a city?

N+S: Architecture, even in programs for private use, always has a public dimension and responsibility towards the urban space or the landscape. With institutional projects, such as a museum, the demand is even bigger. Therefore it is not inaccurate to think that the urban dimension of a building transcends the interior. The history of San Telmo confirms it; the successive uses have been changing —convent, church, military barracks or municipal museum—while its presence in the city and the public spaces that it generates have remained over time.

Gallery at Moritzburg Museum showing new interventions within the castle walls

LSM: For the construction of the Plaza de la Trinidad, which borders the Museum of San Telmo on its western part, Peña Ganchegui, in the 1960s, reused old cobblestones, found in the city council's storage, due to the limitations of the project budget. But by using these old materials with a modern language, he established a unique material relationship with the context, giving new meaning to elements that had lost their significance. Are materials an essential element of integration with the context and a dialogue between epochs? What do you value most when you define the materials in your projects?

N+S: The materials and construction systems that we use in our works are the result of the architectural idea that generates each project: they supplement it and they are its formal support. In other words, the material expression of a building should reflect its relationship with the city, the landscape or the memory of a place. The extension of the Moritzburg Museum was conceived as a folded metal deck that merges with the usually cloudy skies of that place. In the Center for Contemporary Art in Córdoba, prefabricated panels of GCR define a topography whose geometry evokes the ornamentation of the Islamic architecture. In San Telmo, the façade of perforated aluminum panels allows the growth of mosses and lichens in certain places, alluding to the rock and vegetation of Mount Urgull.

LSM: The experience of space varies depending on its materials as they produce different perceptions, smells, tactile sensations, textures, meanings... How do you understand the relationships between different materials? In the reuse and adaptation of heritage, are there materials that inherently hold an element of greater authenticity?

N+S: When speaking about appropriate materials for intervention in architectonic heritage, we would have to distinguish between works of renovation and works of extension. In the renovation or rehabilitation of a historic monument, it is the process itself that leads us to understand the problem through the action of developing and constructing it. We often use similar materials to those of the original building, like stone, stucco, wood, ceramic and copper. When it comes to a new building or an extension, our approach is based on a dialogue with the existing materials. For example, in Madinat al-Zahra, we use white concrete and rusted steel, contemporary materials that "talk" with the stucco and the ceramic of the ancient Hispanic Moorish city. In San Sebastián, the lattice panels of aluminum transform the project in an intervention that links architecture to public art.

Center for Contemporary Art, Córdoba

EROSKI
EROSKI

LSM: In your projects, the use of an outer skin with a special treatment that gives a unique texture to each building is recurrent: in the extension of the Museum of San Telmo, it has much to do with the mimesis with the natural context, in the Congress Center of Mérida, with establishing a more detailed scale, and in the Contemporary Art Centre of Córdoba with integrating the digital world into the facade. Is the exterior facade a reinterpreted mirror of the context in your projects? Which is the relationship that you look for between these two scales of distance and proximity?

N+S: Clearly the works of Mérida, San Telmo and the Art Center in Córdoba are part of a similar concept for the design of the outer skin. In the three cases the expressive value of the material modulates the scale and relationship with the physical environment. In the three projects it comes to collaborations undertaken with contemporary artists in the definition of a texture developed specifically for each occasion: Esther Pizarro in the bas-relief of the city of Mérida, Ferrán and Otero in the green facade of Mount Urgull, and Realities:united in the digital screen in Córdoba. The three projects reflect our interest in the fringe or the limit of where the visual arts, architecture and urban space converge.

TOP
Facade, Center for Contemporary Art, Córdoba
BOTTOM
Facade, Congress Center, Mérida

Facade of San Telmo Museum, San Sebastián

REUSE AND ADAPTATION OF CULTURAL HERITAGE

LSM: In addition to the extension of the Museum of San Telmo, you have many other projects related to the Adaptive Reuse of cultural heritage, including the Museum of Madinat Al-Zahra in Córdoba, the Castillo de la Luz in Las Palmas, and the art galleries Kastner & Ohler in Graz. What about the adaptive reuse of heritage is of particular interest to you?

N+S: We are interested in heritage intervention for its requirement of the taking of a stand in the transformation of architecture in space and time. The rehabilitation of works of the past forces us to read a building as the sum of different juxtaposed texts, in which the new intervention is another chapter of its long history. This also reflects a clear difference between architecture and other artistic disciplines. It is not admitted, in principle, that a pictorial, sculptural, musical, cinematic or literary work of art could be modified by another author, but it has always been assumed that buildings can change use or be extended and transformed by other architects. We could say that rehabilitation and intervention in existing buildings are precisely the condition that distinguishes architecture from other arts.

LSM: Should architecture have 'roots'? How is it possible to dialogue with Time? How do memory and the past, the present and innovation, come together?

N+S: We have referred several times to our work as a dialogue between memory and invention. The process by which an abstract idea becomes a concrete result is constantly nourished by latent images in our memory. Therein probably lies the profound relationship of architecture with time.

View of Joanneumsviertel in historic Graz

Through the glass insertions at the Joanneumsviertel, Graz

LSM: **What is the power of architecture and adaptive reuse that transforms consciousness, transmits values, and generates experiences of a place through its history?**

N+S: Intervening in heritage involves the inquiry of the meaning of the present and the registration of the past. Any new intervention is, on one hand, temporary and, on the other, a reflection of its historical reality. In a work of adaptive reuse it is not easy to determine authorship. It is not already the work of a single architect, but of several throughout its history, which transmits a social and collective experience and value.

LSM: **What is the boundary between what to keep and what not to keep in cities? Do you agree with Rem Koolhaas, when he says that 'preservation is overtaking us'?**

N+S: We have passed from the initial disinterest of Modern architecture for heritage – where historic landmarks were considered as isolated facts, while other buildings inherited from the past should simply be substituted – to the current attitude, especially European, which protects, sometimes in excess, any building of the past. Naturally, we do not agree with these extreme options, but with a balance whose limit lies in the architectural quality of each intervention itself.

LSM: **What is your experience for intervening in UNESCO-protected historical environments as in your project in Graz? What should the balance be between construction and preservation in a historical context, so that it does not become a mere tourist attraction, as is the historic center of Venice, where the inhabitants have moved to the suburbs and only touristic services such as shops and hotels remain in the city center?**

N+S: In Graz, the problem is common to many historical cities protected by UNESCO.

The alternative is often raised in these opposing terms: all new buildings in the old town should be carried out by imitating the forms and materials of an era that is considered the most appropriate to their history and any contemporary intervention would imply the destruction of their identity. Of course we do not agree with this dichotomy.

We understand that the city must remain active and alive so we believe that new interventions require a careful balance between memory of the place, its scale and contemporary needs. Fortunately, in Graz our project was interpreted this way.

LSM: **Where is Adaptive Reuse moving towards? What is the future of the architecture of memory?**

N+S: Adaptive reuse and the transformation of buildings will not be limited in the future only to those considered of historical value because, in our opinion, all architecture—of new creation or of rehabilitation—is always the result of an interpretation of memory.

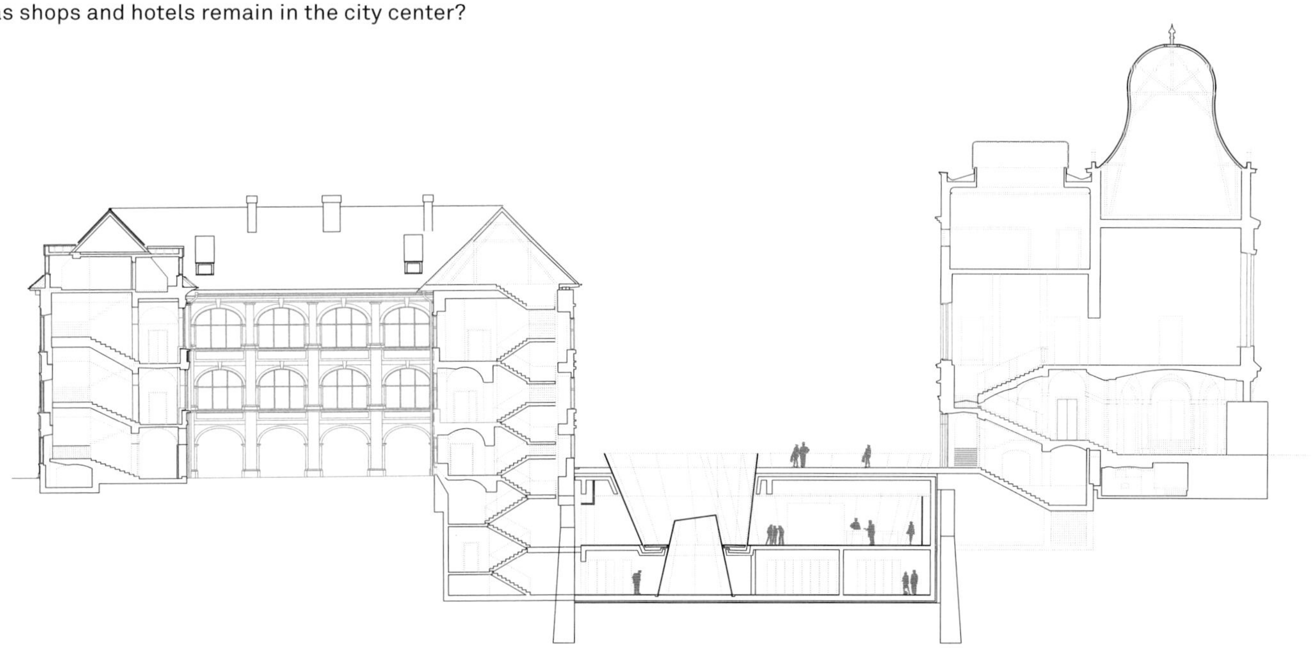

Section through the Joanneumsviertel, Graz

Entrance and Addition, Castillo de la Luz, Las Palmas

Nieto Sobejano Arquitectos was founded in 1985 by Fuensanta Nieto and Enrique Sobejano and has offices in Madrid and, since 2007, in Berlin. Along with being widely published in international magazines and books, the firm's work has been exhibited at the Biennale di Venezia in 2000, 2002, 2006, and 2012; at the Museum of Modern Art (MoMA), New York, in 2006; at the Kunsthaus in Graz in 2008; and at the MAST Foundation in Bologna, Italy, in 2014. They are the recipients of the 2008 National Prize for Restoration from the Spanish Ministry of Culture and the 2010 Nike Prize issued by the Bund Deutscher Architekten (BDA), as well as the Aga Khan Award for Architecture (2010), the Piranesi Prix de Rome (2011), the European Museum of the Year Award (2012), the Hannes Meyer Prize (2012), Honorary Fellow of AIA (2015) and the Alvar Aalto Medal in 2015. Their major works include the Madinat al-Zahra Museum, the Moritzburg Museum, the San Telmo Museum, the Joanneum extension in Graz, and the Contemporary Art Centre in Córdoba. Nieto Sobejano Arquitectos currently have projects in Germany, Spain, Austria, Estonia and Morocco.

NOTES

1 Anne Lorentzen discusses this concept in her paper "Citizens in the Experience Economy," in *European Planning Studies* Vol. 17, No. 6, Routledge, London, June 2009.

2 Chillida, Eduardo. *Escritos*, La Fábrica, Madrid, 2005

3 San Sebastián 2016: Proposed Application for the Title of European Capital of Culture http://www.donostiasansebastian2016.eu/web/guest/proyecto-cultural/proyecto-final

4 Chillida, Eduardo. *Escritos*, La Fábrica, Madrid, 2005

Addition at Castillo de la Luz, Las Palmas

AUTHOR BIOGRAPHIES

Dr. Géraldine Borio is a Swiss-registered architect, an Assistant Professor at the University of Hong Kong, Department of Architecture, and the founder of Borio Lab, an independent research laboratory and architectural-based practice. She co-founded Parallel Lab Research and Architecture (2010–15). Géraldine Borio is the co-author of the book *Hong Kong In-Between* (Park Books, 2015) and the publication *The People of Duckling Hill* (HK Poly U, 2016). The resultant gap and interstitial voids of Asian cities have been her entry points to understand the mechanisms of the built environments. In particular, the urban context of Bangkok, Hong Kong and Seoul have been her testing ground to explore the notion of spatial ambiguity at different scales. Along the way, the shift from in-situ observation and intervention to the making of architecture has created opportunities to test the making of in-between space, buffer zone and threshold.

Cristian Campagnaro, architect and PhD in Technological Innovation, is Associate Professor in the Department of Architecture and Design at the Politecnico di Torino. Since 2017 and with Prof. Paolo Tamborrini, he is the scientific director of the Politecnico's Polito Food Design Lab, which supports research and teaching on food waste, food security, and food safety. Selected in the field of social design by the ADI Design Index in 2015 and 2017–2019, he focused his research on Eco-Design for Sustainability and on Social Inclusion. He oversees and conducts teaching and information actions in the framework of participatory and interdisciplinary workshops involving students, policymakers, public and private social operators, as well as citizens.

Stefano Corbo is an Italian architect and Associate Professor at the Rhode Island School of Design (RISD). He holds a PhD and a MArch II in Advanced Architectural Design from UPM-ETSAM Madrid (Escuela Técnica Superior de Arquitectura). Before joining the faculty at RISD, he taught at several academic Institutions in Europe, the Middle East and China. Corbo has contributed to many international journals and has published three books: *From Formalism to Weak Form: The Architecture and Philosophy of Peter Eisenman* (Ashgate/Routledge, 2014), *Interior Landscapes: A Visual Atlas* (Images, 2016) and, more recently, *Notes from the Underworld* (Schiffer, 2019). In 2012, Corbo founded his own office, SCSTUDIO — a multidisciplinary network practicing public architecture, preoccupied with intellectual, economic and cultural contexts.

Dennis Earle, originally from upstate New York, teaches at Syracuse University's School of Design in Syracuse, New York. He studied the History of Art and Architecture at Yale University prior to earning a Master of Architecture degree at the University of Pennsylvania. Having traveled abroad extensively since early childhood, Earle now works on comparative examinations of cultural traditions and design from around the world and throughout history. His primary focus is on readings of form in design in the context of ancient cultural traditions, and contemporary traditional cultures, and their use of design to both negotiate distinctive relationships to particular physical environments and ecologies, and to give substance to the construction of unique cultural identities.

Nicolò Di Prima is Research Fellow at the Department of Architecture and Design of Polytechnic of Turin. His research focuses on design and cultural anthropology. He is currently working on interdisciplinary research projects dealing with participatory design processes in deep marginality contexts. He has conducted three academic workshop for the Bachelor's degree in Design and Visual Communication (Polytechnic of Turin) focused on co-design and social design issues.

Laura Gioeni is an architect, philosopher, researcher and lecturer. Initially trained at the School of Mimodrama in Milan, experiencing Jacques Lecoq's theatrical pedagogy, she holds degrees in Architecture and Philosophy. For over 20 years she worked as an architect in the field of architectural design, restoration and adaptive reuse. As adjunct professor, she taught classes related to architectural restoration at the Polytechnic of Milan and at the University of Parma. In 2017, she received the Italian National Scientific Qualification as Associate Professor in Architectural Design. She is author of books and essays, including contributions to *The Routledge Companion to Jacques Lecoq* (Routledge, 2016) and to the conference proceedings, *Memories on John Ruskin* (Firenze University Press, 2019). Currently she teaches drawing and art history in secondary schools and is committed to research on the philosophy of architecture. Interested also in dance, she studies and practices Western African traditional dance.

Federica Goffi is Professor of Architecture (2007–present), Co-Chair of the PhD and MAS Program in Architecture and Interim Director at the Azrieli School of Architecture and Urbanism at Carleton University, Ottawa, Canada. She holds a PhD from Virginia Tech in

Architecture and Design Research. She published book chapters and journal articles on the threefold nature of time-weather-tempo. Her book, *Time Matter[s]: Invention and Re-imagination in Built Conservation: The Unfinished Drawing and Building of St. Peter's in the Vatican*, was published by Ashgate in 2013.She edited Marco Frascari's *Dream House: A Theory of Imagination* (Routledge, 2017); *InterVIEWS: Insights and Introspection in Doctoral Research in Architecture* (Routledge, 2019), and co-edited *Ceilings and Dreams: The Architecture of Levity* (Routledge, 2019). Her forthcoming edited book is titled *The Routledge Companion to Architectural Drawings and Models: From Translating to Archiving, Collecting and Displaying* (2021). She holds a Dottore in Architettura from the University of Genoa, Italy. She is a licensed architect in her native country, Italy.

Sally Harrison, AIA is Professor of Architecture at the Tyler School of Art and Architecture at Temple University. She is a registered architect, educator and scholar whose creative work and research explores the social impacts of design. She teaches courses in social activism, architectural and urban design, and urban history/theory. She is the leader and co-founder of The Urban Workshop, an interdisciplinary university-based collaborative undertaking engaged research, design and design-build projects in underserved neighborhoods where questions of social justice, creative expression and community building are played out in the physical environment. Harrison's work is published in numerous books and academic journals, and has received national, international and regional design awards. She is a founding member of the Community Design Collaborative of Philadelphia and the Editorial Board of *Context*, the journal of the Philadelphia AIA. Ms. Harrison received her Master of Architecture from MIT, her BA from University of Pennsylvania.

Lea Hershkowitz is an Architectural Designer with a master's degree in interior architecture from Rhode Island School of Design. She currently works designing new light rail stations for Seattle's expanding sustainable public transit system. Previously Lea worked for IWBI developing and implementing the WELL Building Standard, and as an Adjunct Professor of Design Research at Rhode Island School of Design. Lea's work centers on the ability for design to promote equity, healing, and biophilia. Her master's thesis examined the architecture of confinement in an attempt to adapt prisons into authentic rehabilitation centers rather than stagnant, punitive typologies. Lea has received numerous grants, fellowships, and awards for her work. In 2015, she developed a patent-pending design to adaptively reuse existing mechanical air systems, improving air quality in hospitals.

Caroline Jäger-Klein teaches history of architecture at TU Wien, architectural heritage at UBT Prishtina in Kosovo and researches within an ERC-granted project on Habsburg-Bosnia at the University of Vienna. After her studies in Austria and the US (U of M Ann Arbor), she wrote her PhD on the Austrian architecture of the 19th and 20th centuries. In addition to her theoretical focus, she continued teaching design courses on building in a historical context, her master's thesis topic. She is currently the president of ICOMOS Austria, guiding the South-Eastern-European ICOMOS network and distinguished national expert-in-court on protection and preservation of monuments. The issues of the INTAR-article resulted in an official research cooperation with the Ministry of Higher Education of Saudi Arabia from 2011 to 2014 to document traditional domestic architecture of Hedjaz.

Catherine R. Joseph is an architect and educator. Her design research and work as an educator focuses on developing intersectional and speculative design processes to address adaptability and resilience in the built environment and equity in urban space. She earned her master's degree in architecture from Cornell University and her bachelor's degree in Structural Engineering from Duke University. She is based in Brooklyn, NY.

Brian Phillips & Deborah Grossberg Katz are based in the Philadelphia firm ISA that pursues design and research focused on urbanism, high-performance buildings, and strategic thinking.

Brian Phillips, founder and Creative Director of ISA, is nationally recognized as a design thinking leader in the fields of urbanism, housing, sustainability and city-building. He leads many of the firm's research initiatives, teaches at the Stuart Weitzman School of Design at the University of Pennsylvania, and was named a Pew Fellow in the Arts in 2011. Brian attended the University of Oklahoma and the University of Pennsylvania.

Deborah Grossberg Katz is Principal at ISA and oversees many aspects of the daily work of the office. Deb has wide design expertise including in the fields of adaptive reuse, interiors, environmental graphics, housing and research. She attended Brown University and Columbia University.

Dorothée King is Professor and Head of the Education Department and the Learning Lab at Basel Academy for Arts and Design. After studying art, design and media in Denmark, Germany and England, Dorothée King earned her PhD from the College of Fine Arts at Berlin University of the Arts, where she was a researcher and lecturer. She has also lectured at Rhode Island School of Design; Providence College; the Interface Cultures program at the University for Art and Industrial Design Linz, Austria; and the Banff New Media Institute, Canada. She was a consultant for the TransArt Institute in New York and has been working as a freelance educator, communicator and coach since 2002. Dorothée King's scholarship and teaching are invested in participatory processes, immersive environments, ephemeral materials, multisensory aesthetic experience and the histories and futures of art school education.

Kees Lokman is Associate Professor and Chair of Landscape Architecture at the University of British Columbia. His research focuses on design challenges related to sea level rise adaptation, water and food shortages, and the energy transition. He directs the UBC Coastal Adaptation Lab, which aims to develop novel planning, design, and policy solutions for coastal adaptation based on the co-production of knowledge among researchers, decision-makers, and Indigenous communities. This work has been funded through various agencies and municipalities, including the Pacific Institute for Climate Solutions, Natural Resources Canada, the Dutch Creative Industries Fund, and the City of Vancouver. Recent and ongoing research has been published in various journals, including the *Journal of Landscape Architecture*, *Landscape Research, New Geographies*, and the *Journal of Architectural Education*.

Rafael Luna is Assistant Professor at Hanyang University and co-founder of the architecture firm PRAUD. He received a Master of Architecture from the Massachusetts Institute of Technology. Luna is the winner of the Architectural League Prize 2013, and his work has been exhibited at MoMA, Venice Biennale, and Seoul Biennale. Luna was a co-curator of the Cities Exhibition for the 2019 Seoul Biennale. He has professional experience from the offices of Toyo Ito, KPF, Ateliers Jean Nouvel, Martha Schwartz Partners, dECOI, Sasaki Associates, and Machado and Silvetti. He is pursuing his PhD on Infra-architectural typologies as urban models at L'Accademia di architettura in Mendrisio, Switzerland. His writings have been published in journals such as *Topos*, *MONU*, *SPACE*, *IntAR Journal* and he is currently co-editing an issue for *AD magazine* for September, 2021. He is the co-author of *I Want to Be Metropolitan* and the *North Korean Atlas*.

Célia Macedo studied architecture as her first degree at Universidade Lusíada of Lisbon in Portugal. Following some years of professional experience in architectural practices, both in Portugal and the UK, she graduated from Oxford Brookes University with an MSc in Energy Efficient and Sustainable Building in 2009. Célia is currently engaging in research on the informal settlements of Luanda (Angola) for her PhD in Architecture at Oxford Brookes University, UK. Following two years of research and teaching at the University of Sheffield in the UK, Célia is now a fulltime potter in Portugal.

Gregory Marinic, PhD, is an architectural theorist, scholar, educator, and practitioner. He is Associate Professor in the University of Cincinnati College of Design, Architecture, Art, and Planning SAID. He leads Urbania, a funded research lab speculating on metropolitan futures, and his current research is based in Mexico City. This scholarship focuses on informal settlements in Latin America and transnational urban correspondences between the Global South and North America. His ongoing research examines obsolescence, revitalization, interior urbanism, and post-industrial cities. Dr. Marinic has been widely published in peer-reviewed journals including *AD Journal*, *Journal of Architectural Education*, *AIA Forward Journal*, *Design Issues*, *International Journal of Architectural Research*, and *IntAR Journal of Interventions and Adaptive Reuse*. Prior to academia and establishing his independent practice, Arquipelago, he worked in New York and London architecture firms including Rafael Viñoly Architects, Gensler, Tsao & McKown Architects, Yoshihara McKee Architects, and ABS Architects.

Fabia Mendoza, Ryan Mendoza, João José Santos, Diogo Vale

Fabia Mendoza is a film and art director from Berlin, Germany. Her first movie *The White House Documentary*, 2017 won at the 18th Beverly Hills Film Festival 2018. Over the past six years she collaborated on a variety of projects including 'Another Pussy for Putin'— an act of solidarity art performance for the Russian punk band The Pussy Riots, 2012, and 'Amerikkka,' a photo project in collaboration with Erica Garner, the daughter of the late Eric Garner. Fabia's photographic and cinematographic work has been featured by *Vogue Italia*, *Interview Magazine*, *ID magazine*, *CNN Style*, *Vanity Fair* among others. Her video and documentary material has been featured by BBC World, Arte, ZDF, CNN.

Ryan Mendoza is an American artist who lives and works in Sicily and Berlin. He is the artist behind *The White House* (2015), *the Invitation* (2016), and the *Rosa Parks House Project* (2017). Primarily a painter, Ryan moves between expressionism and realism, engaging Americana and historical reference. Ryan's work often depicts obsessive scenes, illustrating questions of hypocrisy and repression. Ryan has shown with a range of European galleries and museums including White Cube, London, Galerie Lelong, Paris, and Museo Madre, Naples. He is the author of *Tutto è mio*, published in Italian (Everything Is Mine) 2015, Bompiani.

João José Santos holds a B. Arch and M. Arch from Escola Superior Artística do Porto, and he is currently living and working in Berlin. He is specialized in not being specialized as he is moved by arbitrary challenges and mundane curiosity over science and art realms. He independently expresses this in various mediums, involving artifacts about space and the human condition. He continuously looks for opportunities to rationally and physically assist on consequential projects and interventions.

Diogo Vale attained a Bachelor and Master in Architecture at ESAP (Escola Superior de Arquitectura do Porto) in Porto, Portugal. He currently works with various artists in Berlin, from the concept to the exhibition stage, fulfilling the needs/dynamics of itinerary exhibits. Diogo has jumped the boundaries of his architectural training into the area of presentation and social interactions with the architecture space. His intense curiosity in the Art creation processes has led him into approaching architecture as an object for social intervention. In between Germany and Portugal, he provides his input to Art works using Architecture, playing a key role in managing the exhibitions under his responsibility. His outsider architectural skills provide honest technical contributions to the creation of nomadic non-permanent space intervention.

James Patterson-Waterston is director at Vivid Economics, a strategic economics consultancy and leads the Cities and Infrastructure practice. He has expertise in net zero cities and the urban decarbonisation transition, urban and regional economic strategy development; sustainable urban development, and area-based economic assessment. Prior to joining Vivid, James was a consultant with Buro Happold in London and Arup in China, working on large-scale urban planning and economic development projects internationally. James has successfully led important projects for clients including the IFC, World Bank, EBRD, IDB, ADB, United Nations, GGGI, and HM Government. James holds an MPhil in Environmental Planning from the University of Cambridge as well as an MSc in Construction and Development Economics from University College London. He is also undertaking doctoral research, at University College London, into the UK's proposed Freeport policy. James is a member of the Institute of Economic Development and an elected Academician of the Academy of Urbanism (AoU).

Patrick Ruggiero Jr. is an architect and currently lives and works in Los Angeles. His interest in how architecture can positively empower the people that use the buildings we design has led him to work on a wide range of institutional and public-facing projects. His projects range from large-scaled international master plans to art schools, museums, and public spaces. With involvement in stages from conceptual design through the technical detailing of how a project gets built, his strengths lie in bringing a concept and design into reality. An interest in how buildings relate to their context is a strong undercurrent in his work and has driven academic research into issues of the public realm and urban design.

Luis Sacristán Murga is an architect and researcher based in London working across design, technology and urbanism. He is a Project Leader at Heatherwick Studio, where he has been working since 2015 in a multitude of projects, different in scales and contexts. He has contributed to the concept, design development and construction stages for the Google Charleston East campus in Mountain View, currently under construction, and to different projects of Google R+D. Other selected contributions include the IMKAN Pavilion exhibited in Cityscape Abu Dhabi 2018, Olympia London, and Changi Airport T5. Luis has been organising design workshops and participating as guest critic at the Architectural Association since 2013 and has been a Technical Studies Tutor at the Royal College of Art since 2019.

Daniela Sandler is Associate Professor of architectural and urban history at the University of Minnesota. She has a PhD in Visual and Cultural Studies (University of Rochester), and a professional degree in Architecture and Urbanism (University of São Paulo). She has published on grassroots urbanism; public space in São Paulo; squatting and gentrification in Berlin; and the historiography of Brazilian modernism. Her book, *Counterpreservation: Architectural Decay in Berlin since 1989* (Cornell University Press, 2016), investigates how Berlin residents appropriated architectural decay to engage a difficult past, resist gentrification, and create alternative housing and cultural spaces. Her book won the 2019 Antoinette Forrester-Downing Award from the Society of Architectural Historians for excellence in a publication devoted to historic preservation.

Schmidt/Sage/Pinder/Holland/Austin

Dr. Robert Schmidt III is a Reader in Architectural Design at Loughborough University, where he leads LU-Arc and is the Programme Director for the BArch architecture course. He has collected varied academic, industry and personal experiences exploring the built environment across a broad range of cultural and physical territories establishing two key strands of expertise – designing for adaptability and the development of digital co-practices for design. His work has resulted in several funded UK Research Council grants and publications including the book *Adaptable Architecture: Theory and Practice.* He has served on many international research committees and currently leads the Adaptable Futures international research group.

Dr Daniel Sage is a Reader in Organisation Studies and Director of Doctoral Programmes for the School of Business and Economics at Loughborough University. He has a degree in Human Geography from the University of Wales-Aberystwyth and a MA on Space, Place and Politics. His research focuses upon the development of critical social theories through the study of organisations and processes of organising and has been supported by major grants from the EPSRC and ESRC.

Victor Serrano holds a BArch from the School of Architecture at the University of Puerto Rico and a Master of Interior Architecture from the Rhode Island School of Design. He worked in the firm Davis-Fuster Architects where he was involved in the restoration of historic buildings, and with Francesca Russo Architect focusing on the restoration of historic Broadway theatres in New York City. During this time the firm received a New York Landmarks Conservancy Award for the restoration of the Belasco Theatre. His love for teaching was nurtured during his time as a Teaching Assistant at RISD. Today, he lives in Hong Kong, where he has taught at Raffles Design Institute and continues to be a mentor for students at Hong Kong Design Institute (HKDI). Victor describes himself as a curious participant of everyday architecture.

Marie Sorensen is an architect and master planner who uses anthropological methods alongside organizational visioning to define, plan and design facilities that build culture. Marie founded Cambridge, MA-based Sorensen Partners | Architects + Planners, Inc., in 2012 and has designed new construction, renovation, and restoration projects, along with masterplans, for universities, restaurants and hotels, libraries, outdoor recreation, multifamily housing, and diverse commercial clients. As design and technical lead for the firm, Marie foregrounds sustainability and resilience in all of the firm's work. Adaptive reuse projects such as those described in 'Figural Identity in Adaptive Reuse' are emblematic of the attention and wonder with which Marie treats cultures and client organizations with whom she works to sculpt a built future in which they both recognize their identity and embrace the evolution of their culture.

Barbara Stehle (PhD) is an art historian and independent curator. After earning her PhD in Contemporary Art History from the Sorbonne, Dr. Stehle taught at the Rhode Island School of Design for over a decade and worked at several museums in the US and Europe, including the Centre Georges Pompidou in Paris and the Zurich Kunsthaus in Switzerland. She is the founder of Art Intelligentsia. She has given a Tedx talk about "Architecture as Human Narrative" and writes mostly about European art, architecture and women's contribution to the art historical field. Her research on Max Beckmann has been published in major exhibition catalogues, and as a historian of modernism, she is a passionate advocate for the importance of postmodernism and women in art. She is also the art editor of LUXE Magazine and an art advisor for numerous art collections.

Hongjiang Wang is an interior architect, Professor at the Department of Environmental Design of Shanghai Institute of Visual Arts, and Vice Dean of the School of Design of SIVA. He taught in the Design Department of Shanghai Jiao Tong University from 1993 to 2007, has stayed in Design Factory of Hamburg, Germany, for half a year and was a Visiting Scholar at the Interior Design Department of Virginia Tech. He focuses his research on narrative space design supported by spatial interaction. He is now in charge of two funds-supported research as "Interactive Public Arts in Children's Healing Environment," and "Interaction Design Research of Children's Art Therapy" aimed to develop new narrative spatial devices, process and system strategies to strengthen services for children.

IMAGE AND PROJECT CREDITS, INFORMATION

INTRODUCTION: THE SOCIAL AGENDA OF ADAPTIVE REUSE

Image Credits_

fig 01. Militärhistorisches Museum Dresden (6233728639).jpg

https://commons.wikimedia.org/wiki/File:Militärhistorisches_Museum_Dresden_(6233728639).jpg; Attribution: Bundeswehr-Fotos Wir.Dienen.Deutschland., CC BY 2.0 <https://creativecommons.org/licenses/by/2.0>, via Wikimedia Commons

fig 02. Dokumentationszentrum2.JPG, https://commons.wikimedia.org/wiki/File:Dokumentationszentrum2.JPG, Attribution: Chris Baier (chrisglub), http://www.chrisbaier.com, CC BY-SA 2.5 <https://creativecommons.org/licenses/by-sa/2.5>, via Wikimedia Commons

fig 03. *Arvada High School Students march on Earth Day 1970*. Courtesy of the Denver Public Library, Special Collection

fig 04. Main Gate of the Tolentini building headquarters of Università Iuav di Venezia (Iuav university of Venice) designed by Carlo Scarpa.jpg

https://commons.wikimedia.org/wiki/File:Main_Gate_of_the_Tolentini_building_headquarters_of_Università_Iuav_di_Venezia_(Iuav_university_of_Venice)_designed_by_Carlo_Scarpa.jpg, Attribution: Jean-Pierre Dalbéra, CC BY 2.0 <https://creativecommons.org/licenses/by/2.0>, via Wikimedia Commons

fig 05. Taller d'Arquitectura Sant Just Desvern.jpg

("Taller d'Arquitectura" from architect Ricardo Bofill in Sant Just Desvern Catalonia), https://commons.wikimedia.org/w/index.php?curid=2142579

Attribution: De Till F. Teenck – Trabajo propio, CC BY-SA 2.5

fig 06. Lina Bo Bardi, SESC Pompéia (5510960976).jpg, https://upload.wikimedia.org/wikipedia/commons/f/f0/Lina_Bo_Bardi%2C_SESC_Pomp%C3%A9ia_%285510960976%29.jpg, Attribution: paulisson miura from Cuiabá, Brasil, CC BY 2.0 <https://creativecommons.org/licenses/by/2.0>, via Wikimedia Commons

fig 07. Gasometer-hyblerpark-2001.jpg, https://commons.wikimedia.org/wiki/File:Gasometer-hyblerpark-2001.jpg, Attribution: Andreas Pöschek, Viennaphoto, CC BY-SA 2.0 AT <https://creativecommons.org/licenses/by-sa/2.0/at/deed.en>, via Wikimedia Commons

fig 08. Space-gallery 798-art-district.jpg, https://commons.wikimedia.org/wiki/File:Space-gallery_798-art-district.jpg, Attribution: Leeluv, CC BY-SA 3.0 <https://creativecommons.org/licenses/by-sa/3.0>, via Wikimedia Commons

fig 09. Roof pool in Andels Hotel 02, Łódź.jpg, https://commons.wikimedia.org/wiki/File:Roof_pool_in_Andels_Hotel_02,_Łódź.jpg, Attribution: Zorro2212, CC BY-SA 3.0 <https://creativecommons.org/licenses/by-sa/3.0>, via Wikimedia Commons

fig 10. Musée D'Orsay Interior.JPG, https://commons.wikimedia.org/wiki/File:Musee_D%27Orsay_Interior.JPG, Attribution: Sonnickboom, CC BY-SA 3.0 <https://creativecommons.org/licenses/by-sa/3.0>, via Wikimedia Commons

fig 11. I'm Not a Church, St Nikolas, Copenhagen, DK, Attribution: Courtesy of Liliane Wong

fig 12. Zeche Zollverein, Free download, Pixabay https://pixabay.com/photos/zeche-zollverein-eat-ruhr-area-mine-2981131/, Attribution: Not required

fig 13. Rosa Parks House, Attribution: Courtesy of Liliane Wong

fig 14. Flims Gelbes Haus.jpg, https://de.wikipedia.org/wiki/Gelbes_Haus_(Flims)#/media/Datei:Flims_Gelbes_Haus.jpg, Attribution: Von upload by Adrian Michael – Eigenes Werk, CC BY-SA 3.0, https://commons.wikimedia.org/w/index.php?curid=1949092

fig 15. Detention and torture room, Security Prison 21 (S-21), Tuol Sleng Genocide Museum, Phnom Penh, Cambodia.jpg, https://commons.wikimedia.org/wiki/File:Detention_and_torture_room,_Security_Prison_21_(S-21),_Tuol_Sleng_Genocide_Museum,_Phnom_Penh,_Cambodia.jpg, Attribution: Paul Mannix, CC BY 2.0 <https://creativecommons.org/licenses/by/2.0>, via Wikimedia Commons

fig 16. Blick auf den FRAC Nord-Pas de Calais vom Strand von Malo-les-Bains.JPG, https://commons.wikimedia.org/wiki/File:Blick_auf_den_FRAC_Nord-Pas_de_Calais_vom_Strand_von_Malo-les-Bains.JPG

Claus Ableiter, CC BY-SA 4.0 <https://creativecommons.org/licenses/by-sa/4.0>, via Wikimedia Commons

APPROPRIATION

PRESERVATION THROUGH TRANSFORMATION

Authors_ Deborah Grossberg Katz and Brian Phillips; Name of project_ The Granary; Location_ Philadelphia, Pennsylvania, USA; Name(s) of architects/designers_ Interface Studio; Architects_ Brian Phillips, Morgan Ellig, Deborah Grossberg Katz, ViktoriaDiskina; Name of owner_ Pearl Properties; Name of structural engineer_Harman Group; Website address of design firm_ www.is-architects.com

Image Credits_ all illustrations courtesy of Interface Studio
P. 25 © Roberto Arellano

APPROPRIATING ARCHITECTURE

Author_ Dorothée King
Image Credits_ P. 30, P. 34_Shamsia Hassani, Dream Graffiti,2015, copyright Shamsia Hassani, P. 32, P. 33 Top and Bottom_ *Greenpeace Planet Earth First Projection*, 2017, copyright: Greenpeace; P. 36 Drury live in the subway, Berlin, 2017, copyright Michael Ang

COMING HOME

Author_ Leah Hershkowitz
Image Credits_ All images courtesy of the artist, Do Ho Suh. P. 39_ *348 West 22nd Street, New York, NY 10011, USA – Apartment A, Corridors and Staircases (Kanazawa version) 2011–2012*, polyester fabric and stainless steel. Apartment A 690 x 430 x 245 cm / *Corridors and Staircases* 1328 x 179 x 1175 cm. © Do Ho Suh; P. 40_*Rubbing/Loving Project: Kitchen, Apartment A, 348 West 22nd Street, New York, NY 10011, USA 2014*. Colored pencil on vellum pinned on board. Dimensions, overall 363.9 x 843.6 cm (143.25 x 332.125 inches). © Do Ho Suh; P. 41_*Specimen Series: Stove, Apartment A, 348 West 22nd Street, New York, NY 10011*, USA 2013. Polyester fabric, stainless steel wire, and display case with LED lighting. Framed dimensions 74 1/8 x 36 1/8 x 35 inches. © Do Ho Suh. P. 42_*Fallen*

Star 1/5, 2008–2009. ABS, basswood, beech, ceramic, enamel paint, glass, honeycomb board, lacquer paint, latex paint, LED lights, pinewood, plywood, resin, spruce, styrene, polycarbonate sheets, and PVC sheets. Approximately 332.7 x 368.3 x 762 cm (131 x 145 x 300 inches). © Do Ho Suh; P. 43_*Home Within Home Within Home Within Home 2013*, polyester fabric, metal frame 1530 x 1283 x 1297 cm. © Do Ho Suh; P. 44_*Apartment A, 348 West 22nd Street, New York, NY 10011, USA 2011–2014*, polyester fabric, stainless steel tubes. Dimensions 271.65 x 169.29 x 96.49 inches / 690 x 430 x 245 cm. © Do Ho Suh; P. 47_*Wielandstr. 18, 12159 Berlin, Germany – 3 Corridors 2011*, polyester fabric and stainless steel tubes 655 x 209 x 351 cm. © Do Ho Suh; P. 49_*Apartment A, 348 West 22nd Street, New York, NY 10011, USA 2011–2014*, polyester fabric and stainless steel tubes. Dimensions 271.65 x 169.29 x 96.49 inches / 690 x 430 x 245 cm. © Do Ho Suh.

POSTINDUSTRIAL SPECTACLE

Author_ Patrick Ruggiero, Jr. ; Project name_SoMA: The Simulator of Mechanized Authenticity, Bethlehem, Pennsylvania, USA; Design firm_Syracuse University Thesis Project; Owner_The City of Bethlehem, PA; Website of design firm_cargocollective.com/pjr;

Photographer_Jean-François Bedard & Edward Sichta; Image credits_ P. 54, 55 Top & Bottom, 57 by Author, "SoMA": The Simulator of Mechanized Authenticity." (B.Arch Thesis, Syracuse, University, 2013); available from http://cargocollective.com/pjr/undergradute-architecture-thesis; P. 56_Permissions and full resolution courtesy of the photographer, Jeffrey Totaro.

INFORMAL ANNEXATIONS

Author_ Rafael Luna;
Image credits_ All images courtesy by the author.

CITY AS HOTEL

Author_ Markus Berger; Name of project_ PIXEL HOTEL; Location_ Linz, Niederösterreich, Austria; Name of design firm_anytime; Name of owner_ Verein zur Reurbanisierung und Stadtreparatur; Name(s) of architects/designers_ Sabine Funk, Michael Grugl, Jürgen Haller, Richard Steger, Christoph Weidinger and Christian H. Leeb; Year completed_ 2009; Website_ http://www.pixelhotel.at

Name of photographer_ Tollerian; Images_ courtesy of anytime

AUTHENTICITY

FARAWAY, SO CLOSE

Author_ Stefano Corbo; Name of the project_ FRAC Nord- Pas de Calais; Location_ Dunkirk, France; Name of design firm_ Lacaton & Vassal Architectes; Names of designers involved in project_ Anne Lacaton & Jean Philippe Vassal, Florian de Pous (chief project), Camille Gravellier (construction supervision), Yuko Ohashi; Client_ Communauté Urbaine de Dunkerque; Structural and Mechanical Engineering_ Secotrap; Metal Structure_ CESMA; Year completed_ 2013 – 2015; Cost of construction_ 12M Euros net; Website_ www.lacatonvassal.com;

Name of Photographer and Image Credits_P. 78, 80, 81,82 Top & Bottom by Philippe Ruault; P. 83 by Florent Michel, © 11h45m.com

THE PAST EMBODIED IN ACTION

Author_ Laura Gioeni; Name of project_ Cattedrale di Pozzuoli; Location_ Pozzuoli, Napoli, Italy; Name(s) of key architects/designers_ Marco Dezzi Bardeschi (Capogruppo), Gnosis Architettura (Francesco Buonfantino, Antonio De Martino and Rossella Traversari), Alessandro Castagnaro, Renato De Fusco and Laura Gioeni; Name of owner_ Regione Campania; Name of structural engineer_ Giampiero Martuscelli; Electrical_ Domenico Trisciuoglio; HVAC_ Fulvio Capuano; Consultants_ Alessandra Angeloni (geologist), Mario Bencivenni (restoration history and theory), Giovanni Coppola (art historian and archaeologist), Sabino Giovannoni (conservationist), Ugo Grazioso (liturgist), Giorgio Piccinato (town planning), Furio Sacchi (archaeologist), Ferdinando Zaccheo (restoration specialist); Name of contractor_ Rione Terra Pozzuoli Consortium; Year completed_ 2014;

Image Credits_ courtesy by Marco Dezzi Bardeschi

ABSENT MATTER

Author_ Liliane Wong;

Image Credits_ P. 95, 96, 97 Top & Bottom, 98, 99, 100, 101, 103 © Roberto Conte; P. 104, 105 © Fabiano Caputo.

SKIN DEEP CONSERVATION

Author_ Federica Goffi

Image Credits_P. 106 Nils Ole Lund, "The City as Scenography" (37x49) 1983 11 Excerpted from Nils Ole Lund and Christian Olmsen. *Collage Architecture*. © Ernst & Sohn, Berlin, 1990; P. 108 Santa Prassede, a spolia Corinthian column emerges from its Baroque vestment; P. 109 Ground Plan of the Tempio Malatestiano by P. G. Pasini from an article by Charles Hope (The Early Institute of the Tempio Malatestiano, *Journal of the Warburg and Courtauld Institutes*, 1992, LV: 51–155); P. 110 Tempio Malatestiano by P. G. Pasini from an article by Charles Hope (The Early Institute of the Tempio Malatestiano, *Journal of the Warburg and Courtauld Institutes*, 1992, LV: 51–155).

COUNTERPRESERVATION

Author_ Daniela Sandler

Image Credits_ courtesy by Markus Berger

CULTURAL AMBASSADORS

Author_ Hongjiang Wang

Image Credits_P. 119 https://commons.wikimedia.org/wiki/File:Huizhou_Xixinan_Laowuge_ji_Lüraoting_2016.11.13_16-55-13.jpg, https://creativecommons.org/licenses/by-sa/4.0/legalcode; P. 120, Top & Bottom, 122, 123, 125 Bottom Images courtesy by the author; P. 121 https://www.flickr.com/photos/larry1732/38745928451/in/photostream/ Attribution 2.0 Generic (CC BY 2.0); P. 124 Image permission by Mr. Jun Qiu; P. 125 Top, 127 image permission by Wendao Garden Group; P. 126 https://en.wikipedia.org/wiki/ Singapore_University_of_Technology_and_Design#/media/ File: Antique_Chinese_pavilion,_Singapore_University_of_Technology_and_Design_-_20150602-01.jpg

ECOLOGY

BACK TO THE FUTURE

Author_ Kees Lokman

Image Credits_ P. 131 The Big U, Courtesy of Bjarke Ingels Group; P. 133, 134, 136 by Julia Casol; P. 135 Courtesy of H+N+S Landscape Architects; P. 138 Dijkdoorbraak bij Bemmel, 1799, Christiaan Josi, naar Jacob Cats (1741–1799), 1802, source: Rijksmuseum, Amsterdam

BETWEEN RESILIENCY AND ADAPTATION

Author_ Catherine Joseph

Image Credits_ All images courtesy of the author; P. 141 by author, background_ by Aleks Dahlberg at www.unsplash.com; P. 143 by author; P. 144, 146 Top & Bottom graphic by author, background by Frantzou Fleurine; www.unsplash.com

(RE)MADE BY WATER

Author_ Gregory Marinic; Project Name_ New World Mall, Bangkok, Thailand

Image Credits_ All images courtesy of the author; P. 149_Mall; central court, Photograph by Perfect Lazybones; P. 150 Floating market in Bangkok, Photograph by Georgie Pauwels: P. 152_ Mall, escalators, Photograph by Olga Saliy: P. 153_ Mall, koi, Photograph by Olga Saliy; P. 154_ Mall, escalators, Photograph by Olga Saliy.

TAKING ON THE SHAPE OF THINGS

P. 156, 166, 167, 168, Left & Right, 169 Top & Bottom_Reconstruction of the Mother Church 1984–98 | location_ Salemi (TP), Sicilia | client_ Ordinariato Diocesano di Mazara del Vallo (TP) | architects_ Álvaro Siza Vieira, Roberto Collovà, with U.T.Curia Mazara del Vallo | construction administration_ 1°/2° lotto, Roberto Collovà / U.T.Curia Mazara del Vallo – 3° lotto, Roberto Collovà | team_ O. Marrone, V. Trapani, E. Tocco, G. Ruggieri, F. Tramonte, G. Malventano, M. Ciaccio, A. Lo Sardo, K. Muscarella, R. Viviano | contractor_ geom. Melchiorre Armata, Salemi | lighting_ Álvaro Siza Vieira, Roberto Collovà (design), O-Luce Milano (produzione) | name of photographer_ Roberto Collovà

P. 158, 159, 165 Top_Recovery and reconstruction of the buildings of Case Di Stefano 1982–97| location_ Gibellina (TP), Sicilia | client_ Comune di Gibellina| architects_ Roberto Collovà, Marcella Aprile, Teresa La Rocca construction administration_ Roberto Collovà, Marcella Aprile, Teresa La Rocca | design team_ V. Acierno, M. Ciaccio, A. D'Amico, L. Felli, M. Gurrieri, M. Leonardi, S. Marina, F. Nicita, L. Raspanti, E. Tocco, A. Lo Sardo, R. Viviano | name of photographer_ Roberto Collovà

P. 160, 161, 162, 163_Urban systems in the Historic Center of Gela 1993–12 | location_ Gela (CL), Sicilia client: Comune di Gela architect and construction administration_ Roberto Collovà design team_ G.Fascella, L.Foto, A.Molica Bisci, R.De Simone, M.Di Gregorio, M.Enia, S.Perrotta, S.Urbano lighting_ Roberto Collovà (design), O-Luce Milano (produzione) name of photographer_ Roberto Collovà

P. 164, 165 Bottom, 172, 173_Belìce '80, Exhibit at the Museo Civico "Ludovico Corrao" di Gibellina | name of photographer_ Roberto Collovà

P. 170 Top & Bottom, 171 Top & Bottom_The Urban Park of Salemi, Garden of the Carmine (1° intervention): Outdoor Theater 1981/1986 | location_ Salemi (TP), Sicilia | client_ Comune di Salemi | architects_ Roberto Collovà, Marcella Aprile, Francesco Venezia | construction administration_ Roberto Collovà, Marcella Aprile | design team_ Anna Alì, Oreste Marrone | name of photographer_ Roberto Collovà

EQUITY

TACTICAL URBANISM WHERE IT MATTERS

Author_ Sally Harrison

Image Credits_P. 176_Help Build a Playground, by Public Workshop; P. 178_Story time in the Logan Parklet, by PhilaNOMA; P. 180_Street games are age-old urban tactics, by Public Workshop; P. 181_Night guardians, by Public Workshop; P. 182_Light towers, by Sikora Wells Appel/Group Melvin Design

ACKNOWLEDGMENTS: The author gratefully acknowledges Temple University for its generous support of her research, presentation and publication of this work through a Summer Research Grant. This article was originally published in the 2016 ACSA International Conference | Cross-Americas: Probing Disglobal Networks Proceedings.

LUANDA'S NEW FRONTIER

Author_ Célia Macedo; Acknowledgments_ This article arises from the research the author is currently carrying out for her PhD thesis, which looks at the sustainability of the use of earthen building technologies in the peri-urban areas of Angola. The research is being supervised by Prof. Ray Ogden, Dr. Bousmaha Baiche and Prof. David Sanderson. This project was awarded an Individual Doctoral Grant from FCT (Fundação para a Ciência e Tecnologia) – Ministry of Science, Technology and Higher Education, Portugal.

Images_courtesy of Célia Macedo

EMPOWERING ACTIONS

Authors_ Cristian Campagnaro and Nicolò di Prima

Image Credits_P. 193, 195, 198 courtesy of Lilithphoto ©; P. 196 by Sara Ceraolo.

IDENTITY

FLYING TEA ROOMS

Author_ Caroline Jäger-Klein; Name of research team_Dr. Vittoria Capresi (Urban Analysis), Dr. Petra Gruber (Building Structure and Bionics), Dr. Ulrike Herbig (Photogrammetry and Recordings of Architecture), Prof. Caroline Jäger-Klein (History of Architecture), Prof. Erich Lehner (Architecture of non-Western traditions), DI. Irmengard Mayer (Building Research and 3D-Laserscanning), Prof. Hermann Mückler (Social Anthropology) and Arch. DI. Gudrun Styhler-Aydin (Building Research);

Department_Department for the History of Architecture and Building Archaeology (Architekturgeschichte Bauforschung) UNIVERSITY OF TECHNOLOGY VIENNA / AUSTRIA; Website address of University_ www.TUWien.ac.at

Name of photographer_Andrea Rieger-Jandl

A SACRED TRANSLATION

Author_ Dennis Earle; Project name_Holy Trinity Church to Jesus Son of Mary Mosque; Project location_Syracuse, N.Y.; Key architect_ Dennis Earle; Project completed_Ongoing as of summer 2014.

Image Credits_All images courtesy of Dennis Earle

FIGURAL IDENTITY IN ADAPTIVE REUSE

Author_ Marie Sorensen; Project 01_ 50 Moganshan Road (M50), Shanghai, China; Project 02_ Les Halles townhouses, Paris, France, Project artist_Gordon Matta Clark, Project completed 1975 Biennale, now demolished; Project 03_ Westbeth Arts live-work housing, New York City, Project architect Richard Meier; Project 04_ Hamburg, Germany, Project name, Elbphilharmonie, Project architects Herzog & de Meuron.

Image Credits_P. 218_An informal exterior composition in red, turquoise and white as a 'topographical artwork', 50 Moganshan Road, Shanghai, Image Credit Marie S. A. Sorensen, 2006; P. 221 Left_ Complex as Topographical Artwork – Richard Meier's 1970 topography of white paint on brick exteriors at New York City's Westbeth Arts can be understood as a megalithic artwork at the scale of an urban block, Image credit_Marie S. A. Sorensen, 2015; P. 221 Right_ Westbeth Arts, the first publicly funded live-work artist loft project in the United States is an Escher-esque composition of white on brick by Richard Meier, showcasing geometric additions like these park benches, Image credit, Marie S. A. Sorensen, 2015.

LOOKING FOR THE VOIDS IN-BETWEEN

Author_ Géraldine Borio

Image credits_P. 225, 226, 227, 228, 229 by Parallel Lab; P. 230, 232, 233 by Parallel Lab, Anaïs Boileau

LEARNING FROM OLD XINÍNG

Author_ James Patterson-Waterston; Location_Xiníng, Qinghai Province, People's Republic of China; Acknowledgments_ The paper addresses a piece of ongoing research into the adaptation of the urban form of the city of Xiníng. Already the research is demonstrating engineering and environmental value in the existing city grid and building layout, while further fieldwork is due to take place in early 2012.

Image credits_ James Patterson-Waterston

MEMORY AND REDEMPTION

ANTERIOR SPACES AT S.21

Author_ Barbara Stehle; Name of project_ Tuol Sleng Museum of Genocide Crimes; Location_ Phnom Penh, Cambodia; Year completed_1980

Image credits_P. 240, 243, 246, 247 Eva Sutton; P. 242 Drawings for Tuol Sleng Site today by Martin Hojny; P. 244 Architectural drawings by Pen Sereypagna and Vuth Danith; P. 245 Lars Kersten

MALLEABLE REMEMBRANCE

Author_ Victor M. Serrano; Name of project_ Murray House; Location_ Stanley, Hong Kong

Image credits_ Queenie Chow

EVERYBODY'S HOUSE

Author_ Ryan & Fabia Mendoza, João José Santos, Diogo Vale; Name of project_ *The Rosa Parks House Project*; Location_ Detroit, Berlin, Providence; Name of artist_ Ryan Mendoza; Name(s) of key architects involved in project_ João José Santos & Diogo Vale; Website_ www.ryan-mendoza.com; www.whitehousefilm.net;

Image Credits_P. 255, 256, 261 Center Liliane Wong; P. 257, 262, 264 Fabia Mendoza; P. 259 by Elaine Fredrick, Courtesy of WaterFire; P. 260 all, 261, Left & Right João José Santos & Diogo Vale; P. 263 Stefano Corbo

CROYDON'S TOWER

Author_ Robert Schmidt III, Dan Sage,together with James Pinder, Charles Holland, Simon Austin; Name of project_ Croydon's Tower; Location_ Croydon, London, UK; Name of design firm_ The Adaptable Futures (AF) research unit at Loughborough University and FAT architects; Names of key architects/designers involved_ Robert Schmidt III, Dan Sage, James Pinder, Charles Holland, and Simon Austin; Name of owner_ Legal & General, Financial services company; year completed_ project study

Image credits_P. 267 Copyright Getmapping plc; P. 268 Skyscan; P. 269–272 Robert Schmidt III

BETWEEN MEMORY AND INVENTION

Author_ Luis Sacristán Murga; Name of design firm_Nieto Sobejano Arquitectos; Website of design firm_www.nietosobejano.com/; Name of Project_Extension of San Telmo Museum, San Sebastián, Spain; Names of artists involved with the façade project_ Leopoldo Ferrán, Agustina Otero; Names of collaborators involved with the project_ Stephen Belton, Patricia Grande, Pedro Guedes, Joachim Kraft, Juan Carlos Redondo, Alexandra Sobral; Designers_Fuensanta Nieto, Enrique Sobejano; Owner_City Council San Sebastián; Structural Engineer_ N.B.35, S.L Year Completed_2011;

Image credits_P. 274 Català-Roca. Eduardo Chillida en el Peine del Viento. San Sebastián. 1976 – ©Photographic Archive F. Català-Roca – Arxiu Fotogràfic de l'Arxiu Històric del Collegi d'Arquitectes de Catalunya (AHCOAC). With the collaboration of the Collegi d'Arquitectes de Catalunya; P. 276 Top Courtesy of Idoia Murga Castro and Amaya Murga Castro; P. 276 Bottom Author unknown, http://www.guregipuzkoa.net/photo/1079928?lang=es;

P. 278, 279 Top DWGS, 281 Plans, sections site plans, courtesy of Nieto Sobejano Arquitectos; P. 279 Bottom, 280, 287_17 Photographer_ Courtesy of Fernando Alda Fotografia SL; P. 282–283 Name of Project_Moritzburg Museum, Halle (Saale), Germany; Designers_Fuensanta Nieto, Enrique Sobejano; Owner_Stiftung Moritzburg, State – Anhalt; Structural Engineer_GSE Ingenieur-GmbH; Photographer_Roland Halbe Architectural Photography; Section drawing_Courtesy of Nieto Sobejano Arquitectos, Year Completed_2008; P. 284–285, 286 Top_Name of Project_Center for Contemporary Art, Córdoba, Spain; Names of artist involved with the façade project_realities:united; Designers_Fuensanta Nieto, Enrique Sobejano; Owner_Junta de Andalucía (City Council); Structural Engineer_N.B.35, S.L.; Photographer_Roland Halbe

Architectural Photography; Year Completed_2013; P. 286 Bottom Name of Project_Congress Center, Mérida, Spain; Artist involved with the façade project_Esther Pizarro; Designers_Fuensanta Nieto, Enrique Sobejano; Owner_Junta de Extremadura (City Council); Structural Engineer_N.B.35, S.L.; Photographer_Roland Halbe Architectural Photography; Year Completed_2004; P. 288–291_Name of Project_Joanneumsviertel, Graz, Austria; Designers_Fuensanta Nieto, Enrique Sobejano; Owner_Estiria City Council; Structural Engineer_DI. Manfred Petschnigg ZT; Photographer_Roland Halbe Architectural Photography; Section drawing: Courtesy of Nieto Sobejano Arquitectos; Year Completed_2013; P. 292–293_Name of Project_Castillo de la Luz, Las Palmas de Gran Canaria, Spain; Designers_Fuensanta Nieto, Enrique Sobejano; Owner_Ministry of Construction (State); Structural Engineer_N.B.35, S.L.; Photographer_Roland Halbe Architectural Photography; Year Completed_First phase, 2004 & second phase, 2013

COVER IMAGE CREDITS

From left to right

Row 1

a. https://commons.wikimedia.org/wiki/File:Huizhou_Xixinan_Laowuge_ji_Lüraoting_2016.11.13_16-55-13.jpg, https://creativecommons.org/licenses/by-sa/4.0/legalcode
b. Courtesy of Célia Macedo
c. Gasometer-hyblerpark-2001.jpg
https://commons.wikimedia.org/wiki/File:Gasometer-hyblerpark-2001.jpg
Attribution: Andreas Pöschek, Viennaphoto, CC BY-SA 2.0 AT <https://creativecommons.org/licenses/by-sa/2.0/at/deed.en>, via Wikimedia Commons
d. Courtesy of Paul Kaloustian
e. Militärhistorisches Museum Dresden (6233728639).jpg
https://commons.wikimedia.org/wiki/File:Militärhistorisches_Museum_Dresden_(6233728639).jpg Attribution: Bundeswehr-Fotos Wir.Dienen.Deutschland., CC BY 2.0 <https://creativecommons.org/licenses/by/2.0>, via Wikimedia Commons

Row 2

a. Musee D'Orsay Interior.JPG
https://commons.wikimedia.org/wiki/File:Musee_D%27Orsay_Interior.JPG
Attribution: Sonnickboom, CC BY-SA 3.0 <https://creativecommons.org/licenses/by-sa/3.0>, via Wikimedia Commons
b. Courtesy of Do Ho Suh
c. Lina Bo Bardi, SESC Pompéia (5510960976).jpg
https://upload.wikimedia.org/wikipedia/commons/f/f0/Lina_Bo_Bardi%2C_SESC_Pomp%C3%A9ia_%285510960976%29.jpg
Attribution: paulisson miura from Cuiabá, Brasil, CC BY 2.0 <https://creativecommons.org/licenses/by/2.0>, via Wikimedia Commons
d. Courtesy of any:time architekten
e. Main Gate of the Tolentini building headquarters of Università Iuav di Venezia (Iuav university of Venice) designed by Carlo Scarpa.jpg
https://commons.wikimedia.org/wiki/File:Main_Gate_of_the_Tolentini_building_headquarters_of_Università_Iuav_di_Venezia_(Iuav_university_of_Venice)_designed_by_Carlo_Scarpa.jpg
Attribution: Jean-Pierre Dalbéra, CC BY 2.0 <https://creativecommons.org/licenses/by/2.0>, via Wikimedia Commons

Row 3

a. Courtesy of Interface Studio
b. Courtesy of Marco Dezzi Bardeschi
c. Courtesy of Roberto Collovà
d. Photographer, © Roberto Conte
e. Photography by Eva Sutton

Row 4

a. Courtesy of Roberto Collovà
b. Courtesy of Fernando Alda Fotografia SL
c. Blick auf den FRAC Nord-Pas de Calais vom Strand von Malo-les-Bains.JPG
https://commons.wikimedia.org/wiki/File:Blick_auf_den_FRAC_Nord-Pas_de_Calais_vom_Strand_von_Malo-les-Bains.JPG
Claus Ableiter, CC BY-SA 4.0 <https://creativecommons.org/licenses/by-sa/4.0>, via Wikimedia Commons
d. Photography by Elaine Fredrick, courtesy of WaterFire
e. Courtesy of Roberto Collovà

Row 5

a. Photography by Andrea Rieger-Jandl
b. Courtesy of any:time architekten
c. Courtesy of Pixabay
d. Photography by Carol Aizenstark, Stéphane Chalmeau
e. Dokumentationszentrum2.JPG
https://commons.wikimedia.org/wiki/File:Dokumentationszentrum2.JPG
Attribution: Chris Baier (chrisglub), http://www.chrisbaier.com, CC BY-SA 2.5 <https://creativecommons.org/licenses/by-sa/2.5>, via Wikimedia Commons

Editor for the Publisher: Andreas Müller

Production: Amelie Solbrig

Paper: 135 g/m² Condat Matt Perigord

Printing: optimal media GmbH, Röbel/Müritz

Bibliographic information published by the German National Library
The German National Library lists this publication in the Deutsche Nationalbibliografie.
Detailed bibliographic data are available on the Internet at http://dnb.dnb.de.

Library of Congress Control Number: 2021941793

This publication is also available as an e-book PDF (978-3-0356-2503-5).

P.O. Box 44, 4009 Basel, Switzerland
Part of Walter de Gruyter GmbH, Berlin/Boston

Printed on acid-free paper produced from chlorine-free pulp. TCF ∞

Printed in Germany

ISBN 978-3-0356-1828-0

9 8 7 6 5 4 3 2 1

www.birkhauser.com